HAJJ TO THE HEART

Islamic Civilization and Muslim Networks

Carl W. Ernst and Bruce B. Lawrence, editors

Highlighting themes with historical as well as contemporary significance, Islamic Civilization and Muslim Networks features works that explore Islamic societies and Muslim peoples from a fresh perspective, drawing on new interpretive frameworks or theoretical strategies in a variety of disciplines. Special emphasis is given to systems of exchange that have promoted the creation and development of Islamic identities—cultural, religious, or geopolitical. The series spans all periods and regions of Islamic civilization.

A complete list of titles published in this series appears at the end of the book.

HAJJ *to the* HEART

SUFI JOURNEYS ACROSS THE INDIAN OCEAN

Scott Kugle

THE UNIVERSITY OF NORTH CAROLINA PRESS
CHAPEL HILL

Manufactured in the United States of America

Designed by April Leidig
Set in Linux Libertine by Copperline Book Services

The University of North Carolina Press has been a member of the Green Press Initiative since 2003.

Cover illustration by Rudra Kishore Mandal

Library of Congress Cataloging-in-Publication Data
Names: Kugle, Scott Alan, 1969– author.
Title: Hajj to the heart : Sufi journeys across the Indian Ocean / Scott Kugle.
Other titles: Islamic civilization & Muslim networks.
Description: Chapel Hill : The University of North Carolina Press, [2021] | Series: Islamic civilization and Muslim networks | Includes bibliographical references and index.
Identifiers: LCCN 2021038324 | ISBN 9781469665306 (cloth) | ISBN 9781469665313 (paperback) | ISBN 9781469665320 (ebook)
Subjects: LCSH: Muttaqī, ʿAlī ibn ʿAbd al-Malik, –1567. | Muslim scholars—India—16th century—Biography. | Sufis—India—16th century—Biography. | Muslim scholars—India—17th century. | Sufis—India—17th century. | Sufism—India—Gujarat—History—16th century. | Sufism—India—Gujarat—History—17th century. | Islamic learning and scholarship—History. | Islam—South Asia—History—16th century. | Islam—South Asia—History—17th century. | Islam—Saudi Arabia—History—16th century. | Islam—Saudi Arabia—History—17th century. | LCGFT: Biographies.
Classification: LCC BP80.M8985 K84 2021 | DDC 297.4092/254—dc23
LC record available at https://lccn.loc.gov/2021038324

We are proud to announce that this book is freely available in an open-access enhanced edition thanks to TOME (Toward an Open Monograph Ecosystem)—a collaboration of the Association of American Universities, the Association of University Presses, and the Association of Research Libraries—and the generous support of Emory University and the Andrew W. Mellon Foundation. Learn more at the TOME website: openmonographs.org. The open-access enhanced edition of *Hajj to the Heart* can be found at https://manifold.ecds.emory.edu/projects/hajj-to-the-heart.

To my teachers
Bruce Lawrence and Carl Ernst

CONTENTS

xi Note on Dates, Citation, and Transliteration

xv Note about the Digital Humanities and This Book

xvii Acknowledgments

1 INTRODUCTION
Perilous Pilgrimage and Interconnected Lives

12 FIRST SATCHEL
ʿAli Muttaqi's Growth

46 SECOND SATCHEL
ʿAli Muttaqi's Exile

83 THIRD SATCHEL
ʿAli Muttaqi's Maturity

115 FOURTH SATCHEL
ʿAli Muttaqi's Mission

174 FIFTH SATCHEL
ʿAli Muttaqi's Legacy

214 SIXTH SATCHEL
ʿAli Muttaqi's Memory

243 APPENDIX A
Sultans of Gujarat in the Muzaffar-Shahi Dynasty, 1407–1584

244 APPENDIX B
Sufi Lineages of ʿAli Muttaqi and ʿAbd al-Haqq Muhaddith Dihlawi

247 Abbreviations Used in the Notes and Bibliography

249 Notes

275 Bibliography

289 Index

ILLUSTRATIONS

Maps

Gujarat and the Deccan in the sixteenth century 18

Ahmedabad in the sixteenth century 40

Figures

Dargah of Shah Bajan Chishti 19

Flight of Bahadur Shah during Humayun's Campaign in Gujarat 50

Indian Ocean Sailors Fighting Pirates 51

Humayun Routing Bahadur Shah and His Army 55

The Death of Sultan Bahadur Shah of Gujarat 81

Tomb of Shah ʿAbdallah Shattar 121

Dargah of Wajih al-Din ʿAlawi 133

King of Cambay 155

Dargah of ʿAbd al-Haqq Muhaddith Dihlawi 236

The ʿAli Muttaqi Madrasa 239

NOTE ON DATES, CITATION, AND TRANSLITERATION

Verses from the Qur'an—which Muslims believe is the direct speech of God—are set off in italics to mark them as scripture; all translations from the Qur'an are by the author. Dates are given in the Western (Gregorian) calendar without being marked by CE or AD (Common Era or *anno Domini*); when equivalent dates are given in the Islamic calendar, they are marked by AH (After Hijra), the purely lunar calendar that began in 622 CE.

In the main body of the text, names of people are given in transliteration with full diacritics at their first mention and are given in simplified form without diacritics thereafter for ease of reading. Regions and cities are given in transliteration in parentheses at the first instance and thereafter are given only in the common modern spelling, such as Ahmedabad (Aḥmadābād).

Arabic terms are likewise given in italics and with full diacritics at their first mention (and appear in simplified form thereafter) and generally are defined in context the first time they are used. The linguistic origin of terms from other languages—such as Persian (Pr.), Urdu/Hindawi (Ur.), Gujari (Gr.), or Gujarati (Gj.)—will be noted. Terms that are frequently used after being defined in the text, such as "dargah" and "shaykh," are not italicized. Words from Arabic that are common in English are not transliterated and follow common Anglicized spelling, such as "Sufi" (not Ṣūfī), "hadith" (not ḥadīth), and "Qawwali" (not Qawwālī).

The transliteration system is adapted from the *International Journal of Middle Eastern and Islamic Studies*. Letters of Arabic are given below with their representation in roman script with diacritical marks; Persian and Indic terms are transliterated according to a modified Arabic system. The transliteration system for consonants follows the Arabic alphabetic pattern, as do additional characters for terms in Persian and Indic languages.

Consonants in Arabic

ب	b	bā
ت	t	tā
ث	th	thā
ج	j	jīm
ح	ḥ	ḥā
خ	kh	khā
د	d	dāl
ذ	dh	dhāl
ر	r	rā
ز	z	zā
س	s	sīn
ش	sh	shīn
ص	ṣ	ṣād
ض	ḍ	ḍād
ط	ṭ	ṭā
ظ	ẓ	ẓā
ع	ʿ	ʿayn
غ	gh	ghayn
ف	f	fī
ق	q	qāf
ک	k	kāf
ل	l	lām
م	m	mīm
ن	n	nūn
ه	h	*hē*, when voiced at a word's end, is written, as in *nigāh* (sight); as a silent consonant that is not vocalized, it is not written, as in *irāda* (will)
و	w	*wau* a consonant, as in *walī* (saint)
ی	y	*yē* a consonant, as in *ayāt* (signs)

Consonants in Persian

پ	p	pē
چ	ch	chē
ژ	ž	žē
گ	g	gāf

Consonants in Urdu, Hindawi, Gujari, and Gujarati

ٹ	ṫ	ṫā
ڈ	ḋ	ḋā
ڑ	ṙ	ṙā
ھ	ħ	*dō-chashmī hē* for aspirated consonants, as in *pħūl* (flower)
ں	ñ	*nūn ghunna* for nasalized *n*, as in *yūñ* (thus)

Vowels

آ ā

ی ī or ē, depending on pronunciation, as in *shēr* (lion) or *shīr* (milk)

ای ay or ei, a diphthong as in *shaykh* (elder) or *meiñ* (in)

و ū or ō, depending on pronunciation, as in *sujūd* (prostration) or *khusrō* (prince)

او aw, a diphthong as in *awliyā* (saints)

وا wa, a semi-vowel commonly pronounced as ā, as in *khwāja* (master)

َ a *fatḥa* or *zabar*, a short vowel

ِ i or e *kasra* or *zer*, a short vowel, as in *wilāyat* (sanctity)

ُ u or o *ḍamma or pesh*, a short vowel, as in *upar* (above) or *tohmat* (suspicion)

ء ʾ *hamza*, glottal stop, as in *fanāʾ* (obliteration) or two vowels connected as in *khazāʾin* (treasuries)

ِ –e or -ye *iḍāfa* ("of" relation between two nouns), as in *waḥdat-e wujūd* (oneness of being) or *khwāja-ye khwājagān* (master of masters)

و o *wāw* ("and" joining two nouns), as in *bandagī o inṣāf* (humility and justice)

NOTE ABOUT THE DIGITAL HUMANITIES AND THIS BOOK

My forward-thinking publisher, the University of North Carolina Press, has partnered with the equally forward-thinking Emory Center for Digital Scholarship—through the TOME@Emory initiative housed at Emory University's Fox Center for Humanistic Inquiry—to fashion and make available free to all an open-access (OA) *expanded* digital edition of this book, *Hajj to the Heart: Sufi Journeys across the Indian Ocean.* TOME (Toward an Open Monograph Ecosystem) is a collaboration of the Association of American Universities, the Association of Research Libraries, and the Association of University Presses. *Hajj to the Heart* is also available as a regular print book from UNC Press.

This partnership in the digital humanities challenged me to rethink how the Muttaqi community's interaction with its Gujarati and South Asian environment was preserved in material and performance culture. The enhanced OA edition allowed me to include compelling examples of architecture and painting that are related to the Muttaqi community's story in a more expansive way than a print book alone would do. It also spurred me to integrate Qawwali music and sung poetry into the study, a feature made possible by a generous Mellon Foundation New Directions Grant focused on South Asian Sufi music.

These multimedia resources supplement the book's original investigation into archival manuscripts that are largely handwritten and unpublished. In this regard, too, the enhanced OA edition allowed me to expand the study by presenting images of key texts, some of which are exceedingly rare and exist in single manuscripts housed in South Asian archives. These texts are difficult to access and are terribly fragile; the enhanced OA edition allowed me to highlight their importance for conservators and scholars and to offer English-language translations in expanded appendices.

For all of their support and enthusiasm for crafting the OA enhanced edition of *Hajj to the Heart: Sufi Journeys across the Indian Ocean*, I thank Sarah

McKee and the Emory Center for Digital Scholarship; Elaine Maisner, my editor at UNC Press; and Manifold, an open-source platform that makes possible the creation of multimedia-rich online publications.

The OA enhanced digital edition of this book may be located using this link: https://manifold.ecds.emory.edu/projects/hajj-to-the-heart.

ACKNOWLEDGMENTS

Carl Ernst's generous spirit and deep knowledge are wonderful gifts to me, as they are to his many students around the world; he guided me through research about ʿAli Muttaqi's life and legacy. Bruce Lawrence encouraged me to study Chishti texts through a dialectic of reason and passion, *ʿaql o ʿishq*; his relentless quest for truth and wisdom has been a guiding light for me ever since.

I am grateful to many other teachers and colleagues for their support as I wrote this book. At Duke University, Katherine Ewing, David Gilmartin, and Vincent Cornell encouraged this research. At Emory University, Roxani Margariti, a companion of the heart and mind, has a love of the sea that pushed me to adopt a maritime focus; she, Devin Stewart, and Craig Perry refined some chapters with their insights. In India, Muhammad Zubair Qureishi of Ahmedabad and Prof. Suleman Siddiqi of Hyderabad encouraged me with their knowledge and passion for research.

The Charlotte Newcombe Fellowship in Religion and Ethics (from the Woodrow Wilson National Fellowship Foundation at Princeton) supported the writing, while the American Institute of Indian Studies and the American Institute of Pakistan Studies supported archival research. Emory's University Research Committee Grant in the humanities supported revision of the manuscript during summers in Hyderabad and Ahmedabad.

Special thanks go to my students Brittany Landorf, who edited the manuscript when it was in disarray, and Isaac Foster, who helped prepare the music recordings. I am grateful to those friends who contributed photographs relevant to this work and to the archivists at the Casanatense Library in Rome and the Victoria and Albert Museum and the British Library in London who granted permission to include priceless paintings in this work. Archivists in India, Pakistan, and Turkey deserve thanks for their diligent work in preserving manuscripts relevant to the Muttaqi community and allowing me access to them. Outstanding among them are Dr. Rahmat ʿAli and Dr. Nagender Reddy at the Salar Jung Museum and Library in Hyderabad, Drs. Rafath

Rizwana and Fathima Tanweer at the Andhra Pradesh Oriental Manuscript Library in Hyderabad, Dr. Bombaywala at the Pir Mohammadshah Dargah Library in Ahmedabad, and Dr. Zubair Qureishi, who facilitated access to the B. J. Institute of Learning and Research in Ahmedabad. I am grateful to the Sufi custodians who helped me access rare sites and manuscripts in their care, such as the *sajjada nasheens* (hereditary custodians) of the Pir Naseeruddin Dargah in Ahmedabad and the Shah Bajan Dargah in Burhanpur. May lovers of knowledge always thrive.

HAJJ TO THE HEART

Perilous Pilgrimage and Interconnected Lives

Proclaim the pilgrimage among the people!
They will come to you on foot and all kinds of vehicles,
lean on account of journeying through difficult passages . . .
and those who honor the sacred rites of God
should do so from sincere piety of heart.
—Qur'an, Surat al-Hajj (22:27–32)

He finished chanting and closed his Qur'an, for what had begun as a refreshing breeze was quickly gathering force in a storm. The wind goaded dark waves, and menacing clouds obscured the horizon. The sea became the sky and the sky the sea, like two hands united to grip their ship, lifting and tossing them recklessly. He slipped his leather-bound Qur'an into his canvas satchel as his fellow passengers, disoriented and fearful, clung to the ship's wooden planks with increasing desperation. In the twinkling of an eye, their easy passage had become difficult. They had left the Gujarati coastline weeks ago, and their anxiety about pirates and Portuguese marauders had gradually fallen away the nearer they got to Arabia's shores. As they departed the Yemeni port of Aden and tacked northward along the Red Sea coast toward the Hijaz, their expectations had bubbled over into joy.

Yet now, hope sank as every fiber of their ship groaned. Waves crashed overhead like thunderclouds and the deck buckled. The mast snapped. Sails collapsed while the greedy fists of waves pulled them under, thrashing with the bodies of disoriented passengers like nets full of fish. He barely had time to register what was happening: the unthinkable was transpiring before his eyes. The solid ship that was their only protection was splintering into shards as sharp as spears. A verse from the Qur'an coursed through his mind but could barely form on his lips before he leaped into the churning depths—*Upon God I rely, the Lord of the exalted throne* (Qur'an 9:129).

He was a pilgrim, a scholar of scripture, and a lover of God. Yet none of that seemed to matter as the waves closed over his head. The satchel slung over his shoulder, full of his books, dragged him down. Thunderclaps, crashing waves, cleaving wood, and desperate shouts faded. A profound silence embraced him, pulling him deeper.

Grasping his wrist, a hand. Pulling his collar, another hand. Whose hands were these under his shoulders? His face broke through the water's surface as he gasped for air and his arms grasped a wooden plank. The hands held him up until he got a firm hold on the plank, which supported a few of his fellow castaway passengers like a floating anchor despite the storm's cacophony. How many hours did this torture last? His senses were effaced; his mind was numbed as every fiber of his strength went into holding on to the plank. Gradually the storm blew over, the winds calmed, and the waves settled down. Only then did exhaustion overcome him and the several men clinging with him to the plank. He wavered between sleep and death, never loosening his grip.

As day turned to night and night turned to day, his memory slowly returned to him. His name was 'Abd al-Ḥaqq. He was one of countless pilgrims who braved the sea to reach Arabia from South Asian shores. Many perished in the sea's dangers, but not he. From landlocked Delhi, he had never seen the sea until the moment he embarked on the ship, heading to the holy cities of Mecca and Medina. His family of scholars was fond of quoting the poetry of Amir Khusro, the Sufi minstrel of Delhi—"The sea of love moves in strange ways, Khusro! Those who jump in sink but those who drown reach the other side."[1] How could they imagine that their beloved metaphors, when embodied in reality, were so terrifying? His father's voice surfaced in 'Abd al-Haqq's slowly reviving mind, memories of when he taught his son and his circle of disciples from stories by Mawlana Rumi. His rhyming Persian couplets wove narratives, like that of the scholar and the boatman.[2]

Once a scholar stepped into a boat
  And turned towards the oarsman just to gloat:
"Have you learned any grammar?" He said, "No."
  "Then half your life's been wasted just to row!"

Wind steered the boat towards a whirlpool there
The oarsman shouted to him, once aware,
"Have you learned how to swim and keep afloat?"
"I've never learned, skilled captain of my boat."
"O scholar, your whole life has been in vain:
We're sinking fast—what good now is your brain!"

His father had laughed at the punch line and teased his precocious son and fellow students. Would his father laugh now if he saw his son, just on the cusp of maturity, almost drowned in the sea? His father had spent a lifetime teaching him grammar to unlock the secrets of the Qur'an, the Prophet's sayings, and Sufi literature. Chuckling, his father would finish the narrative:

Not grammar but effacement is needed here
If self-effaced, dive in and have no fear!
While corpses can float on a stormy sea
How can the living find security?

These couplets echoed in ʿAbd al-Haqq's consciousness as he drifted toward shore, little more than a living corpse still weighed down by the books in the satchel slung over his shoulder.

ʿAbd al-Haqq survived his ordeal by sea. Though dramatized in this telling, the narrative above follows the facts that he relayed. Many years later, he wrote about his shipwreck and death-defying encounter with the sea in a Persian memoir:

> When I was traveling to the two holy cities [in Arabia], my ship met with a terrible storm and was broken into bits. I, along with some other passengers, clung onto a wooden plank and stayed floating with it for several days. Finally, we were washed up onto shore. I had with me a bundle of books which had become totally drenched. Since we now had to travel from the coast by foot and I had no way to carry them with me, I buried them in the Arabian desert and made a sign at the place so I might find them again later. Then we turned toward Mecca and began traveling by foot.
>
> Along the way, we were overcome by thirst, and water is scarce in the Arabian desert. My companions appealed to me to pray that God might send us water to drink. I said, "I will voice the prayer and you all say Amen." We prayed together until God sent a rain shower, and we filled up

our leather bottles with fresh water. After several days of travel by foot, we reached Mecca. We circumambulated the Ka'ba and ran the track between the hills of Safa and Marwa.

Then some Bedouins approached us bearing a load upon their heads. They asked, "Would you like to buy some books?" When they opened their bundle, I found that the books they had for sale were precisely my books that I had left behind buried in the Arabian desert! I said nothing of this to them, but gave them the price they were asking and took the books. All the pages of the books had stuck together while drying such that one could not open them. I once again soaked the book so that the pages separated from each other, yet in this process not one letter was lost such that the book might become useless to a reader![3]

In danger from drowning and dehydration, 'Abd al-Haqq was more concerned for his books than his own life. He recorded the miracle of abandoning his precious texts when stranded on Arabian shores only to have them carried to him by Bedouins customarily feared for plundering pilgrims. His books, for which he obsessively cared, stood in for his own body, to which he hardly paid attention.

What kind of traveler was this? He was no ordinary merchant or mere pilgrim. His pilgrimage was a quest for religious knowledge, a hajj to the heart. He returned to South Asia years later as a mature Sufi master, brilliant hadith scholar, and prolific author, known as Shaykh 'Abd al-Ḥaqq Muḥaddith Dihlawī, "Our master, the hadith expert from Delhi." He revived hadith studies in early modern South Asia, founded an influential madrasa in the Mughal Empire's capital city, and argued tirelessly that Islamic law and Sufi mysticism were integral to each other. He authored over fifty books, ranging from a biography of the Prophet Muhammad and a history of Medina to invaluable commentaries on prized hadith collections and the most reliable accounts of great Sufis in South Asia. His hagiography of the famous Sufi Shaykh 'Abd al-Qādir Jīlānī (d. 1166) was translated into Persian for popular dissemination by order of no less than Prince Dārā Shikōh (d. 1659), heir apparent to the Mughal throne.

No account of Islam in South Asia neglects to discuss 'Abd al-Haqq's contribution and influence. Yet when he washed ashore in Arabia, he was nobody. How did 'Abd al-Haqq mature into a great religious leader? He left South Asia in despair and matured in Mecca's rarefied air, under the guidance of Sufi scholars there. In Arabia, he searched for learning, piety, mystical insight, and political acumen. He found these qualities unified in the Muttaqi community of Sufi scholars who bridged the distance between South Asia and Mecca; the members of this community taught new reformist ideals of Islamic scholarship fused with mysticism, ideals that they sent back to South Asia through texts, training, and disciples, including most prominently ʿAbd al-Haqq. This community was named after its founding saint, Shaykh ʿAlī ibn Ḥusām al-Dīn ibn ʿAbd al-Mālik ibn Qāḍī Khān al-Hindī al-Muttaqī (lived 1480–1567, hereafter called ʿAli Muttaqi), who crossed the same dangerous sea about six decades earlier, leaving Gujarat to live in exile. He settled in Mecca to teach, write, and train disciples in order to build a reformist Sufi community (in contrast to a distinct Sufi order). Many sailed from South Asia to join him and receive training, braving the perils at sea.

One person's life, when extended through travel and text and taken as exemplary, forms the basis for a network of interconnected lives that persist through time as a community. This book explores how ʿAli Muttaqi established the Muttaqi community that thrived, despite political challenges, over the long sixteenth century, affecting abstract concepts like reform, discipline, piety, and political legitimacy that were central to Islamic society in an era of radical change. Its approach takes inspiration from Richard Eaton's method of viewing "biography not as a genre inherently antithetical to social history, but as a vehicle that could be recovered and mobilized for writing precisely such history," meaning the post-Marxist history of *longue durée* social dynamic, power structures, and political conflicts rather than the bourgeois narrative of great men.[4]

This book documents the life of ʿAli Muttaqi and the Muttaqi community that followed him over three generations spanning one and a half centuries, beginning with ʿAli Muttaqi's birth in 1480 and ending with ʿAbd al-Haqq's death in 1642. It analyzes their collective effort to promote reformist Sufism that fused hadith studies, juridical principles (*qawāʿid*) and Sufi discipline (*adab*) in an ethical program with scholarly, political, and spiritual dimensions. They did this long before most scholars identified Islamic reformism and revivalism as a historically important force in the eighteenth century.

Only through the liminal and forgotten Muttaqi community did ʿAbd al-Haqq mature into the Sufi scholar famed in history, and only through ʿAbd al-Haqq did this community's reformist Sufi teaching flourish back in its members' South Asian homeland. Their journeys of body, soul, and mind over the boundaries of land and sea, political loyalty, and established custom constitute a "Hajj to the heart": an inner pilgrimage toward renewed piety. As the Qur'an says of the Hajj pilgrimage, *Those who honor the sacred rites of God should do so from sincere piety of heart* (Qur'an 22:37). Yet how the Muttaqi community defined "piety" led into subtle debates and bitter disputes with their fellow Muslims from South Asia.

Embarkation: Introducing a Passenger

Undertaking the pilgrimage is a turning point in life for every Muslim who shoulders the material dangers and ritual rigors of its journey. The Qur'an concludes its description of the hajj in verses 22:27-32 by specifying its timing, its conditions of peace, and its requirement of provision. For Muslims in South Asia before the sixteenth century, the Hajj often required land travel, which, though slow, allowed pilgrims to trade, study, and visit holy sites along the way in the major cities of Central Asia, Iran, and Iraq. But in ʿAli Muttaqi's era, embarking on the Hajj almost invariably meant provisioning for a treacherous sea voyage. This was especially true after the Safavid Empire in neighboring Iran became a Shiʿī state in the early sixteenth century and travel overland became difficult. For Muslims from South Asia, the Hajj was a spiritual climax intensified by the dangers of the passage and the difficulty of provision.

Packing one's satchels for the journey was an onerous task and anticipated an exciting adventure. The Qur'an warns pilgrims that making provision for the hajj is only a metaphor for the inward journey of ethical living. *Whatever good you may do, God surely knows of it—Take provision on your journey but know that the best provision is sincere piety, so stay wary in your piety if you have insight* (Qur'an 2:197). In one's spiritual life, the only apt provision is performing good works: doing good is like saving money now for insurance against future downturns and disasters. Yet the Qur'an makes a more profound warning amid the metaphors of banking and trading. It proclaims that good deeds are not enough, for they must be done with sincere intention and purity of heart: *the best provision is sincere piety.*

ʿAli Muttaqi heard these words with deep awareness, words that entered his heart and transformed it. He arrived in Mecca in 1535, one of countless South Asian Muslims who made the pilgrimage at the cusp of the early modern period, but he was a pilgrim with a difference. He was a scholar, well versed in Arabic, scriptural hermeneutics, and hadith studies. He was a Sufi, deeply immersed in mystical devotion and searching for spiritual intimacy with the Prophet and, through him, for the love of God. He was an advisor to rulers, experienced in political diplomacy and social critique. He was a voyager for whom pilgrimage was a metaphor for his whole life as a process, rather than just a one-time event after which he returned safely home. Pilgrimage extended to overtake and color his entire life. He sacrificed all for his ideals and principles, even if they were not popular and won him only continued exile.

This book will explore ʿAli Muttaqi's life, spirituality, struggles, writings, and legacy. His scholarship and writings covered genres like hadith, Sufism, and social ethics. Analyzing the legacy of ʿAli Muttaqi requires us to go on a voyage with him—a voyage of the imagination across the Indian Ocean from the Deccan where he was born; to Gujarat, where he established his authority; to Arabia, where he lived in exile and spread his ideals. He crossed the Arabian Sea five times, voyaging in states of despair, hope, distress, confidence, and serenity. This study catalogs all that he carried in his satchels. More than books, clothing, and food, ʿAli Muttaqi packed his satchels with ideas and ideals. He carried memories both fond and scarred. He carried skills hard-earned through studies and also insights gifted to him in flashes. He carried arguments with his colleagues, the consequences of which cost his followers their reputations and, at times, their very lives.

This study unpacks the satchels of ʿAli Muttaqi to display the burdens that he bore and the hopes that he nurtured. The satchels that held his piety's provision serve as metaphors for the chapters of this book. We can imagine him loading six satchels onto the ship that will carry him through his life's journey: satchels containing his youthful growth, his midlife exile, his mature authority, his contested mission, his dedicated followers, and his reformist legacy that they perpetuated after his death.

Moorings: Time and Place, Sources and Narratives

All voyages are ultimately circular. ʿAli Muttaqi left Gujarat and died in exile in Arabia, but his followers perpetuated his legacy back in South Asia. The coastal region of Gujarat is central to this story, along with its neighboring regions in the Deccan. This book builds on the work of Samira Sheikh, whose analysis of Gujarat left off in 1500.[5] In the sixteenth century, Gujarat thrived as a sultanate and subsequently as an important province of the Mughal Empire. As Jyoti Balachandran notes, "The message was loud and clear: the Gujarat Sultans were central to the functioning of the Muslim community in the region; they had ushered in a new chapter," and the message was broadcast through textual narratives, urban growth in ports and capitals, and architectural monuments.[6] Gujarat's long coastline, rich seaside entrepôts, and Muslim travelers illustrate South Asia's oceanic connections to Arabia and beyond.

The Muttaqi community thrived though sea journeys between Gujarat and Arabia, defining a "maritory" or maritime zone that changes our view of "territories" that otherwise seem disconnected. Sufi support of the sultans of Gujarat is one dimension of the story told in this book, which builds on Balachandran's recent analysis of historical vision offered by fifteenth-century Sufi texts in Gujarat. Another dimension that is more hidden and difficult to decipher is Sufi involvement with hadith scholarship. In Mecca, ʿAli Muttaqi studied hadith with the best scholars of his generation and fused Sufi discipline with hadith studies. He trained a generation in this style of reformist Sufism—a mixture of mysticism, hadith studies, theological knowledge, and political savvy.

In addition to ʿAli Muttaqi himself, this book documents three of his fellow passengers, his primary followers who moved through Gujarat to Arabia and back. ʿAbd al-Wahhāb Muttaqī lived and taught in Mecca (d. 1593). Muḥammad ibn Ṭāhir Pāṭanī transplanted the Muttaqi community's reformist ideals to Gujarat but was assassinated amid partisan conflicts there (d. 1578). ʿAbd al-Haqq, previously mentioned, successfully institutionalized his reformist Sufism in Delhi, deep in the landlocked capital of the expanding Mughal Empire, far from tumultuous coasts. Thereafter, ʿAli Muttaqi's ideals spread in South Asia and beyond the Mughal realm to Southeast Asia, where Sufi scholars in Aceh (in Sumatra) and other regions took initiation into this community. In Delhi, ʿAbd al-Haqq's madrasa and Sufi hospice (*khānqāh*) institutionalized the fusion between Sufism and hadith studies. He engaged with Mughal rulers, a strategy that ultimately did not work. But ʿAbd al-Haqq's institution and Sufi cadres and scholarly followers built a popular base, which slowly altered Islam in South Asia, gradually and indirectly.

The efforts of those in the Muttaqi community played out in a shifting geographic stage. Their story traverses the boundary of land and sea, complicates distinctions between regions like South Asia and Arabia, and transcends the binary of scriptural scholarship versus Sufi mysticism. Their efforts also played out as a chronological drama. Their story crosses an imaginary threshold important to Muslims but unnoticed by others: the advent of the Islamic millennium, "a symbolic occasion of great moment."[7] This occurred on October 19, 1591 (Muharram 1, AH 1000), in the middle of the period considered in this book (which we can conceive of as the "long sixteenth century" favored by historians of early modern world history). Muslims looked forward to its occurrence for the century leading up to it, beginning in 1495–96 (AH 900), with a heady mixture of anxiety and enthusiasm. Christians who were attentive to Islamic discourse predicted that if the Mahdī, the divinely guided religious leader of the last days as expected by Muslims, did not arrive by the year 1500, then all Muslims would renounce their religion under a soon-to-appear world-dominating Christian emperor.[8] Cornell Fleischer demonstrated the importance of apocalypticism and messianism in the powerful early modern

Islamic empires (especially in the Ottoman rivalry with Catholic empires in the Mediterranean world) and challenged other scholars to explore these themes in Safavid, Timurid, and Mughal contexts.[9]

This book takes up Fleischer's challenge in the Indian Ocean context. It inverts Fleischer's focus by examining those who opposed millennial speculation and sought to damper it rather than those who encouraged it and accrued power through it, building on Fleischer's insightful comment that apocalyptic discourse depended upon hadith reports and their interpretation.[10] ʿAli Muttaqi opposed the spiritual and political speculation that the impending millennium sparked in Muslim polities. He and his community wagered their authority as Sufi masters and hadith scholars in a discursive battle against speculative forces, which came to a head in Gujarat, where political instability led to a potent mix of anxiety and opportunity for Islamic movements both millennial and Sufi. For indeed, in 1496 a Sufi revivalist from South Asia proclaimed himself the Mahdi in Mecca and achieved a vibrant following in Gujarat by 1500. Gujarat, with its sea-lane connections to Arabia, was an important theater for millennial debates.

The decades leading up to the Islamic millennium constituted an opportunity for politico-religious reimagining. As a conceptual boundary in time, it helped Muslims integrate into their religious imagination those momentous political, social, and economic changes already at play. For Muslims around the Indian Ocean coasts, 1498 heralded great changes. The Portuguese invaded ports, seized islands, and dominated trade; soon centralizing states, such as the Mughal, Safavid, and Ottoman Empires, arose on land to claim divine mandate. In this era, sea journeys were endangered by the Portuguese, who were not mere pirates who had long preyed upon merchants and pilgrims along Indian Ocean coasts; they were, rather, the vanguard of European colonization, which began not on land but rather on the seas and its strategic islands. Portuguese intervention in South Asian politics contributed to the fall of the sultanate of Gujarat, the coastal polity that ʿAli Muttaqi chose as his home.

ʿAli Muttaqi and his followers are mentioned in every account of Islamic reform in South Asia, but their Sufi affiliations are obscured and their spiritual activities ignored in favor of their important position in hadith studies. Sufism was not a negligible phenomenon of folkloric performance or unorthodox marginality, as some scholars portray it. Rather, Sufis were active agents in political change, social reform, and Islamic scholarship. Sufism was the center of intellectual and political life during the end of the sultanate of Gujarat and the early Mughal period. This book illuminates the Muttaqi community's contribution to Sufism and explains its involvement in social and political affairs. In arguing these claims, this book will center the study of Sufism in Islamic discourses of ethics (*akhlāq*) and disciplined comportment (*adab*), following the lead of Muzaffar Alam.[11] It positions itself against other contemporary scholarly trends, such as seeing Sufism in terms of political power and social capital as in the scholarship of Nile Green, or in terms of bargaining with supernatural forces as in A. Azfar Moin.[12] Moin characterizes Sufis in the Mughal era as supporters of superstition in the form of sorcery, thaumaturgy, astrology, and divination. This book offers a more reasoned assessment—based on a broader foundation of archival sources—on interactions between Sufis and political rulers in the long sixteenth century. *Hajj to the Heart* makes this scholarly intervention by balancing information drawn from Sufi writings—theological, ethical, and hagiographic—with information from historical chronicles that were produced by courtiers.

Sufi ethics, discipline, and comportment provide a lens with which to analyze issues of political power and social relations in early modern Islam in South Asia. Sufis of the Muttaqi community saw themselves as channels for the Prophet Muhammad's inner charisma and outer norms, not merely as scholars of the scriptural tradition of hadith studies. While the Prophet's blessed body might have been inaccessible, the corpus of his traditions was available through textual expertise.[13] Members of the Muttaqi community specialized in hadith studies yet also saw themselves as living exemplars, embodying discourse through their own breathing flesh, performative ethics, and social intercourse.

To tell the story of the Muttaqi community more vividly than its cursory mention in previous scholarship, this book draws on rare manuscript sources in Arabic, Persian, and Urdu. These sources, often unpublished and mostly unedited, include ʿAli Muttaqi's original writings and oral discourses and ʿAbd al-Haqq's account of ʿAli Muttaqi and ʿAbd al-Wahhab Muttaqi's lives and teachings titled *Zād al-Muttaqīn*, or "Provision of the Pious."[14] ʿAbd al-Haqq's writings are crucial in this study, including his letters to Mughal grandees, his critique of the famous Naqshbandi revivalist Aḥmad Sirhindī (d. 1624), and his religio-political advice to Emperor Jahāngīr (ruled 1605–27). This study takes into account the biographies provided by the protagonists and their supporters, in addition to those given by their adversaries in the Shaṭṭārī Order and the Mahdawī movement.

Using fifty manuscript books by ʿAli Muttaqi, in addition to other sources from archives in India, Pakistan, Turkey, Cairo, Europe, and North America, this book provides the most complete treatment of this three-generation community of Sufi scholars. Yet gathering these sources, translating passages, and analyzing them are not enough. This book breathes life into their literary remains to lift them off the page and clothe their lines of script with flesh and feeling. The archival lines traced on paper—by them and about them—call us to imagine them afresh through prose that is more novelistic. Each chapter, conceived as a satchel prepared for a long sea journey, begins with a vignette based on documented facts but presented as dialogue and drama; the narrative vignettes dispense with formalities, such as diacritics and death dates, in order to invite readers into the story and empathize with its characters. For just as sails are mere cloth until the wind blows into them, so academic writing is mere information until readers enliven it with imagination. Only then can readers be moved to embark on a voyage of thought, argument, and inspiration—a true Hajj to the heart.

FIRST SATCHEL

ʿAli Muttaqi's Growth

As the Qur'an recitation faded, hushed expectation settled over the gathering. Hundreds of listeners crowded into the khanqah: the Sufi hospice's wide courtyard in Burhanpur was a sea of people seated to form an open space between the troop of musicians and the shaykh, the elderly Sufi master whose grizzled head was bowed. His turban, the color of marigolds, was the brightest object in the courtyard on that warm night. A sustained note from the *sarangi* strings rang out, conjuring forth the voices of the Qawwali singers. Slow and low they began singing a quatrain in Persian to open the *mehfil-e samaʿ*.[1]

Our raft is sunk, of drowning we're afraid
You support the helpless and dismayed
For the sake of ʿUsman Haruni, your master
O Muʿin al-Din Chishti, come to our aid

The voices of the Qawwals swelled as the drums behind them tapped out a rhythm, first gently on the *tabla* and then, as the singers began to clap percussively, more robustly on the deep-voiced *dhol* and *mridang*.

A young boy watched the musicians intently, as emotion washed over their faces and their throats strained with song. He felt his father's warm presence beside him, calming his fear in this strange and awe-inspiring gathering. His father was looking the other way, toward the shaykh, named Shah Bajan, who raised his head as the song gained momentum, his face luminous as he sank rapt into the vortex of melody and rhyme. "Dark night and frightful waves as storms swirl and roar / Can they know my state, those who stay on the shore?" The father whispered to his son, "Listen carefully, ʿAli! That couplet is by Hafiz Shirazi. They chose it because of the image of drowning in a swirling storm, a *girdab*."[2] But his son was watching Shah Bajan, as the shaykh subtly lifted the corner of his prayer carpet on which he sat cross-legged, otherwise immobile as a statue.

The shaykh looked under the carpet out of the corner of his eye and, seeing nothing there, lowered it back into place. The boy turned to his father, "Why is our shaykh fiddling with . . . ?" "Hush, ʿAli! Mind your *adab*! Focus on the lyrics—clear your heart of everything except the images reflected there." The boy knit his brow in consternation as the tempo accelerated into a new verse.

If pain is from you then no cure I desire
If passion is for you, to hardship I aspire
If I be killed in the path of loving you
Not a cent of blood-money from you I require

The quatrain hovered over the courtyard as his father leaned over to whisper in the boy's ear, "This poem will have a deep impact on our shaykh—it is from our patron saint, Burhan al-Din Gharib."[3] The Qawwals repeated the Persian verses, syncopated against the drum beat, lingering on the word *ʿishq*, or love, rendering it in countless variations. The shaykh's frail body quivered with delight, as this poem was a favorite of his much-beloved spiritual ancestor. The boy observed carefully: the shaykh appeared to be holding inside an enormous energy that surged through him, but he stayed seated with profound gravitas.

The boy saw the shaykh, once again, with frail but nimble fingers, lift the corner of his prayer carpet and peer beneath it. Glancing around his father's form, the boy saw that three gold coins lay where before there had been none. The shaykh slyly picked them up and dropped the carpet's corner back in place, and then he smiled. The boy's mouth fell open with questions as he plucked at his father's sleeve, but his voice was suppressed as drums thundered, shifting from a stately rhythm to a swinging and lilting pace. Their staccato clapping picked up speed as the poetry shifted from Persian to the local Indian tongue. Simple and sweet, the words poured forth—*My lord and savior, helper and protector of all.* Cries burst from the audience as some sobbed and others raised their hands in prayer. "It is our shaykh's own poem," the father exclaimed to his one, "in our own Gujari tongue!"[4]

My lord and savior, helper and protector of all
You who take us across no matter what may befall
A fearful mountain path is before me, steep and tall

With lions lurking and thorns where my feet fall
O jungle's king, over everything ruling, great and small
I give my life and soul to you, now hold me in thrall!

As the musicians sang "I give my life," the elderly shaykh sprang to his feet like a youth and strode across the courtyard, tears coursing down his cheeks. Standing rapt before the singers, who continued to repeat "my life and soul," he tossed a gold coin into the lap of the chief singer, followed by another and another. As the boy watched, engrossed yet fearful, it seemed that the old shaykh was flying though his feet were still touching the ground. Those around him rushed to catch hold of his robe as he sat down again on his carpet. Members of the audience rose to bow before him, offering copper and silver coins, which the shaykh received with benedictions to each and every one as they took the opportunity to kiss his hand or touch his feet. Some remained weeping in their places while others rose to spin in graceful circles, their souls soaring on the winds of melody.

Such ritual assemblies of Sufi music, called *Mehfil-e Samāʿ* (or "Qawwali" in popular parlance) were regular events in the late fifteenth-century Deccan, where ʿAli Muttaqi was born. His father introduced him to the Chishti community and its musical ritual at a young age. ʿAli Muttaqi took initiation as a boy with Shāh Bājan (d. 1507), an innovative Sufi master, hadith scholar, poet, and patron of musicians. The music gave life to lyrics in Persian and Indic languages, rooting Islam in the local environment, even if it always opened and closed with recitation from the Qurʾan, framing this multilingual and interfaith ritual with sacred Arabic.

As ʿAli Muttaqi grew into a youth, he found his ancestral land, Khandesh (Khāndēsh) with its capital of Burhanpur (Burhānpūr), to be both rich and barren. It was wealthy because of its fine industry with cotton that flourished in its iron-rich soil. Its heritage nurtured him, like the rain that the Qurʾan describes falling on the earth and making it vibrate with life. *We created you from dust, then a sperm-drop, then a mucus clot, then a fleshy body . . . then we bring you forth as a child, then nurture you to maturity so that you grow firm. . . . You see the earth barren until we rain down the waters and it quivers, swells, and sprouts with every kind of growth* (Qurʾan 22:5). To understand ʿAli Muttaqi's voyage of life, we must begin with the soil—physical, social, and spiritual—from which he grew. This chapter is a satchel filled with memories—memories of his birth, childhood, youthful struggles, and familiar homeland; it is a satchel filled by ʿAli Muttaqi for his travels. His education and youthful experiences gave him the confidence to reach beyond his birthplace and family tradition.

Burhanpur was known by its residents as Dār al-Surūr, or the "Abode of Bliss." At the northernmost edge of the Deccan plateau, the city was founded with the blessing of a Chishti saint and harbored a deep Sufi tradition. Yet ʿAli Muttaqi was not satisfied with its contemporary forms and wanted to leave the Abode of Bliss, or at least leave its inherited and routine forms of ecstasy. He searched for an authentic voice as a Muslim saint, a search that led him away from the South Asian interior toward its coasts and waterways. His youthful life was unusual in that, even after renouncing worldly life in favor of living as an aspiring saint, he could not easily accept any of the modes of saintly authority that permeated his social surroundings. In the course of his spiritual journey, he explored the various paradigms of saintly authority found in his time, rejecting one after the other. In the end, he estranged himself from his colleagues ritually, ideologically, and even geographically.

The satchel of this chapter will illustrate ʿAli Muttaqi's growth, from tenuous beginnings to maturing as scholar and status-wielding saint. ʿAli Muttaqi's life was woven from contradictions and conflicts with his environment, which gave him a distinct individuality. The values that he affirmed were often at variance with those of his contemporaries and even with those from whom he inherited status and authority, like his father and his first Sufi masters. ʿAli Muttaqi grew up immersed in the rituals of the Chishti Sufi order but rejected them. He came to see sainthood not as a status to be inherited by carrying out a tradition but rather as a quality to be acquired through preparation and labor. He explored authenticity as a saint, in contrapuntal movement to his questioning of the accepted forms of saintly legitimacy that enjoyed social recognition in his local environment. His early life interweaves these two crucial terms that are often in contradistinction: authenticity and legitimacy. However, this will become clear only against the background of Sufi practice that he rejected.

Heritage: Chishti Sufis Spreading Islam in South Asia

Sufism, or *taṣawwuf*, means "Islamic mysticism." Mysticism can be described as "love of the absolute" in contrast to practical accommodation to routine reality.[5] Islamic mysticism seeks spiritual insight and direct experience of God, a search guided by the Qur'an and based upon the example of the Prophet Muhammad, his intimate follower ʿAli, and their spiritual followers (known as *awliyāʾ*—saints or "God's Friends"). It is a way to achieve purity of heart (*ṣafwat al-qalb* in Arabic) and acquire wise insight (*sophia* in Greek, which was absorbed into Arabic), as in the way the ascetic followers of the Prophet Muhammad (*ahl al-ṣaffa*) lived on a bare bench outside the first mosque in Medina.[6] Sufis organized their method of practicing mysticism into socially coherent orders, each called a *ṭarīqa*, or "Way." Over time, the vast majority of Muslims accepted Sufism as integral to Islam and upheld its saints as exemplars.

In the tenth century, Sufis settled in a village called Chisht (in Afghanistan near Herat), where they cultivated Sufism with ascetic rigor, poetic eloquence, and musical meditation; they were known as Khwājagān, or "Masters of Chisht." As the frontier of Sunni rule moved eastward with Turkic invasions into South Asia, Khwāja Muʿīn al-Dīn Chishtī (d. 1236) settled at Ajmer. He taught that a Sufi cultivates "generosity like a river, magnanimity like the sun, and humility like the earth." He distilled universal teachings from Islam, attracting Hindu devotees while extolling Muhammad as the perfect human being and Imam ʿAli as the exemplary saint. He and his companions elevated devotional music to a central practice in Sufism.[7] Two generations later, Niẓām al-Dīn Awliyā (d. 1325) institutionalized the Chishti Order in the capital of the Delhi sultanate. As that sultanate expanded over large swaths of South Asia, its cities were enriched by Muslim migrants from Iran and Central Asia who were fleeing Mongol incursions. Nizam al-Din Awliya's family hailed from Bukhārā (now in Uzbekistan) but were counted as Sayyid descendants of the Prophet Muhammad. He grew up an orphan in northern India, but acquired Islamic learning and later embraced voluntary poverty as the best way to uphold the Prophet's ethical teachings.[8] Chishti Sufis like Nizam al-Din Awliya rigorously upheld that the best provision in the journey of life is not merely piety but rather interior reliance upon God (*tawakkul*) by renouncing worldly acquisitions.[9] This aspect of Chishti teachings would have a great impact on ʿAli Muttaqi during his years of travel, pilgrimage, and exile.

Chishti Sufis cultivated poetry and music while upholding ascetic rigor, which won them fame in South Asia. But they also nurtured Islamic scholarship inflected toward teaching about equality, love, and renunciation. Nizam al-Din Awliya was a hadith scholar and enraged jurists by using these reports to defend the legality of listening to music.[10] Chishti Sufis promoted scholarship and hadith studies but subordinated the literal and political value of such knowledge to the quest for spiritual poverty and humility.[11]

As the frontier of Islamic society moved southward, many Chishti Sufis left Delhi. Burhān al-Dīn Gharīb (d. 1337), a disciple of Nizam al-Din Awliya, settled in the frontier territory of the Deccan. When he first came to Nizam al-Din Awliya's gathering, it was announced that a "poor stranger" (*gharīb*) had arrived, but the shaykh replied, "He is indeed poor now, but the whole world will come to know him."[12] From this first encounter, he earned the nickname Gharib and his future fame was predicted. Nizam al-Din Awliya understood how Burhan al-Din embodied a hadith report in which the Prophet advised, "Live in this world as if you are a stranger or a traveler passing through."[13] Burhan al-Din Gharib took the Chishti engagement with music and poetry to the Deccan when he settled near Daulatabad (Dawlatābād).

Burhan al-Din Gharib fostered the growth of the Chishti Order in the Deccan through his patronage of sung poetry and oral teachings and, later, through adherents' visitation to his tomb.[14] The colorful ecstasies of the Chishti Order shaped ʿAli Muttaqi's early life, for they were prominent in Burhanpur.[15] When the Deccan region of Khandesh—which contained Daulatabad—became independent under the Fārūqī dynasty, its rulers claimed that Burhan al-Din Gharib had blessed their forefather and foretold of his becoming a king. These regional kings—titled "Mīrān" in distinction to the sultans of Delhi—built their capital at the village where Burhan al-Din stayed while traveling from Delhi to the Deccan. Burhanpur was named after the region's greatest saint, and his distinctive Chishti style of performative sainthood became the norm.

Eighty-five years after the founding of Burhanpur, ʿAli Muttaqi was born in 1480.[16] He grew up during the long reign of the fifth king of the Faruqi dynasty, Mīrān ʿĀdil Khān II (ruled 1457–1503). That ruler built the citadel of Burhanpur and established it as the capital of a small but rich kingdom. His magnificent domed tomb is still today treated with reverence.

During the reign of four Faruqi kings before ʿAli Muttaqi's birth, the Sufi admirers of Burhan al-Din fashioned a lively local culture that elevated public ecstasy as the strongest criterion to demonstrate one's sainthood.[17] The leader of this Chishti community in Khandesh was Shah Bajan, the "Master Music Maker" whose given name was Bahaʾ al-Din. His writing demonstrates important aspects of Sufi *adab* and the vernacularization of Islam in South Asia. It contains the earliest examples of Urdu poetry (in a dialect called Gujari), showing how Chishtis used local poetic forms and religious images, including those sometimes associated with Hindi literature and Hindu devotion.[18]

ʿAli Muttaqi's father had him initiated into the Chishti Order at the age of seven at the hand of Shah Bajan. He had built a congregational mosque and Sufi hospice in Burhanpur but was famous for musical sessions featuring his

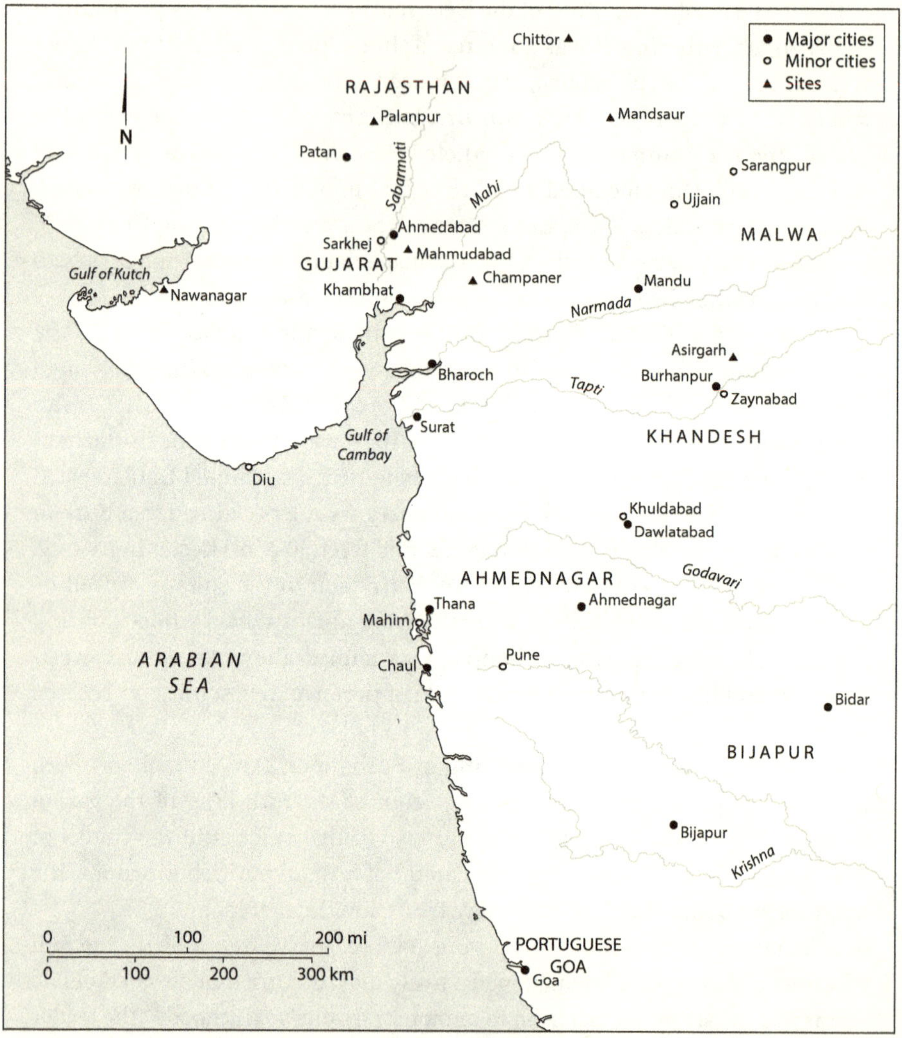

Gujarat and the Deccan in the sixteenth century

original poetry; his popular title, "Master Music Maker," shows that his authority as a saint was intimately linked to his love of God displayed in ecstatic responses to rhyming word and rhythmic sound. As depicted in the vignette that opens this chapter, his miracles centered on paying musicians lavishly despite his commitment to voluntary poverty.

Born in Ahmedabad (Aḥmadābād), Shah Bajan was learned in hadith and trained with Chishti masters famed for their piety (*taqwā*) and reliance on

Dargah of the Chishti Master Shah Bajan in Burhanpur.

God (*tawakkul*).[19] Shah Bajan combined outward rigor with inward love for music and poetry, through which he could reach out to the common people. Chishti Sufis like Shah Bajan brought Islam into their local context, to make its practices meaningful in their society and to translate its values through symbols easily understandable by common people. He cultivated an early form of Urdu—called Gujari in this region—that was enriched by expressions from varied sources and religious traditions. Shah Bajan wrote "Khazāʾin-e Raḥmatallāh" in Persian prose but inserted in it poems he composed in Gujari.[20] Few of his poems have been translated into English, yet they are compelling despite the difficulty in deciphering their archaic language.[21]

Shah Bajan's Gujari poems speak in simple images from daily life yet interlace lines of Persian, restating the meaning in more formal tones.[22] He connected the "local" South Asian spoken idiom to the "universal" Islamic symbolic world invoked by Persian. Despite his simple images and colloquial language, Shah Bajan knew theology and Islamic sciences so well that he expressed in creative ways the essential features of Islam. In the following poem, Shah Bajan begins by urging his listeners to awaken the mind to keep watch over the heart and thereby restrain the actions of the body.[23]

> Of all bad deeds, the heart is the king
> Keep watch over that lazy arrogant thing
> Uphold *shariʿa*'s discipline, that's the best
> Don't let idols into the cavern of your chest
> *Tariqa* is where the Prophet's acts are found
> Follow him with faith, don't just mess around
> The real *haqiqa* is like an ocean vast and wide
> Most who enter drown, few reach the other side

The poem begins by addressing the heart (Gr. *jī*; Ar. *qalb*). In Sufi thought, the heart is the center of the person: if enlightened by a wakeful mind and insight, the heart is the vehicle for good, but if darkened by a selfish nature and lust, then it is the vehicle for evil expressed in our bodily actions. *God has not made two hearts in one chest* (Qur'an 33:4). The human heart can have only one loving orientation: toward the world's pleasures or toward God's spiritual realities.

From this first division into three levels, Shah Bajan elaborates corresponding levels of three. Every person consists of body, heart, and mind. For a person to become a real human being, she or he must understand the relationship between matter, soul, and spirit. Becoming a real human means following religious duty (*sharīʿa*), joining an order for mystical training (*ṭariqa*), and realizing ultimate reality (*ḥaqīqa*). This spiritual realization is the fruit of following the *shariʿa* and cultivating *tariqa*, but it is achieved by only a few who realize that their ego is passing away such that God alone is real. This is what Shah Bajan means when he says *haqiqa* is "an ocean vast and wide / Most who enter drown, few reach the other side."

Chishti Sufis like Shah Bajan explored commonalities with other religious communities. His poetry reveals this pursuit, through words and images, of a common foundation for ethics that is wider than one's own dogmatic community. Shah Bajan was a pioneer in this movement and wrote his poems to be sung. He called some of his sung poems *jikri*, a Gujari pronunciation of *dhikr*, or meditation that repeats God's names. In South Asia, some Sufi orders demanded silent *dhikr*, while other orders favored group *dhikr* with only a drum to keep rhythm or chanting only in Arabic. In contrast, Chishti Sufis taught that *dhikr* is good whether in Arabic or in another language, yet devotional music is better when singing poems in the local language accompanied with a variety of instruments, both Indic and Iranian.[24]

Shah Bajan's lyrics reveal the importance of *adab*. *Adab* is the term for "literature" in Islamicate cultures, but its deeper meaning is multidimensional in ways not always acknowledged in Western scholarship. Marshall Hodgson, the historian who asserted the importance of Sufism and literature to understanding Islamic civilization, recognized that *adab* began as courtly discourse, implying both literary eloquence and refined manners.[25] For Hodgson, *adab* stood in contradistinction to the *shariʿa*; it represented a discourse of courtly norms and aristocratic prerogatives that prevailed against the more restrictive vision of "piety-minded" jurists and hadith scholars. His analysis is suitable for the Abbasid period (eighth through the eleventh centuries). However, Hodgson codes *adab* as "literature" when his analysis passes from Arabic to Persian and Asian vernacular languages; indeed, he uses Persianate literature as a segue to analyzing arts and architecture in general, pairing them as literary and visual components of a wider "aesthetic culture."[26] In this sense, the indigenous term for "literature" in Persian and Urdu is *adabiyāt*, constructed from the plural and understood as "products of eloquent refinement." Courtly etiquette remained important, but it was increasingly coded as *ādāb*, again constructed from the plural and understood as "behaviors of refined manners." However, as Sufism grew and developed toward the end of the Abbasid period, it mediated between court and mosque. The Sufi hospice (*khanqah*) and saint's tomb (*dargah*) became sites for the rejoining of piety and propriety, fervor and fluency, reverence and refinement. Sufis appropriated literary and musical forms from aristocratic culture that radiated from the court, adapting these forms to their own uses; in Sufi hands, literature and music became tools for training in a moral system that was both deeper and more popular than juridical Islam. Sufism recreated the original multivalent meaning of *adab*, constructed from the singular and understood as "discipline" that leads to outer refinement and inner piety. Sufism restored ethics to the meaning of *adab*.[27]

Like *adab*, the term *akhlaq*, meaning "ethics," is also a complex notion in Islamic civilization. Following Hodgson's insights, Muzaffar Alam studies both courtly and Sufi approaches to ethics in South Asia. For him, *adab* is courtly refinement that produced *akhlaq* literature, the formal ethical system that addresses governance outside of the narrowly juridical *shariʿa*.[28] Composed by court scholars, *akhlaq* is an elite discourse whose user may be trained in jurisprudence or literature but have a philosophical orientation to the maintenance of justice. While focusing on *akhlaq*, Alam largely ignores *adab* in his treatment of systematic ethics and political philosophy in South Asia. However, Sufis in South Asia developed *adab* as ethical literature linked to practical discipline on a popular level, parallel to how court scholars developed *akhlaq* as philosophical literature on an elite level. Barbara Metcalf has reflected on how Sufi authors and leaders have made the concept of *adab* "a key to central religious concepts of South Asian Islam."[29] Nizam al-Din Awliya is a classic example: he bridged courtly and popular audiences so effectively that certain sultans perceived him as a threat, while other sultans relied on him as an indispensable support. He did not write books, but his oral discourses were recorded in a new genre of ethical literature, *malfūẓāt* or "oral teachings." His followers in the courtly orbit wrote texts in genres as varied as political theory and lyric poetry. The breakup of central authority of the Delhi sultanate in the fourteenth century both created regional sultanates with their own provincial capitals and increased the importance of vernacular languages. Sufis responded to both stimuli and strove to preserve the ethical content of *adab* as "refined manners" by stressing moral discipline rather than aristocratic etiquette. Within this wider civilizational perspective, Shah Bajan's Sufi poetry in Gujari takes on new importance as an example of *adab*, discipline that both shapes moral character and inspires eloquent words.

Chishti Sufis nourished an emerging style of vernacular poetry and, similarly, had a decidedly localizing penchant when it came to pilgrimage. They advocated visiting shrines of South Asian saints, which largely eclipsed the pilgrimage to Mecca. For instance, Shah Bajan started on the Hajj, but partway there a dream informed him that his intention was accepted and he must return to South Asia. His aborted pilgrimage confirmed a trope among Chishtis: it was a higher ethical duty to stay local in both place and style than to make the long journey to Mecca or adopt Arabizing airs that would separate one from the local populace. This vernacular attitude among Chishtis might be termed a religious ideology of confirming the particularistic against the universal in Islamic devotion.

In Burhanpur, ʿAli Muttaqi attended musical sessions with Shah Bajan as a child, as depicted in the fictional vignette that begins this chapter. In these Qawwali assemblies, ʿAli Muttaqi witnessed the dramatic displays of ecstasy and trance that they could inspire, giving him his first taste of spirituality and his early notion of the role of saints. ʿAli Muttaqi attended these assemblies to cultivate his spiritual sense at the same age that he attended school to hone his rational faculties.

Dissatisfaction: Rejecting a Chishti Heritage

When ʿAli Muttaqi was around fifteen years of age, his father died. He then left Burhanpur to seek employment, having completed the traditional course of religious and literary training. He presented himself as an educated young gentleman at Mandu (Māñḍū), the capital of Malwa (Mālwā), a prosperous kingdom just north of Khandesh. Mandu was the colloquial name for Māñḍawgāṙh, meaning "Fortress of Joy" (Persian sources translate its Indic name as Shādīyābād). ʿAli Muttaqi arrived at the court of Ghiyāth al-Dīn Khiljī (ruled 1469–1500), whose reign was peaceful and prosperous: according to the historian Farishta, even the mice and birds in Mandu's palace had monthly stipends assigned for their welfare![30] Like Deccan kingdoms that gained independence from Delhi, the rulers of Malwa patronized a new elite class of courtiers, soldiers, artists, and builders.[31] ʿAli Muttaqi was one of many talented people attracted to their court. He spent his early twenties at court, amassing enough wealth to move his mother and family to Mandu. Records about his early life are vague, but it seems his householding success was short lived.

Hagiographic sources say that ʿAli Muttaqi's worldly success tasted bitter to him, and while still young he resigned from his position at the Malwa court. What caused his sudden change of heart? At this time, Sultan Ghiyath al-Din Khilji was aging, and his two sons spawned a bitter rivalry. Before the sultan died, the younger son attacked the elder, who served as prime minister. In retaliation, the elder son slew his brother and his whole family, despite their taking refuge in their father's palace. The elder son was crowned Sultan Nāṣir al-Dīn (ruled 1500–1512), and a few days later his father was poisoned.[32] ʿAli Muttaqi witnessed both fratricide and patricide at Mandu and may have been caught up in factional fighting. He never related the exact causes but committed himself to renouncing worldly ambition.

The young ʿAli Muttaqi returned to Burhanpur in hopes of continued Sufi training but found that Shah Bajan had died. He renewed his initiation with Shah Bajan's son, ʿAbd al-Ḥakīm, but was unmoved by the Chishti rituals that had so charged his childhood. The emotional outpouring, eloquent poetry, and ecstatic music of Burhanpur now failed to stir him. Thus, he began reaching back into his Chishti lineage, beyond the immediate examples of his master, to find a model that struck him as authentic. He recorded quotations from past Sufi masters whom he admired, titling this collection from his early life "al-Jawāhir al-Thamīna," or "The Precious Jewels."[33] ʿAli Muttaqi's youthful search brought him to a new role model: the master of the master of Shah Bajan, named Shaykh ʿAzīzallāh Mutawakkil (d. 1506), whose epithet means "Reliant on God Alone."[34] His reputation glowed in Mandu, where ʿAli Muttaqi heard of him.

ʿAzizallah Mutawakkil was born in Gujarat and traveled to the Deccan. When he learned that people in Daulatabad "were worshipping only in outward form while relying on Brahmins for their daily affairs," he headed to Mandu.[35] ʿAzizallah never accepted gifts of food or money, relying solely on God for daily provision.[36] When he was about to cross the Narmada River and arrive at Mandu, he announced that he would enter the city on the condition that the ruler would not meet him, send him gifts, or seek his blessing. The sultan of Malwa complied and ʿAzizallah settled in Mandu, whose residents looked to him as a patron saint, while traveling often to Burhanpur. He lived in strict isolation, emerging from his room only on rare occasions when others were in need. He followed the Chishti rule of not saving for the future. Each night, he would clear his home and distribute any goods found there to the needy—even excess water. This ascetic style of devotion appealed to ʿAli Muttaqi: he asked leave of his master, Shah Bajan's son, and followed the example of ʿAzizallah Mutawakkil. He traveled as a form of training to discipline the self and minimize his reliance on other people and worldly comforts. As he traveled, ʿAli Muttaqi met different spiritual masters from diverse Sufi communities. From his viewpoint as a wandering ascetic, most of them were comfortably self-satisfied. ʿAli Muttaqi considered Sufism, as it existed in his local environment, to be in grave need of reform. In this opinion he was not alone, for there was a movement raging in Gujarat and the Deccan that confirmed his ideas: the Mahdawi movement. He was attracted to this vibrant movement, which elevated the ideals of Sufi communities while critiquing their acquired forms.

The Mahdawi movement was a complex religious and social movement that grew out of Chishti ideals. The leader of the movement, Sayyid Muḥammad Jawnpūrī (d. 1505), claimed to be more than just another Sufi master or Muslim saint. Instead he declared himself the Mahdi who would come to revive the Muslim community, to correctly interpret the Qur'an, and to establish social justice. As the Mahdi, he claimed to embody the ethical virtues of the Prophet Muhammad in a way that replicated the Prophet's presence, as if the Prophet's personality had appeared again (though without the gift of revelation). This intimacy with the Prophet, which approached total identity with him, would wipe away all the routine forms of religious authority and social legitimacy in Islamic society like so much rust that had crusted the face of a mirror. Those who accepted Sayyid Muhammad's claim to be the Mahdi renounced their position, property, and family. They joined Mahdawi circles (*dāʾira*) in shantytowns outside cities where they engaged in intense spartan devotions, scrupulously fulfilled ritual obligations, and shared their wealth.

Their leader claimed that the Prophet Muhammad embodied both the outer ritual forms and their implicit inner ethic, yet the Arab Muslims of his time could not apprehend this inner ethical meaning of revelation. Therefore, the Prophet had announced the future coming of the Mahdi, who would embody the Prophet's ethics and make explicit what the Prophet had left implicit. This was the teaching of virtuous excellence (*iḥsān*), which had been the goal of saints to convey for almost a millennium. However, none could convey it completely, because no saint was the replica of the Prophet in bloodline, mindset, and spirituality, until the advent of the Mahdi. Sayyid Muhammad Jawnpuri left Jawnpur to wander with his followers. In accord with hadith reports relating to the future Mahdi, he made the pilgrimage and in Mecca announced publicly his claim to be the Mahdi. Returning to Gujarat, he made two public announcements and attracted followers who set up a huge camp to hear his discourses on Qurʾanic interpretation and ethics.

In this way, Sayyid Muhammad Jawnpuri tried to rescue Sufi ideals from the limited domain of Sufi orders. He rejected the rituals of popular practice and their mediation through past masters. He claimed to exclusively represent spiritual training in its complete form (*takmīl-e ṭarīqa*). He did not rely on any horizontal connection to a mediating saintly guide but rather gave up his ego to be absorbed in the spiritual personality of the Prophet Muhammad. His followers consequently rejected the routinized sources of religious authority: they jettisoned Sufi lineages, distanced themselves from allegiance to any single legal method, and even called into question many of the hadith reports about the Mahdi himself. They tried to rebuild the prophetic community around a living exemplar in the Mahdi, as the early Islamic community had grown around the Prophet's guidance in the moment. Their new community repudiated the institutions that seemed to them to have become alienated from the spirit of the Prophet, in favor of radical renunciation of wealth, social status, and scholarly pride.

ʿAli Muttaqi became involved with the Mahdawis. They impressed him with their ascetic lifestyle and devotional practices, and he had extended discussions with them. He may have had acquaintances in this movement, accepted hospitality at their camps, or joined them as a renunciant member of their liminal community. In his view, the Mahdawis advocated the strict ascetic regime of ʿAzizallah Mutawakkil. Externally, they refused to save money and food from day to day to live in sole reliance on divine providence and withdrew from habitual social and family relations. Internally, they cultivated an intense form of ritual meditation with the goal of waking ecstasy, which Sayyid Muhammad Jawnpuri termed "seeing God in this world with one's eyes."

This movement grew amid criticism and persecution, advocating revival of the *shariʿa* around the charismatic Mahdi. Spurred by expectation of the millennium (marked by the year 1000 in the Islamic calendar), the Mahdawi movement advocated total rejection of Islamic society as it had historically evolved and a total withdrawal from routine forms of social life in favor of building a radically new and just society. In this call for a new beginning, the Mahdawis were both utopian and absolutist: they held that Muslims who did not accept Sayyid Muhammad as the Mahdi promised at the end of time were actually infidels. As a seed community that would revitalize and recreate the true Muslim community once again, as the Prophet Muhammad had done almost a millennium before, they claimed for themselves the title of true Muslims.

Sayyid Muhammad Jawnpuri died in 1505, when ʿAli Muttaqi was in his midtwenties. Conflict intensified between followers of the purported Mahdi and his detractors. Accusations of infidelity flew between the Mahdawis and their Sunni opponents, erupting into sharpened rhetoric between the sultan of Gujarat and the Mahdawi camps. Violence and denunciation shocked ʿAli Muttaqi and led him to doubt the Mahdawis, whom he had admired. The Mahdawis persisted in building a schismatic community within the wider Sunni community that ignored or questioned their mission; in response, ʿAli Muttaqi concluded that their ideals for reviving the *shariʿa* and reforming Sufi devotional practice were indivisibly linked to their project to build a separate community. This nullified any benefit of their ideals, since their program for reform could never spread widely in the general society, bound as it was to the doctrine of the Mahdi.

At first, ʿAli Muttaqi made these conclusions viscerally rather than intellectually. He wrote that, despite his initial interest in Mahdawi practices and adherents' ascetic way of life, he grew increasingly skeptical that Sayyid Muhammad Jawnpuri was the Mahdi. In this way, ʿAli Muttaqi is like the famous Mughal-era historian ʿAbd al-Qādir Badāʾūnī (d. 1605), who penned the earliest record of the Mahdawis by a Sunni opponent.[37] ʿAli Muttaqi's rancorous debate with the Mahdawis will be detailed in this book in the fourth satchel. At this point in his life, ʿAli Muttaqi had no role model in his local environment from his Chishti community or from the Mahdawis. He continued to wander: his outward rootlessness expressed his inward confusion as he failed to find a personal model upon whom to base his aspirations.

From Gujarat, ʿAli Muttaqi traveled northward through Sindh to Multan. The hagiographic sources are vague about the chronology or itinerary of his travels. He unmoored himself from his Chishti heritage, a "continental" Sufi movement that spread from Delhi to its satellite towns and distant provinces on the pattern of the sultanate of Delhi's imperium. He rejected the Mahdawi alternative, which was like a politicized version of the Chishti Order that morphed under the pressure of millennial expectations. In his wanderings, ʿAli Muttaqi searched for something new, exhibiting "coastal" movement that abandoned mainland fixities in favor of fluidity and exploration. Sindh was where the Gujarati coastline met the Indus River delta; traveling from there upriver led one into the land of five rivers, the Punjab. Traversing this coastal and riverine system, he minimized intake of food and social intercourse to build up inner stamina and spiritual insight.

ʿAli Muttaqi traveled to hone his inner resources. He was "thoroughly dissatisfied with the outward formalities of inherited saintly authority and the way masters trained disciples among his contemporary Sufi colleagues, so he traveled to Multan to search for the authentic principle [*maqṣūd-e aṣlī*] of spiritual development."[38] ʿAli Muttaqi did not intend to meet a new master in Multan but was rather discovering for himself in the journey what were the real principles of Sufi practice. His travels were a direct form of training in ethical nonattachment that eschewed elaborate ritual forms (as in Chishti devotion) and an ideological framework (as in Mahdawi renunciation). This was an experiment in "the death of the will" and later inspired his written work on what to do if one has not found an acceptable saint as a guide.[39] ʿAli Muttaqi's biographer describes these travels at length to show how he systematically limited his desires down to the minimum that would support his life.

In Multan, the major city on the Indus and a center of Sufi scholarship, he met the man who could serve as his model of sainthood. Ḥusām al-Dīn Muttaqī became his spiritual guide, embodying inward sincerity and outward asceticism while orienting his spirituality to strengthening the Sunni community against schism. Upon meeting him, ʿAli Muttaqi concluded that his youthful training in the Chishti Order had little benefit and many pitfalls. He began again, to mine his own experience and find the criteria of saintly authenticity under new guidance. He settled outside of Multan with Husam al-Din for an intense two-year discipleship. His overriding concern in this period was the "preservation of his faith" from all the youthful experiences that had distracted him: showy musical devotion, worldly ambition, and sectarian adventurism.

Biographical sources do not name Husam al-Din's formal affiliation to a

Sufi order. He used the nickname "Muttaqi" (meaning the "Pious One") rather than a formal moniker (*nisba*) relating him to an order. The Suhrawardi Order had long dominated Multan, and its members cultivated scriptural studies and avoided musical gatherings.[40] Husam al-Din shared those opinions but protested how Suhrawardi leaders dabbled in politics and built powerful family dynasties, so he seems to have not belonged to that order. Husam al-Din advocated the "death of self-will," which was vividly described in the Qadiri Order; he may have been a Qadiri, for that order had newly flourished near Multan.[41]

Husam al-Din did not initiate ʿAli Muttaqi into an order. Rather, he gave the principles that underlay all the orders. He trained ʿAli Muttaqi for two years, allowing the latter to systematize intuitions he had gleaned from his travels and his rejection of other spiritual guides. ʿAli Muttaqi, who underwent Sufi training that fused devotional insight to the acquisition of knowledge and rational endeavor, was Husam al-Din's only known disciple. Under Husam al-Din's tutelage, he filtered his experience of Sufi methods of training through the lens of the example of the Prophet Muhammad and his exemplary virtues. Husam al-Din called this "the devotional method of scrupulous caution and wariness of God" (*ṭarīqat-e waraʿ o taqwā*). ʿAli Muttaqi began to articulate the ethical principles that should underlie any spiritual training, no matter to what Sufi lineage it might outwardly belong. These principles centered on the concept of "self-willed death and the death of self-will."

ʿAli Muttaqi admired how Shaykh Husam al-Din reduced outward devotion to a means of cultivating inward sincerity. The shaykh expressed this heightened attention to sincerity in his scrupulous attention to money, food, dress, and the outer mode of life. More extreme in his nonattachment than ʿAzizallah Mutawakkil, Husam al-Din would not accept food from others, whether given or bought. To keep aloof from any possible pollution, he stubbornly farmed his own food on a tract of *kharāj* land, rather than accepting land from the state or religious endowments. He insisted on paying the full 10 percent tax to the state on all produce from such lands in order that his food would have no taint of selfishness or illegality about it.[42] His ritual attention to the source of his food was matched by his attention to the method of eating, for he authored a text on how to eat like the Prophet Muhammad.[43] When the Mughal prince Bābur (then ruler of Kabul in Afghanistan) invaded Punjab in 1524, he besieged Multan, throwing the government into disarray and inflicting the population with famine; since there was no legitimate administration to collect agricultural taxes, Shaykh Husam al-Din gave up agriculture completely and lived off fish that he caught himself.

His exacting attention to ritual and legalistic piety might cast doubt upon whether Husam al-Din was a saint at all, for he attracted no community of disciples, gave no public teachings, and exhibited no miracles. However, his attention to piety made him consider issues of social justice in ways uncommon in his South Asian environment. He saw a Sufi's sincerity bound up in how taxation was gathered and used and how public money was spent. He critiqued the ways that his contemporaries participated in political power by currying favor with rulers. He refused to lean against the wall of the dargah of Multan's most revered saint, Bahāʾ al-Dīn Zakariyā (the grand master of the Suhrawardi Order, d. 1262), or rest in its shade; this monument had been built with money from the public treasury, which Husam al-Din thought should be spent on feeding the hungry and caring for orphans.[44] Building tombs for revered saints was one of the major ways that rulers courted favor with powerful Sufi communities, who could in turn grant them popular support.

Husam al-Din taught a pared-down version of Sufi devotion, in which inner spiritual states were concealed by acquisition of knowledge. He based this Sufi method on "The Revival of Religious Disciplines" (*Iḥyāʾ ʿUlūm al-Dīn*) by Abū Ḥāmid al-Ghazālī (d. 1111) and the commentary on it, "ʿAyn al-ʿIlm."[45] He set ʿAli Muttaqi reading, memorizing, and meditating upon these books, in addition to a commentary on the Qur'an. He placed his disciple in an isolated cell and would come to visit him only in order to bring these books to study. This training carefully balanced the acquisition of outer textual knowledge with the illumination of inner experiential knowledge: both had to be pursued together, but the balance was hard to maintain. He would come to ʿAli Muttaqi's cell with books stacked on top of his head and knock; if no answer came he would leave his disciple in deep meditation, but if he came to the door, they would settle down to read and discuss together.[46]

Husam al-Din composed a short treatise, "Preserving the Faith" ("Ḥifẓ al-Īmān"), which reveals his teachings. He most likely wrote it as a result of his intensive studies with ʿAli Muttaqi.[47] The author explained, "I have spent some time reading through religious books, and have gathered together these beneficial morals about preserving one's faith. Perhaps this will be helpful for those Muslims who are not expert enough to read them all for themselves." He drew from at least twenty-seven basic works in Sufi devotion and Islamic doctrine to define faith (*īmān*) and document all its outward signs. He laid out what causes faith to ebb away and become eclipsed by selfishness, leading to false claims of faithfulness. Finally, he detailed the means by which a sincere person can keep their faith firm. Although he addressed his book to the general population of Muslims, he felt that many Sufis suffered from weak faith. A person's faith may crumble at the time of death, and this will happen if one puts his or her faith in inauthentic religious practices (*bidʿa*). Faith crumbles because Sufis "search for cosmic reality" rather than stay content with revealed scripture. These were both indirect critiques of his contemporary Sufis and the saints to whom they looked for guidance. Husam al-Din further pronounced that if someone experienced such an "eclipse of faith" it was as if they were infidels, even if some faint stirring of faith caused them to insist on calling themselves Muslims.[48] Such an eclipse of faith occurred especially when a Sufi might claim sainthood in an act of self-aggrandizement or purposeful display of miraculous actions.[49]

With such strong pronouncements, Husam al-Din gave ʿAli Muttaqi clear reasoning and vocabulary to make sense of his feelings of dissatisfaction with current forms of sainthood. It provided him with outward criteria to measure the authenticity of anyone who claimed to be a saint (or who was recognized by others as a saint). The teacher and student saw themselves continuing and even intensifying the project of al-Ghazali: to assert that Sufi practices express the inner dimension of the *shariʿa* that is given its outer form by the legal and scriptural disciplines of knowledge. However, they surpassed even al-Ghazali, for he dealt mainly on the level of rhetoric, framing Sufi ideals within the prose of legal norms and hadith reports for the purpose of defending Sufi practices from those who might claim that is was "heterodox" or beyond the bounds of the *shariʿa*. In contrast, ʿAli Muttaqi claimed that the disciplines of knowledge must saturate Sufi training, moving beyond merely rhetorically framing Sufi practices. He insisted that Sufi saints should be first recognized as scholars. Without this training, they had no personal authenticity and their claim to being saints was socially dangerous.

Shaykh Husam al-Din imparted this method of tempering Sufi devotion with the study of the religious disciplines to ʿAli Muttaqi. He taught that reading books of religious knowledge was a kind of *dhikr*, as was memorizing texts, correcting them, copying them for publication, and researching them. ʿAli Muttaqi's primary disciple, ʿAbd al-Wahhab Muttaqi, would later express this ideal when he advised his disciple ʿAbd al-Haqq,

> The man who is always engaged in good deeds is always engaged in *dhikr*. Saying prayers is *dhikr*; reciting Qur'an is *dhikr*; studying religious knowledge is *dhikr*. Any good action is *dhikr*. One should be doing such good things at every moment. But the actions of one who abandons seeking knowledge will never benefit themselves or others. To choose to sit in isolation and perform *dhikr*, that is like taking medicine to cure a specific

illness. You only need it from time to time, as you feel sick. . . . But seeking knowledge is such an important form of worship that if anyone lays it aside, they must reflect on their conscience and review their state of *taqwa*.[50]

Husam al-Din's teaching contrasted with the Chishti Order's emphasis on emotional presence over rational inquiry. Nizam al-Din Awliya taught that immersing oneself in God is the true goal and everything not related to it is an obstacle, even learning hadith from books.[51] Pursuing scriptural knowledge could be a form of egoism that veiled the Sufi from God's presence. Chishti Sufis adopted this attitude, making poetry, music, and love their focus, even if they read and taught from books. Husam al-Din Muttaqi countered that scriptural knowledge was the key to finding God's presence. Following him, continuous learning and pursuit of knowledge formed the cornerstone of ʿAli Muttaqi's subsequent career and prepared him to revive hadith studies as a vehicle for Sufi training.

In contrast to those whom he warns against in "Preserving the Faith," Husam al-Din called his own Sufi method "the way of scrupulous caution and wariness of God." These two interlinked terms were the basis of Husam al-Din's spiritual vocabulary. *Taqwa* or wariness is the connection between the human heart and the divine presence: it is a relation of fear and awe that leads to wariness. In Husam al-Din's view, *taqwa* encompassed the sincerity of a saint's orientation to God, which was the foundation of faith. *Waraʿ* is extreme caution, so as not to trespass the bounds of humility and legality in any thought, word, or action. Whereas wariness is an inward relationship to the divine that is invisible to others, scrupulous caution is an outward demeanor and a visible way of behaving with others. As manifested in Husam al-Din's life, caution made him extraordinarily scrupulous about the sources of his money and food. He passed on to ʿAli Muttaqi this pious emphasis on food and its purity and minimal intake.

Husam al-Din offered ʿAli Muttaqi practical training rather than demanding total devotion to his person like many other Sufi guides. He gave ʿAli Muttaqi a rigorous advanced education in scriptural disciplines and, more importantly, gave him an ideology that placed the acquisition of such knowledge as the center of Sufi training. However, he did not initiate ʿAli Muttaqi into a discrete order, granting him no title or relic to mark his formal discipleship. This was not the usual Sufi training according to the model of master and disciple. Rather, Husam al-Din treated his disciple like a pupil, offering him training on the model of teacher and student. A teacher offers students knowledge and the tools to acquire knowledge themselves. In contrast, a master demands absolute obedience from disciples, whose task is to subjugate their own will rather than to self-consciously seek knowledge. Husam al-Din behaved as if Sufi training on the model of master and discipline was no longer viable; rather, what remained was to acquire training in the *shariʿa*: conforming to its dictates would involve devotion that limited one's ego. He did not demand that ʿAli Muttaqi stay with him until his death or act as his spiritual successor. Husam al-Din lived until 1553, while ʿAli Muttaqi left his company after only two years to return to Gujarat with the intent to live authentically as a saint back in his home environment.[52]

Alienation: Experiments in Authenticity

Setting out from Multan, ʿAli Muttaqi traveled as an experiment with this pared-down method of Sufi devotion, "the way of scrupulous caution and wariness of God." He was not traveling toward a pilgrimage place, neither the Hajj's goal of Mecca nor a local saint's shrine. He was traveling toward his heart's sincerity. Outward movement was merely a method to strip away everything that obscured this goal. ʿAli Muttaqi systematically limited his intake of food; at first, he would carry enough food to last him two or three days, but after some time that same amount would last him for four or five days. If he stayed in a town, he conscientiously avoided sleeping in mosques and rented a room to avoid being obliged to accept gifts of food and money from others, the origins and legal purity of which was unknown. He swore to rely only on God to provide for his needs, yet concealed this oath to remain aloof from anyone offering help.[53]

This ascetic practice was ʿAli Muttaqi's experiment in the "death of self-will." This experiment gave him the certainty that he had experienced for himself the ultimate criterion that marked the real passage into being a saint. In the liminal state of the open road, there was no master present to whom to attribute this transformation and no fellow disciples present to witness it. ʿAli Muttaqi expressed his ideal of authentic sainthood in negative terms by stating what it was not: it was not a state marked by social distinctions such as inheritance, dress, or bodily postures as in dance or trance. It was not a state that an act of will or self-assertion could claim. It must be earned indirectly and could never be demanded. The only positive expression he could make embodied in its very language the ultimate negation: one could achieve sainthood only through "dying to yourself before your actual death."

By this expression, he meant that the only way to become a saint was through a profound gesture of surrender. This is an ultimate paradox: to achieve something valued above all else, one must relinquish the very desire to achieve it. This paradox cuts to the core of psychological experience framed as "mysticism."[54] Intent and desire lead to struggle and self-assertion, which in many cases cause the failure to arrive at a desired result. This is especially true when the object of desire is abstract, remote, and of ultimate value (like sainthood). If one can loosen the bondage of intentionality, then one can attain one's goal without self-aggrandizing effort. ʿAli Muttaqi used the metaphor of death to illustrate his own abandoning of will, volition, and ambition to encourage others who admired him as a saint to do the same.

Sufi literature offers a long tradition of paradoxical sayings that try to lure the will into just such a spontaneous gesture of surrender. A Sufi master who would become very dear to ʿAli Muttaqi, named Abū'l-Ḥasan al-Shādhilī (d. 1258 in Humaithara, Egypt), said, "If you must willfully plan, and how can you avoid willfully planning, then plan only not to willfully plan." Al-Shadhili focused only on the will's propensity to plot and plan for its own benefit rather than on critiquing the very ontological existence of the will. However, an earlier saint, Bāyazīd Bisṭāmī (d. 874–75), phrased the same idea in a more radical critique: when asked by a divine voice, "What do you want?" he answered, "I want only to not want at all."[55] These admonitions to abandon self-will permeate Sufi teachings, and ʿAli Muttaqi likely learned the emphasis on death of the volition from the Qadiri Order. One of the primary texts taught in this order is "Openings of the Unseen" (*Futūḥ al-Ghayb*) by ʿAbd al-Qadir Jilani . It contains this remarkable section on voluntary death and rebirth as the dramatic passage into sainthood.

> If you have died to the demands of other people (God have mercy on you) then may God make you die to your own desires. If you have died to your own desires (God have mercy on you) then may God make you die to your own will and planning. If you have died to your own will and planning (God have mercy upon you) then may God grant you a whole new life. At that moment, you are revived with a life after which there is no presence of death. . . . You will become the most unique person, the wellspring of sanctity, the hidden core of the hidden, the very secret of the secret. At that moment, you inherit the innermost legacy of the Prophet and Messenger of God. His spiritual authority is sealed with your person. From you, the anonymous saints go forth to lift away anxiety and

> distress. The rains of bounty and blessing will fall through you, and by your being calamities and afflictions will be lifted from the shoulders of all the people. You will bear the weight of the land and all its people.[56]

This language of death is not about suicide in its destructive mode. It urges one to seek a fuller life under the guise of not requesting anything by one's own will. In his Persian commentary on this Arabic text, ʿAbd al-Haqq wrote, "By requesting that death in which there is no sign of life, I want that life in which there is no sign of death. This is absolute death to the self and its willfulness and desires."[57] The death of self-will became a foundation of ʿAli Muttaqi's method for those who followed him. Echoing Shaykh ʿAbd al-Qadir Jilani, he taught that "the Sufi is the land that everyone, good or bad, can walk over; the Sufi is a cloud that casts shade on everyone equally; the Sufi is rain that gives water without calculating any return."[58]

To achieve this dissolution of the ego, ʿAli Muttaqi advocated a frontal assault on the body and its volition while excluding other metaphoric avenues that existed in Sufi communities for acting out this same drama of being-close-to-death. His advocacy of the death of self-will contained within it an implicit critique of his contemporary Sufis, suggesting that they followed established forms of Sufi rituals and enjoyed traditional legitimacy but lacked the underlying alchemical experience of psychological death that would make them efficacious and preserve them from egoistic abuses. The drama of institutional Sufi rituals would have required him to adopt uncritically the practices of a wide community. Such acceptance would have run counter to his position of extreme caution and suspicion of relying upon others. In contrast, his frontal assault on the will through bodily discipline required no community and—as his life history demonstrates—no spiritual guide to impart the training to cultivate it.

Through his solitary travels, ʿAli Muttaqi eased himself into the experiments with the "death of self-will."[59] He crafted for himself props to keep his attention constantly on the presence of death, such as his "death satchel" (Ar. *kharīṭa*; Gj. *jhōlī*). Earlier, Sufis would commonly carry a small bag with their devotional items, which served as an outer symbol of their commitment to the mystical path. Nizam al-Din Awliya mentions this "little purse of derwishes" called a *kinf* (or its Arabic diminutive form, *kunayf*) in his oral discourses.[60] However, ʿAli Muttaqi pushed this symbol to extremes; he saw individual experience of death before one's death to be the sole criterion of a person's sanctity. Upon granting disciples the status of his authoritative representatives, ʿAli Muttaqi would give them a shoulder bag like his own "death satchel" in place of a patched cloak (*khirqa*), the traditional symbol for attainment among other Sufi communities. A century later, Shaykh ʿAbd al-Haqq described this bag, how to wear it, and how ʿAli Muttaqi and his community would grant it in place of a traditional cloak.[61]

His oral teachings also testify to how ʿAli Muttaqi considered his experience of death as the touchstone of his sainthood. In his old age, a rumor spread that he was dying, though he was actually healthy at the time. Admirers rushed to see him before he passed away. When they arrived, they expressed surprise that he was lively, since they had heard that he was on the brink of death. ʿAli Muttaqi smiled and begged their forgiveness; he explained how such a strange rumor was not a simple error but confirmed his authentic sainthood. He said, "I am a man who has already sipped the drink of death and has seen what lies beyond it—I've stood before God to be judged but was sent back for second lease on life to be made useful for God's purposes. Such a man is never far from the mindful presence of death."[62] He referred them to his earlier youthful rigors of ascetic denial and not to his old age or impending death. Having long ago "sipped the drink of death," he had abandoned his own will in order to live as God's saint.

ʿAli Muttaqi's travels led him back to Gujarat. There, his heightened rhetoric of saintly authenticity implicitly rejected his Gujarati colleagues and their current forms of Sufi authority. A saint is the center of a devotional community of Sufis, and ʿAli Muttaqi tried to build such a community in Gujarat. He searched for allies and colleagues, but this would be a difficult struggle as his ideology conflicted with those around him. Ultimately, he was unable to remain in Gujarat and would choose a life of exile in Mecca for political, religious, and scholarly reasons.

His newly forged identity as an authentic Sufi master was expressed in his adopting the title "Muttaqi" for himself. Muttaqi means "the Pious One" or "the One Aware of God," and it is a term with deep roots in the Sufi tradition. The early Sufi sage al-Ḥakīm al-Tirmidhī (d. 869) noted that even some people called "Muttaqi," despite their piety, are tempted and often defeated by ego (*nafs*).[63] Al-Tirmidhi wrote extensively on disciplining the egoism of the soul (*adab al-nafs*) and understanding the spiritual anatomy of the heart.[64] In his short treatise called *Natures of the Egos* (*Ṭabāʿi al-Nufūs*), he analyzes the ego that develops in different kinds of persons and their various activities.

> The ego continuously wages war against the believer and weaves deceits until it wrests him away from righteousness and alienates him from his center. They are like two chess players who come together over the board

> to duel, dividing the pieces between themselves. They play the game, removing the other's pieces from the board one after the other, until one of them relentlessly removes all the pieces of the other player and takes him into captivity. Desire is the chessboard of the ego which continuously strategizes and moves against the pieces belonging to the true One, taking piece by piece until it leaves the believer's heart empty of the true One and captures it. The arrogant one is deluded and befuddled by the deception of the ego, and plugs up the ears of his heart from hearing what messages come to him. Then desire [*hawā*], from the dark shadow of the ego, throws up object after object before the ego, and the ego casts these images into the heart. If the heart accepts these images and craves, then it is deluded by the arrogance of the ego. The ego keeps up this game relentlessly until it finds the opportunity to drive the heart into a corner, overcome it, and take it into captivity.[65]

According to al-Tirmidhi, Muslims known for their piety (*taqwa*) are prone to continuous deceit by the ego, ending up arrogant and proud. ʿAli Muttaqi, however, adopted his honorific name the "Pious One" after his traveling experiment with the death of volition, through which he claimed to have subdued the overweening impulses of his ego. His ego was dethroned: in the Manichaean chess match that al-Tirmidhi imagined between the vulnerable soul and the crafty ego, ʿAli Muttaqi claimed to have engineered a checkmate. Indeed, the term "checkmate" comes from the Persian-Arabic hybrid term *shāh māta,* or "thus died the king."

With this new confidence, ʿAli Muttaqi decided to settle in Gujarat. He did not return to Mandu, where his mother and family lived, or to Burhanpur, where his religious teachers and previous guides were active. His decision to settle in Ahmedabad reflected a program of action. From the capital of Gujarat, he could contact diverse communities of the religious elite. Alienation from his surroundings and emerging confidence in his own spiritual authority incited him to write. However, since writing a text is a display of ambition and authority, the task did not come easily to him. ʿAli Muttaqi claimed that he authored his first text at the inexorable urging of divine will, thus denying his own authorial ambition. Once his pen began to move, it never stopped. He wrote continuously for the rest of his life (whether composing, editing, or copying), even in his sick bed until the moment of his death.

His first composition, "Exposition of the Ways to God" ("Tabyīn al-Ṭurūq"), reveals that he was digesting his experiences of death by relating them to the variety of Sufi practices that surrounded him.[66] In this initial foray, he ignored the terms of his own experience, the "death of self-will," as the means to gain distance from one's own selfish desires. Instead, he inverted this idea and wrote about closeness to God (*qurb ilā ʾllah*) as the common goal of all aspirants to sainthood. This text was ostensibly a commentary on the famous saying by Najm al-Dīn Kubrā (d. 1221), "The paths to God are as numerous as the variety of beings in creation." ʿAli Muttaqi argued that since the methods for spiritual training are numerous, they are of little importance.[67] What is important is that these methods be based on a solid foundation, which is legal rectitude, performing religious obligations, and avoiding religious prohibitions as charted in the *shariʿa*. Although he began by urging the reader to engage in supererogatory acts of worship, he ended by stressing that such acts were ultimately invalid unless based on the scrupulous observation of the *shariʿa*.[68] "Obligatory acts of worship are not complete and perfect means of closeness to God, without supererogatory acts of worship to supplement them. Without supererogatory worship as an expression of love, these acts of obligatory worship only save the actor from punishment, rather than gifting him intimacy. Performing only the obligations is the 'path of being saved.' In contrast, performing obligations and completing them with optional acts of worship (in prayer times and in every moment) is the 'path of approaching intimacy' step by step."[69] In his initial text, ʿAli Muttaqi advocated a mildly reformist perspective on Sufi practice. His reformist perspective had not yet crystallized into a reform program. *Taqwa* was more important than ritual or forms of *dhikr*, and *dhikr* included acts of teaching, social service, and charity, which were probably more meritorious than contemplative *dhikr*.

ʿAli Muttaqi asserted that those who engaged in Sufi rituals should downplay the distinctiveness of each lineage and adhere to the *shariʿa*. ʿAli Muttaqi's reformist rethinking of Sufi practices set up a dynamic of distance and intimacy. He perceived that his intimacy with God was proportional to his distance and alienation from the people surrounding him. This is exactly the danger of pride that al-Hakim al-Tirmidhi warned against:

> *Taqwa* is defined by the Prophet of God when he said [in a hadith report], "Do not snub others or consider them less than you—just be like brethren, worshippers of one God." Then he continued, "For indeed *taqwa* is just here" while he pointed to his chest. Thus, we know that *taqwa* means purity of heart to avoid holding others in contempt or belittling them or having no empathy with them, thus keeping aloof from their problems and refusing to give them good counsel and effective help so that they might worship God, and to encourage them in good deeds. Indeed, the

> person with *taqwa* is like a man who exits the bathhouse having cleansed himself of all filth and impurity and wearing clean white clothes. If he sees dirt being blown around by a wind, he rushes to cover his head, his beard and his clothes in order to avoid getting coated in dirt! Such it is with the Muttaqi, the person with *taqwa*, who has purified his heart and his chest.[70]

Al-Hakim al-Tirmidhi lampooned Muslim devotees who thought their piety made them better, cleaner, and purer than other Muslims around them.

In just this way, ʿAli Muttaqi became alienated from masters of the Chishti Order and other orders with their distinctive, popular styles of devotion and who through popularity enjoyed positions of power. Later, he described his state of singular despair at the spiritual alienation he felt for all surrounding him in Gujarat.

> That neighborhood of conscientious poverty lies abandoned and its homes sag in despair. Its folk have all departed, leaving for other places or passing away. Only the impostors and hypocrites have prospered, those who are busy with envy, lies, and worldly ambitions. They distract themselves with listening to music that is forbidden, and erupting into dance that can only lower their dignity. They engage only in forgery, selling themselves, impassioned anger and rivalry, malice, cheating and hatred, envy and greed, pride and dissimulation. They approach others with enmity. They gaze upon young men with love and sit around with kings in luxury and with scholars in flattery. Those impostors themselves embody such deceitful and lowly qualities, so how can it be legal to take them as spiritual guides and Sufi masters? How can one pledge allegiance to them and wear a cap from their hands?[71]

This elegy to his times served as an introduction to his advice to all who desired to sincerely pursue sainthood. For them, he defined intimacy with God (*qurb*) and then defined the saint (*walī*) as one whom the experience of closeness and intimacy with God has indelibly touched. He expanded on the idea that one's distance from the people gauged one's nearness to God, as if to justify his own alienation from these local Sufis who maintained intimate contact with people, engaged in populist styles of devotion, and entertained mass followings.

His first text, though small, reveals ʿAli Muttaqi's approach to the practical contours of Sufi practice. It differs from the work of most of his contemporaries, who saw the clearest expressions of closeness in poetry and the most efficacious expressions of intimacy in ecstatic behavior. His sobriety and moderate ascetic discipline were so outside the routine for saints of his time that he acquired notoriety and popular respect. Crowds flocked to him as he walked through Ahmedabad, wishing to receive his blessing. He slammed the door of his house on the crowds and installed a lock to keep them away. He employed a servant to console people with blessings and prayers that came "from the shaykh" who refused to come to the door. And he left his home only for communal prayers on Fridays.[72] This reclusive behavior increased his popular acclaim in Ahmedabad, the city that would become the center of his world.

Embedding: Setting Roots in Gujarat

To understand ʿAli Muttaqi's growth, we must explore the sultanate of Gujarat, the region in whose nourishing soil he was transplanted. This kingdom—its prosperous lands and profitable seas with its glittering capital of Ahmedabad—was the center of his world. The sultanate of Gujarat comprised a world of power, wealth, and cosmopolitan ambitions that has not received the scholarly attention that it deserves. Samira Sheikh has demonstrated how the sultanate has often been overshadowed by the Mughal Empire. Scholars (mainly architectural historians and scholars of trade) are attracted to Gujarat under Mughal rule.[73] Yet the history of Islamic culture in South Asia is enriched by a focus on the earlier sultanate of Gujarat located as pivot between continent and sea: Gujarat connected North India and the southern Deccan and also linked South Asia to Arabia.

In the late medieval period, the sultanate of Gujarat was ruled by the Muẓaffar-Shāhī dynasty. It is named after Muẓaffar Shāh, the regnal name of the adventurous administrator who founded the dynasty in 1411. He was formerly known as Muẓaffarkhān and had been appointed governor of Gujarat in 1391, when it was a province of the sultanate of Delhi under the Tughlaq dynasty. However, centralized rule was tenuous. In 1351 the Deccan region asserted independence as the Bahmani sultanate. Situated between the Deccan and Delhi, the province of Gujarat also began to feel political tremors. Khan had to fight to assert his rights as governor—despite his appointment from Delhi—against the previous governor, who toyed with open rebellion. Muzaffarkhan embodied upward mobility in the Tughlaq regime: his father had been a Hindu Rajput, the son of a village chief, who helped a Tughlaq prince who got lost while hunting in Gujarat. That prince mounted the throne as Fīrōz Shāh Tughlaq (ruled 1351–88), and Muzaffar Khan's father rose to a

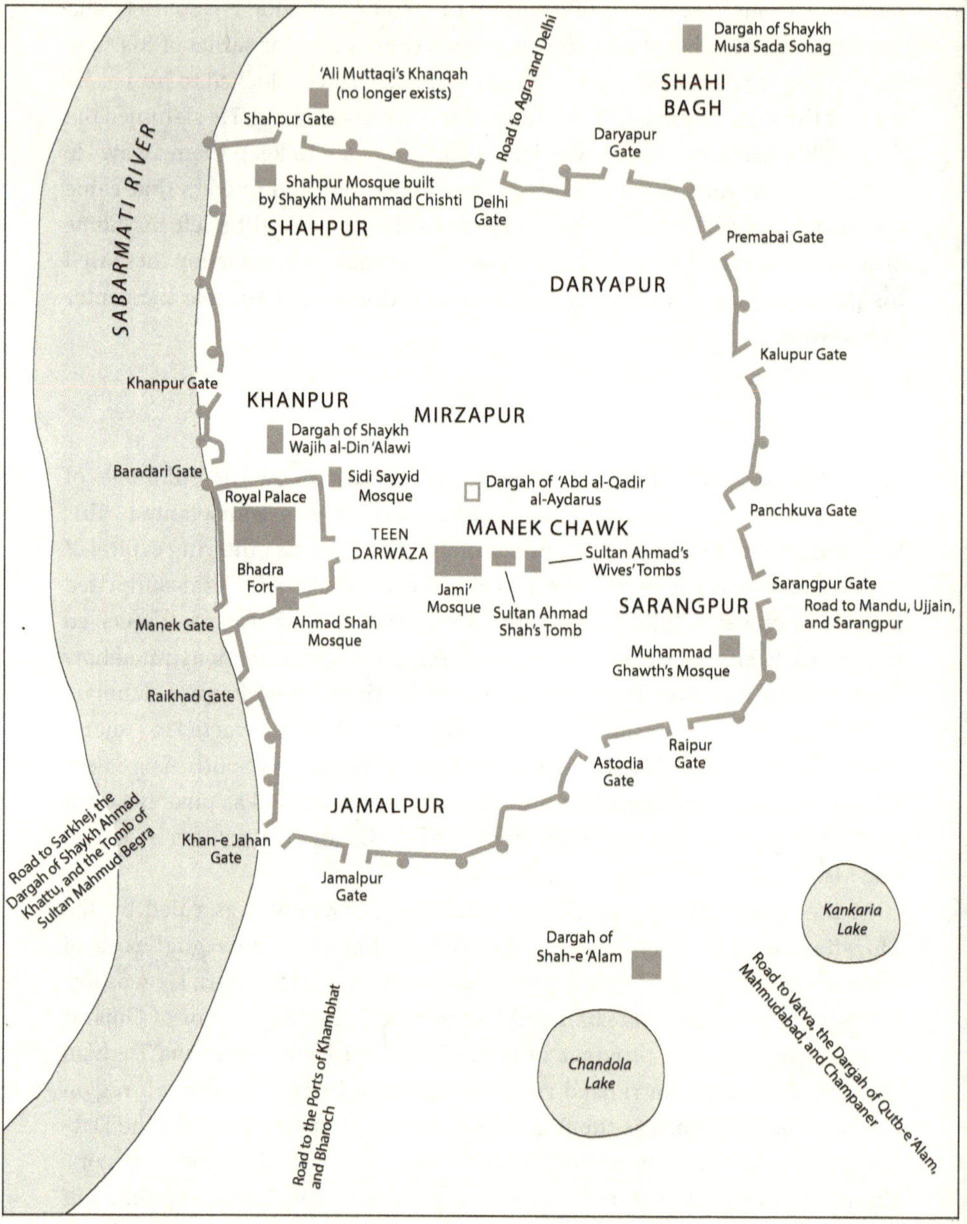

Ahmedabad in the sixteenth century

prominent position as his cupbearer in Delhi, converting to Islam and ranking as nobility.[74]

Muzaffar Khan grew up in Delhi with administrative knowledge, military skill, and loyalty to Sufi ideals. When he asserted his rights as governor of Gujarat, his son was appointed prime minister in Delhi, but as civil war broke out in Delhi, centralized rule almost disappeared. Muzaffar Khan made a pilgrimage to Ajmer to visit the tomb-shrine of Muʿin al-Din Chishti; such visitation (*ziyārat*) had long been a symbol of seeking spiritual blessings to become a ruler. He and his son harbored ambition to take over the throne in Delhi from their power base in Gujarat. Their plans were thwarted in 1398 when the Central Asian conqueror Timur sacked Delhi and carted off its wealth and human skill to his capital at Samarqand.

After Timur's sack of Delhi, Gujarat became effectively an independent realm, and its governor took the title Muẓaffar Shāh (ruled 1407–11 as sultan). His son urged him to march on Delhi, but Muzaffar Shah knew that the days of centralized rule from Delhi were over. The son revolted, imprisoned his father in 1404, and declared himself sultan in order to seize the throne of Delhi. This futile goal was abandoned when the son was poisoned by his relatives, who reinstated Muzaffar Shah. He gave his name to the Muzaffar-Shahi dynasty, whose lineage of sultans of Gujarat are given in appendix A. He abdicated in 1411 a few months before his death to allow his grandson Ahmad to take the throne.

Aḥmad Shāh became sultan at age nineteen and founded a new city, Ahmedabad (formerly a town called Ashaval). He moved the capital of Gujarat from Patan (Pāṭan) (Ar. Fattan; formerly Gj. Anhilwād, Ar. Naharwāla), which looked northeast toward Delhi and the wider Gangetic plain. In contrast, his new capital, Ahmedabad, was on the Sabarmati River, facing southwest toward the Gulf of Cambay and the Arabian Sea. Ahmad Shah reoriented Gujarat as an independent sultanate toward its twelve port-cities and their maritime trade and overseas links to Arabia. From Delhi, Sikandar Lōdī (ruled 1488–1517) gazed with envy at Gujarat's ports and their revenue from trade and manufacturing, saying, "The magnificence of the kings of Delhi rests on wheat and barley; the magnificence of the kings of Gujarat rests on coral and pearls."[75]

Ahmad Shah's intimacy with Sufis mirrored his political vision. Muzaffar Shah's father had close ties to Sufis from the Suhrawardi Order. According to legend, he and his brother converted under the guidance of Shaykh Jalāl al-Dīn Makhdūm-e Jahāniyān, whose grandson Sayyid Burhān al-Dīn Quṭb-e ʿĀlam (d. 1453) settled in Ahmedabad and married the daughter of a noble of Gujarat; his son Shāh-e ʿĀlam (d. 1475) and their descendants became religious leaders over many generations.[76] The sultanate was reputed to prosper through the blessing of these Suhrawardi saints who were Bukhari sayyids, descendants of the Prophet Muhammad who lived in Bukhārā (now in Uzbekistan).

Muzaffar Shah showed respect to Sufis from the Chishti Order with their reputation as spiritual guardians of South Asian rulers.[77] Ahmad Shah added to this a special fondness for Shaykh Aḥmad Khaṭṭū (d. 1445) of the Maghribi Order linked to Shaykh Abū Madyan Shuʿayb (d. 1198, a Sufi master popular in North Africa and Yemen). Ahmad Khattu helped Ahmad Shah lay the foundation of the capital, near his own residence at Sarkhej (Sarkhēj). He was the principal "Ahmad" who gave his name to the city, along with three others: Sultan Ahmad Shah himself, Qāḍī Aḥmad Jūd (disciple and successor of Ahmad Khattu), and Mālik Aḥmad.[78] Legend asserts that the four pious Ahmads were aided by twelve Sufis known as Bābā (an endearing honorific for a *darwēsh* or *qalandar*) who were remotely associated with the Chishti Order. While this book focuses on how the sultans of Gujarat interacted with Sufis and fostered Islamic culture, their stable rule had lasting impact on Hindu, Jain, and other religious communities in Gujarat.[79]

Gujarat was already dotted with Muslim tombs related to Sufi, Ismāʿīlī, and legendary figures. The sultans of Gujarat patronized new ones, now clustered around the growing capital of Ahmedabad. The tomb-shrine (*rawḍa*; Gr. *rōza*, Ur. *dargāh*) of Ahmad Khattu became a place of royal residence and burial as well in the era of Mahmud I (ruled 1458–1511), who led Gujarat to its zenith.

He was known as known as Maḥmūd Bēgṛā, or "Mahmud of the Buffalo Horns," referring to either two curved buffalo horns (like the shape of his macho mustache) or two fortresses that he conquered (Girnār and Chāmpānēr).[80] In either case, his nickname implied masculine vigor. He built a new capital at Champaner with a magnificent multistoried congregational mosque (*jāmiʿ masjid*), constructed in 1509.

His strength was acknowledged by the Lodi sultans of Delhi (who began to honor him with gifts like an independent sultan) and the Bahmani sultans of the Deccan. He received emissaries from the new Safavid Empire in Iran, a major trading partner of Gujarat in the Arabian Sea and Persian Gulf.[81] During his fifty-three-year reign, the sultanate of Gujarat prospered and patronized Sufis and Islamic scholarship on the Qur'an and hadith. The sultans invited scholars of hadith from Egypt and Arabia to Gujarat to serve in court.

His successor, Sultan Muẓaffar Shāh II (ruled 1511–26), zealously acquired a copy of *Fatḥ al-Bārī*, or "Disclosure of the Creator," the esteemed commentary on the hadith collection *Ṣaḥīḥ al-Bukhārī*, written by Ibn Ḥajar al-ʿAsqalānī (d. 1449). Arrival of such texts were important events during which sultans would publicly display deference to the Prophet's legacy and value its scholars. Similarly, ship captains carried the multivolume hadith commentary of *Fath al-Bari* on their dangerous voyages across the Indian Ocean in the belief that God would not destroy a ship bearing such blessed cargo.[82] Arriving in Gujarat, hadith scholars expected generous reward and political postings as administrators or treasury officers. New connections from Arabia to the sultanate of Gujarat supplemented and nourished the ongoing devotion of South Asian Muslim scholars to hadith and Qur'an commentary.

Despite the growing importance of hadith scholarship, Sufi leaders remained crucial figures in the religious life of the sultanate. Many Sufis were also scholars of the Qur'an and hadith, and they came to the fore when Sultan Muzaffar II died in 1526. His death sparked rivalry that would have enormous impact on ʿAli Muttaqi. Of the sultan's six sons, four aspired to the throne: Sikandar, Nasīr Maḥmūd, Bahādur, and Laṭīf. Prominent Sufis predicted that his third son, Bahadur, would take the throne.[83] But the ailing Sultan Muzaffar II did not raise Bahadur's rank to signal his favor, and Bahadur fled in fear of his brothers. At Ajmer, Bahadur sought refuge in the blessings of Muʿin al-Din Chishti's dargah. Sultan Muzaffar II delayed naming a successor as his health failed, hoping that Bahadur would return to Gujarat.[84] As the sultan died, civil war broke out between his eldest son, Sikandar, and his youngest, Latif. Sikandar failed to show deference to Sufi leaders in Ahmedabad and appeared to lose popular legitimacy.[85] He proclaimed himself sultan but was poisoned after just three months.[86]

The minister who poisoned him raised to the throne a boy from the royal family, to rule in name as Maḥmūd Shāh II but in fact to be a puppet of the regent minister. This internal chaos in Gujarat was mirrored by external warfare in North India. From Ajmer, Bahadur procured support from the sultan of Delhi, Ibrāhīm Lōdī (ruled 1517–26) but got caught up in the chaos of the Mughal invasion. Bahadur was present at Panipat where the Lodi army was defeated; he was fleeing with Lodi commanders when news reached him of his father's death. As Prince Babur occupied Delhi, Bahadur evaded Mughal interception and returned to Gujarat, announcing his claim to the throne. Bolstered by Sufi leaders and popular support, Bahadur dethroned the boy-puppet and displaced his rival brothers. He was crowned as Bahādur Shāh in 1527. The story of his father's death, his sibling rivalry, and his political triumph through his appeal to Sufis and scholars illustrates the vibrant environment of Gujarat. The sultanate of Gujarat was a crucible that alloyed Sufi leaders, hadith scholars, and political patrons, which proved to be fertile ground for ʿAli Muttaqi's growth.

Bahadur Shah was reigning when ʿAli Muttaqi settled in Ahmedabad. In keeping with his practice of alienation, ʿAli Muttaqi socialized with few companions. He built a small community of like-minded Sufi and religious scholars. His friends were Qāḍī ʿAbdallāh Sindhī, his son Qāḍī Ḥamīd Muḥaddith, and his brother Raḥmatallāh. Qadi ʿAbdallah came to Ahmedabad along with his family to escape some catastrophe in Sindh.[87] He was a jurist but had a Sufi perspective, and he befriended ʿAli Muttaqi. He and his brother became disciples and then successors. ʿAli Muttaqi was also friends with Miyān Ghiyāth, who lived in Bharoch (Bharōch); he exhibited a limitless generosity, giving people whatever they might need, whether money, clothes, food, medicines, tools, or books—his house was always full of things to give away.[88] His piety focused on scrupulousness in the details of the *sunna*, which probably attracted the friendship of ʿAli Muttaqi.[89]

In another step toward maturity, ʿAli Muttaqi decided to marry, but records do not identify his wife or mention whether ʿAli Muttaqi allied with a notable family of Ahmedabad. The couple had a son who died in childhood. At this point, ʿAli Muttaqi revealed that he had never set his heart on building a household. After his son's death, he said to his wife, "I now have no need for this marriage since our son has disappeared. I married you out of duty to produce a son and to raise him well. Now that he has passed beyond this world, on the day of resurrection he may plead for me before God as my son who died before he came of age. You are free to do as you please, whatever you decide."[90] She asked to stay in his company to draw water and carry it for his ritual baths. It is not clear whether she stayed on as his wife or simply as a follower. However, he must have treated her with ample kindness, for many of her relatives joined them as followers of ʿAli Muttaqi and servants in his household. He lived just outside the Shāhpūr Darwāza in Ahmedabad, in a house with a mosque in its compound.

His fame reached the ears of Sultan Bahadur Shah, who requested his audience repeatedly. ʿAli Muttaqi turned down the requests. Finally, the sultan sought the mediation of Qadi ʿAbdallah Sindhi, whom he knew to be his close friend. Qadi ʿAbdallah begged ʿAli Muttaqi to see the sultan, even if only once. ʿAli Muttaqi complained that he might see the sultan dressed in a manner against the *shariʿa*, and then he would have to chastise him, ruining the whole meeting and perhaps placing his life in danger. Qadi ʿAbdallah reassured him that the sultan wanted only to see him—on any condition, even if he refused to say a word—and that the qadi himself would be present to speak with the sultan and distract him with stories. Finally, ʿAli Muttaqi agreed to meet the sultan and gave him some admonition. Despite his stern approach to the meeting, ʿAli Muttaqi seems to have won Bahadur Shah's trust and confidence.[91]

This narrative is crucial in ʿAli Muttaqi's hagiography. It reveals his wariness of the sultan, whom he considered decadent. It shows his courage in giving strong advice to a ruler, foreshadowing his later role as a reformer. It displays his virtue of scrupulous caution in refusing royal gifts. Finally, those who witnessed the scene or spread the news of it would see the sultan's acceptance of ʿAli Muttaqi's criticism to be proof of the latter's status as a saint. ʿAli Muttaqi became a patron and advisor to Sultan Bahadur Shah, showing that he understood himself to be one of the saintly pillars of the sultanate of Gujarat. He also grew close to one of Bahadur Shah's chief ministers, Aṣaf Khān, who was a soldier and administrator famed also as a scholar and paragon of virtue.[92] Yet this apparent success was an illusion, as the second satchel will reveal. A political calamity was brewing like a dark storm on the horizon, and its winds would carry ʿAli Muttaqi far away into exile.

SECOND SATCHEL

ʿAli Muttaqi's Exile

Total pandemonium broke out at the port when news of the battle spread. The prime minister, Asaf Khan, commandeered every boat in the harbor sheltered between the Gujarati mainland and the fortified island of Diu. His officers hustled palanquins bearing the ladies of the palace *zenana* onto boats, followed by chests of treasure and royal furnishings—whatever riches could be carried from Ahmedabad. Asaf Khan lowered the huge iron chain that hung from a tower, called Pani Kotha, on the island to a tower on the mainland, a defense over the water at the entrance to the harbor. The escape route was clear for the ships to leave, as soon as his command might be given.

Beyond the island's fortress walls, the Arabian Sea shimmered listlessly, dull in the off-season when winds lagged. In the opposite direction, the view east along the coast toward the capital and countryside was full of commotion. Carts of refugees rushed along the roads toward the port but were repulsed by royal guards under command to keep the docks clear of commoners. Black smoke, like unseasonable storm clouds, filled the horizon to the south, rising from the flaming pitch-soaked wood of Gujarat's naval fleet in the Gulf of Cambay; hundreds of ships burned. Beyond the smoke-filled horizon, a black storm of vultures and kites picked over the dead soldiers of the decimated Gujarat army that lay along the road toward Malwa and Delhi.

While crowds of refugees blocked the roads leading to Diu, a lone barque slipped into the harbor from the South. Alarms were raised and guards rushed to the dock to intercept it. As guards lowered their spears and aimed their *bunduqs*, a shaykh stood at the gunwale of the small boat as it nudged against the dock. The guards hesitated. The shaykh slipped a ring of carnelian inscribed with Arabic off his finger; he handed it to their commander and asked him to deliver it to the prime minister. A few minutes later, Asaf Khan himself rushed over to embrace the shaykh, ordering guards to escort his ragged party ashore. Shaykh ʿAli Muttaqi, along with his family and followers, starved and parched by the chaotic rush from Ahmedabad, were finally safe. The shaykh surveyed the port, glancing west toward Arabia, and then asked the prime minister for the latest news.

The sultan of Gujarat, Bahadur Shah, had miscalculated badly. His success in conquering Malwa had gone to his head. He had occupied its capital at Mandu and boasted of next taking Delhi, but this incited its Mughal ruler, Humayun, to invade Gujarat preemptively. As the two mighty armies clashed, Bahadur Shah lost his nerve and fled the army camp at night for the safety of his fortress at Champaner, citing the need to secure the treasury. At dawn, news of his flight spread through both armies, causing Gujarati morale to collapse and provoking a Mughal charge. Defeated in battle, Bahadur Shah abandoned his fortress on the borderlands and fell back to the Gulf of Cambay, citing the need to protect his royal family and capital. At the port of Khambhat, two rivers meet—the Mahi flowing from Baroda and Sabarmati flowing from Ahmedabad—and join the wide gulf that opens onto the Arabian Sea. There Bahadur Shah had built a proud fleet—hundreds of warships—to protect his trade routes and ward off Portuguese marauders. Fearing that Humayun's army would advance to confiscate his ships, he ordered his remaining soldiers to torch the fleet that he had built at great cost to the royal treasury and the kingdom's merchants and peasants. As Bahadur Shah watched them burn, the prime minister ordered all that remained of the sultan of Gujarat's family and wealth loaded onto the few ships that were left at Diu, the legacy of six generations of the Muzaffar-Shahi dynasty ruling the richest province of South Asia. He now paced the dock, waiting for enough news to make a decision.

Before the prime minister could finish his account, a riot of cheers and jeers arose from the crowd, which parted for a cavalry contingent that galloped onto the docks holding high the crimson parasol of the sultan, now smeared with mud and dust. Bahadur Shah rode directly to his prime minister and then noticed Shaykh ʿAli Muttaqi. He dismounted and quietly urged his minister to continue preparing the ships while he conferred with the shaykh.

In private in a room of Diu's fort, the sultan broke down before the shaykh. He said, "I am the divinely appointed and legitimate ruler, but see what disaster has befallen me!" He unleashed a torrent of regret and sorrow, blaming himself and his conduct—"I have been disobedient and arrogant! Now the Muslims under my rule are caught in grave tribulations and face terrible trials because of me." He sat with the shaykh until late in the night, recounting all the catastrophes that occurred while continuously offering his repentance and detailing his faults, begging for absolution and spiritual support.

While the sultan sobbed and raved, the shaykh sat on the balls of his feet, in exactly the same position he was in when the sultan had approached him. Shaykh ʿAli Muttaqi remained silent as a stone, refusing to look at the sultan. He was so still, it was as if he were not breathing. When Sultan Bahadur Shah finally lapsed into silence, Shaykh ʿAli Muttaqi rose and, without a word, walked slowly toward the dock where he boarded the last ship to leave the harbor.

Though dramatized in this retelling, this narrative about the docks of Diu is conveyed by ʿAbd al-Haqq Muhaddith Dihlawi in his biography of ʿAli Muttaqi, "Provision of the Pious" (*Zād al-Mutttaqīn*). He heard it from the son of a companion of ʿAli Muttaqi who accompanied the shaykh on the fateful flight from Ahmedabad and attended him during the sultan's unsuccessful audience.[1] This narrative poignantly portrays ʿAli Muttaqi as an exile rather than a routine pilgrim as he sailed toward Mecca. The Qurʾan urges those who struggle with pilgrimage and exile to take heart and deepen their faith. *Those who have faith, are exiled, and then struggle for the sake of God—as well as those who give them shelter and aid—are the true believers. For them is forgiveness and provision most generous* (Qurʾan 8:74). ʿAli Muttaqi traveled far to train himself in the discipline of "dying to self-will" and along the way discovered a new model of Sufi authority that he felt was authentic. Armed with this new training and perspective, he settled in Gujarat to exercise his authority. But all too soon, he was forced to pack his bags again and to embark on a much longer and arduous voyage into exile. Yet he turned adversity into advantage through his skill.

This chapter is a satchel full of skills—skills in hadith scholarship and Sufi insight. These pious skills were highly portable and deeply respected wherever displayed in the Indian Ocean world that ʿAli Muttaqi inhabited. With them, he found ample shelter and aid, and in exile in Arabia, he was able to rebuild his authority, deepen its roots, and extend its scope. Before his crises and exile, ʿAli Muttaqi was drawn into the circle of political forces in Gujarat. Sultan Bahadur Shah was ruling in an age of prosperity and expansion that was, nonetheless, fragile.

Pilgrimage: Empowering Exile in Mecca

To understand ʿAli Muttaqi's loss in exile fully, we need to consider Gujarat during the reign of Sultan Bahadur in detail. ʿAli Muttaqi saw the sultanate of Gujarat as his natural arena of activity and respected the Gujarati sultans' long tradition of patronizing religious scholars and paying respect to those who upheld the *shariʿa*. Like most Sufis in Ahmedabad, he loyally supported the independence of Gujarat against any threat, whether by land or by sea.

On land, the sultans of Gujarat traditionally rivaled the sultans of Malwa, their neighbors inland to the east. Sultan Bahadur Shah (ruled 1527–35) ably handled Malwa and its smaller neighbor to the south, Khandesh, through a combination of military victories and strategic marriages.[2] But the very year he took the throne, a new threat appeared from the north—the Mughals under Babur (ruled in South Asia 1526–30) and his son Humāyūn (ruled 1530–40). ʿAli Muttaqi saw the Mughals as barbarian invaders from Central Asia, the bastard sons of Timur; in his eyes, they had no dynastic, legal, or religious legitimacy, though they wrested power from the previous rulers of Delhi.

Since becoming sultan in 1527, Bahadur Shah spent most of his energy competing with the Mughals. Upon Babur's death in 1530, Bahadur Shah seized the opportunity to conquer the fortresses of Mandu and Chittor (Chittōrgāṙh), which had acted as buffer zones between the two polities. He also accepted refugees from Delhi: Afghans from the collapsing Lodi dynasty and dissident Mughal princes like Babur's son-in-law Muḥammad Zamān Mīrzā.[3] These military and diplomatic maneuvers caused Humayun to suspect that Gujarat plotted to advance north. He organized a preemptive invasion in 1534. Bahadur Shah and his ministers turned to ʿAli Muttaqi to bless their actions and policies, but he was critical of the sultan's military ambition.

This was a highly personal issue for ʿAli Muttaqi because Bahadur Shah had retreated from Mandu in the face of the Mughals. As they conquered Mandu, ʿAli Muttaqi's former home and residence of his mother and other extended family, they razed the city and massacred its inhabitants to discourage resistance in Gujarat, a policy that followed their Mongol heritage.[4] While ʿAli Muttaqi arranged the affairs of his wife and companions in the port of Diu, he assumed from reports and rumors that his mother and family had been butchered in Mandu.

In this hasty retreat from the Mughal threat, Bahadur Shah torched his own newly built navy. This illustrates how precariously he faced danger from both land and sea, for he had built the fleet to stave off Portuguese marauders who were threatening his ports. The Portuguese menace was not new; Bahadur

Flight of Bahadur Shah during Humayun's Campaign in Gujarat in 1535, a miniature painting by Dharmdas in Lahore, circa 1590. (Nasli and Alice Heeramaneck Collection, Museum Associates Purchase M.78.9.6, Los Angeles County Museum of Art.)

Indian Ocean Sailors Fighting Pirates, a miniature painting by an anonymous Portuguese artist in 1540. (Biblioteca Casanatense in Rome, ms. 1889 c. 35.)

Shah's ancestors had strategized to control ports and sea trade routes. The farthest extent of their coastal authority was the southern island port of Mahim (Mahīm) (now part of Bombay), where the Sufi scholar ʿAlī Mahīmī (or Mahā'imī, d. 1431) had served as a judge in the Gujarati administration.[5] Sultan Ahmad Shah I had arranged his son's marriage with the daughter of the ruler of Mahim, and in this way the sultans kept close control of other port cities.[6] When the Bahmani sultans of the Deccan threatened to take Mahim in 1431, Sultan Ahmad countered their attempts with daring naval and army maneuvers.[7] After the Bahmani sultanate broke up, the Bijapur sultans administered the Konkan coast; in 1494, a Bijapur officer seized ports at Mahim, Dabul, and Chawl to set up a pirate state. The next sultan of Gujarat, Mahmud Begra, sent the same land and sea assault, but a storm wrecked the ships on the shore, where the Bijapur officer's men imprisoned the admiral and slaughtered the Gujarati sailors.[8] Diplomatic pressure induced Bijapur to execute its rogue officer and to release the admiral, who returned laden with rich gifts to pacify the sultan of Gujarat.

In 1498, the balance of land and sea power shifted, altering South Asian politics forever. The Portuguese admiral Vasco de Gama landed on the Malabar coast of South India and established port-forts, which anchored the Portuguese net of sea-control from ports in Aden and Hormuz, at the mouths of the Persian Gulf and the Red Sea. From here, the Portuguese cut off trade from Egypt and Arabia through to the Indian coastline from Kerala to Gujarat. They were so effective that the Mamluk sultan of Egypt combined naval forces with the sultan of Gujarat, Mahmud Begra, to drive off the Portuguese.[9] In 1509, the Portuguese defeated the combined Muslim fleet off the coast of Diu (the chief port of Gujarat in the sixteenth century, along with Surat).[10] This naval defeat ended effective cooperation between Gujarat and the Mamluks, whose naval commitment was "feeble."[11] The Portuguese sacked and burned Goa with a violence that stunned Mahmud Begra, so he decided to pursue an independent diplomatic course. He freed Portuguese prisoners and acknowledged Goa as theirs to keep them from encroaching farther north toward Gujarat. His successor, Muẓaffar Shah II, pursued a similar policy. The Portuguese desired another port farther north and applied diplomatically to build a fortress at Diu. Now just a sleepy town attached to the Gujarat coast by bridges, Diu was then an island and harbor well protected and lucrative, about a two-week sail from the coasts of East Africa and Arabia. The Portuguese officer in South Asia, interpreter, and travel writer named Duarte Barbosa (d. 1521) described the strategic position of this port that the Portuguese knew as Dīū-ye Bandar-e Rūmī or "Diu the Port of the Turks," referring to the Turkic ethnicity of the sultans of Gujarat:

> There is a promontory[,] and joining close to it is a small island, which contains a very large and fine town.... It has a very good harbor and is a port of much trade in merchandise, and of much shipping from Malabar, Baticala [modern Karwar port in Karnataka], Goa, Dabul and Chawl. The people of Diu sail to Aden, Mecca, Zayla, Barbara and Mogadishu and Barawa [all ports in Somalia], Mombasa and Hormuz, and to all parts of the kingdom [of Gujarat].... This town gives such a large sum of money as revenue to the king for the loading and unloading of such rich goods that it is a subject of marvel and amazement.... The king keeps a Moorish governor in this place ... [who] makes much artillery and has many rowing barges, very well arranged ... and has had constructed in the port a very strong and fine bulwark in which he has very good artillery with many lombards [cannons], and he always keeps with him many men-at-arms to whom he pays very good appointment.[12]

Considering its strategic importance and the competence of its governor, Mālik Ayāz, it is not surprising that Muzaffar Shah II denied the Portuguese their request to build their own fort on the island. Not used to being refused, the Portuguese raided Diu but were repelled in 1520, while Malik Ayaz tried to cement an alliance with the expanding Ottomans, who were pressing to conquer the Mamluks in Egypt and take over the trade from the Red Sea through the Indian Ocean.[13] This tense situation prevailed as Bahadur Shah became the new sultan.

Bahadur Shah did not consider the Portuguese to be a dangerous enemy, as his ancestors had.[14] He ignored their previous policy out of greed to control more land while encouraging the Ottoman ruler Sulayman the Magnificent (ruled 1520–66) to wage naval war against the Portuguese. He welcomed an Ottoman naval contingent, just in time to repulse a Portuguese attack on Diu in 1531, in what is heralded as "the first transoceanic victory in Ottoman history."[15] But the victory was pyrrhic for Bahadur Shah, who relied on the Ottoman naval force, whom he later hired as mercenaries of Gujarat and who proved to have flexible loyalties. Bahadur Shah was obsessed with expanding Gujarat's continental boundaries; his success in conquering Malwa and Khandesh caused him to overreach by dominating the kingdom of Ahmednagar (Aḥmadnagar) to the south and challenging Mughal rule in the north.[16] This provoked the Mughal ruler Humayun and pushed rulers in the Deccan to ally with the Mughals against Gujarat.

Bahadur Shah behaved arrogantly toward neighboring sultans and misjudged the Mughal imperium, expecting its ruler to behave like one sultan among many rather than as a burgeoning emperor who could depose rival sultans. When Bahadur Shah was besieging the fortress of Champaner to subdue its Rajput ruler, he wrote to Humayun urging him to gallantly delay invading Gujarat while its sultan was "fighting infidels." Humayun ignored this request, seeing no difference between Rajput infidels and Sunni Muslim rivals: all opponents needed to be subdued systematically in his growing imperium. When he was a young prince, Bahadur Shah had been present with the Lodi army when the Mughals defeated it in 1526. He should have known that the Mughals were not like the ethnic Afghan rulers in South Asia, who were content to rule a regional sultanate surrounded by many other sultans considered equals. Rather, the Mughals had imperial ambitions linked to their Timurid legacy and competed imitatively with the Safavid Empire in Iran. From the opposite perspective, the first Mughal ruler described Bahadur Shah as a renegade prince before he claimed his throne and a "bloodthirsty and audacious young man" in his personal account titled the *Babur Nama*. Babur lived for only a few years in South Asia and left his eldest son, Humayun, to consolidate Mughal rule.

In 1535, Humayun defeated Bahadur Shah at Mandsaur (Mañdsawr, a town in Malwa, midway between Ahmedabad and Delhi) and then again at Mandu (the capital of Malwa, recently conquered by Gujarat). Bahadur Shah abandoned his chief defense in the fort of Champaner, thus losing ten years of revenue wealth from Gujarat.[17] His only hope was to instigate insurrection behind the Mughal lines. He sent secret correspondence to the Afghan commander, Shēr Shāh Sūrī, offering military and monetary aid if he would march from Bihar (Bihār), take Delhi, and quickly attack the Mughals.[18]

In the face of the Mughal invasion, Gujarat's pious and able prime minister, Asaf Khan, abandoned the capital; he rushed to Diu to load the royal family and treasury on a fleet of ten ships. They also carried a contingent of 2,000 Yemeni, Turkic, and Ethiopian guards, as well as lesser nobles like Qayṣar Khān and Shams Khān. The sailing season was over, but the desperate refugees prepared to venture out to sea anyway.[19] Then Bahadur Shah burst into the port, having given up defending the capital. In his final audience with ʿAli Muttaqi, Bahadur Shah petitioned consolation but received none. The Sufi scholar boarded a ship and headed away from Gujarat, toward a life of exile, and the sultan was left to fend for himself.

Hadith: Exploring the Heart of the *Shariʿa*

ʿAli Muttaqi left no record of his desperate voyage out of Gujarat, stating only that he arrived in Mecca and settled in a strange land. However strange, it was a land that held promise for him. For in making the pilgrimage and circumambulating the Kaʿba, he was ritually circling the center of the world. He actively turned exile into the acquisition of authority through additional Sufi training and connection with new lineages. He undertook further scholarly training that would be highly respected back in South Asia. In Mecca, he found the resources to reconstruct his shattered world.

During that long off-season voyage, ʿAli Muttaqi pondered the loss of his home, family, and country. Mughal forces had razed the city of his mother. Bahadur Shah's capital was under Mughal control, and his army lay scattered in retreat. As the coast of Gujarat disappeared behind him, ʿAli Muttaqi assumed that his former patron, Bahadur Shah, had been dethroned and soon would be killed. He had considered Gujarat to be the natural arena for his newly found authenticity as a saint, bolstered by popular and royal recognition. Now all that lay in ruins behind him.

ʿAli Muttaqi did not intend to settle permanently in Mecca but instead considered this a chance to consolidate his training in hadith studies. While still

Humayun Routing Bahadur Shah and His Army at Champaner Fort in 1535, a miniature painting by Farrukh Chela in 1603–4. (*Akbar Nama*, vol. 1, folio 61, British Library Or.12988.)

in Gujarat, he had developed a keen interest in hadith studies but had been unable to find a worthy teacher. In his youth, he had witnessed many hadith scholars from Egypt, the Hijaz, and Yemen settling in South Asia to teach. The florescence of small, independent courts in the Deccan in addition to Gujarat fueled this trend.

In Gujarat, ʿAli Muttaqi had met the hadith scholar Wajīh al-Dīn Muḥammad ibn Suwayda (d. 1504), who had emigrated from Egypt to Ahmedabad. The sultan of Gujarat gave him the title "Mālik al-Muḥaddithīn," the king of hadith experts. Those hadith scholars with credentials from respected circles—like those of Ibn Hajar al-ʿAsqalani—enjoyed high social standing.[20] This king of hadith scholars in Gujarat arrived by 1492, and from him ʿAli Muttaqi learned of the circles of rigorous hadith studies that drew students from all corners of the Islamic world to Arabia.[21] ʿAli Muttaqi's flight to the ritual heart of the Islamic world was thus also a journey to the scholarly center of hadith studies. When he arrived in Mecca, he joined the scholarly circle of Abū'l-Ḥasan al-Bakrī (d. 1546). ʿAli Muttaqi became close friends with him and his son Muḥammad Abū al-Makārim al-Bakrī (d. 1585). They secured for ʿAli Muttaqi a place among the most renowned scholars in what is called "the era of consolidation and analysis" of hadith in the late Sunni tradition. Solidifying in the fourteenth century—during Mamluk rule in Egypt and the sultanate of Delhi in South Asia—this tradition was characterized by a new stability and creativity as scholars integrated allegiance to Sufi orders into their loyalty to a school of law.[22] Within this tradition, the fifteenth century witnessed a renaissance of hadith scholarship, beginning with al-ʿAsqalani.

As a notable Sufi and scholar, Abu'l-Hasan al-Bakri introduced ʿAli Muttaqi into the circle of the great jurist and hadith scholar with Sufi attachments Ibn Ḥajar al-Haythamī (d. 1566). ʿAli Muttaqi joined as a student but quickly showed himself to be an emerging master. Al-Haythami referred to ʿAli Muttaqi as an equal while interpreting obtuse phrases in hadith reports, saying that ʿAli Muttaqi was actually his teacher rather than his student, as it outwardly appeared.[23] When ʿAli Muttaqi entered the gathering, al-Haythami would rise from the seat from which he taught and greet the younger ʿAli Muttaqi as his peer.

Under the watchful eye of al-Haythami, ʿAli Muttaqi honed his skills in hadith compilation and interpretation. He began his lifelong project of reworking the collections of Jalāl al-Dīn al-Suyūṭī (d. 1505). ʿAli Muttaqi undertook to combine al-Suyuti's "The Comprehensive Collection" (*Jamʿ al-Jawāmiʿ*, also called *al-Jāmiʿ al-Kabīr*) and "The Small Collection" (*al-Jāmiʿ al-Ṣaghīr*). Most importantly, he sought to reorganize the whole collection by gathering the reports under a topical rubric related to their content and meaning. ʿAli Muttaqi selected these rubrics from the topics of legal manuals to encourage jurists to consult the reports on which to base their legal decisions. In contrast, al-Suyuti—like many previous hadith scholars—ordered the reports in his collections by alphabetical index following the initial letter of the first word in the report. This system made using the compilation dependent on accurate prior memorization of the report's content, which was a considerable limitation. His colleagues greeted ʿAli Muttaqi's exacting work of reordering and interpreting the hadith reports with great accolades. Abu'l-Hasan al-Bakri said, "Al-Suyuti has earned the gratitude of the whole world [for his hadith collection], yet ʿAli Muttaqi has topped him, earning the gratitude of al-Suyuti himself [for refining that collection]."[24]

ʿAli Muttaqi also produced smaller and less systematic compilations of hadith reports, some based some on the works of al-Suyuti,[25] while others drew from the works of different masters.[26] He continued the tradition of selecting forty hadith reports that he found especially moving to circulate in one slim volume with Persian commentary.[27] ʿAli Muttaqi contributed to the technical study of hadith interpretation with an abridgment of a text on uncommon terms and strange locutions in hadith reports.[28] He drew from his vast knowledge of Prophetic reports to address specialized subjects. He collected reports pertaining to the virtues of the Prophet.[29] And he compiled collections about the personality of the Mahdi, as the fourth satchel documents in detail.

He found this new community in Mecca alienating at first. Al-Bakri's circle of students drank coffee, a recent innovation.[30] At first, ʿAli Muttaqi recoiled from drinking coffee, suspecting that its stimulating qualities made it *ḥarām*, like intoxicants. Yet al-Bakri cajoled him into drinking it since all-night *dhikr* had become tightly associated with energizing coffee. This custom was recorded and defended by a Sufi scholar in Ahmedabad who was born of a Yemeni father and Gujarati mother, the venerable ʿAbd al-Qādir al-ʿAydarūsī (1570–1627, also named Abū Bakr Muḥyī al-Dīn). His book *al-Nūr al-Sāfir ʿan Akhbār al-Qarn al-ʿĀshir* ("The Light Unveiled, with Events of the Tenth Century Regaled") is one of the earliest works to record ʿAli Muttaqi's biography; it includes Arabic poems in praise of coffee, noting that a veritable fatwa war raged over whether the beverage was licit.[31] As a Sufi and merchant, al-Aydarusi quoted jurists and doctors about the medical benefits and legality of coffee, along with Sufi poems in praise of its salubrious effects.

It was relatively easy for ʿAli Muttaqi to adjust to coffee as a minor innovation, but it was far harder for him to confront how these notable scholars amassed wealth and social status. He admired their scholarship and was indebted to them for giving him access to teachers, but ʿAli Muttaqi openly criticized their luxurious lifestyle. He reprimanded Muhammad al-Bakri, the son of his friend and teacher, for building a rich mansion, saying, "If his own father had never acted so ostentatiously, why should the son?"[32] The Ottoman administration gave generous stipends to scholars and Sufis in Mecca, a policy to justify their adoption of the title "Protectors of the Two Holy Cities" after 1517. Many religious leaders grew wealthy by supporting their protectorate. Although the Ottoman governor at Mecca allotted a stipend to ʿAli Muttaqi, he did not accept it for his personal use and refused to allow his closest disciples to use the funds. Rather, he accepted the money to distribute among his followers who were studying law or hadith and had no aspiration to follow Sufism.[33]

In addition to hadith studies, ʿAli Muttaqi also received new Sufi training in Mecca. Abu'l-Hasan al-Bakri introduced ʿAli Muttaqi to an Egyptian Sufi master, Muḥammad ibn Muḥammad al-Sakhāwī. Most likely, he was the son of Shams al-Dīn Muḥammad ibn ʿAbd al-Raḥmān al-Sakhāwī (d. 1497), the prolific Egyptian jurist and hadith scholar who belonged to the Shadhili Order and frequented Mecca; he wrote an account of hadith scholars of his era (*al-Ḍawʾ al-Lāmiʿ li-Ahl al-Qarn al-Tāsiʿ*, or "Lighting Up the Memory of Scholars in the Tenth Century") and a biography of his hadith teacher al-ʿAsqalani. Despite the fame of his ancestor, Muhammad ibn Muhammad al-Sakhawi is obscure; even ʿAbd al-Haqq, who tried to collect all information about ʿAli Muttaqi, knew little about him, perhaps because al-Sakhawi did not live in Mecca and ʿAli Muttaqi took initiation while he was there for the Hajj.[34] ʿAli Muttaqi did not need a master to offer him spiritual guidance and Sufi discipline, for he had already received this for two years under Husam al-Din Muttaqi. Rather, the valuable gift he received from al-Sakhawi was his lineages: the Qadiri, Shadhili, and Madyani Orders fused together in an initiation that we can call "the triple *tariqa*." ʿAli Muttaqi's disciples preserved the record of his lineages, reproduced in appendix B.

Husam al-Din Muttaqi had not given ʿAli Muttaqi a firm pedigree in an institutional lineage, but al-Sakhawi compensated for that shortcoming. Prominent in the lineage that al-Sakhawi granted to ʿAli Muttaqi is the figure of Shaykh Aḥmad Zarrūq (d. 1494).[35] He was a reform-oriented Sufi, jurist, and social critic who opposed a popular revolution in Morocco against the Marinid dynasty in 1465. Exiled from Fez, Zarruq went on the Hajj and then pursued theological and legal studies in Cairo, where he studied with the elder al-Sakhawi.[36] He took initiation with a reform-minded Sufi, Shaykh Aḥmad ibn ʿUqbā al-Ḥaḍramī (d. 1490), in Cairo. Under al-Hadrami's influence, Zarruq fused Sufism with Islamic law to avoid ritual extravagance and charismatic authoritarianism, teaching to "be a jurist first, then a Sufi; don't be a Sufi first, then a jurist."[37] His Sufi master ordered Zarruq to return to Morocco to spread reformist ideals, but he was ostracized. Abandoning his homeland, Zarruq traveled across North Africa to teach jurisprudence, initiate disciples, and write texts until he finally settled in Miṣrāta, a key trading town in Tarabulus (Ṭarābulus, now Tripolitania), on the coastal region of western Libya, while his network of students and disciples spread through Egypt and Arabia.

ʿAli Muttaqi's life mirrored Zarruq's life in profound ways. As he joined the Sufi circle of Abu'l-Hasan al-Bakri, ʿAli Muttaqi read the devotional text favored by him, "The Book of Wisdom Sayings" (*Kitāb al-Ḥikam*) by Ibn ʿAṭāʾallāh al-Iskandarī, the Sufi jurist of the Shadhili Order (d. 1310 in Cairo), with its many interpretations, including those by Zarruq. This was the beginning of ʿAli Muttaqi's intense engagement with the ideas, writings, and spirituality of Zarruq, whose persona guided him to fuse scriptural studies with Sufi training.

ʿAli Muttaqi plunged into this elite circle of reform-oriented Sufis concentrated in Cairo and Mecca, hadith scholars and jurists who also pursued Sufi training with vigor. In this atmosphere, he was able to combine hadith studies and Sufi devotion in ways that were impossible in Gujarat. By combining them, he sought to transform both. Here, he found a Sufi community that upheld the ideal of the scholar-saint. This ideal gave expression to the inner conviction that ʿAli Muttaqi had been cultivating ever since he had rejected his Chishti heritage.

ʿAli Muttaqi was a powerful force in these scholarly circles, whose leading figures acknowledged him as a saint who embodied their ideals. ʿAli Muttaqi demonstrated his burgeoning authority as a scholar-saint by silently persuading al-Haythami, his apparent superior and teacher in hadith sittings, to become his disciple through a Sufi initiation.[38] This was an astounding feat, since al-Haythami was a stern man who was outspoken against most activities associated with Sufis, as reflected in his work titled "Refraining the Riffraff from Forbidden Frivolities and Musical Sessions."[39] At the initiation, ʿAli Muttaqi gave his teacher a signature "death satchel" in front of thousands of his hadith students to symbolize his entrance into the community and his relationship with ʿAli Muttaqi as his saintly guide. This event was a crowning achievement for ʿAli Muttaqi since it embodied his ideal of saintly authenticity, bringing divergent methods of scholarship and spiritual insight together. His relationship with al-Haythami symbolized the attainment of this goal and illustrated the model he desired for his future community of followers. This was the heart of his Hajj, which had begun in exile and despair.

In Mecca, ʿAli Muttaqi blurred distinctions between scholarship and Sufi devotion; he strove to integrate the pursuit of religious knowledge with one's intellect and the burnishing of religious insight with one's heart. He considered every action that benefited one's self (or better, that benefited others) to be *dhikr*. He would prepare special black ink for his students as a form of *dhikr*.[40] His relating hadith reports to others was the highest kind of *dhikr*. He saw the authenticity of his own sainthood wrapped up in his scholarly teaching and writing, which he held up as the highest proof of his spiritual authority.

He expressed this ideal repeatedly in his compositions but perhaps nowhere as clearly as in the short treatise titled "The Ultimate Perfection, on the Best of all Meritorious Action." Here, he argues that teaching and learning are the most highly rewarded devotional acts.

> This treatise could also be rightfully called "The Most Beneficial Labor, on the Virtue of Teaching and Learning." People will gain different levels of blessing in the next life according to their different virtuous actions performed in this world. The most virtuous actions are those that give benefit to others even after the actor has died. . . . Of all these actions, imparting knowledge to others is the most virtuous action. Spreading knowledge has the widest benefit and the longest lasting usefulness, when compared to building water channels, planting date palms, founding a mosque or a fortress, or granting an institution a copy of the Qurʾan. Knowledge is the cause of revitalizing the *shariʿa* and rectifying people's souls. If one builds a fortress or plants a tree or digs a water channel, surely this construction will eventually grow old and decay after his death. In contrast, knowledge never fades, and once taught, it never dies away. Teaching knowledge is even loftier than dying as a martyr in defense of Islam. . . . Learning and scholarship include many different activities, which are all means to the same end. One may teach full-time, lend books, or give them as charity. Even helping a single student to acquire paper, pen, and ink is helping to spread knowledge and partakes in its virtuous reward. However, the one activity which is essential and upon which all the others rest is teaching basic literacy to children. The one who imparts basic literacy has a share in all the further benefits of learning that the child might reap, including what he might later teach to others.[41]

According to this analysis, the greatest blessing ʿAli Muttaqi could give himself and others was to spread knowledge of the *shariʿa*: his special kind of knowledge was hadith, and his mission was to make reports accessible to jurists, Sufis, and rulers. To his last day, he continued to revise and compile hadith, as his supreme form of *dhikr* and moderate form of asceticism.[42] He recorded a story "about a Sufi who left the company of other Sufis and began to sit with the scholars and their students. Someone observed this change of behavior and asked him why he had left the company of other Sufis and preferred the company of those engaged in learning. He answered, 'Because the Sufis consign themselves to drowning in absorption with the divine, while the scholar reaches out his hand to pull up the drowning man and save him!'"[43] Although veiled, this story is autobiographical: it shows the underlying rationale that ʿAli Muttaqi discovered for his total change of life since rejecting his Chishti community in Burhanpur. He upheld his new authority as a master teacher of hadith as the proof of his authentic sainthood, in contrast to those "ignorant ones among the Sufis" who claimed to carry out devotions or follow a saint without authenticating their actions with scriptural knowledge. He alleged that other Sufi communities did not teach knowledge, and he denounced those who did not see learning as a method of cultivating spiritual insight. Some went so far as to prohibit their followers from learning the religious disciplines "as if they were the enemies of scholars, and of knowledge itself, claiming that it is injurious to their faith."[44]

ʿAli Muttaqi engaged these Sufi communities in the style of argument that became his hallmark. He investigated what hadith reports or traditional sayings they relied on and then reinterpreted them to counter their arguments. He followed this with an illustrative analogy drawn in the simple lines of caricature.

> Perhaps these Sufis who praise ignorance and shun learning base their rationale on the saying of the masters that "knowledge is the greatest veil of God." However, in their ignorance, they don't realize that the intention behind this saying is to send them on a mission of acquiring knowledge! Knowledge is a veil for those who endeavor to attain it while they brag and boast of their attainment and all the worldly trifles it brings them. In reality, those who claim to love God and the Prophet but refuse to pursue knowledge are like a person afflicted with passionate love for a sweetheart to such an extent that he is helpless without his beloved. Imagine that this man was informed that his sweetheart was behind a

> high wall, and that the only way to reach his beloved was to climb the wall. Imagine that upon hearing this news, he says, "This wall is a veil, an obstacle between my beloved and me, so I'll turn my back on it and reject it!" Upon hearing this logic, all the people around him would tell him that he is an idiot. He should clearly work to climb the wall to reach his lover, rather than turn his back on the wall altogether. Those who desist from acquiring religious knowledge are all idiots like this man. Sufi masters have said that "knowledge is the greatest veil of God" since such painstaking effort is required to master it.[45]

This conscious effort to blur the popular distinction between Sufi worship and scholarly effort became a pillar of his teachings. It reflected his sense of authenticity as a saint, bolstered by his newly found affiliations in Mecca.

Integrity: Training Disciples and Reforming Genres

His success in Mecca made ʿAli Muttaqi feel that he had transformed losses of exile into gains of authority. He gained expertise in the scriptural field of hadith and gained initiation into a community that fused three Sufi orders. Most importantly, he gained an ambitious circle of colleagues who, along with ʿAli Muttaqi himself, aspired to reintegrate the study of religious disciplines with the internal work of spiritual refinement. Outside the environment of ecstatic devotion and existential philosophy that dominated South Asia, ʿAli Muttaqi was able to articulate an alternative and carefully delineated mode of sainthood.

ʿAli Muttaqi aimed to reform Sufism by highlighting principles that undergirded its institutions while de-emphasizing its outward ritual practices. This approach was parallel to his work in hadith studies. He applied the methods of hadith scholarship to Sufi training while insisting that Sufi devotion be fused with training in the scholarly disciplines, like hadith studies. In this way, he singled out knowledge as the pivot that brought together and balanced disciples and disciplines in his reform program.

As mentioned above, ʿAli Muttaqi's lifelong project in hadith studies was to edit al-Suyuti's mammoth collection of Prophetic reports, single out the operative principle in each report, and then group reports together that embodied the same principle. He transmitted all such reports together under one rubric, taken from the field of jurisprudence. He sought to identify the legal and moral principle within the text of each report. He designed this project to facilitate the practical use of hadith reports, above and beyond the literal memorization and personal transmission of reports as a sort of ritualized blessing.

Similarly, ʿAli Muttaqi tried to find the principles behind every form of Sufi devotion. Inspired by Zarruq's juridical reform of Sufism, his project was implicitly critical of the inherited forms of Sufi devotion. In laying out the principles to be safeguarded, ʿAli Muttaqi necessarily charted the distance between those principles and the practices of his contemporaries. This operation took its most extreme form in ʿAli Muttaqi's experiments with the "death of self-will," as detailed in the first satchel. These experiences confirmed for him his own authenticity as a saint who had undergone Sufi training and successfully embodied its highest ideals. He highlighted the death of self-will as the founding principle of Sufi practice, the principle from which all forms of worship and ascetic discipline ultimately derived. From that vantage point, he could evaluate whether any form of devotion led to this central experience, actually or only rhetorically, directly or merely metaphorically. He judged that Sufis should avoid or limit those devotional practices that only indirectly led to selflessness. They should also avoid or vocally denounce those persons who claimed to be saints but did not embody this principle of the "death of self-will."

As previously illustrated, ʿAli Muttaqi experimented with these methods of self-denial before he arrived in Mecca. But it was in Mecca that he became acquainted with Shaykh Zarruq and his small epistle on the death of self-will. ʿAli Muttaqi preserved that Arabic text, titled "Traveling the Path of Spiritual Cultivation with No Reliable Fellow Companion," analyzed here from the only known manuscript of this work, which is preserved in Gujarat.[46] The digital edition of this book provides a full translation in appendix C.

Zarruq wrote his epistle to benefit those who had not found a spiritual guide to show the way or a sincere companion to give sound advice. Sufi masters described the path of traveling toward God in countless books in different ways, saying, "The paths to God are as numerous as the variety of beings in creation." It is bewildering to examine the variety of good deeds, from the very Islamic ritual recitation of "No god but God" to the very universal offering of help to one's neighbor. Zarruq argued that all good deeds and Sufi practices could be distilled into a single principle: to give one's life for God. In accord with the Arabic proverb "Whoever marries a beauty has to pay the dowry," those who want to be intimate with God must abandon their own egos: "You should desist planning and choosing for yourself to earn eternal repose with God and a life without anxiety and care."

This short epistle illustrates a spiritual paradox about human will. Even the resolve to let one's self-will die involves willpower. The very term used by Zarruq (and ʿAli Muttaqi after him), *al-mawt al-ikhtiyārī*, captures this ambivalence. It could be translated in two ways, each valid and each contradictory: the "death of self-will," or a "self-willed death." To make sense of such a paradoxical phrase requires a wider perspective, taking into view how sainthood came to be seen as a state of being-close-to-death.

In the Islamic tradition, this paradox comes into play when religious specialists struggle to embody and display for others a state of being-close-to-death. Those who favored music and poetry displayed this being-close-to-death in the drama of ecstasy, involuntary motion, and trance. Those who placed their faith in Sufis saw being initiated by a master as the necessary gesture of surrender that rhymes with death. However, these metaphoric solutions to the problem of reaching the threshold of death did not satisfy ʿAli Muttaqi. He was characteristically more direct, even blunt. If being-close-to-death was the necessary passage for self-transformation, then one must push the self to the brink of death.

One of the many commentaries that ʿAli Muttaqi wrote upon the texts of Zarruq was on his epistle about the death of self-will. Titled "My Lord's Guidance in a Spiritual Guide's Absence," ʿAli Muttaqi's commentary was written three-quarters of a century after Zarruq's death. It is analyzed here from rare Arabic manuscripts in Ahmedabad and Cairo.[47] The digital edition of this book provides a full translation in appendix D.

ʿAli Muttaqi begins his commentary with a statement from Zarruq's teacher, al-Hadrami: "Spiritual training is no longer valid in the sense commonly understood, and all that's left is benefiting from the shaykh's own aspiration and state. You should follow the scripture [*kitab*] and the example of the Prophet [*sunna*], no more and no less."[48] ʿAli Muttaqi reinforces this message by citing a hadith report: "Those who are ascetically abstinent in this world, God teaches them without study and guides them without teachers, giving them spiritual insight to remove their blindness." Thus, learning without study and being guided without teachers happens when one refuses to rely on one's self-will and volition. To this point, the Prophet Muhammad taught, "Die before you die" and "Consider yourself among those in their graves." ʿAli Muttaqi's commentary couches Zarruq's radical ideas in the framework of tradition; he compares them to hadith and rephrases them in rhyming Arabic aphorisms. For example, he writes that the death of self-will is "the elixir of willful volition in the alchemy of blissful salvation." ʿAli Muttaqi turns also to popular analogies and parables to make his point. The death of self-will is like an alchemical elixir that transforms anything it touches from base metal to gold:

"The will to die to one's self-will is one among the goals of will itself. Yet it is, like an elixir, an object that transforms other objects. If the elixir is dribbled upon a piece of brass, it transmutes the metal into purest gold, raising its value exponentially from what it was before. . . . The person who has died to self-will is like a spiritual alchemist whose wise use of an elixir transports him effortlessly to the fulfillment of whatever he had desired." Moving from analogy to parable, he echoes the story of the Prophet Job (Ayyūb). After quoting an Arabic aphorism—"purity dwells in the hearts of those who dwell on trash heaps"—ʿAli Muttaqi asks his reader to consider a paradoxical story. "If a person ends up on a stinking, rotten trash heap and wants to get free of the stench, he or she has two choices. The first choice is to climb down off the trash heap, wash out one's clothes and bathe, and then consider oneself clean. That is relatively easy. The second choice is much harder and requires intense effort. One could stay right there, dwelling on the trash heap, and cure its overwhelming stench with a powerfully fragrant perfume. The only fragrance powerful enough is that emitted by the death of self-will."

By the end of his brief text, ʿAli Muttaqi not only comments upon this text but also mines the sources of Zarruq's inspiration. Zarruq had made his career writing commentaries on "The Book of Wisdom Sayings" of Ibn ʿAta'allah al-Iskandari. Following Zarruq, ʿAli Muttaqi made the genre of the wisdom sayings or aphorisms (Ar. *ḥikam*, singular *ḥikma*) the centerpiece of his teaching method. Wisdom sayings condense deep insight into few words and also blur the distinction between different genres of devotional literature.[49] ʿAli Muttaqi used them to fuse Qur'anic verses, hadith sayings, and Sufi maxims in order to communicate advice and insight to his followers. He also used them to explicate the principles that underlie Sufi rituals and technical terminology in order to refresh and revive Sufi practice.

To honor Zarruq's admiration for aphorisms, ʿAli Muttaqi composed his own and spiced his commentary with them:

> Death is the only store in which shop both rich and poor.
>
> The greatest of miracles bequeathed is rising to walk though you're deceased.
>
> A virtuous quality that's of the highest worth is to have died while still walking the face of the earth.
>
> The only way taking a life is not a crime is sacrificing your spirit before the body's appointed time.

> The only killing that leads to life beyond end or start is giving up one's soul before the body falls apart.
>
> The way to gain advantage and protect against other people is to abandon all the qualities that typify other people.

ʿAli Muttaqi knew that human reason is crafty and that fear drives us to reason away death in any way possible. How to cut through the distraction of routine common sense and hold our attention on the reality of imminent death, so that we no longer fear but actually welcome it? Only language that is honed and crafted to distill a message into its most condensed and rhythmic form can fulfill this function.

Thus, ʿAli Muttaqi argues through aphorism, parable, and analogy that the essence of Sufism is to give up one's egoistic volition in loving surrender to God's creative will. He praises Sufi masters who help their disciples internalize this insight. He encourages readers to find a principled master whose personality is in accord with both their own disposition and the *shariʿa*, for that will ensure that this insight gets conveyed directly and deeply. Beneath this framework of respect for tradition, ʿAli Muttaqi's epistle is written specifically for those who do not have a spiritual guide. He quotes with approval Zarruq's vivid description of how one must enact death, not just through Sufi initiations or musical trances but through the very limbs of one's body. This method turns the will against the body itself, denying its most basic urges and habitual motions, like eating, drinking, sleeping, standing, even moving. This is a total erasure of bodily habitus that one has learned since birth. ʿAli Muttaqi tries to address this apparent paradox of how the will can overpower the body, leading in a contradictory motion to the death, not of the body, but of the will that began the operation.

ʿAli Muttaqi also wrote another small treatise on the subject, titled "Reminders of Death for Gradually Passing Away."[50] In it, he uses the image of alchemy to describe the "paradox of intention" through which the greatest aims can be achieved only by abandoning the will to achieve them.[51] The process cannot be an achievement of the ego; it must come as a gift from above. This process means opening a space in the human personality for the workings of a transcendent force that Sufis call "divine solicitousness" (*ʿināyat allāh*). ʿAli Muttaqi hoped that as Sufi saints-in-the-making experienced the social power of their role, they would abandon the ambition and self-will that drove them to take on Sufi discipline in the first place. If self-will persisted within a person who bore the socially prestigious distinction of being a saint, it could lead to abuses of power like fostering sectarian movements, bidding for political power, or indulging in personal aggrandizement through the garb of piety.

The expression "the death of self-will" is purely negative. Similarly, this immediate reduction of Sufi training down to the experience of "dying before death" is a negative analysis, declaring what the ultimate experience is not rather than describing how one could achieve such an experience. To balance this, ʿAli Muttaqi also built a method of training disciples to open them up to this ineffable experience: the death of self-will. Just as those who are dead to their own will act in full accord with the Prophetic example of the *shariʿa*, so a method of spiritual training that aims to evoke this death of self-will must be limited by and vitalized through the *shariʿa* itself.

To achieve this end, ʿAli Muttaqi insisted that all his disciples first acquire thorough training in religious learning in its linguistic, scriptural, and legal aspects. He argued that Sufi affiliations were a vehicle for the pursuit of knowledge in all its dimensions. He stressed the priority of outer knowledge first, which would lead to the pursuit of inner knowledge.

> There are two kinds of knowledge: inner knowledge and outer knowledge. Each has its own distinct starting points and its own ultimate goals. Inner knowledge is also called ethics [*akhlaq*]. . . . Each kind of knowledge further divides into two categories: that knowledge which is essential and obligatory for each individual, and that knowledge which is obligatory for the community as a whole but not for each individual. In the dimension of inner knowledge, what is essential is what makes one's outer actions sound and efficacious. The rest consists of details and elaborations on the subtle points of Sufi practice that should be left to specialists in the community and are certainly not required for every individual. A person should first endeavor to acquire what is essential of outer knowledge and only then get what is essential of inner knowledge. Without this essential inner knowledge, hypocrisy and pride may adulterate a person's outer knowledge.[52]

Unlike many of his contemporaries, he did not see studying religious disciplines as basic training, as a first step that was necessary but separate from the real training of Sufi devotion. Rather, he saw it as integral training. Studying the religious disciplines was not just a first step before spiritual training; it was already spiritual training in its very essence. However, ʿAli Muttaqi felt that only a saintly teacher like himself could bring out these dimensions in Islamic learning. His teaching method was effective: many of his leading disciples admitted that they came to him originally only for external training in hadith. It would take up to a year before the student realized that his spiritual training had already begun, without his having ever intended to become "a Sufi."

In this way, ʿAli Muttaqi fused scholarly training with Sufi training. His home in Mecca was both a madrasa and a khanqah in one building. He intentionally "disguised" his Sufi training in the form of scholarly teaching. He was trying not only to limit who could claim Sufi training but also to insinuate Sufi training into would-be jurists and hadith scholars, such as his disciples Muhammad ibn Tahir Patani and the brothers ʿAbdallah Sindhi and Rahmatallah Sindhi. He tried to balance the acquisition of religious knowledge (which was a form of social prestige and power) with virtue and selflessness, without which it could not lead to social justice. To illustrate this ideal fusion, he quoted one of the principles of Zarruq: "One who follows the Sufi path while neglecting jurisprudence is a heretic, while one who learns jurisprudence while neglecting the Sufi path commits transgression. However, one who combines both has attained realization of the Truth." ʿAli Muttaqi explained this principle (based upon a saying by Anas ibn Mālik, a companion of Muhammad who relayed many hadith reports): "The first is a heretic because he believes in a good thing that nonetheless negates the wisdom of revelation and the legal rulings derived from it. The second is corrupted because his knowledge eclipses the inward orientation that prevents him from rebelling against God and alienates him from virtues upon which religious actions must be based in order to be purely for God. The realization of the third is because he is upright in Truth, adhering to the essence of the True One."[53] ʿAli Muttaqi insisted that his disciples first become his students for several years, in order to establish this firm basis of legal rectitude.

When his students made the transition to becoming disciples, their explicitly Sufi training began. Then ʿAli Muttaqi would introduce them to the texts of Zarruq, whose writings elucidated the operative principles of Sufism (*qawāʾid al-taṣawwuf*). He positioned Zarruq's texts as the ideological linchpin that held together scriptural learning and Sufi practice. This reduced the whole medieval elaboration of Sufi devotion to an elegant but irrelevant set of rituals, and he recommended that the sincere disciple should avoid attachment to them. In a short but incisive text, ʿAli Muttaqi tried to construct an authentic lineage for his tempered style of Sufi devotion, titled "The Tightest Bond of Forefathers and Descendants on How to Be a Sufi as Derived Directly from the Qur'an, the Prophet's Example, and Our Pious Ancestors."[54] He demonstrated how scripture provides the basic vocabulary for Sufi practice and how the Prophetic hadith specify its essential forms. In the final section of this work, he extracted the sayings of the pious ancestors, *al-salaf al-ṣāliḥ*, that support Sufi practices. Strategically, he included Zarruq as a "pious ancestor," even though he was only two generations senior to ʿAli Muttaqi. In this way, he projected Zarruq as a legitimate figure rooted in a tradition that cut through medieval accretions and revived that style of Sufi practice that derived directly from scripture and the Prophet's actions. In the end, he condensed the tradition even more tightly by eclipsing mention of Zarruq and delving right to the practice that he saw as the essence of being a Sufi: "I have displayed for you all these various definitions of being a Sufi and all the ideas of who is a Sufi, in all their different kinds and types. However, if you ask me what is the best way to achieve this station, I would answer: simply the death of self-will. I have written a treatise on this process, which you should read to understand it and practice it yourself."[55]

For the benefit of his disciples, ʿAli Muttaqi also authored teaching texts based on Zarruq's "Uṣūlī approach" to Sufi practice. Usuli scholarship began in jurisprudence, as medieval reaction to diversification of decisions by various legal schools. Usuli scholars endeavored to explain the legal principles by which decisions were formulated and to check that all decisions were based on firm scriptural roots.[56] Zarruq adopted the terms "root" or authentic source (Ar. *aṣl*, plural *uṣūl*) and "principle" or systematic rule (Ar. *qāʿida*, plural *qawāʿid*). He borrowed these terms from juridical scholarship and applied them to Sufi practice to articulate the principles of spiritual cultivation under the guidance of a saint just as jurists explicated the principles of jurisprudence. This involved a bold but delicate extension of Usuli scholarship into the field of Sufi practice. Zarruq hoped that his "Principles of Being a Sufi" would guide the outer actions of Sufis which fell under the jurisdiction of law and legal sanction, just as "The Book of Wisdom Sayings" of Ibn ʿAtaʾallah had come to guide their inner lives.[57] His principles would both limit their actions and link them to "root" behaviors sanctified by scripture and Prophetic example.

ʿAli Muttaqi wrote many books to make Zarruq's intricate texts more accessible. These are not commentaries but rather condensations of the original works intended to popularize their content. ʿAli Muttaqi saw his own reform program in such continuity with Zarruq's "Usuli approach" that he did not need commentaries on Zarruq's texts but had rather integrated them into his own ideas. He reworked Zarruq's two basic texts, "The Principles of Being a Sufi"[58] and "The Foundations of the Path,"[59] for use among his disciples: these two texts together neatly pruned the Sufi tradition of all the wild growth that over the last few centuries had obscured its main trunk and roots and inhibited the production of its fruit. ʿAli Muttaqi wrote of the bewildering multiplicity of devotional methods, such that "all the Sufis are on a single path, but they are different depending on their states and stages. It is as if they drink from the same water, but get nourishment from different types of food."[60] He saw Zarruq's texts as channels that protected that one source of water and ensured its purity.

In addition to reworking texts by Zarruq, ʿAli Muttaqi also wrote his own version of the principles of being a Sufi. These efforts were modest: he felt that this genre did not need expansion through creative elaboration but rather demanded only internalization and implementation. ʿAli Muttaqi's constant emphasis on practice could extend to almost anti-intellectual extremes. He felt that the composition of Sufi texts had already gone too far, and he himself wrote only for specific purposes: to limit which books might be in circulation among disciples, to limit the very need for books, and to reintegrate those ideas that had gained independence through Sufi books back into their appropriate setting enmeshed in the religious disciplines. He wrote his own work on "essential principles" as a reminder to his disciples, not as a fully conceptualized text. "The Provision of the Seekers" is such a reminder, in which ʿAli Muttaqi reduces Sufi devotion to five basic principles: doing constant *dhikr*, opposing the selfish ego, refusing to depend upon the world, relying absolutely upon God, and staying satisfied with whatever one has at the moment.[61] He weaves all these principles around two key terms: cautious abstinence (*waraʿ*) and renunciant reliance upon God (*tawakkul*). All these principles, he stressed, are best apprehended and applied through intense study of the Prophet's life and, consequently, the hadith corpus.

> The vast reservoir of hadith reports contains the Prophet's example of worship and daily activities; they include his legal transactions, virtues, stories, encouragement, and warning. Whoever embodies all these different facets of the Prophet's example can be said to follow the Prophet in word, deed, and spiritual state. The essence of hadith studies and its primary aim is just this: to follow the Prophet's example. One achieves this by embracing poverty and minimizing one's dependence on the world, knowing that these choices show love for God. For the love of God has a concrete sign—that is the love of the Prophet himself and following his example.[62]

ʿAli Muttaqi tried to fuse scriptural learning with spiritual training, for both were required to love and follow the Prophet. This was a project to implement the warning of Zarruq and his teachers that classical Sufi training was no longer valid and all that remained in the present age was firm adherence to scripture and the Prophet's example. The spiritual guide must conceal Sufi training within this form, and Sufi aspirants would progress in insight only through the guide's attention and concentration that flowed to them through scriptural and legal studies.

ʿAli Muttaqi's position with regard to Sufi training was conveyed most forcefully to his closest disciple, whom he chose to be his successor (*khalīfa*), ʿAbd al-Wahhab Muttaqi. In turn, he preserved their position for posterity when he wrote,

> In former times, Sufi masters were absolute guides. They established the bond between the master and his disciples on the master's absolute authority. They would place a disciple in isolation, then feed and nourish him according to a strict regime that would benefit him. The master would endeavor to help the disciple with full concentration; he would give each disciple a special litany to recite as *dhikr*, and provide each with special rituals to perform according to the disciple's personal spiritual state. The disciple would not come out of isolation except for obligatory congregational prayers or bodily necessities. All the time, the disciple would stare at his feet while sitting in a corner, never looking right nor left. Other than his litany, the disciple would utter nothing. Once or twice a day, the master would check on his disciple to ask about his states, thoughts, desires, or visions, and to make further demands according to the disciple's own needs. The master might change his diet and intake of water, or set limits to his thought pattern or behaviors. In this way, the master would prudently cure each disciple's spiritual diseases and personal weaknesses. Some disciples would take a year in isolation, some only six months or less. The disciple would emerge from isolation as a perfected and actualized master himself. This is what "spiritual training in the reality of the term" means. This was the old way of training disciples, which these days has become invalid.[63]

ʿAbd al-Wahhab Muttaqi contrasted the old method of training and the new method of the Muttaqi community in the triple *tariqa*. The assertion that the old ways had passed away was a foundation of their reformist ideology; they assumed that a newer, subtler method now needed implementation.

ʿAli Muttaqi and his community believed that the personal attention of the master to the individual state of each disciple had created a bewildering array of rituals, exercises, and litanies. Masters had provided these as skillful means to achieving the death of self-will, yet all these means were ancillary to the *shariʿa*. Disciples mistook these tools for the foundational principles and adhered to them with partisan fervor to such an extent that Sufis not only were jealously partisan to their own lineage or sub-lineage but also dismissed those jurists and scholars who did not pay deference to those rituals in which the Sufis placed so much hope and pride. The result was a cleavage between different religious specialists and subsequent loss of devotional intensity and ethical insight in all quarters. ʿAbd al-Wahhab Muttaqi continued to explain the new method of training.

> In contrast, training by "the master's attention and concentration" is still possible. This means that the master can focus his lofty aspiration and spiritual state upon the disciple [without discrete rituals]. Nowadays, the master outwardly teaches the rulings of the *shariʿa* and the comportment of the Sufi path, while inwardly fixing upon the disciple's progress his own powerful and intense spiritual concentration. With his actions, words, or spiritual state, the master guides the disciple and tries to lead him to perfection. In this way, too, after some time the disciple may feel the effect of the master's presence; the illumination and purity of the master's spiritual state begin to seep into the disciple and affect him indirectly. This is the method of "benefiting by aspiration and spiritual state." This type of training remains possible in the present era. All the masters of today agree that disciples should be set upon the Sufi path by this method. Yet even this method remains rare today.[64]

This new method involved paring away all the outward rituals of Sufi initiation and training. There would be no shaving of the head, no dramatic display of submission in taking allegiance to a master, no change of dress or occupation, and no long period of isolated meditation or ascetic rigor. Instead, the master endeavored simply to teach the commandments of the *shariʿa* and to specify the virtues necessary to live up to them, weaving spiritual insight and personal transformation into this scholarly training.

The best illustration of these somewhat abstract distinctions is the life story of ʿAbd al-Wahhab. In the beginning of their relationship, ʿAbd al-Wahhab had no inkling that his teacher had singled him out as a disciple. In his perception, ʿAli Muttaqi took him on as an assistant because of his strong calligraphic hand, and they spent time copying books and editing the master's hadith compilations while discussing scriptural studies. ʿAbd al-Wahhab recounted his early days.

> ʿAli Muttaqi's method of training a disciple was not to remove him abruptly from the style of life that he was currently leading. He would instead leave

> him exactly in the condition in which he first found him. The master himself would remain engaged with the disciple from within his own conscience, working on the disciple, examining him to find just the right way to train him. He would continue to keep his attention firmly focused upon him for some time, until, without the disciple knowing it by any sense, the disciple found that he had reached a place where he had never ever been before! . . . I had been in the service of ʿAli Muttaqi [as a student and a scribe] for two years before I was ever aware that the master was turning his spiritual attention to me. During this time, he never mentioned any litanies that I should recite as *dhikr* and never assigned me any spiritual exercises or ascetic disciplines or periods of isolation. He mentioned nothing openly related to Sufi practices: he would just keep me busy with the work that we were engaged in together. We spent most of our time copying books and writing out his own texts. Such was the power of the master's concentration that he had me participate in his work while he took on the work of working spiritually upon me! Only after two years, it became evident to me that I no longer inhabited the same condition that I had once been in. I had arrived at a new place altogether, a place I had never even imagined before.[65]

This method of tempered Sufi training consisted of an arrival with no dramatic departure and a transformation through grasping basic principles rather than through submission to laborious ritual. ʿAli Muttaqi had described his own "unimagined arrival" at a state free of selfish cares without having willed himself to arrive there: "Very slowly and gradually, with the helping care of an actualized master, and with his companionship, blessings, and spiritual aspiration, the disciple finds that he himself has (as if by himself) emerged from the dark murk of his former mean life. He has taken on the virtuous qualities [of the master and of the Prophet]. This method of training disciples is most direct, easiest, and kindest. This was the method of my own master [Husam al-Din Muttaqi]."[66] Because it did not make use of anything outside scripture and the *shariʿa* built upon scripture, ʿAli Muttaqi felt that this new method of Sufi training was safe from the dangers of ego, social rivalry, and partisanship. Only Sufi training of this type could encourage a rapprochement between religious authorities who looked to the outward form of scriptural dictates and those who looked toward the inward experience that scripture might inspire.

If Sufis strove to embody humane virtues, their most glowing example was in the Prophet Muhammad, so a method of Sufi training that relied upon hadith studies would be the most direct path to gaining illumination from the

Prophet's virtuous qualities. ʿAli Muttaqi himself thought of his reformed Sufi training as the "most direct, easiest, and kindest" route to attaining closeness with the Prophet, and through the Prophet to the divine source of prophecy itself. Before Sufis could aspire to become saints, he asserted, they must become scholars in hadith.

Although ʿAli Muttaqi elevated the mastery of hadith to be the primary condition for Sufi training, he did not reject Sufi texts but rather made the genre of the wisdom sayings the centerpiece of his teaching method. ʿAli Muttaqi tried to wean his disciples away from extensive prose works and offered them instead a diet of wisdom sayings that he had filtered, examined, and carefully crafted. As the intellectual content of Sufi training, he taught "The Book of Wisdom Sayings" by Ibn ʿAtaʾallah al-Iskandari. He relied on the commentaries of Zarruq (who penned about twenty commentaries on the slim text over his lifetime) and was especially fond of the fifteenth commentary. The pithy and abstract style of wisdom sayings was in perfect accord with ʿAli Muttaqi's reform program. Wisdom sayings were independent of the biography of a particular saint (unlike *maktūbāt*, or letters written by a Sufi master) and not beholden to parochial concerns of a given community (unlike *malfūẓāt*, or recorded oral discourses of a master). Wisdom sayings had the rhythm and rhyme of poetry but eliminated the emotional exuberance and appeal to passion that poetry inspired. They elicited a response of cogitation and silent meditation rather than demanding to be sung or set to music. In these ways, they were an important means of limiting and pruning Sufi devotion while preserving a way to talk about "progress" along the path of spiritual refinement.

ʿAli Muttaqi rewrote Zarruq's fifteenth commentary on "The Book of Wisdom Sayings" by organizing both the aphorisms and the subsidiary commentary according to legal and ethical topics in order to integrate their spiritual advice with the concerns of jurisprudence.[67] This topical reordering reveals a certain ideological program. He started with those wisdom sayings that deal with inner attitudes and with customary rituals that were obligatory and common to all Muslims. Only then did he mention specifically Sufi rituals and practices, addressing the spiritual states that constituted the main topic in most Sufi manuals. He began with chapters on seeking knowledge, then repentance, then sincerity; this list follows the three main topics of Zarruq's own compositions. ʿAli Muttaqi reordered the aphorisms of "The Book of Wisdom Sayings" to make them amplify his reformist agenda, not in the obvious medium of commentary but in the subtle forms of listing and categorizing.

The genre of wisdom sayings is a very Arabic genre. With their rhythm spanning the fields of prose and poetry (like the *sajʿ* medium in literary Arabic), wisdom sayings resonate with the cadence of the Qur'an. Their power is very hard to recreate in another language, since this resonance would be absent. Yet ʿAli Muttaqi intended to popularize this genre beyond the confines of the Arabic-speaking world; he wanted even South Asians, with their love of Persian metaphysical poetry, to switch allegiance to the *hikam* as the purest vehicle to communicate Sufi ideals. He attempted to integrate the very Arabic *hikam* into the types of texts quoted by Persian and Indian Sufis. For example, in his notebook of quotations, "The Precious Jewels," he juxtaposed wisdom sayings by Ibn ʿAta'allah with quotes from the most beloved of Persian Sufi poets like Saʿdī Shīrāzī (d. 1291) and ʿAbdallāh al-Anṣārī (d. 1088). While in the circle of his disciples, he advocated exclusive attention to the wisdom sayings, for the wider reading audience of Sufis who did not necessarily agree with his reform project he was satisfied with simply drawing equivalencies between the *hikam* and Persian poetry.

Not content simply to expand the readership of the wisdom sayings, ʿAli Muttaqi strove to expand the genre itself by composing his own *hikam* in Arabic. His wisdom sayings that extol the virtues of the "death of self-will" conform most closely to the inimitable style of Ibn ʿAta'allah. Wisdom sayings were the perfect vehicle to capture the paradoxes inherent in that enterprise, and he liberally spiced his two treatises about the experience of self-willed death with them.

More surprising are ʿAli Muttaqi's experiments with this genre. He composed a number of proverbs in the style of the *hikam*, in which the first line states a problem or issue, and the second line responds with a scriptural quotation from the Qur'an or hadith that answers the first line, illustrates it, or contradicts it. Whereas Ibn ʿAta'allah composed his wisdom sayings through the medium of Sufi terminology, and while Zarruq expressed rules and principles in the form of wisdom sayings through the medium of juridical language, ʿAli Muttaqi wrote his through the medium of scriptural phrases. ʿAli Muttaqi felt that each passing generation that composed wisdom sayings pared a little more off the outer rind of Sufi practice and penetrated a little further into the inner source of spiritual insight. For ʿAli Muttaqi, there was no need to become distracted by either Sufi terminology or legal definitions. He sought to link his wisdom sayings directly to the source of revelation, getting at the intimate connection between the Prophet and the words revealed to him.

ʿAli Muttaqi wrote two texts in this style, "Divine Gifts from on High" and "The Wisdom of Spiritual Insight," and his method of composition is evident when these texts are placed side by side. At first, he extracted phrases from scriptural sources that suggested principles for guidance along the path of personal transformation. It is as if he were trying to illustrate that the Qur'an and reports about the Prophet provided all the necessary principles for Sufi training. The experience of Sufis and saints confirmed these principles by putting them into practice. There would be no need, therefore, to venerate the person of a saintly guide, since everything the saint experienced or taught was already presented as guidance in scripture. Examples of this first step in his composition include these two maxims: "Incessant recollection of death collapses your self and makes you oblivious to its desires," and "The rational one prepares for death before it descends, so seek and you will find."[68] ʿAli Muttaqi specifies that only those who already know scripture well enough to recognize the full verse or report from which the phrasing comes can taste the true spiritual delight of these pithy extractions. The reader must be accomplished in scriptural interpretation to appreciate fully how the non-scriptural wording resonates with the scriptural phraseology. Out of modesty, he wanted to add few words of his own to what he saw as the brilliant words of scripture. His works in this mode also expressed his ideology of fusing the Sufi quest for illumination with the scholarly quest for scriptural understanding.

These high demands on the audience must have severely limited who could read his *hikam* and derive any wisdom from them. ʿAli Muttaqi therefore reworked the whole collection, expanding the scriptural guidance into a denser clothing of prose, further structured by rhyme. The total collection reached over 800 sayings in "The Wisdom of Spiritual Insight." He organized them into chapters to encourage disciples to read them as they would a manual of Sufi guidance. In the margin, he included the full verse or hadith report that the aphorism tries to magnify, in order to open his wisdom sayings to a wider audience. He also introduced the whole collection with a discussion of the word "wisdom" (*ḥikma*) in its multivalent meanings. It means wisdom in the general sense, especially the wisdom inherent in God's having destined events as they happen. Yet it also means human ingenuity in expressing this wisdom in sayings or teachings. Furthermore, ʿAli Muttaqi brings out a deeper meaning, in that *ḥikma* also means the underlying principle behind an event. In this way, he illustrates how the genre of wisdom sayings is a tool in his search for principles of Sufi practice.

Wisdom is a great gift that lifts away sorrow and trouble;
Whoever is granted wisdom has been granted a great benefit.

The saints from horizon to horizon are hidden in tissues of humanity just like us;
What kind of Prophet is this who eats and walks through markets just like us?

The hearts of saints ascend though their bodies rest tranquil;
Do you look to the mountains and think their masses inert?[69]

ʿAli Muttaqi's admiration for Ibn ʿAtaʾallah went beyond his skillful use of the wisdom sayings. He found Ibn ʿAtaʾallah's text "The Book of Illumination on Desisting from Selfish Calculation" irreplaceable as a tool to teach his disciples how to rely upon God in all situations.[70] In this brief book, Ibn ʿAtaʾallah had described in discursive prose the meanings that he had previously encapsulated in his more enigmatic and evocative wisdom sayings. He explained how to rely absolutely upon God to provide for one's needs, to make one's decisions, and to sustain one's whole life. His emphasis on leaving aside the ego's propensity to plot and plan expressed more moderately ʿAli Muttaqi's exhortation to struggle toward the "death of self-will." For this reason, he taught the text in his reformed Sufi method and also translated it into Persian for a wider audience.[71]

In another short tract, "The Red Sulfur of the Greater Spiritual Alchemy," ʿAli Muttaqi connected his own expression of "death of self-will" to Ibn ʿAtaʾallah's expression of "desisting from selfish calculation."[72] ʿAli Muttaqi illustrated the six beliefs that lead a person to depend upon God alone (as first presented by Ibn ʿAtaʾallah) by comparing them to the six aromatic roots of alchemy (Ar. *ʿaqāqīr*, singular *ʿaqqār*). These six medicinal herbs are the constituent elements of the legendary "red sulfur" that can magically transform lead into gold. Similarly, the six beliefs that direct one to reliance upon God (*tawakkul*) transform the soul through a psychological death, from being bridled with passion to being a perfect instrument for divine will. Such a spiritual death will guide one to perfect inward contentment and the greatest reward, just as material alchemy reputedly leads to outer riches and worldly comfort.

Most authors compared the mythical "red sulfur" to the person of a realized saint, yet ʿAli Muttaqi evoked this image in a very different way. He wrote about the constituent elements that make the "red sulfur" efficacious. These are the six principles that lead one to develop a spirituality that would allow one to embody the ideals of sainthood. He refused to reify the person of the saint and resolved instead to distill from that person, through his reformist chemistry, the necessary principles that would result in his becoming so spiritually potent. This search for principles that undergirded Sufi training and that could limit its expressions was the central motif of ʿAli Muttaqi's project of reform.

In Mecca, ʿAli Muttaqi operated at the center of a new circle of Sufi scholars who fused hadith studies with Sufi discipline to make an integral whole. This fusion constituted a project of reform internal to Sufi communities. Through it, ʿAli Muttaqi tried to reshape the role of the Muslim saint, to limit who could claim to be a saint, and to define what would be such a saint's overt social signs. He engaged in this difficult internal reform in hopes that revitalized Muslim saints would reform society as a whole. In this way, reform within the Sufi community would spread more widely into social and political fields.

Withdrawal: Martyrdom between Land and Sea

This chapter has unpacked ʿAli Muttaqi's satchel full of skills in Sufism and hadith studies. These he perfected while living in exile in Mecca; through them he turned a terrible loss to his advantage. As he sailed away from a Gujarat devastated by Mughal attack, he assumed that its sultan, Bahadur Shah, was doomed. Yet uprisings against the Mughal garrison prevented Humayun from collecting taxes or co-opting the government. Mughal forces quickly retreated north, fearing that the Afghan chief Sher Shah Suri (ruled 1538–45 as sultan of Delhi) would invade Delhi from his stronghold in Bihar.[73] The Mughals abandoned Gujarat after plundering its treasury. Bahadur Shah survived. Nobles, merchants, and peasants rallied around him, the symbol of a resiliently independent Gujarat.

Heading into exile, ʿAli Muttaqi withdrew his spiritual protection from Bahadur Shah's reign. In his arrogance, Bahadur Shah failed to heed advice from his spiritual counselor, relying on the Portuguese and their artillery instead. After recovering from Mughal devastation, Bahadur Shah allowed the Portuguese to fortify the port at Bassien in 1534 in exchange for promises of military aid. A year later, he granted them the right to build a fort at Diu. Bahadur Shah then agreed that all ships bound from Gujarat had to call at Portuguese forts to pay for a protection certificate (*cartaz*) and that Gujarat would not build warships or trade with Deccan kingdoms in horses or arms in what became an interregional maritime "protection racket."[74] Gujarat thus abandoned profitable relations with other Islamic kingdoms like Bijapur, whose major port at Goa had been conquered by the Portuguese in 1510.[75]

ʿAli Muttaqi had been critical of Bahadur Shah's reliance on the Portuguese to support his ailing campaign against the Mughals, for it was foolish for a sultan of Gujarat to abandon the seaways while invading the limitless continental expanse. When the Portuguese reneged on promises of aid, Bahadur Shah had built a fleet to drive them off the Gujarati coast but subsequently torched his ships while retreating before the forces of Humayun. He pursued this desperate policy even though Humayun did not chase Bahadur Shah to Diu from Khambhat (K̲h̲ambh̲āt; Ar. Kambāyat; Eng. Cambay), where the ships were docked, but rather stayed inland at Champaner to secure the fort's treasury.

At Diu, ʿAli Muttaqi refused to console the defeated Bahadur Shah, once his patron and friend. His refusal implies a criticism of the sultan's negligence in depending upon the Portuguese and giving them footholds on the Gujarat coast. ʿAli Muttaqi never encountered the Portuguese personally, but the European invaders were present in political, military, travel, and trade relations at this time. Some of ʿAli Muttaqi's fellow Sufis fell prey to Portuguese piracy.[76] ʿAli Muttaqi saw Bahadur Shah's capitulation to be a betrayal of Muslims, because the Hajj routes were threatened by Portuguese crusading naval policy, which combined capturing trade routes with terrorizing Muslim pilgrims and targeting Muslim holy sites. The flotilla that carried ʿAli Muttaqi to Mecca, along with the prime minister, Asaf Khan, and the royal family and treasury, was lucky to have arrived without being plundered.[77]

With such virulently anti-Muslim instincts driving Portuguese trade relations and political alliances, Bahadur Shah's policy of negotiation and cooperation with the Portuguese was short-sighted. ʿAli Muttaqi, like most jurists and scholars, upheld the view that the sultan's legitimacy rested on protecting Muslims' safety and ability to fulfill religious obligations free of threat. Portuguese crusading and piracy morphed quickly into colonial domination, threatening the livelihood and religious freedom of Muslims in Gujarat and beyond. Farther south along the coast, in Malabar, another Sufi scholar, Makhdūm Zayn al-Dīn Maʿbarī (d. 1583), mirrored ʿAli Muttaqi's life experience. He lived in Calicut (Kozhīkōde), which, like Gujarat, thrived on trade with Arabia. Calicut bore the brunt of Vasco da Gama's incursions. The Portuguese built coastal forts farther north, in Gujarat, because they were driven off by the zamorin of Calicut, a Hindu ruler with close Arab allies. Zayn al-Din's book *Tuḥfat al-Mujāhidīn fī baʿḍ Akhbār al-Burṭughāliyīn* ("Gift for Holy Warriors, about Reports Pertaining to Portuguese Foreigners") is dedicated to the sultan of Bijapur, who he hoped would come to the defense of Muslim merchants along the coast after the Portuguese wrested Goa from Bijapur's control.[78] This book is a history of Malabar's Muslim community (the earliest history of that South Asian region, ironically written in Arabic) and an indictment of Portuguese piracy and colonialism. ʿAli Muttaqi never wrote explicitly about the Portuguese, but the two Sufi scholars were part of the same network. The two probably met in Mecca, for Zayn al-Din, like ʿAli Muttaqi, was a student of the hadith scholar in Mecca Ibn Hajar al-Haythami.

The personal connection between these two Sufi scholars from Gujarat and Malabar mirrors actual military coordination of their era. Malabar's corsairs joined with the Ottoman fleets and navy of Gujarat in 1538 in an organized attack on the Portuguese, termed "an enormous transoceanic coalition, linking Istanbul with allies across the entire breadth of the Indian ocean from Shihr and Gujarat to Calicut and Sumatra."[79] This grand alliance fell apart at Diu when, on the verge of victory in besieging the Portuguese island fortress, the Ottoman and Gujarat forces descended into squabbling and distrust. By that time, Bahadur Shah had recently died, but his lack of commitment to repelling the Portuguese doomed this promising alliance. The opinions of the younger, more explicit Zayn al-Din from Malabar reflect those of the older ʿAli Muttaqi, whose assessment of the Portuguese remained implicit in his withdrawal of support for Bahadur Shah.

The naïveté of Bahadur Shah's policy with the Portuguese had ended his life. The commander of the fort at Diu, Nuno da Cunha (d. 1539), assassinated Bahadur Shah, along with many of his ministers, during a parley at sea in 1537.[80] Bahadur Shah sank into the sea, his head crushed flat by a Portuguese oar or skewered with a boarding pike. He died as he lived, trapped between land and sea, not knowing in which direction his true enemies lurked. A poetic phrase that serves as a chronogram records the date: *Sulṭān al-barr shahīd al-baḥr*, or "Ruler on land, martyr at sea."[81] ʿAli Muttaqi was not alone in blaming Bahadur Shah for his defeat and ruin of Gujarat. The worldly chronicler Muḥammad ibn ʿUmar al-Makkī al-Āṣafī Ulūghkhānī—in his history of Gujarat zealously titled "Victory for One Who Loves Muzaffar and His Family"—expressed the ambivalence that all Gujarati loyalists must have felt as Bahadur Shah vacillated between announcing jihad against the Portuguese and beseeching military aid from them. The historian Ulūghkhānī assessed him either as a hero for his rhetoric who was granted by God the noble death of a martyr, or as a fool for trusting the Portuguese who deserved the death he received by their treachery.[82]

By the time Bahadur Shah was killed, ʿAli Muttaqi was living in exile and reconstituting his life through new skills. Bahadur Shah had ruled for ten years and died at thirty-one years old. His body was never recovered from the sea's grip for an honorable burial under the soil. This "martyrdom" was not mourned by ʿAli Muttaqi. He had already withdrawn his support and hoped to invest his potent guidance in Bahadur Shah's successor. Despite his exile in Mecca, ʿAli Muttaqi perpetuated his connection to Gujarat in expectation that his Sufi reforms could create efficacious saints to act as the sound foundation for a revitalized state after the catastrophe of Humayun's Mughal invasion. After Bahadur Shah's death, ʿAli Muttaqi returned to Gujarat twice in order to project himself as just such a scholar-saint who could sustain the sultanate of

The Death of Sultan Bahadur Shah of Gujarat in 1537, a miniature painting by Lal in 1603–4. (*Akbar Nama*, vol. 1, folio 66, British Library Or.12988.)

Gujarat. What began as a reform internal to a Sufi order spread outward into a delimitation of who could be an authentic saint, then to what that saint's role in society should be, and then to the furthest limit of how such a saint could be the catalyst for a revitalized Islamic society. Sultan Bahadur Shah's disaster led to new opportunity for ʿAli Muttaqi to put his principles into action in an overseas mission, as will be revealed in the next chapter.

THIRD SATCHEL

ʿAli Muttaqi's Maturity

The shaykh sat in the courtyard of the palace. His inner voice whispered to his chest, "*Inna ʾllaha maʿ al-sabirin*—Surely God is with those who are patient."[1] Glancing up at the noontime sun with concern, he released a sigh. Just when would this young sultan finish washing?

This was the shaykh's first visit with the new ruler, a distant nephew of Bahadur Shah who was crowned as Sultan Mahmud Shah III. The shaykh had been in Mecca when the former sultan was martyred at sea. After much intrigue and warfare between pretenders and kingmakers, Mahmud Shah III gained the throne. The crown must have dwarfed his head, as the boy was only eleven. "Patience is the key," the shaykh reminded himself. "You stayed away for a long time, watching developments carefully and showering this new sultan with prayers from afar"—he had prayed that the young sultan survive and thrive, that he might grow in wisdom and strength, and that he would repel the infidel Farangis from the west and the uncouth spawn of Timur from the north. For so long, he had invoked God to help this boy sultan uphold the *shariʿa* and succeed in Gujarat where his uncle had failed. "Yes, you stayed away for a year after his coronation, praying that he would break free of those selfish ministers who kept him in a gilded cage, like a little songbird, to rule in his name. So be patient with him now."

Shaykh ʿAli Muttaqi had waited in Mecca until ships arrived from Gujarat with charitable gifts from the treasury for Asaf Khan, the prime minister in exile, for the shaykh to distribute to the scholars, Sufis, and poor in Arabia. Cash began to flow in again for the Muẓaffarī Madrasa, the college in Mecca endowed by the sultans of Gujarat as a sign of their legitimacy and prestige.

These were all good signs. Then the invitation came—the boy sultan requested the shaykh to return to Ahmedabad.

He cautioned himself, "Even as he's showing signs of maturity, you took your time to meet him, so what is the rush now?" He had accepted the invitation to meet only when the new sultan, with a palanquin to transport the shaykh to the palace, came in person to where ʿAli Muttaqi tarried in Ahmedabad. When ʿAli Muttaqi had mounted the palanquin, the young sultan surprised him by joining the bearers to raise it up on his own shoulder! The sultan had not protested when the shaykh refused to enter the palace quarters and asked to remain in the courtyard so as to not lay eyes on luxuries that contravened the *shariʿa*. The young sultan had respectfully seated him in the shade of pomegranate trees, where they sat on the same couch to chat. "Yes, he's no longer a boy, yet not quite a man. But there are good signs. When I observed that the time for noon prayer had arrived, without hesitating he suggested that he would be honored to pray with me as imam. Servants laid the carpets and rushed out to give us complete privacy. He then strode off to make his ablutions and prepare for prayer, but what could be keeping him for so long?"

At least a half hour passed. Finally, the shaykh rose from his couch in the shade and walked across the courtyard into the fierce sunlight. His shadow was beginning to extend: the time for prayer was passing swiftly. He traced the footsteps of the sultan through an archway and into a smaller courtyard garden, heard the sound of water splashing, and followed it into a shaded alcove. There Mahmud Shah III, less a sultan than a troubled boy, was slumped against the cistern wall, trembling. His cap was lying in a deep puddle, his head dripping wet, his sleeves rolled up, his pant legs drenched. The stream of water coming from a fountain spigot in the wall was left open, filling the cistern to overflowing. A brass ewer and pitcher lay dented on the ground where they had been thrown. The boy sultan scrambled to stand, but the shaykh stopped him. "Stay seated—I'll sit with you." The shaykh knelt before him on the wet ground as the sultan wiped at his eyes, stammering, "I was making my *wuḍuʿ* ablutions but . . ." The shaykh quieted him, "I know." "But the water, it did not . . ." "Baba Mahmud, I know." "It did not clean me like it should have . . ." the sultan continued frantically, "because the water is not pure, or the vessels are filthy, or . . . or the whole palace is poisonous." The shaykh asked, "Or you are polluted, is that what you think?" The young sultan lowered his gaze in shame.

"Baba Mahmud, you are not polluted," the shaykh said quietly but firmly. "I do not sit with polluted people," he continued as he picked up the ewer and pitcher. The sultan watched him carefully as the shaykh stood and leaned over the cistern wall. He scooped some water with the ewer, swirled it to rinse the vessel, and poured out the water on the flowerbeds that grew around the courtyard. This he repeated three times. Then he rinsed the pitcher three times, pouring out the water at the roots of the rosebushes. He then filled the pitcher to the top with water and turned to the sultan with a smile. "Baba Mahmud, this is pure water, a blessed and subtle substance, highly revered in our *shariʿa*. Any doubts that you harbor in your mind about this are merely the whisperings of the tempter in your breast, the tempter who is in every human breast. Say with me, *I seek refuge with the Lord of humanity . . . from the harm of the creeping tempter that whispers in the chests of humanity.*" The shaykh recited Surat al-Nas quietly over the pitcher, blowing over the water. "Yes, you know the verse from the Qur'an. That whispering of doubt is the voice of Shaytan. Now take this water and drink a sip—and let it wash away any trace of doubt that sullies the clean slate of your heart."

The sultan rose to his feet while the shaykh held the pitcher to his lips. He took a sip of water and began to breathe easier. The shaykh paused for a moment, imagining all the blood this boy had shed to survive to this point, all the trauma he must be carrying. "Would you like to know how our Prophet—may peace and blessings be upon him—used to make ablutions?" The sultan nodded. The shaykh held the pitcher above the ewer. He took the boy's right hand and, pouring a gentle trickle of water, he washed it. Then the left. He kept pouring gently, just enough for the boy to rinse his mouth and nostrils, his face and forearms, his ears and hair, and then his feet and ankles. "If you opt for the Prophet's method for *wuḍuʿ*, then you can wash easily, without wasting a drop." He handed the pitcher to the sultan, who stared in amazement: not even half of the water in the pitcher was used.

"If you adopt this method, then God will preserve your mind from all that burdens you. Inshallah, all will pass away." The sultan gazed at him with gratitude and asked, "Will you come every day to pray with me?" The shaykh answered, "I will come and pour water for you myself. Now pick up your cap before the shadows indicate that noontime has passed."

This dramatized account is based on an oral narrative that ʿAli Muttaqi told his successor, ʿAbd al-Wahhab, and was later written down by ʿAbd al-Haqq Muhaddith Dihlawi.[2] The event was so pivotal to the career of Sultan Mahmud Shah III that it became part of the lore of the sultanate of Gujarat. The more worldly minded historian Ulughkhani narrated it to mark the beginning of the sultan's reign.[3] It was a key moment in ʿAli Muttaqi's life, expressing his last hope for political independence of the sultanate.

This narrative displays ʿAli Muttaqi's newfound maturity, acquired through his exile in Mecca. He was now a hadith expert with rare skills and recognition from the best masters of Prophetic reports in Arabia. He was also a Sufi master with admired initiations in multiple Sufi orders. He combined these separate kinds of authority in a new model of sainthood that implied innovative principles of Sufi training, one that radiated that subtle charisma of someone who felt that he had died to self-will and remained a vessel through whom divine aid and guidance could flow to others. The result was Sufism of a rarefied kind, called the triple *tariqa*. He forged its reformist vision while in exile in Mecca and desired to apply it in Gujarat.

The reform project had institutional and political dimensions, which will be unpacked from the satchel of this chapter. As ʿAli Muttaqi matured and began to exercise greater authority, his project of reform was the grain ripening on the wheat stalks of his hopes and aspirations, planted long ago and tended carefully until they might bear fruit. *The righteous are like a crop that is sown, whose seeds sprout then grow tall, then firmly thicken and mature on their stalks, to the delight of the faithful sower and the consternation of the disbelievers* (Qur'an 48:29). Seeds are useless until they sprout, grow, and bear fruit. In the same way, principles are useless until they are embodied in personalities and actions. ʿAli Muttaqi developed the principles for his Sufi project of reform. He then strove to embody them as a scholarly saint.

This chapter is a satchel full of actions through which ʿAli Muttaqi embodied the principles he articulated. These actions constituted his maturity, the ripening of his program for Sufi reform. His reformist Sufism was based on principles that would temper sainthood with the *shariʿa* sciences like hadith and jurisprudence, and embodying these essential principles would empower him to influence Gujarat from afar. After a few years in Mecca, he was invited back to Gujarat with revived authority and a mandate to institutionalize reformist Sufism back in South Asia.

Foundation: Critiquing Sufism from Within

On an institutional level, ʿAli Muttaqi solidified his reformist vision by fusing three Sufi orders—the Qadiri, the Shadhili, and the Madyani—into the triple *tariqa*. As noted in the previous chapter, Ahmad Zarruq had previously advocated a single initiation into these three lineages as the unifying force of a Sufi community. ʿAli Muttaqi took initiation in them as a fused and integral set. He led this community by presenting himself as a scholarly saint. In that role, he sought to refine the reformist content of the triple *tariqa*, to strengthen its community of disciples, and to popularize it beyond its origin among elite scholars.

ʿAli Muttaqi received initiation into these three orders simultaneously from Shaykh Muhammad al-Sakhawi. Their fusion was, at least partly, an inherited form of Sufi legitimacy. However, ʿAli Muttaqi actively sought ways to strengthen the fusion between the orders as a method to temper Sufi devotion and to purify it of practices he thought inauthentic. His use of wisdom sayings integrated this genre derived from the Shadhili Order, while his writings on death and rebirth took its rhetoric from literature of the Qadiri Order. Beyond the realm of texts, ʿAli Muttaqi offered disciples initiation into all three lineages together, rather than to any one individually. He hoped that each would strengthen the others and that the combination of three would limit any possibility of partisanship, exaggeration, or innovation. He hoped that this fusion would prune ritual forms from within these lineages, rather than compound the ritual forms promoted by each one.

From within allegiance to a Sufi single order, it was difficult to institute a reform of ritual practices. Loyalists to tradition cited honored masters in their own order who practiced rituals in a distinctive way and interpreted opposition to those rituals as disloyalty to the ancestral masters of that lineage. This is why the triple *tariqa* was so crucial to ʿAli Muttaqi's reform program. When opposing any particular devotional practice or ritual form that he perceived as illegitimate or inauthentic, he fell back upon the other two lineages to offer a contrasting example or to counter any charges of disloyalty to the tradition. Examples of his reform from within Sufi orders include his rejection of Sufi music and his nuanced avoidance of existential philosophy.

From the perspective of Sufi devotional life in South Asia, ʿAli Muttaqi's most dramatic reform was denouncing music. When South Asians began to convert to Islam in large numbers, devotional music gatherings became a virtual training ground for Islamic customs and a model of a casteless but ordered society.[4] Despite the historical importance and popularity of music, ʿAli Muttaqi opposed the practice as it existed in Gujarat and wider South Asia. Some jurists resisted the practice because they felt that music and poetry were irreverent and sensual, but ʿAli Muttaqi opposed it because he believed that Sufis used it as a shortcut to saintly authority.[5] He judged devotional music not in terms of music itself but rather in terms of a saint's interaction with the wider public. He accepted that devotional music might be acceptable in private sittings or individual meditation but objected if it were a venue for showy displays of ecstasy and rivalry for public acclaim. ʿAli Muttaqi considered a saint's attendance at such sessions as pandering to the "animal urges" of the masses to demonstrate one's sainthood in order to demand fealty, favors, or submission. Juridically, he noted that music's legality was open for debate, but sociologically, he condemned the habit as a temptation toward self-aggrandizement.[6]

With this condemnation of music, ʿAli Muttaqi included all manner of large devotional gatherings. He critiqued aspiring saints' custom of sponsoring public feasts and poetic recitations.[7] He also decried the vivacious ritual of *shāhid-bāzī*, or gazing at young men to contemplate the beauty of creation.[8] This ritual was popular among Sufis in Burhanpur, in both the Chishti and Shattari Orders, judging from the acerbic condemnations of the practice that arose from jurists and reform-minded Sufis in that city.[9] These gatherings publicly displayed sainthood to a populist and mixed audience, which blurred the distinction of scholar and unlettered or Sufi and uninitiated.

ʿAli Muttaqi pointed out the theological and experiential reasons for aspiring saints to avoid the public displays associated with listening to music. Part of his internal reform of Sufi devotion was to limit expressions of love mysticism. Love for God is an essential dimension to a Sufi's personal experience. In a treatise dedicated to the subject, ʿAli Muttaqi argues that true love does not lead to the overt displays of love-madness that were expected in popular culture.[10] In "Warning to Lovers," he argues that true love of God manifests in particular signs in a saint's comportment. The true lover conceals passion from the gaze of others, refraining from bragging, sighing, weeping, or lamenting. Similarly, the lover must love death, for one can stay constantly with the beloved only after death. In a wisdom saying, he wrote that "death is a cord that leads lover to beloved," so the true lover waits expectantly for death. Love entails obedience to the beloved's command, and since "the Qurʾan is a love-letter from God," the lovestruck Sufi needs to study the letter and acquire the knowledge to understand it. ʿAli Muttaqi undermined the allure of love by deflating the essential vocabulary of that tradition. He argued that "union with the beloved" (*ittiḥād*) does not imply the mingling of two distinct essences but actually means "to desire nothing but God and think of nothing but God."

The boldness of this reform program emerged against the backdrop of the loyalty by which South Asian Muslims adhered to devotional music and love poetry. Earlier Chishti Sufis limited music by restricting its audience and frequency but did not question the ritual at its foundation as ʿAli Muttaqi did. When ʿAbd al-Wahhab Muttaqi's disciple ʿAbd al-Haqq first encountered these reformist ideas, he questioned their very applicability to the South Asian context.

> ʿAbd al-Haqq complained to his master that, "in Delhi and its environs, the practice of *samaʿ* involves complex and bizarre rituals that are very popular with the masses. While living there, it is next to impossible to stay aloof and avoid such practices. If someone tries to denounce *samaʿ* there, or even just tries to avoid practicing it, one would have to run contrary to the entire Sufi community and all the Muslims. All the townspeople would be suspicious of such a person. All the common people would accuse him of contradicting the great saints of the past, and lay blame against him! In those environs, people come together in huge gatherings: worthy people mix with unworthy ones, while the righteous sit with the corrupt. All kinds of people mix freely while participating in these rituals. What should one decide in such a case?"[11]

ʿAbd al-Haqq doubted that he could denounce devotional music without suffering a virulent backlash. ʿAbd al-Wahhab ordered ʿAbd al-Haqq to simply never practice *samaʿ* in the way that his fellows did in contemporary South Asia. ʿAli Muttaqi had called it "a habit of the common Sufi [*darwesh*], not a foundation of the path," such that none are obliged to practice it.

Just as ʿAli Muttaqi designed his fusion of three Sufi orders to curb the social excesses of musical gatherings and limit the experiential hyperbole of love, he also hoped it would restrain the speculations of reason and imagination. Through his reform program, ʿAli Muttaqi addressed a saint's relation with doctrine and ideology and sought to limit the teaching of existential philosophy and cosmology (*ḥaqāʾiq wa raqāʾiq*). Existential philosophy stressed the creator's continuity with creation by postulating that all of material existence consisted only of the qualities of the divine, in various combinations and permutations that had taken on congealed, physical form. From this perspective, spiritual insight consisted of recognizing the true origin of all material forces and their true composition: all that exists is essentially from God, with God, and in God. The only real existence is God, and the fabric of being consists of the qualities of God. Ibn ʿArabī (d. 1240) had systematized these cosmological and philosophic ideas, framing in them the terminology and practices of Sufi communities. His teachings permeated Persian Sufi poetry and Indic devotional music, as well as Arabic theological works, in a popular form called *waḥdat al-wujūd* or "the oneness of being."

ʿAli Muttaqi did not oppose these ideas in their essence but rather decried their popularization as an independent religious ideology. He argued that one's first allegiance must be to the Qur'an as a whole, while admitting that cosmological speculations were subtle suggestions hidden within a few of its verses. Therefore, he argued, only an elite few should learn cosmology, consisting of those who had studied the Qur'an, hadith, and legal traditions so thoroughly that their loyalty to the outward structure of the *shariʿa* was beyond question. Only these few were qualified to discourse on subtle cosmological issues. ʿAli Muttaqi feared that if Sufis publicly expounded them, these ideas might form the basis for a religious ideology in which the physical universe, since it emanated from God and was in continuity with divine being, might be seen as giving direct access to God. This would open the possibility for ambitious religious seekers to claim direct connection to God without reference to the Prophet Muhammad and the revelation he relayed.

"Sugar-coated poison" is how ʿAli Muttaqi characterized the elaborate theological texts and alluring poetic compositions that elevated this philosophical outlook to a position of prime importance among Sufis. "If you beware of their dangers it is beneficial to read them, though for most they are deadly rather than beneficial."[12] Though seemingly derived from Qur'anic verses, such texts could undermine the authority of the scripture itself, if Sufis misunderstood their subtleties and took them as absolutes. More importantly, they sidelined the authority of the Prophet, upon whose veracity the convincing power of the Qur'an depended. While not banning such texts, ʿAli Muttaqi tried to limit them and to give his disciples the scholarly training that allowed them to read such texts in a reformist context.[13] He eliminated any mention of Ibn ʿArabi by name, knowing that disciples and scholars bore partisan opinions about him based on his reputation more than his ideas. When quoting Ibn ʿArabi's ideas, he would only write, "It has been said," in order to equivocate and focus attention on the idea itself rather than refer to the ideological debates that might engulf it.[14] Furthermore, he would refrain from mentioning such ideas if he thought his listeners did not have the scriptural knowledge to properly contextualize them or if any were present who might be tempted to adopt extremes.[15]

In a more complicated discursive strategy, ʿAli Muttaqi sought to appropriate the popularity of Ibn ʿArabi and channel it into his own reformist Sufism. When he quoted Ibn ʿArabi by name in his writings, he cited only the simplest orthodox passages that expressed nothing speculative or controversial.[16] He stressed that Ibn ʿArabi and his followers were simply good Muslims who conformed to the basic values: they prayed and fasted, while starting all their theological works with "In the Name of God." Therefore, he taught that there was no need to elevate them to positions of ideological importance or to denounce them as unbelievers. He authorized only those whom he trusted to understand correctly to delve into their existential thought, while general Muslims were best served by a careful silence about their names, reputations, and theories. In this way, he tried to mute the "polemical image" of Ibn ʿArabi and slip past the arguments of both his proponents and detractors. ʿAli Muttaqi saw these polemics as a major obstacle to the rapprochement he so desired between Sufis and scholars.

ʿAli Muttaqi built the foundation of his reformist Sufi community in the safe haven of Mecca and chose ʿAbd al-Wahhab to be his successor and representative there. ʿAbd al-Wahhab took on the nickname "Muttaqi," as if his life continued the life of ʿAli Muttaqi. In fact, ʿAbd al-Wahhab was himself the embodiment of ʿAli Muttaqi's reformist teachings: his biographer calls him "not just a reflection of the completeness of his Shaykh but an essential co-participant in his very spirit."[17] ʿAbd al-Wahhab practiced *fanāʾ fiʾl-shaykh*, or absorption in the personality of one's spiritual guide, which had been so difficult for ʿAli Muttaqi.

ʿAbd al-Wahhab was born in Mandu around 1536. His father, Walīʾllāh, had the reputation of being saintly and scholarly but died when ʿAbd al-Wahhab was young. The boy moved to Burhanpur, where he lived as an orphan, perhaps studying in a madrasa that would have supported his basic needs. He left in his teens to wander extensively in Gujarat, the Deccan, and South India as far as Adam's Peak in Sri Lanka. He searched for teachers and spiritual guides but never stayed with anyone for long and never found satisfaction. In 1556, around the age of twenty, he arrived in Mecca for the Hajj. He worked as the scribal assistant of ʿAli Muttaqi and later became his closest disciple. While ʿAli Muttaqi lived, ʿAbd al-Wahhab was his constant companion and amanuensis and considered it disrespectful to marry. He remained unwed until he reached his forties to better serve his master. He returned to Gujarat at least once but lived mostly in Mecca, where he died in 1593.[18]

ʿAbd al-Wahhab lived in almost complete self-abnegation in his eleven years under the care of his guide. He molded his personality into a replica of ʿAli Muttaqi's. He considered this abnegation as essential to his personal path to spiritual refinement, but he never made it obligatory for others.[19] Like ʿAli Muttaqi before him, ʿAbd al-Wahhab fused his authority as a teacher with his authority as a saint. He spoke of scriptural knowledge as the key to maintaining the most basic spiritual virtue of pious wariness of God (*taqwa*). "Knowledge is a general and universal good, while *dhikr* is a specific and conditional good. *Dhikr* is like medicine that you take only occasionally when you need a cure for a specific ailment. The disciple should take recourse to *dhikr* periodically, especially when in isolated retreats [*khalwa*] during auspicious times to gain peace of mind and freedom of heart. . . . However, being engrossed in knowledge, learning and teaching is a general good and is always relevant [to spiritual advancement]. . . . If one abandons knowledge and neglects learning, then any action one performs will come to nothing."[20] ʿAbd al-Wahhab concealed any miraculous deeds, visions, or spiritual disclosures that would occur to him, though visions at the tomb of the Prophet Muhammad seemed to be a regular element of his spiritual life.[21] His admirers in Mecca and Yemen would regularly praise him by saying, "ʿAbd al-Wahhab follows in the footsteps of Abū'l-Abbās al-Mursī" (d. 1287), who was the second axial saint of the Shadhili Order after Abu'l-Hasan al-Shadhili. When questioned about the meaning of his identification with al-Mursi, ʿAbd al-Wahhab would only say, "How do I know what others mean by such praise?"[22]

Before he met ʿAli Muttaqi, it was reported that ʿAbd al-Wahhab performed miracles and showed interest in alchemy and enchantment. His discipleship under ʿAli Muttaqi, though, purged him of any such displays of spiritual power, which he later considered "selfish."[23] When asked why he ceased performing miracles when he joined the circle of ʿAli Muttaqi, he replied,

> Everything I have is from the blessing of ʿAli Muttaqi as a gift that I do not deserve. He established my sense of religion and straightened my ability to follow the law. He placed me firmly on the foundation of Islam. Before I met him, I vacillated between many different spiritual methods and states. God knows where I would have ended up if I had not met ʿAli Muttaqi! In his company, I discovered the way of religion, faith and worship, and learned the importance of following *shariʿa* steadfastly. This is the key to everything one can achieve, and it is the final stage on the path of spiritual refinement.[24]

In this tribute to his master, ʿAbd al-Wahhab recapitulated the basic contours of his reform-minded vision of who the saint should be. Being a saint was the final stage on the path (*ṭariqa*) of spiritual refinement, and saints were to limit their activities and social status to the role of exemplary teachers. They were to spread scriptural knowledge and demonstrate how to live within the bounds of juridical norms. This was scholarship as the highest form of worship and the true marker of being sincere as a saint. Exile and alienation were intrinsic elements of this sincerity, as ʿAbd al-Wahhab wrote in "Bishārat al-Ḥabīb fī Faḍl al-Gharīb," a commentary on the Prophet Muhammad's recommendation of travel and estrangement (*ghurba*) in the pursuit of scholarly knowledge and virtuous excellence.[25]

Despite his praise of isolation and estrangement, ʿAbd al-Wahhab lived at the center of the community of Sufi scholars, for the triple *tariqa* thrived after ʿAli Muttaqi passed away. The reformist power of this fusion of three lineages is dramatically illustrated in the experience of ʿAbd al-Haqq. His biography reveals how ʿAli Muttaqi's reformist Sufism operated in practice. ʿAbd al-Haqq arrived in Mecca for the pilgrimage, already a fully trained Sufi disciple from his childhood, boasting of two initiations into the Qadiri Order and zealously devoted to Shaykh ʿAbd al-Qadir Jilani. He imbibed a South Asian vintage of Qadiri devotion, steeped in emotive love, Persian poetry, and existential philosophy. ʿAbd al-Wahhab Muttaqi first accepted him as a student of hadith, without mentioning any Sufi terminology or advice. After a period of study, ʿAbd al-Wahhab initiated him in the triple *tariqa*, to wean his disciple from overbearingly clinging to one lineage and its founding saint, Shaykh ʿAbd al-Qadir Jilani. ʿAbd al-Haqq later admitted that

> I used to be excessively and zealously devoted to ʿAbd al-Qadir Jilani. I used to never look to other masters or even mention their names, so absorbed was I in turning toward Shaykh ʿAbd al-Qadir, for he is always present for those who turn their attention toward him. Shaykh ʿAbd al-Wahhab had told me, "You are certainly from among Shaykh ʿAbd al-Qadir's disciples and servants. However, it is the duty of one who seeks the truth to learn from every beneficial source, and also to teach whoever can learn from you [regardless of their lineage]. Never close upon yourself the door of seeking or bar the way of learning from others. From whatever source you may draw benefit, you may ascribe the blessing to the presence of your Shaykh [ʿAbd al-Qadir]."[26]

His master insisted that ʿAbd al-Haqq not reduce his triple *tariqa* into just one of its lineages, for such partisanship committed him to some rituals that the reformist Muttaqi community was trying to pare away. He criticized ʿAbd al-Haqq for being too eager to learn any new litany or ritual from the Qadiri Order. Instead, he taught that one order should balance and temper the others: "One should never believe that absolute perfection lies in one place and one place only; whoever claims this will induce others to denounce him and weaken his own faith."[27] ʿAbd al-Wahhab argued that one could have a constant spiritual orientation to Shaykh ʿAbd al-Qadir without that preventing oneself from taking initiation into other lineages, for each lineage had a spiritual method that was beneficial.[28]

ʿAbd al-Wahhab's own Qadiri style was very moderate compared with the other Qadiri masters whom ʿAbd al-Haqq met and admired, for its fusion into the triple *tariqa* tempered it against exaggerations and accretions. ʿAbd al-Wahhab Muttaqi urged ʿAbd al-Haqq to disavow Qadiri extremists who would modify their statement of faith to attest, "I am satisfied with God as Lord, with Islam as religion, with Muhammad as prophet . . . and with ʿAbd al-Qadir as master." These Sufis would supplicate ʿAbd al-Qadir while facing his tomb in Baghdad, which ʿAbd al-Wahhab found to be an inauthentic practice that distracted dangerously from ritual orientation toward Mecca.[29] In addition, he tried to curb ʿAbd al-Haqq's eagerness to read the texts of Ibn ʿArabi and his admirer ʿAbd al-Karīm al-Jīlī (d. 1403, a descendant of Shaykh ʿAbd al-Qadir), which expounded existential philosophy and an emanationist vision of the cosmos.[30] In his final testament, he firmly prohibited ʿAbd al-Haqq from discussing with others in South Asia "cosmic existential realities" and other such expressions of existential philosophy.

In this way, ʿAli Muttaqi hoped that his community's fusion of three Sufi orders would become a powerful resource for purging Sufi communities of what he regarded as extremist practices, political partisanship, and burdensome ritual. The tension between ʿAbd al-Haqq and his master, ʿAbd al-Wahhab, illustrates the strategies for reform within the Muttaqi community and the resistance to it from other Sufi groups. As a hadith scholar and as Sufi master, ʿAbd al-Wahhab stepped into ʿAli Muttaqi's shoes and perpetuated his ideals of reform. His later followers recorded intimate interactions and conversations with him and were proof that ʿAbd al-Wahhab never demanded personal subjugation from his disciples or signs of formal allegiance. He spoke principles that would convince disciples rather than pronouncements that would subdue them. He trusted his scholarly training, limitation of textual sources, and institution of the triple *tariqa* to achieve these reforms. He never exercised absolute control over the mind or heart of his disciple, for he believed that—as ʿAli Muttaqi and Ahmad Zarruq asserted before him—the method of Sufi training by domination and submission was no longer valid.

Expansion: Seeds of Social Reform

The personality of ʿAbd al-Wahhab and his interactions with ʿAbd al-Haqq vividly illustrate the triple *tariqa*'s reform of Sufi training. Through it, ʿAli Muttaqi intended to promote the ideal of the scholar-saint as the ideal center of Islamic society. From this center, his reformist vision expanded beyond the saint, his circle of immediate disciples who aspired to sainthood themselves, and the circumference of a Sufi community that admired him. He hoped that reform within his Sufi community would continue to expand, affecting classes throughout society. His reform aimed to eliminate specialized rituals that held disciples distinct and separate from other people in society. By fusing the role of saint with the roles of hadith scholar, jurist, and administrator, ʿAli Muttaqi sought to limit the role of saints and to intensify their effectiveness. He embraced the apparent contradiction that in making saints more disguised within their overt role as teacher or jurist, their spiritual potency would have a wider reach and a deeper effect in society.

Conversely, ʿAli Muttaqi hoped to infuse other social classes with some semblance of Sufi training. The authentic saint should cast reflections in every corner of the social world by performing beneficial acts that would not be recognized as "miracles" but rather as duties fulfilled. The saint who had died to his own self-will was granted a new life; his selflessness made him the axis around which daily life pivoted and revolved. The renowned ʿAbd al-Qadir Jilani addressed such a transformed person with the following commission: "The rains of bounty and blessing will fall through you, and by your being, calamities and afflictions will be lifted from the shoulders of all the people. You will bear the weight of the land and all its people."[31] To radiate the light of sainthood among all levels of society, ʿAli Muttaqi tried to provide reformist Sufi guidance to people of all types and classes. His tempered Sufi practice, pared of its baroque accretions and specialized ritual forms, could weave more effectively into all levels of society. Insinuated into the daily lives of common people, this reformed Sufi teaching would reinvigorate the moral fabric of Islamic society.

This project is evident in his five-part series on soul training (*sulūk*), or how to pass through life with spiritual sincerity and ethical integrity. All five of these treatises have a common theme: people achieve salvation by carrying out their common duties in this world, not by rejecting the world or transcending it. This theme is commensurate with ʿAli Muttaqi's insistence that performing one's duty with sincerity is *dhikr*, whether that duty be outwardly religious, apparently professional, or simply charitable. Spiritual advancement comes not from opposing the world or the ego but from orienting the ego in the world so that one does not act out one's own selfish will. In these five small treatises, ʿAli Muttaqi tried to find simple ways that various classes of people could limit their own will to power through their everyday duties, illustrated with examples from the Prophetic hadith.

His ulterior motive was to limit the social purview of Sufi institutions. While encouraging piety in all classes of people, he tried to discourage overtly virtuosic exertions. He discouraged classes of common people who were not scholars from renunciation and asceticism that might pull them out of their routine and into a social movement. He further tried to discourage common people from seeking vicarious benefit from emotional attachment to a saint, whether buried in a shrine or alive at the helm of a social movement. Instead, he recommended that people learn contentment with their lot in life. ʿAli Muttaqi argued that only those who know the limits set by the Prophet and the revelation he delivered could negotiate the path to sainthood. More simply, one must be a scholar first and a saint second. In this way, his deeply held conservatism comes out clearly through these five treatises, for scholars are necessarily an elite minority.

After summarizing the first four treatises, this book will focus only on the fifth and last one about soul training for rulers because it explains how ʿAli Muttaqi aimed for direct intervention in the political and social order of Gujarat, as he became the advisor to Sultan Mahmud Shah III. The first class whom ʿAli Muttaqi addressed was common young men who were reaching maturity, as the young sultan would have been had he not been destined to rule. ʿAli Muttaqi encouraged them to marry and instructed them how to live a devotional life while supporting a wife and raising a family. He wrote that marriage is a religious duty, despite the fact that he terminated his own marriage, telling his wife she should separate from him after their infant son died. He noted that in the hadith, working to support a family is a lofty form of worship equivalent to staying long hours in the mosque or fighting jihad. Married men should earn their upkeep through labor and spend spare time with his wife and children; ʿAli Muttaqi left no room for married men to visit saint's tombs, attend devotional music, or isolate themselves for contemplation.[32]

From the class of common men, ʿAli Muttaqi then turned his attention to women in the second treatise, the longest of the five. Women played a largely unacknowledged role in both Islamic scholarly circles and Sufi communities. Most Sufi hagiographies included stories about saintly women, many of whom were relatives of publicly revered male saints, who often extolled the role of female relations as spiritual guides. Ibn ʿArabi is one illustrious example.[33] Closer to ʿAli Muttaqi's heart, Ahmad Zarruq's grandmother was a saintly jurist who inspired him at an early age.[34] More germane is the example of ʿĀ'isha Bāʿūniyya (d. 1517 in Damascus), a female jurist, poet, and Sufi master in the Qadiri Order who wrote books and issued fatwas in the same circles in Arabia that ʿAli Muttaqi inhabited two decades later.[35] Few Sufi authors have written analytical treatises on the topic of how women participated in the largely male world of Sufis, despite these examples. ʿAli Muttaqi addressed this intriguing question, but his patriarchal conservatism hindered him from dealing squarely with how women could become saints or play active roles in Sufi communities.[36]

ʿAli Muttaqi's patriarchy affected his view of men in addition to women. He asserted that "real men" were those who rejected worldly ambition and mastered their selfish impulses. Men who fulfilled other patriarchal goals—like sexual prowess with women, virility in fathering children, success when competing with other men for power, or status in amassing wealth—were really "eunuchs" from the spiritual point of view. His third treatise in this series addresses "soul training" for real men (*rijāl*). [37] In his oral discourses, he taught that "the work of real men is to take control of their own hearts."[38] Such men provide for family out of duty but do not rely on family for spiritual fulfillment, which comes only from complete absorption in God and teaching religious knowledge. ʿAli Muttaqi's rigid patriarchy was shared with most scholars and jurists, as members of an elite male class. In his conception, only a clear hierarchy of power could ensure social stability and religious sincerity. He quoted a hadith, saying that women in their homes are under the command of their husbands, but women who step out of the home are under the command of the tempter (*shayṭān*). This he juxtaposed with the statement that a man who has not submitted himself to the authority of a spiritual guide has submitted to the authority of *shaytan*. In equating these two statements, ʿAli Muttaqi reinforced a hierarchical authority structure, setting up a continuity from patriarchal authority of men over women and children to spiritual authority of a Sufi master over his disciples. The master is like a husband or father for the men who submit to his religious authority, while the man is like a master for his wife, who submits to his social and legal authority. This pervasive hierarchy set up reciprocal relations of command and compliance, active assertion and passive obedience.

It may seem strange on the surface, then, that ʿAli Muttaqi tried to move the social role of Sufi master out of this economy of power by equating him with a teacher. As noted earlier, a teacher's authority was in continuum with students; their experience in a common field separated them, but they were not distinguished by an incommensurable gap of power like that which separated a master from disciples or a saint from followers. By insisting that the Sufi master act as a teacher of scriptural knowledge, ʿAli Muttaqi had tried to curtail access to charismatic authority and dramatic displays of social power (whether through miracles or through leading social movements). He even insisted on the right of a disciple to evaluate the rectitude of publicly acknowledged masters and thereby judge their sainthood as sincere or inauthentic.

Such a move may seem to disrupt the hierarchical power structure outlined above. However, 'Ali Muttaqi had not intended to empower disciples or liberate students. Rather, he meant to limit Sufi masters by curbing their ability to claim authority from a transcendent source. Just has he placed women under the social authority of men, and men under the religious authority of masters, he placed saints under the scriptural authority of the Prophet and thereby curtailed their will and ambition. He wanted to give disciples and saints a set of common standards that would set limits upon the behaviors of saints and bring them in line with his model, derived from the Prophet's example.

'Ali Muttaqi turned his attention from the domestic domain of marital duties and gender relations to the more public domains of the state and administration. He wrote his fourth treatise on soul training for soldiers and military men. His audience included mercenaries as well as the nobility of Gujarat, who were military commanders as well as courtiers. 'Ali Muttaqi praised them as embodying heroic qualities, upon whom the security of the people depended. However, 'Ali Muttaqi argued that martial and heroic characteristics like courage and self-sacrifice must take on a transcendent reference if they were to be virtues, and not merely the instrumental qualities of hired mercenaries. They must die to their own self-will before they risk their actual lives in fighting.[39] 'Ali Muttaqi pictured soldiers as the most obvious social analogy to saints (in the long Islamic tradition of elevating military martyrs to the status of holy persons). They provided a natural illustration of his will to embrace death in order to achieve a transcendent goal.

As in his earlier treatises, 'Ali Muttaqi elevated daily routines to the status of religious rituals. For a soldier, the highest form of spiritual training was the apt performance of duty and constant practice in arms. Any appeal to devotional activities to escape the rigors of that military life was a sure sign of hypocrisy and vice. He instructed them to hide their spiritual aspirations: they should not wear distinctive clothes or markers of spiritual dedication. He advised against soldiers wearing the garb of devotional communities, as Catholic orders did in the Crusades and during Portuguese naval expansion. He avoided building a special Sufi ritual that would pervade the whole military, as in the Ottoman Empire where the Janissary corps took allegiance to the Bektāshī Order.

Sufi allegiance could have built cohesion among the soldiers of the Gujarati kingdom, who came from widely divergent ethnic groups (East Africans, Yemenis, Turks, and indigenous South Asians), just as it did among the slave corps of the Ottoman polity. However, ʿAli Muttaqi chose to take a psychological approach focusing on the death of self-will. He emphasized how the limitation of self-will channeled the vocational courage of soldiers into self-transformation. Externally, this transformation would take the form of legal rectitude and scrupulous performance of professional duties.

ʿAli Muttaqi may have intended this spiritual advice and strategic thinking especially for the personal slave army of the sultan. ʿAli Muttaqi's friend the minister Asaf Khan built up a corps of soldiers loyal only to Sultan Mahmud Shah III. These special corps were free from court partisanship and political ambitions.[40] This project alone restored independence to the sultan after bitter civil war. ʿAli Muttaqi may have entrusted Asaf Khan with transmitting these teachings among this elite corps of the military.[41] This leads us to his final treatise in this series on soul training.

ʿAli Muttaqi wrote the fifth treatise in this series to admonish the sultan to refine his spirituality by staying within the bounds of Islamic law and social justice. ʿAli Muttaqi was concerned to protect the sultan from his own military corps and also to protect him from his own royal ego. Society depended on a just sultan at the political level, exactly as it had to center on an authentic saint at a popular level. In a more dramatic way than with any other class, the spiritual ambition and ethical cultivation of rulers affected the salvation of society as a whole.

> This is a treatise designed to give advice to rulers, to show them how to behave with a view to their spiritual fulfillment. Whoever puts this advice into practice, God may elevate him to the status of a true ruler in this world and the next. By the natural law of divine will, every land is ruled by a prince: subject under him are his ministers, their nobles, and then common people. If not for rulers and their hierarchy, common people would come to pieces and foreigners would conquer the land. Therefore, someone must guide the rulers to elevate and enlighten their conduct in wielding worldly power, benefiting them in the next world as well. If they do not accept wise guidance, then not only will they lose the benefit of the next world but even this world will come to naught in their grip.[42]

Returning to his common theme, he portrays the sincere and just performance of one's duty as the surest means of spiritual fulfillment and the firmest guarantee of salvation.

ʿAli Muttaqi offered worldly kings the model of the first successors of the Prophet Muhammad (*al-khulafāʾ al-rāshidūn*) as their exemplars for combining worldly power with spiritual fulfillment. Rather than praise the successors for being kings in a golden age that can never return, he asserted that any ruler can achieve their exalted status by administering justice within the limits and norms of the *shariʿa*. In this way, he tried to guide the ruler away from making radical claims to religious authority granted directly from God, as some Gujaratis feared from the Mahdawi movement if it would turn to politics. In addition, Shiʿi rulers in the Deccan claimed to administer justice on behalf of the occulted Imam by rejecting the first three successors. ʿAli Muttaqi, as a staunch Sunni, tried to block the ruler's recourse to such transcendent claims.[43]

> All people belong to one of four categories. There are those who have power in the other world but none in this world: they are the Muslims who suffer impoverishment [*fuqarāʾ*, an epithet for Sufis] yet have patience in their lack of material means. There are those who have authority in this world but none in the next world: they are rulers who travel the path of oppression and coercion with no sense of justice. There are those with no authority in this world and none in the next world: they are the poor who have no patience in their poverty and deny that their Lord cares for them. Lastly, there are those who have authority in this world and authority in the next: they are the four rightly guided successors to the Prophet, those kings who are just, and those who follow in their ways. To achieve such a lofty status, you must follow the advice in this treatise and put it into practice.[44]

ʿAli Muttaqi positively assessed the role of the sultan in wielding worldly power. Not only was the sultan's personal power necessary for the good of society, but his manner of wielding power was also the key to his own spiritual success. This contrasted with other Sufis' attitudes toward rulers in South Asia. Chishti Sufis usually refused to defer to worldly rulers, lambasting them as tyrants. Chishtis extolled the saints as the true rulers whose power was their poverty and whose grandeur was their modesty. They praised the paradigmatic saint Muʿin al-Din Chishti as the true "sultan of India" who cared for the needy, unlike supposed worldly kings.

Such idealization of a saint as "the true sultan" contains implicit condemnation of worldly rulers. Later Chishti Sufis struck a truce with rulers who were eager for legitimacy by accepting state patronage in exchange for veneration and patronage. Others charged that the only value of worldly power lay in renouncing it as a condition for personal salvation and as an ethical lesson for others. This was the approach of the Mahdawi movement, which grew out of the Chishti Order.[45] All of these various responses to worldly power projected the saints as the real successors of the Prophet.

In contrast, ʿAli Muttaqi saw wielding worldly power as potentially good; it was the key to salvation of the society as a whole and for the sultan himself. The ruler must use his conduct in wielding power in this world for justice, in the hopes of earning merit in the next world as well as benefiting those he ruled. Therefore, ʿAli Muttaqi tried to rationally lay out the four foundations of political power, so that the ruler could control and deal justly with each.

> The four foundations of worldly power are the treasury, the army, distribution of money to the army, and the administration of justice without oppression. Each foundation has different levels to it, with differing importance and priority. The army is more important than the treasury, since nobody can collect treasure or taxation without an army. Distributing money among the army is actually a more powerful force than the army itself, since a small army that is well maintained and well motivated can defeat a much larger army that argues among itself over scarce funds. Ruling justly and avoiding coercion is actually a stronger force than distributing money among the army. A large army that is well paid by money coerced from the people can be easily vanquished by a smaller army that is well paid by funds raised by just means [and therefore supported by the common people].[46]

Such advice on capturing and maintaining political and financial power has been common in the genre of "mirror for princes" since classical times.[47] Authors of this genre were mainly ministers, courtiers, or literati who urged rulers to maintain a firm grasp on power, administer it justly for the common people, and grant the author position as an invaluable advisor. ʿAli Muttaqi's short treatise is different in that its author was a Sufi scholar. His intent was to urge the sultan to be just in exercising his absolute power and also to care for his own spiritual fulfillment through such just administration.

ʿAli Muttaqi did not order the ruler to show deference to Sufi saints, patronize the custodians of saint's tombs, or revere holy madmen (who sometimes took the liberty of mocking rulers as "court fools"). He recommended that the ruler acquire virtues himself rather than seek the mediation of saintly figures. The only way the ruler could do this would be to voluntarily limit his absolute power by following the limitations of the *shariʿa* in waging war, collecting taxes, and running courtly ceremonies. This would be the best insurance of justice in the administration.

He had no illusions that the ruler could become a saint, in the affective sense of active spiritual authority (*wilāya*), contradicting the sketch of sixteenth-century South Asia recently drawn by Azfar Moin.[48] That would be impossible without voluntary poverty, asceticism, and contemplative isolation that would endanger the state and jeopardize the welfare of common Muslims. However, the ruler could gain some saintly virtues through cultivating sincerity and the apt performance of his worldly duties. This would be enough, for it would place the sultan's worldly authority in harmony with the saints' spiritual authority. The axial saint is the absent presence in ʿAli Muttaqi's treatise. He never explicitly mentions saints (*awliyaʾ*) in his advice to the ruler, though he mentions holy people (*fuqaraʾ*) as those who wield authority over the spiritual states of others through their reliance upon God alone.

Despite this apparent absence of the saint, ʿAli Muttaqi saw social stability as the fruit of harmony between worldly and spiritual powers. The saint and the sultan should not be opposed as contradictory sources of power. The sultan should embody certain saintly virtues that were conducive to a just administration, enough to guide him in his worldly duties without distracting him or leading him to renunciation, abdication, or subjugation before other mediating saints. In parallel, the authentic saint must embody certain postures of worldly authority in the guise of a scholar, judge, and advisor to rulers. The saint must temper spiritual aspiration with social responsibility. The resonance between such a scholar-saint and a just ruler would ensure stability and prosperity for the society that they protected. The just ruler would present the outer form of power, while the authentic saint would provide the inner potency of this power.

ʿAli Muttaqi wrote this fifth treatise, "The Most Superior Station," as guidance for Mahmud Shah III. He desired to keep the young sultan from the egoistic faults and self-aggrandizement that had pushed the previous sultan Bahadur Shah over the brink into disaster. However, ʿAli Muttaqi was not content to advise the sultan of Gujarat from afar but returned to visit him and deliver his advice in person. A close friendship developed between them, which opened new possibilities for ʿAli Muttaqi. He had found stability in Mecca, where he established a reformist method of Sufi training; now, he felt these skills and networks might nourish the spiritual and political regeneration of the sultanate of Gujarat. The next section addresses the spiritual dimension of this regeneration, as he endeavored to limit who could claim the social capital of being a saint in the Sufi tradition.

Discrimination: Sainthood under Analysis

In Mecca, ʿAli Muttaqi had begun to articulate in writing the criteria by which an authentic saint could be recognized. This would set up a clear framework to valorize his own brand of saints and to critique other, competing demonstrations of sainthood. Returning to Ahmedabad, ʿAli Muttaqi's program for reform led to a critical stance against competing saints, their Sufi followers, and the social movements that grew up around them. He took an assertive stance and offered a forceful critique of popular forms of Sufi devotion that he felt were inauthentic when compared with his reformist Sufism.

From his center in Mecca, ʿAli Muttaqi embodied the principles of his reformist Sufism. As he prepared to return to Gujarat and project his authority there, he confronted the religious movements that grew out of Sufi orders and pushed certain ideals of sainthood to extremes. ʿAli Muttaqi critiqued them in a vocal announcement of his own counter-legitimacy, with a theological argument based on his concept of inauthenticity (*bidʿa*). At the same time, his critical opposition to these movements was also an attempt to give new stability to the Gujarati regime that was recovering sovereignty under the young sultan Mahmud Shah III.

ʿAli Muttaqi expounded the criteria for judging the authenticity of alleged saints. He wrote a short text, "The Clear Proof about Recognizing the Saint," in hopes that people would use it to identify true saints from incomplete Sufis (or worse yet, false and inauthentic saints) by scrutinizing their inner character and outer comportment. This would be the first step in enabling others to become true saints themselves, if they would have the sincere aspiration and ability.

> This is a small treatise on how to recognize the fully realized saint [*wali*], the one who is approaching that state [*wāṣil*], and the one near to approaching it [*mutaqarrib*]. All these are names that are very similar and almost synonymous but contain distinctions. The least benefit of this treatise is that a person who has not yet reached the stage of sainthood [*wilaya*] may read it and understand what that state contains, and thereby know who the saint really is. If one acquires that knowledge, then it is possible that, by the grace of God, one might attain that state of sanctity.[49]

ʿAli Muttaqi posited that there are many degrees of holiness before a person became fully realized as a saint. Common people may not understand these subtle distinctions, but a person armed with acute reason and scriptural knowledge could distinguish them. Such a person could recognize those dangerous figures who had acquired some semblance of sainthood but had not yet passed beyond the demands of their selfish natures.

The terms used to describe saints have deep resonance in poetry, song, and folklore, but ʿAli Muttaqi tried to strip them of such popular metaphoric resonance to make them analytic terms as he defined the principal characteristics of the authentic saint. In honing such analytic terminology, he followed the example of Zarruq; indeed, he quotes several of Zarruq's principles of being a Sufi.[50] In a short text called "The Greatest Hope in Soul Training and Arriving to God," he describes how a person actually becomes a saint by overcoming selfishness:

> You must all know the true meaning of the terms intimacy with God [*qurb*] and arriving to God [*wiṣāl*]. Intimacy with God and arriving to God means worshipping God and nothing but God, by obliterating all the obstacles that separate you from God. Only that is the desired meaning. Individual existences separate from God are so many and so varied, and each is an obstacle to intimacy and arriving to God. However, one can summarize these obstacles into four different classes: the obstacle of the world, the obstacle of people, the obstacle of the ego, and the obstacle of the tempter [*shaytan*]. Al-Ghazali clearly laid out the method of overcoming each of these obstacles in *Minhāj al-ʿĀbidīn*.[51] One overcomes the obstacle of the world through asceticism. One overcomes the obstacle of other people through isolation and aloofness (tempered by its legal conditions), by refusing to turn to others with requests and demands except for the bare necessities. One overcomes the obstacle of the ego by grasping firmly the reins of strength and resolve. One overcomes the obstacle of the tempter by acknowledging the snares and devious possibilities of getting tricked. When a person's heart begins to be purified through these methods, then it begins to empty of selfishness, fill with virtuous qualities, and radiate manifestations of divine qualities. The heart begins to shimmer brightly and become illumined as it enters the intimate presence of God. After this, a person will experience states and stages which have no end. The "death of self-will" eases and facilitates the cure of the heart, which means dying to the self before the self actually dies.[52]

Such internal spiritual development has no outward manifestation except simple ethical benevolence and respect for the actions enjoined by the *shariʿa*. Any outward displays of seemingly "saintly" behavior is thus a cause for scrutiny and suspicion. Miracles or exercises of power, social or political, are at best a distraction for the true saint and at worst a cause of temptation and backsliding. "The goal is only for a person to remain in a state where nothing remains inside him except for God with no trace of otherness or alienation. It is no loss to such a steadfast person if no miracles or supernatural powers appear in his actions. You must know that such miracles and disclosures do not demonstrate one's spiritual superiority. Rather, the only cause for superiority is constant awareness of God [*taqwa*]."[53] Drawing from the Qur'an 49:13, ʿAli Muttaqi returned to the theme of *taqwa* continually in his writings. It was the singular principle of spiritual development and also the explanation for arrested development. *Taqwa* appeared in degrees in various persons, and those without complete fulfillment of *taqwa* were the locus for miracles and outward demonstrations of spiritual potency. Such an appearance of miracles was a temptation that could lead to false saints and social movements centered on them, resulting ultimately in personal aggrandizement and social discord.

> Those traveling the path of spiritual development are in different stages of completeness, according to their level of *taqwa*. From the disciplines of knowledge [both religious knowledge and rational knowledge] we know that some who strive on the path are still far from their ultimate goal. This separation gives rise to their miraculous workings and wondrous disclosures of spiritual power. We know from the sayings of the great saints that such miracles are not necessary and essential for achieving sainthood. They say that "this world is the place of struggle, preparation and testing, while the next world is the place of reaping fruits of one's labor and getting rewards for one's deeds." Just as the next world is not a place of struggle, so this world is not a place of reward, for rewards are guaranteed only in the next world. Reward for one's sincere actions, by their very nature, do not need to appear in this world. [If rewards appear,] they show that the person through whom they manifest is lacking full preparation and does not have a full share [of sainthood]. . . . This means that ecstatic states of deep immersion [*istighrāq*] or actions that yearn toward self-obliteration [*istihlāk*] do not advance one upon the spiritual path toward sainthood. The sole cause for advancement is effort and struggle. The manifestation of such miraculous ecstasies actually impedes real spiritual work. In fact, such ecstasy should be an experience of the next world after death. If ecstasy does not appear in this life, then surely it will come in the next life [as a reward for sincerity] in complete perfection, free from any trace of trickery or temptation to deceit. People once asked a certain saint why they never saw him performing miracles or revealing supernormal spiritual states. He replied, "I want to meet God and receive my full reward [after death]; I don't want to lessen my reward by requesting anything here and now!"[54]

Since any outward and socially recognized mark of sainthood was a sign of incompleteness, ʿAli Muttaqi emphasized the need for discrimination, suspicion, and scrutiny. He urged his reader to trace others' actions back to their principles to ascertain the authenticity of the actor. Although the importance of *taqwa* is common to all Sufi writings, as is elaborating on stages of the path of spiritual development, ʿAli Muttaqi used these motifs for an uncommon purpose. He aimed to limit those who might endeavor to become saintly. He coupled these motifs to lay the framework for a critique of alleged saints.

The urge to critique others' claims to sainthood may seem, on the surface, to be unworthy of a true saint. ʿAli Muttaqi himself characterized true saints as those whose extensive generosity and forbearance allowed them to critique others by giving a gift or words of blessing. It was this very quality of benevolence that separated them, in inward experience and in manifest behavior, from all other types of people in society.

> Society consists of four different categories of people. There are common people who are corrupt, common people who are righteous, special people [who experience an urge toward sainthood], and the most special of the special people [who achieve sainthood]. . . . You can recognize these four types of people by their virtues and ethical comportment manifest in their every action. . . . Imagine that someone spits on the face of another. If he forgives the one who spit on him with forbearance and patience, the man is clearly one of the special people. Yet if he takes delight in being spit upon and repays the one who spit on him even more kindly by giving him a gift or a blessing (if he has nothing to give), then clearly you know that he is of the most special people. With this example, you can extrapolate the criteria of judgment for yourself in any case.[55]

If such limitless patience in the face of personal injury and insult was the basic behavioral criterion for authentic sainthood, then how could ʿAli Muttaqi justify his own exacting critique of the behavior of other "alleged saints" who certainly never confronted him personally, let alone injured his person or his dignity? ʿAli Muttaqi, at least on the mute level of emotional reaction, distinguished between injury to his person and transgression against a principle. The latter was a matter of truth, not a matter of his person, reputation, or property. He considered his zealousness in safeguarding what he saw as truth (especially religious truth with scriptural foundations) as a clear sign of his sainthood, just as his potentially giving a gift to one who spat on him would be a clear sign.[56]

This urge to critique alleged saints is consonant with ʿAli Muttaqi's reformist fusion of hadith studies and Sufi devotion. The discipline of hadith rested on the premise that scholars can distinguish true reports about the Prophet's words and deeds from those that are unreliable, weak, ambiguous, or outright forgeries. Scholars performed this act of critique not by referring to the content of the ostensible report but by examining its route of transmission (*isnād*): how it passed from one stage of narration to the next while keeping its authenticity intact. ʿAli Muttaqi imported this critical method into the examination of saints and Sufis. He urged others to assess ostensible saints not by the content of their miracles, their social prestige, or the zealousness of their followers but by their adherence to the fundamental principles of wariness, scrupulousness, and sincerity. Hadith scholars also performed operations of critique against people who claimed to transmit reports about the Prophet, called *jarḥ wa taʿdīl*, or tearing apart a reporter's credentials or judging them sound. In Sufi literature, such operations are rare. Hagiographers included everyone they possibly could under the umbrella of sanctity, and saints themselves rarely spoke out in open criticism of each other. In contrast, ʿAli Muttaqi denounced vociferously those whom he perceived as inauthentic saints and illegitimate religious leaders.

ʿAli Muttaqi's reform within Sufism addressed what form of training could lead disciples to potentially achieve sainthood and what legitimate forms a saint's social role could take. He further asserted how the saint's presence should filter out beyond his person into the various classes of society, transforming the apt performance of duty into spiritual fulfillment. At its most risky apex, his reform measures challenged the political life of the court and the very military-financial foundations of the sultanate of Gujarat. Yet this whole series of reforms rested upon the limitation of who could claim sainthood, leading ʿAli Muttaqi to critique many of his fellow Sufis who claimed the title of saint through channels other than the reformed training that he advocated. ʿAli Muttaqi built his acerbic critique of these rivals from the technical vocabulary of legitimacy and authenticity, but its ultimate contest was over love: the saint's singular love of God and its concomitant expression in love of neighbors and strangers. ʿAli Muttaqi believed his critique to be an expression of his love and care for his fellow Muslims, whose spiritual destiny and social welfare only his brand of reformed Sufi practice could protect. He authored a short work, "Warning to Lovers on the Signs of Sincere Passion," in which he tries to debunk the claims of would-be saints to love God out of his own love of the wider Muslim community and his safeguarding of their spiritual well-being.

> I have written this treatise because those who falsely claim to be lovers of God and the Prophet have clearly grown numerous in this age. Yet one

> finds none of the signs of sincere passion and true love in them. They spend their whole lives in false claims and ignorance. Very few people raise an alarm or complaint so that the people might realize that they are not really lovers of God. Many common and unlearned people place great faith in these false lovers, while those with true insightful knowledge have not confronted them with a straight answer. . . . Therefore, their pride and self-deception grows more intense day by day. If a person has pursued the love of God and the Prophet to its fullest state and has proficient knowledge of the signs and conditions of divine love, he must speak publicly to them with advice, for their own well-being. Still they do not accept such advice. They say, this one who complains about us is not a lover, but we are from the band of lovers! . . . I write these few lines so that you may distinguish sincere love from that which is feigned or self-deceiving.[57]

While his words of critique may sound bitter, ʿAli Muttaqi insisted that they came from the sweet longing of sincere love of God, the Prophet, and the community of Muslims. When harnessed to his reformist sense of caution, scrutiny, and care, the expressions of love (so vivid in devotional poetry, music, and contemplation) revert to a form at once diminished in size and charged in intensity. They take the form of guarding the rights of God over those who claim divine love and evaluating the criteria of those who claim affective spiritual authority in society.

ʿAli Muttaqi aimed to prevent the dilution of the social power of sainthood, in the same way that counterfeit coins of impure metal dilute the overall value of a country's currency, even if some individual coins remain pure. "Un-minted silver will never fit in anyone's purse. You should be that silver which is minted into pure coin so that the money changer can weigh you and deem you valuable."[58] His program for reform shows how widely ʿAli Muttaqi perceived the currency of sainthood to circulate in society, far beyond the bounds of Sufi rituals and explicitly religious affairs. He thought of himself as the ultimate money changer of Sufism, who checked the purity of coinage as it circulated through the markets, certifying what was pure and discrediting what was counterfeit or adulterated.

The next chapter documents in detail ʿAli Muttaqi's vociferous critique of saintly leaders of popular movements in Gujarat, especially those of the Shattari Order and the Mahdawi movement. His actual confrontations with these leaders were guided by his theoretical conception of sainthood and his reform program for Sufism. In his mind, his critique of other Muslim leaders was eminently justified, for it demonstrated the true mettle of his own authenticity. Without it and the benefit it might accrue to common Muslims, his sense of being a saint would be a purely subjective state, affecting no one and accountable to nobody. In this way, he set himself up to guide the spiritual regeneration of Muslim rule in Gujarat. Yet his reform program also had political aims, which the next section addresses.

Engagement: Social Reform between Saint and Sultan

ʿAli Muttaqi conceived of himself as an authentic scholar-saint, in a position of social power and ethical sincerity confirmed by his leadership position in a reformist Sufi community. In a patriarchal metaphor and in accord with his treatises, he thought of himself as a "real man." He illustrated his experiment in governing as a saint to be like a marriage with two wives. His first wedding was to the next world (*ākhira*), as a saint concerned with virtue. Now, he was getting engaged to a second wife, this world (*dunyā*) of political power and social competition. He argued that a scholar-saint should be able to hold two wives in equilibrium. He thought that he could act as a channel to bring the divine order of the next world into the political order of this world and to infuse his Gujarati society with the virtue he embodied.

Historical chronicles detail the important role ʿAli Muttaqi played in Gujarat's political life by supporting Sultan Mahmud Shah III after he was called to the throne in 1538.[59] The new sultan was a boy overshadowed by nobles who clashed in political jockeying unleashed by the assassination of Bahadur Shah, who had no sons when the Portuguese murdered him at sea. As a minor princeling confined by the Faruqi ruler of Khandesh, Mahmud Shah III was extracted by force by Gujarati nobles from Burhanpur who promoted his ascension, since they believed he was a malleable cub. Soon they fought among themselves over who would act as regent. Before him, several claimants to the throne had been installed, but they had all been quickly deposed or killed. One was an exiled Mughal prince who declared he had been adopted by Bahadur Shah's mother and thus had legitimate claim to the throne of Gujarat; he staged an unsuccessful palace coup in Ahmedabad yet escaped with the treasury while threatening to rouse a Mughal army to take Gujarat by force.[60] Another was a nephew of Bahadur Shah who ruled as sultan of Khandesh; he took the throne of Gujarat but was poisoned after only six weeks as ruler.[61] In the midst of such machinations—fueled by both internal feuds and external threats—the young sultan's fate did not seem promising.

Although he was just a boy, Mahmud Shah III played the nobles' ambitions against each other. He prompted one after the other to seize the regency from his current dominator, weakening one only to fall under the control of another. To end his confinement, he escaped the capital by trickery and appealed to provincial nobles to help him take power for real. With their help, he conquered Ahmedabad, defeating rival forces and executing those nobles who had confined him. He raised his own servants who had been loyal during his weakness to positions of nobility.

Through this bloody path, Mahmud Shah III gained independence by 1540 when he was around thirteen years old. Yet his mind was completely gnawed by suspicion against Gujarati nobles, so he ordered a new city to be built thirty-six kilometers distant from Ahmedabad, called Mahmudabad (Maḥmūdābād).[62] There he centralized his rule, surrounded only by loyalists, safe from palace intrigue and vested interests of the nobles.[63] Until Mahmudabad could be completed, Mahmud Shah III was in a tenuous position, not knowing whom to trust. For instance, he allowed a minister who had exploited him, ʿImād al-Mulk, to govern Surat but still suspected him of conspiring with other nobles to depose him. Mahmud Shah III ostensibly encouraged ʿImad al-Mulk to go on the Hajj, but as the minister arrived at the port of Surat to catch the boat, he was executed.[64] Even after his rule stabilized, the young sultan remained psychologically scarred: he ordered that, if any women in his harem should become pregnant, she should drink medicine to ensure an abortion so that no son would be born to rebel again him.[65]

ʿAli Muttaqi stayed in Mecca during these years of instability, consolidating his own authority and gaining confidence in his ideals of reform. When Mahmud Shah III emerged as an independent ruler, ʿAli Muttaqi returned to Ahmedabad between 1539 and 1541.[66] He gained the confidence of the new sultan, as the story at the opening of this chapter illustrates, by cleansing the sultan of misgivings by teaching him how to wash his face and hands for prayer. As the secular chronicler Ulughkhani wrote,

> ʿAli Muttaqi came to Gujarat from Mecca to visit Mahmud Shah III and paid special attention to his psychological needs and fulfilled all his necessities. Once he was present with the sultan during prayer times, and he observed the sultan during his ablution. The young sultan was taking so much time washing that he used a huge amount of water, which would have sufficed others for a full bath with some left over! ʿAli Muttaqi knew what his weakness was but kept silent for a time. Then the shaykh asked the sultan directly about his doubts and misgivings, and the young ruler confided in him and complained of his many anxieties and fears. ʿAli Muttaqi said, "Inshallah, all these will pass away." The

> shaykh stayed with him until the next prayer time came. When the sultan went to make ablution again, ʿAli Muttaqi took from his hand the pitcher and poured the water for him, showing him how to make ablution according to the Prophet's practice. The sultan accepted his direction with politeness even though it was very difficult for him to carry out his ablutions with only a minimum of water; still, he forced himself to have patience at the hand of the shaykh and obeyed his advice. . . . ʿAli Muttaqi would stay with the sultan before his prayers and would pour water for him and help him keep his ablutions within the Prophet's pattern for a number of days. The shaykh's blessings were thereby concentrated upon the sultan, and his condition improved under the influence of the shaykh's powerful determination. Soon the young sultan was taking a full bath with the amount of water that would have barely sufficed him before for washing his face and hands.[67]

This incident marked ʿAli Muttaqi's rehabilitation in Gujarat and his entrance into a position of actual power rather than symbolic power. Yet its details are unfathomable unless it is placed in this history of Mahmud Shah III's youthful and bloody political struggles.[68]

Wasting water stood metaphorically for the blood that the sultan had spilled in coming to power. Whether the issue was guilt over killing many of his kingdom's nobles or the continuing anxiety that, faced with further machinations, he would have to shed more blood, the young sultan was disturbed by his own rise to power. By inviting the sultan to wash with minimal water, ʿAli Muttaqi indirectly raised the issue of his own authority in a bid to have Mahmud Shah III accept him as patron and protector.

Sultan Mahmud Shah III fought to subdue his impulse toward independence that he had won only through such terrible civil strife; he experienced great difficulty in placing trust in an elder authority. He could not easily transfer allegiance to an authority, after having struggled so hard against regent after manipulative regent. Yet in the end, subjugating himself to a saintly authority augmented his political potency rather than diminished it. Allowing ʿAli Muttaqi to pour water for his ablutions encapsulated this entire process. From ʿAli Muttaqi's perspective, this act was also highly charged with spiritual power.[69] By encouraging the sultan to change his method of washing from one that reinforced his own fears to one that expressed devotion to the Prophet, ʿAli Muttaqi freed him from personal limitations so he could grow into a strong ruler. He hoped that Mahmud Shah III's rule would embody the norms of Islamic custom and law and establish social justice.

As this historical narrative suggests, a relationship of intimacy and confidence grew between the saint and the sultan. It is not clear if Mahmud Shah III became a formal disciple of ʿAli Muttaqi, though historical chronicles imply this. He did defer to ʿAli Muttaqi, refusing to wear rich clothes of state that the shaykh thought were forbidden by the Prophet's example and bearing the shaykh's palanquin upon his own shoulder.[70] In turn, ʿAli Muttaqi accepted favors and money from the new sultan, whereas he never accepted money or even praise from others. He clearly saw his relationship to Mahmud Shah III as extraordinary, meriting a relaxation of his previous abstention. There were critical political and social reasons for ʿAli Muttaqi to go so far out of his way to offer psychological support to the young Mahmud Shah III.

ʿAli Muttaqi perceived the need to have a strong ruler in Gujarat, to keep order both on land and in the sea-lanes connecting South Asia to Arabia. After this initial visit to Ahmedabad and his positive reception, ʿAli Muttaqi returned to Arabia. From his position in Mecca, he guided the young sultan to appoint a new governor of Surat to replace the noble whom he had murdered after ordering him to take the pilgrimage. Mahmud Shah III appointed Khudāwand Khān (also known as Ṣūfī Āghā Turk), who was known for his opposition to the Portuguese and knowledge of naval warfare. Khudawand Khan built a fortress at Surat to protect the port, despite assault by the Portuguese, who, having failed to stop his fortifications, proffered him bribes to turn it over to them, bribes that were ineffective.[71]

In 1538, during the first year of Mahmud Shah III's reign, the Ottoman sultan Sulayman the Magnificent sent a fleet to Aden in Yemen; the Portuguese had attempted to seize that port in raids from their South Asian strongholds, and the Ottoman forces needed it to defend their trade through the Red Sea and their claim of legitimacy as protectors of Mecca and Medina. From Aden, the Ottoman fleet sailed to Gujarat under the command of Sulaymān Pāshā to expel the Portuguese from Diu. Sultan Mahmud Shah III delegated Khudawand Khan to cooperate with the Ottoman forces with personnel and supplies.[72] However, the two naval commanders quarreled, and without strong central leadership from the Gujarati government, the siege against Diu broke down.[73] The opportunity to curtail Portuguese interference in the Arabian sea-lanes was bungled at a turning point in world history. ʿAli Muttaqi could not have foreseen that Portuguese incursions would initiate European domination and usher in the modern era; however, he clearly saw their effects in endangering trade, pilgrimage, and scholarly patronage that had kept the connection between Mecca and Gujarat so lively.

ʿAli Muttaqi played a crucial role in this Arabian Sea connection that was so important for legitimacy and prosperity for the sultanate of Gujarat. He promoted pilgrimage to Mecca, offering free hospitality to Muslims from Gujarat who came to Mecca for the Hajj or for extended study of hadith and Sufism. When he returned to Mecca, ʿAli Muttaqi accepted large donations from Sultan Mahmud Shah III to distribute to worthy students and travelers. This started a tradition: the sultan sent a sum of money each year in a ship, so that ʿAli Muttaqi could distribute it to those he deemed worthy of support.[74] In addition, Sultan Mahmud Shah III granted funds to build a new compound for ʿAli Muttaqi and his followers in Mecca. The compound had a wide courtyard and many rooms for those who came to stay with him and study hadith, thus integrating the functions of madrasa and khanqah.[75] Through these acts of generosity and patronage, ʿAli Muttaqi gained renown in Mecca, which spread to the Sulayman the Magnificent, who assigned ʿAli Muttaqi a yearly stipend from Istanbul. He refused to accept it for himself, agreeing only to distribute money to worthy students and scholars who were not involved with Sufi training.[76]

In their relationship of mutual trust and cooperation, both ʿAli Muttaqi and Sultan Mahmud Shah III benefited. The young sultan was not slow to translate his newly discovered sense of purpose and confidence into political gains. He gathered around himself a new cabinet of loyal nobles and refurbished the navy after the ignoble failure of Ottoman-Gujarati forces. By 1546, Sultan Mahmud Shah III organized a new offensive against the Portuguese.[77] Two years later, he recalled the minister Asaf Khan from exile in Mecca (where he had fled with the treasury and royal harem at the defeat of Bahadur Shah). He reappointed Asaf Khan as prime minister, and the minister organized a personal army, loyal only to the sultan and not any Gujarati nobility; this secured Maḥmūd Shah III's position once and for all.[78] Asaf Khan's return to Gujarat strengthened ʿAli Muttaqi's connections to the new court at Ahmedabad, for while exiled in Mecca, he had become very close to the shaykh. Asaf Khan had patronized scholars and Sufis in the holy cities besides acting as ambassador for the sultans of Gujarat.

As ʿAli Muttaqi witnessed Asaf Khan return to Ahmedabad with treasury and royal family, a utopian idea dawned upon him: ʿAli Muttaqi aspired to implement reform directly through the court. He returned to Ahmedabad for a second time in the same year that Asaf Khan arrived. His intention was to place the sultan's rule on righteous foundations by implementing *shariʿa* in the court. He imagined that a righteous ruler would be a strong ruler, in contradistinction to the Mughals, whom he saw as illegitimate marauders with the backing of adventurous but inauthentic Sufi leaders, as we will document in the next chapter.

Upon arriving, ʿAli Muttaqi requested Sultan Mahmud Shah III to appoint him as "enforcer of the Shariʿa" (*ḥākim al-sharʿ*), who would review court rituals and procedures to eliminate any practices that he found contrary to legal norms and religious custom. The sultan assented and set up ʿAli Muttaqi with a staff of his followers in the court house (*maḥkama*). Other hadith scholars had dreamed of this position, but ʿAli Muttaqi actualized it with both scriptural knowledge and Sufi authority.[79] From this position of power, he intervened in courtly and religious life in Gujarat and encountered deep conflicts that would push him, once again, off the shores of South Asia.

FOURTH SATCHEL

ʿAli Muttaqi's Mission

The minister slammed his financial register on the desk in frustration, blasting account papers in a flurry across the room. He punched its massive leather cover with his gold-ringed fist. As he rose from his desk, his officers scurried about, gathering papers off the silk carpet. "The state cannot be run like this! We will come to ruin. Ours is the richest kingdom in India, but the treasury's key is in the hands of a so-called saint who doesn't know the difference between fingering a rosary and pocketing a rupee!" His assistant approached gingerly. "Your eminence, you asked me to bring a woman to your chambers? She is here." The minister asked, "You're sure she can be trusted?" The assistant smiled, "A little silver secured her trust—she will do your will." "Then give her this," replied the minister and handed him a velvet bag, small but weighty. "And send her to the office of Shariʿa Compliance to speak with the deputy there, as I instructed. Do it tonight." His assistant bowed low and backed out of the office.

The minister leaned out his window, gazing west from where ships approached over the Arabian Sea. The sun reclined on horizon, throwing shadows over the Sabarmati River dotted with barques and bales of cargo, the signs of trade that was the very lifeblood of Gujarat. He remembered the young sultan's joy when the shaykh had first arrived from Mecca, thinking it a blessing to bolster his tenuous rule. The minister originally supported Sultan Mahmud Shah's initiatives to send huge sums of money to Mecca to support the Sufis and scholars of the holy cities. Even the world-weary minister was relieved to feel that the kingdom now had a legitimate ruler, after so much chaos and violence, who was backed up by the army of prayer, as Sufis were called.

Who could have imagined that this Sufi scholar would step right off the dock and turn the kingdom on its head? On his first day in the capital, he had attended court to bask in the joy that the young sultan exuded. After the thundering *nawbat* drums, the drone of the court musicians, the Persian panegyrics of court poets, and a formal welcome from the sultan, he was seated next to the royal throne. That sly shaykh sat quietly for a dramatic pause and then asked the sultan, "Do you know why I have come?" The sultan answered, "How should I know?" The shaykh answered, "I came on a mission to weigh your rule in the balance of the *shariʿa* so that nothing remains but what conforms to it." The sultan accepted his proposal, as stunned courtiers stood at attention. The sultan naively ordered all his courtiers to refer decisions to Shaykh ʿAli Muttaqi, whose expertise in hadith and pious wisdom would steer the ship of state.

The minister sighed. That scheme might have worked in Medina under the Prophet's early successors, he thought to himself, but this is Ahmedabad! We are Muslims, yes, but we are not fools lost in the maze of hadith, chasing after "I heard him say that his father heard so-and-so say that the Prophet, peace be upon him, once mentioned . . ." What could the Prophet have said about world trade, global banking, cotton cloth, silk brocade, monsoon crops, commerce with Brahmins and Jains, amity with Sadhus and Shiʿa, or the ancient rites of Persian kingship? Ahmedabad is the center of the world, not some holy oasis of date palms and camel hides. This shaykh's insistence on religious *shariʿa* and negligence of administrative law have choked the state. Taxes are in arrears. Soldiers' salaries are stalled. Advance orders to craftsmen in gold, silver, and silk are in abeyance, while their families begin to starve. Land grants to temples are suspended, and all who depend on them are thrown into doubt.

The minister smiled at the setting sun. The day was cloudless, but a secret storm was brewing. In politics, the most fearsome storms come not from wind and waves but rather from ambition and resentment. The shaykh took hold of the reins of state but then despises those employed in the world's affairs, mused the minister. The shaykh deputed a loyal follower to deal with the courtiers and officials corrupted by the dirt of the real world. He orders that follower to attend court, examine our affairs, and report matters to him. All the while, he stays in his cell surrounded by books, cozy in prayerful isolation. The shaykh passes his decisions to his deputy, who announces them in court. It was just as the clever poet al-Mutanabbi said: "Wrongdoing comes from the ego's nature, so if you find / A man free of ego, perhaps he's not the wrongdoing kind." The ego does only what is in its nature to do! As the Arabs say, *janasa man jalasa*—one takes on the character of the company one keeps. Bad influence makes bad characters. Spending time with courtiers and politicians surely makes this deputy, seeming so holy and pious on the outside, susceptible to greed? Let him take the bribe this woman I sent will offer him, lying that it is given on behalf of her husband, a wealthy aristocrat administering land-grants in the countryside. The deputy will take the jewelry now and give a decision on taxation later that favors her, all in the name of Shaykh ʿAli Muttaqi.

While he contemplated his plot, a knock on his office door pulled him back to reality. The room had darkened, and he realized he had missed the sunset prayer. His assistant entered, bowing, "Your eminence, it is done." The minister stormed out of the room, shouting behind him, "Go, alert the sultan—even in his bedchamber—that I must have an audience at once!"

When news reached ʿAli Muttaqi that the sultan had stripped him of authority and reauthorized the minister of state to run financial affairs and court protocol, he rushed to the palace. The sultan listened politely to his protests and entreaties but did not look him in the eye. Rather, the sultan felt the weight of a velvet bag's load—of golden, gem-encrusted jewelry that had been recovered from the reception room of the office of Shariʿa Compliance—as it pressed against his belly, where he had tucked it in his sash, so as to not be swayed from his weighty decision. Seeing the sultan's disposition changed, ʿAli Muttaqi walked straight out of the palace and toward the port, intending to sail to Mecca on the first ship. Outside the city, a group of courtiers arrived to pacify him, and the shaykh lectured them on the nature of the world: "It is reported that the Prophet—peace and blessing be upon him—has said, 'The best among you is not the one who leaves this world in favor of the next nor the one who leaves the next world in favor of this, but rather the best among you is the one who engages this world and earns the next.' This hadith allows for worldly ambition but on condition that it is done with *adab*, proper discipline, to scrupulously limit what one needs from the world so that God might bless his worldly affairs."

While the courtiers delayed the shaykh's departure by pretending to listen to his admonition, the sultan arrived. He beseeched, "Please stay in Gujarat as a blessing to the kingdom and pray for our welfare!" The shaykh answered, "God has dignified Mecca as the place where prayers are answered, so it is better if I pray for you and your kingdom from there." No matter how they cajoled, the shaykh remained unmoved. His impassive face turned westward, and he silenced them with a poem as he set off for the port of Khambhat:

With a blessed house and good neighbors,
Staying in Mecca seems good to me.
Let me settle there in that neighborhood!
To live near the Lord is to live carefree.

ʿAli Muttaqi's mission to Gujarat started with promise and ended in disaster. Arriving in Ahmedabad, he secured an audience with Sultan Mahmud Shah III. Earning his trust, the saint positioned himself as spiritual advisor to the ruler and requested that he be appointed as "Enforcer of the Shariʿa" with powers to review court protocol, political ritual, tax revenues, and ministerial decisions. The young sultan was relieved to have a saintly buffer between himself and the courtiers whom he so viscerally distrusted; he also wanted expiation for his guilty conscience, since he had executed many nobles in his struggle to come to power. The sultan handed over the keys to the treasury to ʿAli Muttaqi, who set up an office in the palace from which he set about disciplining nobles, reining in courtiers, and scrutinizing the operations of governance.

Immediately upon implementation of this reformist project, serious problems arose. As the vignette recounted above illustrates, most nobles resented saintly intrusion in their domain of worldly power. Those who did not oppose his reforms out of jealousy remained skeptical about their efficacy for good governance. Historical chronicles that record these events are sympathetic to the nobles' point of view, advocating the realist position that government requires certain practices that might seem immoral from the standpoint of religious propriety yet are for the greater good of public welfare and social justice. ʿAli Muttaqi clearly differed with this view on ideological grounds. He felt that good government was one that implemented the *shariʿa* over and against any compromise or convenience. His reforms rested on the faith that divine providence would support a *shariʿa*-bound government centered on the scholar-saint, even if practicality seemed to work against it.

ʿAli Muttaqi persisted in the face of the grumbling opposition of some the most powerful nobles in the court, leading to a disastrous end. Eventually, in a strategy to undermine his mission to reform society based on how he imagined sincerity of heart and fidelity to the *shariʿa*, courtiers accused him of taking bribes. Later in this chapter, all the details of this dramatic incident will be recounted. The sketch above is based on the account of the historian Ulughkhani, in his history of Gujarat written in Arabic, which covers politics, trade, social change, and notable biographies for almost two centuries (from the independence of the sultanate of Gujarat in 1396 until its definitive conquest by the Mughals in 1573).

The historian was "secular" in the premodern sense of the world: he was oriented to worldly concerns and had little patience for theocracy, while not being against religion itself. Ulughkhani was an administrator turned historian who represents the cosmopolitan society that thrived during the sultanate of Gujarat.[1] Ulughkhani left an invaluable record of Gujarat in Arabic, a manuscript unknown to Indian historians until it was found at the Calcutta Madrasa and published in 1910. His history includes the activities of Sufis and Islamic scholars inasmuch as their personalities impacted worldly affairs. Ulughkhani begins his biographical account of ʿAli Muttaqi with fulsome praise but swiftly changes tone. He narrates the incident described above from the viewpoint of the courtiers, nobles, and clerks who resented a saint meddling in affairs of state.[2] These were Ulughkhani's informants, and they probably mumbled cheers under their breath as the shaykh departed, walking out of their city to the port. ʿAli Muttaqi's own supporters, like ʿAbd al-Haqq Muhaddith Dihlawi, recorded the incident differently. ʿAbd al-Haqq emphasized that the shaykh stayed firm to his just principles and scriptural learning, while courtiers and government officials plotted against him.[3]

During his time in Gujarat, ʿAli Muttaqi conflicted not only with administrators but also with competing religious leaders who challenged his ideals. He confronted the two major religious movements of the time: the vibrant Shattari Order, which was gaining ascendancy at the time, and the Mahdawi movement. Both of these movements grew out of Sufi communities and pushed certain ideals of sainthood to extremes; they also became steeped in the political turmoil of Gujarat. ʿAli Muttaqi projected his authority as a reformist scholar-saint, but it was tenuous and contested. He thought himself to be the guardian of the treasury of sainthood. Just as he scrutinized the legitimacy of the requests for payment from the treasury, he also tested the purity of the coinage that flowed out to meet the needs of the kingdom. For this reason, he critiqued Islamic leaders who he felt were inauthentic or heretical or who would misuse the social capital of Sufism for their own popularity and acclaim. His goal to limit who could claim legitimacy as a saint led him to clash with various rival movements, for he attained his sense of authenticity by rejecting popular forms of sanctity as recognized and celebrated in Gujarat and wider South Asia. This chapter is a satchel containing confrontations and conflicts, denunciations and persecutions. It explores how ʿAli Muttaqi and his community confronted other religious leaders—Sufis of the Shattari Order and revivalists of the Mahdawi movement—with subtle theology, scriptural scholarship, and state persecution.

In looking back over his experiment with governance, ʿAli Muttaqi exonerated himself through the metaphor of marriage. A man's marriage to two wives fails because of the nature of his wives, not because of his own failings. A first marriage is always spoiled by engagement to a second woman, "for two wives cannot live in peace." Before we assess his political engagement for success or failure, we need to explore how his stint as "Enforcer of the Shariʿa" in Gujarat pushed him to critique those who he thought abused their reputation as saints.

Confrontation: Battling the Shattari Powers

In the early sixteenth century, the vivid Shattari Order rose to power and fame by supporting the early Mughal rulers. This Sufi order developed as a branch of the Kubrāwī Order in Central Asia, where it was known as the ʿIshqī Order or "Path of Ardent Lovers."[4] Perhaps ʿAli Muttaqi had this irony in mind when he wrote his short treatise critiquing those who insincerely claimed to be "lovers of God," as quoted in the previous chapter.[5] This order entered South Asia with Shāh ʿAbdallāh Shaṭṭār (d. 1485), who settled at Mandu, the capital of the sultanate of Malwa. The sultan patronized him, and his disciples spread the order under his name as the Shattari Order. Shah ʿAbdallah Shattar was buried in the royal complex of the College of the Heavenly Vault (Madrasa-ye Bām-e Bihisht), which included a monumental victory tower, a Sufi khanqah, and an Islamic school whose architecture included white marble walls with inlay of precious stones cut into geometric and vegetal designs, a craft derived from inlay work in ivory and mother-of-pearl; this architectural style would later be adopted by Mughal royalty for the tomb that Queen Nūrjahān (d. 1645) built for her father and, one generation later, made famous in the Taj Mahal.[6] The grandeur of Malwa now lies in ruins, but the complex's eight-meter high plinth still attests to its ambition and scale. The tomb of Shah ʿAbdallah Shattar still exists, open to the sky in a walled courtyard that once was part of the khanqah, where Sufis could stay and worship with royal patronage.

From his center in Mandu, he trained many disciples and spread his new teachings such that the Shattari Order took his name. His epithet *shaṭṭār* means "clever" or "quick," and this description was apt for the community that followed him. Adherents quickly adjusted to the South Asian environment and cleverly supported the nascent Mughal Empire when it was still

Tomb of Shah ʿAbdallah Shattar in Mandu. (Photograph by Jayanti Rajagopalan.)

struggling to control Delhi and the Gangetic plain.[7] Their leader was Shaykh Muhammad Ghawth of Gwalior (Gwāliyar), who had a reputation as a spiritually vivid and politically powerful saint whose Islamic spirituality had a distinctly South Asian flavor. He helped consolidate Mughal rule and systematized the teachings of the Shattari Order. He embraced Yoga and advocated it as a devotional path complementary to Sufism.[8] He calibrated his technique of *dhikr* to astronomical expertise and, like Brahmin astrologers, leveraged this knowledge to advise political rulers in exchange for patronage. He also accepted Indian music and poetic arts as being totally compatible with Sufism and was the Sufi master (or also adoptive father, in some legends) of the great singer Tansen. Muhammad Ghawth's enthusiasm for existential philosophy helped him blur the distinctions between Islam and Hinduism in ways that other Sufi communities were reticent to do.

In his early teens, Muhammad Ghawth spent years in a mountain retreat in Bihar, where ascetic rigor pushed his consciousness to extremes. He recorded visionary experiences, possibly fueled by radical fasting, which culminated in his ascension through the cosmos into the heavens and to the throne of God. His experience echoed that of the Prophet Muhammad but also differed from traditional accounts of that Prophetic miracle.[9] For example, Muhammad Ghawth met Khiḍr, the legendary ever-youthful embodiment of wisdom and immortal companion to the Prophets, and Khidr led Muhammad Ghawth in his ascension. Since Muhammad Ghawth published his experience as the transcendent culmination of his many Sufi initiations, his ascension gave him great fame. This event occurred shortly before Babur conquered Delhi. Muhammad Ghawth's ascension to the divine throne coincided perfectly with Babur mounting the political throne.

Muhammad Ghawth and his Shattari Order sided with the Mughal rulers after Babur's initial success. Its leaders helped displace Afghan chiefs of the Lodi dynasty, who upheld the last vestiges of the Delhi sultanate. After settling in Gwalior (about halfway between Delhi and Mandu to the south), Muhammad Ghawth refused to bless and support the Lodi regime that had recently conquered that town's strategic citadel. After Babur defeated Ibrahim Lodi, the last of the Delhi sultans, Muhammad Ghawth helped engineer the Mughal conquest of Gwalior, a bastion of survival for the Lodi regime.[10]

Babur died after ruling only five years. He had ties to the Naqshbandi Order from Central Asia, as did many of his family and soldiers who followed him into South Asia. By the era of Humayun, the Mughals were losing their Central Asian perspective and increasingly relied on South Asian Sufis, especially Shattari leaders. The new Mughal ruler, Babur's son Humayun, depended even more heavily on the Shattari leaders to support his tentative rule. Muhammad Ghawth's colleague Abū'l-Fatḥ Sarmast (d. 1538), who was a disciple of his same master, cursed Afghan strongmen who held out for a return of Lodi rule and accompanied Humayun's army to fight them in Bihar. In Delhi, Muhammad Ghawth's older brother, Shaykh Bahlūl (d. 1538), gave Sufi initiation to Humayun and connected him to Muhammad Ghawth. Both brothers were famous for their supernatural abilities through *daʿwat-e asmā'*, or "invoking the names of God."[11] Shaykh Bahlul was known in Indian sources as Shaykh Pħūl, but in Humayun's court he was given the overtly political title Jahāngīr, "He with the World in His Hand." Under his influence, many Sufis with ties to the court joined the Shattari Order; at least two prominent Sufis were "obliged" to take Shattari allegiance in order to remain at court.[12] Shaykh Bahlul took on the role of advisor and confidant to the Mughal ruler, fomenting discontent in Humayun's extended family that traditionally relied on Naqshbandi Sufis in Central Asia for spiritual guidance.[13] As Humayun's grip on power slipped, his half brother, Mirzā Hindāl, rebelled, and Shaykh Bahlul was sent on a diplomatic mission to convince him to desist but was assassinated.[14] Soon after, Humayun was dislodged by the Afghan warlord and Lodi loyalist Sher Shah Suri. In defeat, Humayun turned to Muhammad Ghawth for guidance and consolation. When Humayun fled to Iran in exile in 1542, Muhammad Ghawth took refuge in Gujarat. From there, he wrote letters to Humayun, counseling patient persistence and foretelling his successful return to the throne.[15] Theology alloyed with politics in this powerful nexus between the Shattari leader and the Mughal emperor, a nexus that ʿAli Muttaqi vowed to confront and break.

ʿAli Muttaqi met Shaykh Muhammad Ghawth in Ahmedabad when the Shattari leader had reached a zenith of fame and prestige. ʿAli Muttaqi's suspicion of his legitimacy developed into open confrontation. By the end of this imbroglio, ʿAli Muttaqi summoned all his resources as a scholar-saint, empowered by an official position in the government, to denounce Muhammad Ghawth's spiritual experiences as "nothing but ecstatic boasts and fantastic claims." The incident is one of the best documented instances of Sufi persecution of other Sufis.[16]

ʿAli Muttaqi denounced Muhammad Ghawth in theological terms, specifying exactly how Muhammad Ghawth's performance of sainthood was inauthentic and dangerous. His critique was informed by his reformist ideals, and he expressed them to a wider audience among Sufis, scholars, and courtiers in Gujarat. However, critique is a function of competition, and competition rests on an unspoken similarity between the two competitors. Both ʿAli Muttaqi and Muhammad Ghawth, despite their apparent differences, shared an unspoken similarity. From their youth, both were dissatisfied with the routine legitimacy of their initiation into a Sufi order, with its lineage of masters leading back to the Prophet. They both pursued extremes of introspection in an attempt to arrive at a fuller justification for their saintly authority. From this point, they diverged and conflicted.

ʿAli Muttaqi was driven to investigate the "grounding principles" of being a Sufi that undergirded any initiation; in contrast, Muhammad Ghawth explored the upper limits of spiritual experience that are potentially within any initiation. In one visionary experience, the Prophet granted Muhammad Ghawth an initiation that made him surpass other saints.[17] Muhammad Ghawth wrote down and spoke about these experiences, which singled him out as the most efficacious channel for divine power in his age, over and against other contemporary saints. These bold claims climaxed in his experience of ascension, in which he followed in the very footsteps of the Prophet Muhammad in his passage into intimacy with God.

Muhammad Ghawth's major disciple, Wajīh al-Dīn ʿAlawī (d. 1590), bolstered these claims by asserting that his master's spiritual authority was absolute and his transcendent initiation was unique.[18] As Wajih al-Din recorded the lineages granted to him from all his previous masters, the lineages led to the Prophet (in the typical pattern of Sufi lineages).[19] Yet he claimed that his initiation with Muhammad Ghawth was more efficacious, more vivid, and more powerful because it was empowered by his ascension. It led back to the Prophet horizontally through a chain of mediating saints, but it also recreated the Prophet's experience vertically through ascension and direct initiatory contact with God.

ʿAli Muttaqi's critique of Muhammad Ghawth centered on these transcendental initiations. He questioned their theological justification and the ways in which Muhammad Ghawth translated them into social power as he built a popular movement around his Shattari ideals. Following his analytic method, ʿAli Muttaqi reduced Muhammad Ghawth's claims to a fundamental assertion: that a saint can ascend to heaven upon the footsteps of the Prophet and return to tell about it. He attacked this assertion with hadith. He relayed a little-known report of the Prophet showing that anyone who claims to have ascended above the earth through the heavens to the divine throne is surely misled. "The tempter [*shaytan*] has a throne placed between the heavens and the earth; if he wants to afflict someone with being the cause of discord [*fitna*] then he reveals to that person his throne."[20] A false throne in a false heaven is the basis for false claims of spiritual potency.

ʿAli Muttaqi wielded this hadith like a double-edged blade, for he cited it in the context of the story of a famous Sufi, Muḥammad ibn Khafīf of Shiraz (d. 982), who bragged of his ascension experiences but was humbled upon hearing this hadith. The report silenced his claims and led him to true spiritual insight through his sincere repentance; he later became a respected hadith scholar and sober Sufi respected by Sunni scholars:

> Shaykh Muhammad ibn Khafif was once sitting in the company of all the masters of Shiraz, when the topic of conversation turned to witnessing God through visionary encounters [*mushāhida*].[21] Each one said something about the topic according to his own spiritual state, but Ibn Khafif stayed silent. One shaykh, Mu'ammal Ḥassās, urged him to add something to the discussion. Ibn Khafif answered, "They've already said every good thing that there is to say on this topic." Mu'ammal insisted, "In any case, please say something as well." Then he answered, "You have all offered skillful answers from a hundred different artful sciences, but none

> of these are the real truth directly told. Visionary encounter means just this: that the obscuring veil should be lifted up so that you can see God directly with your own eyes." They asked him, "From what authority do you say this? How did you come to know it?" Ibn Khafif said, "I stayed in the wastelands around Tabūk in Arabia and I was struggling very hard with ascetic exercises for I had nothing at hand. I offered up intimate pleas to God [*munājāt*]. Suddenly, the veil was lifted and I saw God sitting upon the divine throne. I fell into prostration before God and said, 'My Lord, what a place is my place, what a station is my situation!'" When all the others heard this, they fell silent. Mu'ammal said, "Get up now—let's go visit some other shaykhs!" He took Ibn Khafif's hand and led him to Ibn Saʿdān, a hadith scholar. They greeted him and Ibn Saʿdan praised Mu'ammal greatly. Then Mu'ammal asked the hadith scholar, "Why don't you tell us that report related from the Prophet in which he said, 'The tempter has a throne placed between the heavens and the earth; if he wants to afflict someone with being the cause of discord then he reveals to that person his throne.'" Ibn Saʿdan explained how this report was recited person by person back to the Prophet himself, who had said these very words. Hearing this, Ibn Khafif cried out, "Repeat it to me again!" As he heard it over and over, he was beside himself with weeping, ran outside, and disappeared for many days. When he finally returned to town and was asked where he had been all these days, he replied, "I've been saying over again all the prayers that I had said since that day [I had witnessed the false throne], because I now see that I had been worshipping the tempter all this time! None of my prayers were valid until I ventured back to that very place where I had seen him and lowered my head and cursed him there on the spot!"[22]

When younger, Ibn Khafif pursued rigorous austerities and extreme fasts in Syria before moving to Iran, where he is credited for spreading Sufism in cosmopolitan Shiraz; there, he became an expert in hadith and exemplar of sober scholarly Sunni Sufism of the type that ʿAli Muttaqi's reform movement aimed to generate.[23]

ʿAli Muttaqi did not name Muhammad Ghawth specifically while relating this story, but the Shattari master was the object of his critique. ʿAli Muttaqi expected him to hear Prophetic reports that contradicted his own experience and to respond positively by curbing his claims, as had Shaykh Ibn Khafif long before. ʿAli Muttaqi must have mobilized this story from one of the foundational sources of Sufism, *Kitāb al-Lumaʿ* by Abū Naṣr al-Sarrāj (d. 988). This first Sufi manual was written during the era of Ibn Khafif and relayed the same warning story about Satan's throne.

> I have heard that some Sufis in Syria claim to see spiritual realities in this world through vision of the heart just like we will see spiritual realities in the next world through vision of the eyes. . . . [al-Sarraj mentions that there is a hadith in which the Prophet says that he saw the throne of God.] . . . I witnessed some of them who took upon themselves severe austerities, sleep deprivation, extreme fasting and long isolation in retreats, efforts that were accompanied by strange occurrences. They fell victim to the tempter who appeared to them in an imaginary form seated on a throne from which radiated intense light. Some of them took counsel with learned teachers who could recognize the snares of the enemy and informed them of the true nature of this experience and guided them rightly, returning them to upright conduct. A similar story is told about a disciple of Sahl Tustari who said to him one day, "Oh my teacher, at night I see God with the eyes of my head!" Then Sahl knew that this was from the snares of the enemy and he replied, "My dear, when you see him the next night, wish for a lightning bolt to strike!" It is said that the next night when he saw the vision of God he wished for a bolt of lightning and when it struck, the throne flew away and the radiant lights dimmed to darkness. That disciple was released from this experience and never saw such visions afterwards.[24]

ʿAli Muttaqi cited these stories so that Muhammad Ghawth might limit his claims and refine his *adab*, to refrain from making public pronouncements about ascension experiences. In ʿAli Muttaqi's opinion, a visionary experience was no fast ticket to selflessness; rather, it was the fastest way to inflate the ego with the delusion of having gained power. It led to social discord, since a saint's reference to his or her own ascension transcended acquired religious knowledge and thus threw its value into doubt. As Ibn Khafif boasted, scholarly knowledge of scripture and hadith could offer "a hundred different artful sciences, but none of these are the real truth directly told." ʿAli Muttaqi was wary of ascensions because they appeared to transcend acquired religious knowledge, to denigrate the effort to acquire such knowledge, and even to eclipse the source of such knowledge.

In ʿAli Muttaqi's view, Muhammad Ghawth's vision of the heavenly throne indicated that he had arrived at a dangerous level of temptation; his insistence on speaking openly about his vision revealed that he was hopelessly captivated by selfish urges to acquire power. ʿAli Muttaqi ascribed Muhammad

Ghawth's demonstrated spiritual power to the effects of satanic magic. His miraculous experiences were a grave personal temptation that led to social division and strife (*fitna*). ʿAli Muttaqi circulated this Prophetic report about the throne of the tempter to confront Shaykh Muhammad Ghawth's claim to esoteric knowledge and manipulation of supernatural forces.[25] He critiqued Muhammad Ghawth's ascension narrative and also the social ramifications of his ascension claim, for it garnered him great social prestige from his practice of "invoking the names of God" (*daʿwat-e asmāʾ*) in alignment with astrological forces to subdue political rulers on earth (*taskhīr-e mulūk*).[26] This Shattari practice has been sorely misunderstood by scholars. The historian Azfar Moin mistranslates *taskhīrāt* as "spirits," whereas the actual practice involves prayers which align names of God with planets to subdue (*taskhīr*) forces in the social world, especially political rulers.[27]

When Muhammad Ghawth took refuge in Gujarat, his reputation preceded him, and the ability of his Shattari colleagues to influence politics was widely known. For instance, Shaykh Waliʾllah in Mandu advised his son to avoid taking initiation from "certain persons prominent these days in Gujarat . . . [who] indulge in invoking the divine names and attempting to captivate kings." The son who received this advice, ʿAbd al-Wahhab, eventually became ʿAli Muttaqi's major follower.[28] One disciple asked ʿAbd al-Wahhab Muttaqi whether reciting God's names in alignment with stars and planets to affect worldly events was an authentic method of reaching intimacy with God. He answered by repeating ʿAli Muttaqi's ethical critique of such practices, questioning not the ritual itself but the ambitions that it expressed. He replied, "Sufis who habitually indulge in this practice neglect to polish their ethical comportment. Most of them are truly rude and selfish people who bear grudges against others. From anyone who might slight them or oppress them, they are sure to take retribution."[29]

ʿAli Muttaqi also criticized Muhammad Ghawth's supposed political miracles as the clearest expression of his ambition for power. To counter Muhammad Ghawth's powerful use of miracles and visions to harness popular acclaim, ʿAli Muttaqi developed the concept of *istidrāj*, or spiritual backsliding. He dedicated a whole section of one book to "an exposition of the difference between miracles that confirm prophethood, miracles that appear in sainthood, and alleged miracles that are actually spiritual backsliding."[30] He stated, "Steadfastness in worship is greater than performing miracles, for with miracles there is still the fear of backsliding [*istidraj*] and selfishness, for nothing is dearer to a human being than the ego. Until one passes beyond self-interest, one can never reach the goal."[31] Similarly, in his treatment of the famous wisdom sayings of Ibn ʿAtaʾallah, he organized a chapter on backsliding, relating this aphorism: "It is to be feared that God does good for you yet you persist in doing bad, for that can lead to your backsliding."[32]

In his writing and teaching, ʿAli Muttaqi mobilized concepts that were basic to discussions of Sufism in South Asia, in an environment saturated with holy men of various religions who commanded popular awe with miracles. Long before ʿAli Muttaqi, the Chishti teacher Nizam al-Din Awliya warned about the spiritual and social dangers of backsliders or "retreaters" who succumbed to *istidraj*. He taught, "There is the traveler, the standstill and the retreater. . . . The traveler is the one who treads the [Sufi] path; the standstill is the one who stops along the way. . . . Every time that the traveler lapses in his obedience, he becomes stationary. If he quickly resumes this work and repents, then he may again become a traveler. If, God forbid, he remains at a standstill, then he may become a retreater or a backslider."[33] Although Nizam al-Din Awliya mentioned spiritual backsliding, he ended his discussion of it quickly by invoking God's protection from such a terrible spiritual condition that could lead to hardening of the heart and enmity against God.

In contrast, ʿAli Muttaqi developed this concept as a social critique, describing in detail the powers that accrued to the Sufi backslider. In his exposition, backsliding or *istidraj* leads to the production of supernatural events and the experience of extraordinary visions as a result of the ego's ambition. He contrasts *istidraj*, as a mark of corruption, with *karamāt*, which are true miracles granted to saints as an embodiment of selflessness. ʿAli Muttaqi explained that people who engage in worship, meditation, and ascetic rigors develop an inward concentration and spiritual potency; in this process, they experience extrasensory phenomena, control their appetites, and empower their bodies in unusual ways. They may even find that they can control or manipulate events of the world by their will. These events are popularly known as "miracles" (*khawāriq al-ʿāda*), but they are not really miracles in the true sense of the word. Even non-Muslims, he asserted, can generate such magical effects. These do not symbolize a saint's authentic selflessness any more than paint smudged on a person's hands are the marks that one is a skillful painter.

These supernatural events mark the ethical boundary between spiritually potent egoists and authentic saints. They are a great temptation, and how supposed saints deal with miracles is the litmus test of their sincerity. If a saint promotes his own miraculous powers or actively cultivates them, that is a sign of inauthenticity.

> When people become close to God, they are chosen as the locus of the appearance of God's absolute power. This power appears in the world

> as supernatural events. In reality, they are the workings of God; they appear through the actions of the saint, although the saint really has no claim on them. . . . Common people think that the saints perform miracles in and of themselves, but real saints know that this is a divine reprimand holding them at the threshold that requires than to persevere until they are final granted success in banishing the objects of worship in themselves [and the very idolatry of the self]. Real saints know that this passing beyond the self is the only real miracle. Real saints forbid themselves from paying any attention to all the actions that the common people know as "miracles," since these are tainted with the ambition of their egos and are an obstacle to true sincerity. They wipe out any claim of their ego self to knowledge of the result of an apparent miracle, because they know that the only benefit they will receive is in the next world, not in this world.[34]

In this definition, ʿAli Muttaqi refines the general theological concept of *istidraj*. Previous Sufis had used the term to denote the supernatural actions of people who did not follow Islamic legal custom; because of this doctrinal lapse, such a person's "miracles" became a sign that he was a hypocrite (*zindīq*) or fraud (*makkār*).[35] ʿAli Muttaqi reverses the elements of this definition. For him, the ethical comportment of the supposed saint is the root cause for declaring whether he really follows the *shariʿa* or not. Rather than using *istidraj* as a blanket denunciation of non-Muslim miracles or heretical miracles, ʿAli Muttaqi forges the term into an ethical criterion to determine whether a saint is sincere. If he is sincere, then his sanctity is authentic, and if this is authentic, then he necessarily follows the *shariʿa*. But if a supposed saint promotes his miracles, then he is not sincere, his sanctity is inauthentic, and he can be safely declared a heretical innovator (*mubtadiʿ*).

ʿAli Muttaqi also disparaged Muhammad Ghawth's ideology of spiritual leadership. Shattari saints, including Muhammad Ghawth, claimed to wield a superior method in training disciples for spiritual development. The name of their lineage, Shaṭṭār, means one who reaches the goal "swiftly and effortlessly."[36] His ascension was an experiential confirmation of the reality of existential philosophy—Muhammad Ghawth not only ascended vertically but also dissolved existentially, allowing his illusory independent existence to melt, stage by stage, into the vast divinity of the oneness of being (*waḥdat al-wujūd*). He claimed to be able to spark in disciples and followers the same existential transformation, quickly and effortlessly.

Ultimately, ʿAli Muttaqi criticized Muhammad Ghawth not because he taught the radical immanence of God as aspect of existential philosophy, but because he taught it openly and widely rather than limiting it to disciples qualified in scholarship and committed to the *shariʿa*. Muhammad Ghawth crafted existential philosophy's terms of radical immanence into the ideological pivot of his spiritual method. For ʿAli Muttaqi, it was a perspective on the world that could be tasted by only a few, only after they had trained their intellects, honed their reason, humbled their egos, and attended to their obligatory worship. In other words, only realized saints could see the world as unified in its reliance on undifferentiated primal reality, which is the existence of God. He denied that unitive philosophy was a quick means to achieving sanctity and contended that it was instead perspective on the world that resulted from personal sanctity.

In his teachings, ʿAli Muttaqi distinguished between "*tawḥīd* as actions" to make an object unified and "*waḥdat* as existential unity" as an abstract concept. The first stresses ritual action and ethical comportment, while the second stresses a philosophic system.[37] In ʿAli Muttaqi's teachings, there are four levels of *tawhid*, meaning to acknowledge apparently discrete things to actually be one. The first level, "*tawhid* of faith," is common to all Muslims; it is to declare the oneness of God and serve that single God by believing in the revelation and Prophetic example that demonstrates God to be so. Other levels of *tawhid* are the realm of religious specialists, including Sufis. "*Tawhid* of knowledge" is a philosophical and rational perspective: knowing that there is no ultimate reality except God and that all existing things subside through the force of the names of God. All worldly objects and events can be traced back to their archetypal being in the shifting light of the divine names; ʿAli Muttaqi asserts that this is a beginning Sufi's perspective. Sometimes the light of these names shines clearly so that the knowers' own existence does not veil them from seeing the reality of these names, such that they lose self-consciousness and act in ways that transgress the bounds of religious custom. These ephemeral experiences of selflessness do not mean that the darkness of ego has yet been cleared, and they can still fall victim to subtle acts of infidelity and egoistic passion. The next, more advanced level is "*tawhid* of spiritual states." This is when the act of unifying becomes not just the quality of verbal belief or rational knowledge but the very quality of one's essence. In this stage, most all of the dark matter of ego and personal need will be eclipsed by the brightness of the divine light that sustains a person. Every action will reflect this light, rather than proceed from egoistic will; this is the highest stage of spiritual completion attainable by humankind. Beyond this is the "*tawhid* of divinity," the simple fact that God is now exactly what God was, originating from no otherness, proceeding to no otherness, and sustained and sustaining through no otherness.

Through these teachings, ʿAli Muttaqi set up criteria to critique the assertions of Muhammad Ghawth. He assessed that the Shattari leader's rhetoric of existential unity conflated two different levels of *tawhid* while betraying the level in between. ʿAli Muttaqi placed him in the middle level of "*tawhid* of knowledge" and accused him of trying to leap directly into contact with the last level, "*tawhid* of divinity." In ʿAli Muttaqi's view, Muhammad Ghawth knew rationally that there is no real existence but God's existence; he had experienced this through transitory states of self-abnegation and then concluded that he was personally in touch with that divine expanse of pure existence to the point of purposefully identifying his ego with God, as depicted in his ascension narrative and embodied in his ritual of *dhikr.* Yet according to ʿAli Muttaqi's criteria, this was self-delusion, for he had not yet passed through "*tawhid* of spiritual states" by abandoning the last vestiges of personal ambitions by upholding the boundaries of the *shariʿa.*

ʿAli Muttaqi pointed to various teachings of the Shattari community as evidence of this ethical flaw. For example, once a disciple asked Wajih al-Din ʿAlawi about the true meaning of sincerity (*ikhlāṣ*). He replied in Gujari, "*Ikhlas* is saying that the God that I seek is nothing but the essence of my very soul."[38] In this teaching he uses the familiar theme of Shattari devotion, that the ego is in essence nothing but the Being of God, to explain the most central ethical principle. In contrast, ʿAli Muttaqi held that the final evidence of having reached these upper limits of *tawhid* is conspicuous silence about divine reality, constancy in rituals of everyday religion, and ethical teaching based on scriptural sources.

These theological and ethical differences set ʿAli Muttaqi and Muhammad Ghawth on a collision course. The dangers were further augmented because of their difference in political loyalties. Although Muhammad Ghawth settled in Ahmedabad, he was a known partisan of Humayun, who supported the Mughal regime even when it was temporarily toppled from power. ʿAli Muttaqi, in contrast, remained loyal to the sultanate of Gujarat with its proven record of respecting Sunni scholars and being blessed by long-established Sufi orders. In ʿAli Muttaqi's view, both the Shattaris and the Mughals whom they supported were new arrivals with wild ambitions and unproven credentials.

Once he settled in Ahmedabad, Muhammad Ghawth advertised his presence and began to train disciples. Very quickly, local Sufis with scholarly learning complained about his teachings.[39] Their alarm increased as Wajih al-Din ʿAlawi, the renowned hadith scholar and Qadiri Sufi, became Muhammad Ghawth's disciple. Complaints reached ʿAli Muttaqi, as the "Enforcer of the Shariʿa" and a leading Sufi authority. He investigated Muhammad Ghawth's teachings. He sent spies to sit in his circles and listen in to his teachings, and he also read his books, like the concise "Ascension Narrative" (Miʿrāj Nāma) and the massive "Keys to Heaven's Treasuries" (Kalīd al-Makhāzin), his theological treatise on existential philosophy and Sufi cosmology. ʿAli Muttaqi ordered Muhammad Ghawth to attend a public hearing where he would, in the presence of leading Sufis and scholars, recant his claim to have ascended into heaven and wash the ink off pages of his books that made false claims. Muhammad Ghawth managed to wriggle out of this humiliation since his disciple, Wajih al-Din ʿAlawi, defended him.

During the critique and persecution, Muhammad Ghawth's disciples and sympathizers countered that ʿAli Muttaqi was distracted by the formalities of legal and ritual custom. His attention to external form, in their view, compromised his claim to sainthood. In response to this spirited defense, ʿAli Muttaqi broadened his critique to include the motives of Muhammad Ghawth's followers: he singled out the most ardent supporter, Wajih al-Din ʿAlawi, as self-serving and partisan. Although both were hadith scholars, Wajih al-Din did not at all share ʿAli Muttaqi's reform agenda or his reification of the *shariʿa*. Rather, he taught that, "for the purpose of achieving intimacy with God, there is no need of study and the acquisition of scriptural knowledge. If a problem arises and you need a judgment [about the external form of religious duties], then just go consult a qualified jurist."[40] He established a madrasa in Ahmedabad in 1528, and among his pupils were Muḥammad ibn Faḍlallāh Burhānpūrī and Shaykh Ṣibghatallāh from Bharoch. His remained the premier madrasa for a century and a half; Wajih al-Din taught scriptural studies yet saw no need for a reform program that fused Sufi training with scholarly learning. In fact, he may have resented it as a blurring of professional boundaries or a bid for political influence. Wajih al-Din represented a powerful juridical family with a reputation for being pillars of piety in the capital. Many students of Wajih al-Din who entered his madrasa seeking scriptural training became Shattari disciples. All four of Muhammad Ghawth's sons were educated by Wajih al-Din at the madrasa; this gave Muhammad Ghawth's order scholarly legitimacy that he personally lacked. Shaykh Wajih al-Din's resistance to this reformist project will become clearer in the discussion of ʿAli Muttaqi's disciple Muhammad ibn Tahir Patani in the fifth satchel.

In defense of his Sufi master, Wajih al-Din claimed that ʿAli Muttaqi was a mere ascetic rather than a truly realized saint, yet he had to couch this critique in a compliment. During his public discourses, Wajih al-Din said, "Shaykh ʿAli Muttaqi was an angel in human form. There was no more pious and God-fearing person on the face of the earth, so far above my own humble state! He attained this spiritual excellence through his own strenuous efforts

Dargah of Wajih al-Din ʿAlawi at Khanpur in Ahmedabad.

and painful struggles. In contrast, I received my spiritual state through inward unveiling due to the power of my spiritual guide [Muhammad Ghawth]. What a difference there is between the spiritual gift given by serving a guide and the spiritual acquisitions attained by one's own struggles without a guide!"[41] Wajih al-Din explained that would-be saints engage in strenuous exercises and ascetic privations only before they find a spiritual guide. A guide frees his disciples from their own egos and gives them the insight to immediately grasp selflessness.[42] He implied that a saint known for outward rectitude was inwardly imperfect and still prisoner of his ego. In Wajih al-Din's counter-critique, ʿAli Muttaqi was incomplete because he had never found a real saintly guide.

During this public discourse, a follower of Wajih al-Din offered that ʿAli Muttaqi had a guide in Shaykh Husam al-Din Muttaqi. Wajih al-Din answered, "Husam al-Din was nothing but an ascetic! He was known only for ascetic rigor and God-fearing piety." He told the story of how Husam al-Din Muttaqi died of starvation, which hagiographers thought too damning to narrate fully. Wajih al-Din's intent in recounting this tale is just the reverse of hagiography—he meant to strip both the shaykh and his disciple of the status of sainthood.

> Shaykh Husam al-Din was a man so scrupulous that he could find nothing to eat but fish! In the end, he left even the fish as impure! You see, there was a Hindu temple just a short distance from the river where

he would get the fish, and worshippers used to take the leftovers of the ritual food [Gj. *prasād*] from the temple and feed it to the fish. When he heard of this practice, Husam al-Din said to himself, "Maybe the fish have eaten of this stuff and gotten contaminated—I refuse to eat them!" He sat around wondering what else to eat that would be pure, but he couldn't find anything else. In the end, he gave up eating altogether! Somebody quoted to him the verse: *Do not drive yourselves by your own actions to destruction* [Qur'an 4:29]. Husam al-Din answered, "Only a murderer is guilty of killing." Eventually, he died of starvation. After his death, someone saw him in a dream. Husam al-Din was sitting on a golden throne with a jeweled crown on his head but looked depressed. The dreamer asked him, "Why so sad?" The shaykh said, "The Prophet Muhammad said to me [when I got to heaven], 'Oh Husam al-Din, you left that world with external purity but you came into this world without internal purity!'" From this dream vision, you can tell that he was never blessed with the inner tranquility of absorption in God [*istighraq*] and remained alienated from pure union with God.[43]

Wajih al-Din narrated this whole story to his disciples to disqualify Husam al-Din Muttaqi, whose scrupulous piety in external matters led to distraction in ritual details and an unsanctimonious death. Wajih al-Din even accused Husam al-Din of suicide, a grave sin. If Husam al-Din never reached a level of true sainthood, then how could one expect it of his disciple, ʿAli Muttaqi? Wajih al-Din iterated this point in his lectures, saying, "There are so many ways to prepare yourself to reach intimacy with God, so why go starve yourself?"[44]

With such a damning story, Wajih al-Din impugned ʿAli Muttaqi's reputation and then expanded on it with a full assault against reformist Sufi training. In retrospect, the Shattari community emerged from this imbroglio with the upper hand. ʿAli Muttaqi tried to force his opponent to publicly admit his error, but Muhammad Ghawth wriggled out of making any confession. ʿAli Muttaqi demanded that Muhammad Ghawth wash the ink off the pages of his books that describe his heavenly ascension and cosmology of divine immanence, but his opponent slipped out of Ahmedabad to the port of Bharoch. ʿAli Muttaqi sent two letters charging governors with the task of chaining up Muhammad Ghawth and sending him back to the capital to confront his accusers, but his opponent had well-placed supporters while the patience of courtiers was wearing thin with ʿAli Muttaqi's stint as "Enforcer of the Shariʿa."

Eventually, the Shattari Sufis won this confrontation through attrition. ʿAli Muttaqi, the strongest theological mind from among Muhammad Ghawth's detractors, left Gujarat never to return. Muhammad Ghawth came back to Ahmedabad, and the remaining scholars and Sufis who had opposed him accepted his dissimulation as he restated that his ascension was a dream vision rather than a bodily experience. Muhammad Ghawth made Gujarat into a stronghold of the Shattari Order. He raised funds to build a monumental mosque in the quarter just inside the gateway of Sārangpūr Darwāza in Ahmedabad's walled city.[45]

His disciple Wajih al-Din ʿAlawi advocated Shattari teachings in his madrasa in the Shahpur quarter of Ahmedabad. Wajih al-Din would say, "Follow the external teachings of the Prophet like ʿAli Muttaqi, but embody the inward spirituality of the Prophet like my shaykh, Muhammad Ghawth!" Wajih al-Din's discourse shaped ʿAli Muttaqi's image in most hagiographies: few sources mention ʿAli Muttaqi's critique and persecution of Muhammad Ghawth directly. The lone exception was ʿAbd al-Haqq Dihlawi, who righted the image of ʿAli Muttaqi by rewriting his biography in both *Akhbār al-Akhyār* and *Zād al-Muttaqīn*.

ʿAli Muttaqi's confrontation with Muhammad Ghawth reverberates in the present since the Shattari leader's reputation is hotly debated among scholars today. The historian Azfar Moin and the literary scholar Aditya Behl offer differing assessments. Azfar Moin seems to have accepted ʿAli Muttaqi's critique without examining the subtle theological debate that shaped it. Moin's assessment is broad and stereotyped, not based on reading of Sufi literature and Islamic theology about sainthood and its social manifestations. Moin depicts Shattari Sufis as ambitious and powerful magicians, masking this judgment with the technical term "thaumaturge." He does not analyze the literature they produced, which was deeply immersed in Islamic theology, Qurʾan interpretation, and Sufi ritual; he is interested, after all, in how Mughal rulers exercised power by interacting with sacred power—whether sacred power took the form of Islamic rituals, Sufi practices, magical performances, or occult beliefs. Moin notes correctly that most Mughal chronicles present the Shattari Sufis as charlatans dabbling in sorcery and trickery for thinly veiled political ambitions. He looks at the world through the lens of Mughal rulers and is not interested in Sufi leaders and their communities per se. Inverting this perspective, this book focuses primarily on Sufi leaders who built the Muttaqi community and its reformist ideals, while their interaction with rulers (the sultans of Gujarat and later the Mughals) is important but secondary. Moin strives to balance information drawn from Sufi writings—theological, ethical, and hagiographic—with information from historical chronicles that were produced in royal courts.

Azfar Moin's assessment of Shattari Sufis, in particular Muhammad Ghawth and his brother Shaykh Bahlul, is skewed because the Mughal sources he relies upon are skewed. Babur's family members held traditional allegiance to the Naqshbandi Order and so were suspicious of the Shattari leaders; they favored importing Naqshbandi advisors from Central Asia rather than relying on South Asian Sufis from the Shattari, Chishti, or Suhrawardi Orders, as revealed in sources written by Humayun's half-siblings Gulbadan Begum and Mirza Hindal. Yet Babur, and Humayun after him, depended upon Shattari leaders to help stabilize their precarious rule: "The last entry in Babur's annalistic account of his life, made a few months before his death, recorded that he received a visit from Shaykh Muhammad Ghawth Shattari. . . . In their South Asian territories, they [early Mughal rulers] began by collaborating with local influential Sufis such as Muhammad Ghawth and his older brother, Shaykh Phul [Bahlul], in order to establish themselves in the local political and moral economy."[46] However, Humayun's son Akbar (ruled 1556–1605) consolidated Mughal imperial power. Sources from Akbar's mature years dismiss the Shattari leaders.[47] We can date Akbar's maturity to the period after 1570 as he consolidated his personal power over against his Mughal relatives, built his new imperial capital at Fatehpur Sikri, and conquered Gujarat to solidify his empire's commercial prosperity and fiscal viability. By that time, the Shattari leaders' usefulness had dissipated because Mughal rule was firmly established and imperial authority was centralized in the person of the emperor. For this reason, Moin rightly observes that "when Akbar's chronicles were written in the 1590s, the political and spiritual landscape had changed so much that the Shattari brothers [Muhammad Ghawth and Shaykh Bahlul] were given but brief mentions and ridiculed as magicians and sellers of sainthood."[48]

After 1570, Akbar was above relying on any living saint from the Shattari or any other Sufi order. Azfar Moin internalized the dismissive judgment of voluminous Mughal sources of a later period; in contrast, he notes a few sources written by Babur's or Humayun's circle that present respectful deference for the Shattari leaders, but he does not consider them realistic portrayals of a dynamic, innovative, and complex Sufi community.[49] Furthermore, Moin speculates that the Shattari leaders, as "aspiring holy men," built their Sufi community on millenarian models (like Sayyid Muhammad Jawnpuri) or legendary martyred warriors (like Salar Masʿud Ghazi), but this not plausible.[50] The Shattari leaders took as their model the founder of their order, ʿAbdallah Shattar, and their immediate Sufi master, Ḥajjī Ḥamīd Ẓuhūr al-Ḥaqq; in the remote past, all of these Shattari Sufis saw the paradigmatic mystic Bayazid Bistami as their exemplar both in their ideology of ecstatic love and their charismatic chain of initiation. Shattari Sufis in Gujarat discouraged persecution of the Mahdawis, but this followed from their theological stance of accepting all religions as manifestations of the divine and their policy of minority protection, for they had survived persecution themselves.

In contrast to the historian Moin, the literary scholar Aditya Behl upholds Shattari Sufis as paragons of composite culture and religious syncretism in South Asia. He positions Muhammad Ghawth's community as a useful countercurrent to contemporary Hindu Nationalist politics and Islamic fundamentalism. As a literary scholar, he translated the popular romantic epic infused with love mysticism *Madhumālatī*, composed in 1545 by Mīr Sayyid Manjhan, a poet and disciple of Shaykh Muhammad Ghawth.[51] This poem was both cosmopolitan and vernacular, with Sufi symbolism expressed through Hindu imagery, in a dialect of Hindi written in Persian script. This genre blossomed in the fifteenth and sixteenth centuries, cultivated by poets belonging to communities as varied as the Chishti and Suhrawardi Orders and also the Mahdawi movement. The finest example of this genre is by the Shattari Shaykh Manjhan. Behl masterfully translated this poetry to challenge identity politics of the contemporary world; however, he does not assess how controversial the Shattari Sufis were in their own era.[52] This book does just this by revealing how they clashed with ʿAli Muttaqi's program for reformist Sufism.

Millennialism: Expecting the Mahdi

While ʿAli Muttaqi confronted the Shattari Order, another storm loomed on the horizon in Gujarat; it was not an atmospheric storm at sea but rather a psychological storm across the land. The final century of the first Islamic millennium began with restless expectation that the Muslim community would experience radical change. Past compromises and established authorities might be abandoned if the Mahdi appeared to usher in the "End of Time" as the Islamic calendar careened toward its 1,000-year mark. ʿAli Muttaqi opposed the Mahdawi followers of Sayyid Muhammad Jawnpuri, who announced that he was the expected Mahdi of the last days.

ʿAli Muttaqi critiqued the Shattari Order vehemently, but he denounced the Mahdawi movement violently. The Shattari Order was new to South Asia and innovative in its teachings, but it competed with other Sufi orders in a shared field of familiar concepts, terms, and techniques. In contrast, the Mahdawi movement grew out of Sufi communities and took on the more complex role of social reform and radical millenarianism.[53] ʿAli Muttaqi opposed the Shattari Order as an outsider, with clearly divergent political loyalties. However, his relationship to the Mahdawi movement was more complicated. As a young man, ʿAli Muttaqi was involved with the movement to some extent, and his aspiration to become a saint emerged only as he grew disenchanted with the Mahdawi movement. Interestingly, he opposed the Mahdawis without acknowledging his early experience with them.

In many ways, Mahdawi theological assertions were more complex than those of the Shattaris. Sayyid Muhammad Jawnpuri claimed to have a unique and absolutely transcendent connection to the divine and to be "the Mahdi of the End of Time," which implied that he knew the true interpretation of the Qur'an intuitively. This authority meant that he was qualified to decide legal matters beyond the historically developed structure of the four Sunni schools of law. In a debate with legal scholars, Sayyid Muhammad was reported to have said, "Taken in a wider sense my religion is identical with that of God, while from the point of view of adhering to a legal authority [*taqlīd*] I follow the religion of the Prophet and obey the Qur'an. As the Prophet Muhammad was deputed to prohibit idolatry [*aṣnām*], my mission is to reject materialism [*ajsām*].[54] I come to remove the differences among the various schools of Muslim jurisprudence: had the great masters of the juridical schools been my contemporaries, they would have followed only my exposition of the truth of God."[55] In Mahdawi theology, Sayyid Muhammad was not just one saint among many; he was a saint beyond sainthood whose spirituality matched the Prophet Muhammad's, action for action and attitude for attitude. He was the "seal of sainthood based on the paradigm of Muhammad" (*khātam-e wilāyat-e Muḥammadī*).[56] The Shattari leader, Muhammad Ghawth, implied that his transcendent connection to God overshadowed the routine and historically bound norms of the *shariʿa*. In contrast, the Mahdawi leader, Sayyid Muhammad, claimed that his transcendent authority revived the *shariʿa* as practiced by the Prophet.

In accord with this transcendent leap to a higher authority, Sayyid Muhammad insisted that Islamic society must make a radical break with the past and begin anew. This radical break would begin when Muslims testified to their faith that Sayyid Muhammad was the promised Mahdi of the End of Time. Believers in him would separate from Muslim society, as it had existed in incomplete and compromised form, and would be inducted into a new, liminal community that would revive Islamic society from within. Having made this fundamental break, the Mahdawis were acute social critics; they claimed that religious scholars and Sufis were morally bankrupt, implying that political rulers of their time were illegitimate.

How did Sayyid Muhammad make his radical transcendent claim to authority from God? Mahdawi sources relate that Sayyid Muhammad began his life as a Chishti Sufi. During his training, he met Khidr, who taught him the method of silent and constant remembrance of God within each breath (*dhikr-e khafī*).[57] Sayyid Muhammad returned to his Chishti master with this new intensified form of meditative devotion. According to Mahdawi sources, his master confirmed that Sayyid Muhammad was specially chosen to propagate this *dhikr*, which the Prophet Muhammad had known but not vouchsafed to his followers, in expectation of transmitting it directly to the Mahdi.[58] Hearing this affirmation, Sayyid Muhammad taught this *dhikr* to his Sufi master in a dramatic reversal of traditional authority (that normally flowed from elders to younger disciples). This form of meditation became the center of Mahdawi devotional life. As a result of its constant practice, Sayyid Muhammad claimed to have purified his soul to the point that he could "see God through these worldly eyes." He taught his closest companions this *dhikr*, so that they, with steadfast practice, could also enjoy direct witness of God's presence in the world. Khidr embodied the metaphorical leap that allowed a vertical connection to God.

Sayyid Muhammad traveled through Gujarat's ports in 1494 and sailed to Mecca. He was convinced that his human attributes were absorbed into those of the Prophet Muhammad and that he witnessed God's presence with his worldly eyes. He officially declared his mission as the Mahdi at the Kaʿba in 1496 (the first year of the tenth Islamic century). Returning to Gujarat, he announced his mission publicly in 1500.[59] In response to his preaching, Gujarati nobles joined his community, including ministers such as Iʿtimād Khān and Shēr Khān as well as the governor of Palanpur (Pālanpūr, a town 150 kilometers north of Ahmedabad on the strategic road to Rajasthan [Rājasthān]).[60] In addition, almost all of Ahmedabad's craftspeople were reported to be Mahdawis. Even Sultan Mahmud Begra's sisters, the princesses Rājī Sūn and Rājī Murādī, joined the movement.[61]

The sultan also wanted to hear Sayyid Muhammad, but his court ministers feared that his powerful oratory about the renunciation of wealth and worldly ambition would affect the sultan and ruin affairs of state; they schemed to prevent him from meeting the charismatic preacher.[62] If the princesses led the sultan to join the Mahdawi movement, it would have threatened to unbind the tight association of Muzaffar-Shahi royalty with Sufis and Sunni Islam, which was the basis of the sultanate of Gujarat. This tight bond is concretized in architectural stone carving: the dynastic motif of an oil lamp (Ar. *sirāj*; Gj. *diyā*) emitting tendrils of light and hanging by a chain, often from a solar lotus or flanked by a gateway (Gj. *torana*). This motif was carved into royal tombs both male and female, into mosques as both exterior decoration and interior sacred symbol, and into dargahs of Sufis who were loyal to the sultanate of Gujarat.

Some Sunni scholars thought Sayyid Muhammad Jawnpuri's teachings were heresy, and like the ministers of state, they were worried about the rapid spread of this devotional movement. When Sayyid Muhammad said, "I can show you the complete vision of God with the very eyes in your head," some scholars of Ahmedabad wrote a fatwa calling for his execution.[63] A learned scholar of his time, Muḥammad Tāj Ganj-e Shakarī, drafted this fatwa and sent it to a highly reputed Sufi, Ḥasan Muḥammad Chishtī (whose mosque is located near ʿAli Muttaqi's home at Shāhpūr Gate). The Chishti master reprimanded the scholar, "You spend your whole life studying religion, but all you can do with it is write a fatwa to execute a descendant of the Prophet?" Under censure, the scholar rescinded his order to execute Sayyid Muhammad.[64]

Scholars and Sufis in Ahmedabad received Sayyid Muhammad with great ambivalence. Shaykh Jī Bukhārī examined Sayyid Muhammad and pronounced, "He's certainly a great man and a master of high spiritual states, however he exclaimed to the masses some lofty expressions understood only by the special saintly few, and does not respect the general rule of the hadith: speak to each person according to his level of understanding."[65] Another Sufi, Shāh Chālinda, interviewed the Sayyid and declared, "He is a complete Sufi and spiritually very lofty, but in a state of spiritual intoxication he says things that will cause dissent in our religion [*fitna*] and cause to be shed much innocent blood."[66]

The young ʿAli Muttaqi never met Sayyid Muhammad Jawnpuri, but he witnessed the later growth of the movement and subsequent shedding of "much innocent blood." Sayyid Muhammad died in 1505, after having left Gujarat to pursue his mission in Sindh and Afghanistan. While he preached in Ahmedabad, attracting followers who believed he was the promised Mahdi and sparking reactions from scholars and Sufis alike, ʿAli Muttaqi was growing up in Mandu and Burhanpur. When ʿAli Muttaqi renounced worldly life and came to Gujarat, he encountered the followers of the Mahdi at the height of their zeal. This was the time when Sayyid Muhammad's son Sayyid Maḥmūd and his closest companion, Sayyid Khundamīr, were setting up renunciant communities that were called Mahdawi circles (*da'ira*) in Gujarat.

As he wandered through Gujarat in his youth, ʿAli Muttaqi held discussions with Mahdawis and may even have joined a *da'ira* for some time. He wrote, "I have engaged these followers of 'the Mahdi' in discussion and sat with them for a long time, for in my youth I was attracted to their claims and desired to learn from them."[67] Contemporary leaders of the Mahdawi community assert that ʿAli Muttaqi had joined the *da'ira* of Shāh Dilāwar (d. 1538).[68] Some of ʿAli Muttaqi's extended family joined the movement. In any case, ʿAli Muttaqi admired their extreme renunciation and complete reliance on God's provision (*tawakkul*), for this mirrored his own personal state of devotion at the time. Their discourse of reviving the *shariʿa* through heightened ethical behavior may have inspired him as well.

While he respected Mahdawis' ideals and ethics, ʿAli Muttaqi harbored suspicions about their theology. From the point of view of faith and reason, could Sayyid Muhammad actually be the promised Mahdi? His followers practiced a pared-down spiritual discipline and intense commitment to virtue that ʿAli Muttaqi appreciated, but were these valid if rooted in a theology based on untenable claims about their leader? Could he really have the same spiritual character as the Prophet Muhammad, as the Mahdawis upheld? Was it true that his every action was inerrant and his every word the true interpretation of the Qur'an? When ʿAli Muttaqi became a disciple of Husam al-Din Muttaqi in Multan, the scholarly Sufi gave him a new perspective on these troubling questions. His training in the texts of al-Ghazali made ʿAli Muttaqi feel that Sufi devotion had to be tempered to uphold the worldview of the Sunni community. The goal of Sufi training was not just inward illumination or heroic virtue; these were good only when fused to the wider goal of maintaining social order. In Husam al-Din's teaching that was based on the thoughts of al-Ghazali, authentic Sufi practice led to legal rectitude, obeying civic authority, and avoiding any act or expression that might go beyond the bounds of the Prophet's discrete and historical legacy. In striving to absorb and master these teachings, ʿAli Muttaqi entertained deeper doubts about the Mahdawi movement. He questioned whether the *shariʿa* could be revived through an absolute chiliastic social critique like that which the Mahdawis leveled against the institutions of Islamic society.

Returning to Gujarat after his two-year stay in Multan, ʿAli Muttaqi witnessed the social strife precipitated by the Mahdawi movement's rapid growth, sparking political and religious resistance. Amid such discord, he wondered whether the Mahdawi community could ever transform the whole Islamic society from within, as was members' idealistic goal. Mahdawi leaders increasingly denounced those who opposed them; in order to highlight the need for followers of the Mahdi to make a complete break with the surrounding society, some Mahdawi leaders began to label as infidels (*kāfir*), rather than true Muslims, those who did not accept Sayyid Muhammad's claim. Sayyid Mahmud became the Mahdawi leader after the death of his father, Sayyid Muhammad Jawnpuri; he settled at Rādhanpūr (a town 160 kilometers from Ahmedabad, near Patan on the strategic road to Sindh) to preach that his father was the promised Mahdi and that only those who believed in him were real Muslims. Once his claims became well known, Sunni scholars there sent complaints to the sultan of the time, Mahmud Begra.[69] They alleged that Sayyid Mahmud was spreading propaganda by calling Muslims "infidels," while many people were heeding his call. They alleged, "It is therefore necessary for the ruler to suppress him and put down this religious disturbance; otherwise, many people will turn to him and be misled into heresy."[70]

In 1513, Sultan Mahmud Begra ordered Sayyid Mahmud to be incarcerated in Ahmedabad. Some Mahdawi leaders wanted to meet this persecution with force: Sayyid Khundamir visited Sayyid Mahmud twice in prison and said, "If you give us permission, we will break open the prison and rescue you!" He refused and ordered his colleagues to do everything that was legal in the *shariʿa* to secure his own release. This proved more effective. The sultan's sisters, who were Mahdawi followers, staged disruptive lamentation in the palace courtyard, keeping a hunger strike while petitioning for his release. After forty days, the sultan released him and sent him by royal palanquin back to his *da'ira*. However, Sayyid Mahmud died soon after of gangrene from the chain wounds on his ankles.[71]

Despite pressure upon him from members of his family and some nobles, Sultan Mahmud Begra moved to suppress the Mahdawi movement. He might have been threatened by the movement's spread beyond the common people into the ranks of soldiery and nobility. Sayyid Muhammad Jawnpuri had made no overtly political claims and insisted that his teachings were purely spiritual, yet the discourse generated by the term "Mahdi" was implicitly rebellious. According to hadith reports, the Mahdi's title would be "the representative of God on earth" (*khalīfat allāh*). This had been the title of the first leaders of the Muslim community after the death of the Prophet, who were military and governmental rulers. From the sultan's point of view, any popular movement centered on a Mahdi sounded like rebellion against the legitimacy of his own rule.

It is not certain whether ʿAli Muttaqi was in Ahmedabad during the crisis of Sayyid Mahmud's incarceration. He was surely present a decade later when violence escalated between the Mahdawis and the military forces of the new sultan, Muzaffar Shah II (reigned 1511–26). The new sultan harassed the Mahdawi *da'iras* more vigorously to suppress their proselytizing. The next leader of the movement, Sayyid Khundamir, had to move his *da'ira* as many as twenty times to avoid persecution. In the days of Sayyid Muhammad Jawnpuri, the Mahdawis had considered it a virtue to suffer exile and accepted harassment with nonviolent resignation. However, this resolve eroded under generations of oppression. Sayyid Khundamir advocated taking up arms to protect their communities from assault. Once Sayyid Mahmud died as a martyr from his prison wounds, Sayyid Khundamir resorted to violence. In the eyes of the sultan, this tactic confirmed that the Mahdawi movement posed a political threat. In 1524, the governor of Patan, ʿAyn al-Mulk, led military forces against the *da'ira* of Sayyid Khundamir, who fought for two days until martyred.[72] This marked a low point for the fortunes of the Mahdawis in Gujarat, and Sayyid Khundamir's descendants fled to outlying principalities like Palanpur and Jalore (Jālōr), which mark the border between Gujarat and Rajasthan.

ʿAli Muttaqi witnessed violence erupt over the question of whether or not Sayyid Muhammad was the promised Mahdi. He saw how a delicate theological point about sainthood became the kernel of a social movement that could rip the fabric of society. He tried to ascertain the truth of the theological matter to answer his doubts about this social strife. He consulted all the reputable scholars in Gujarat and North India, asking for an authoritative statement as to whether Sayyid Muhammad could be the Mahdi, but he found no reliable answer.[73] He decided to investigate the matter himself, using all the resources of hadith scholarship and Sufi literature at his disposal. He soon became an inveterate enemy of the Mahdawi movement and its most dogged critic.

Once sympathetic to the Mahdawi cause, ʿAli Muttaqi turned acrid critic. He thought Mahdawi followers betrayed their own saintly exemplar, Sayyid Muhammad Jawnpuri, by insisting that he was the Mahdi and that only his followers were true Muslims. He pursued his inquiry into the Mahdawi movement while resident in Ahmedabad during the reign of Bahadur Shah. As advisor to the sultan, he thought that the welfare of the realm depended on the stability of the state and that the Mahdawis weakened society from within while external forces had begun to erode the state from without. Portuguese disruption of trade and pilgrimage routes between Gujarat and the Red Sea ports made up a major external force.

During Bahadur Shah's reign, the conflict between the Gujarat state and the Portuguese had reached the level where the sultan began to use jihad rhetoric: in 1527–28, a Portuguese ship ran aground near Bharoch, and the sultan's forces forced the crew to "accept Islam" or face execution. Despite his rhetoric, Bahadur Shah slowly conceded to Portuguese demands and signed two separate peace treaties acknowledging the Portuguese presence in the Indian Ocean basin (in 1534 and the following year). While naval power and statecraft could restrain Portuguese threats, ʿAli Muttaqi felt that it was up to religious authorities to suppress the internal threat represented by the Mahdawi movement.

Mahdawi sources tell a different story: ʿAli Muttaqi turned against Mahdawis out of malice and spite. Present-day Mahdawis relate that ʿAli Muttaqi had joined the *da'ira* of Shah Dilawar, who established *da'iras* in Ahmedabad, Patan, and Maharashtra, eventually becoming the fifth leader of the movement. According to these narratives, ʿAli Muttaqi betrayed the Mahdawis because he could not live up to their ascetic ethic of masculinity. Mahdawi preachers used to use the metaphor of "being a real man and not an impotent eunuch" to encourage followers to renounce the world.[74] They were fond of quoting a Prophetic hadith: "The real man is he who renounces the world; all other alleged men are really impotent." This rhetoric justified why Mahdawis refused to pray in congregations led by a non-Mahdawi: a "eunuch" was legally banned from leading communal prayers, and any Muslim who had not "renounced the world" by becoming a follower of the Mahdi was not a real man. A dramatic example of this discourse is found in the speeches of Miyān Muṣṭafā Gujarātī, a Mahdawi scholar who debated with the religious authorities in Emperor Akbar's court.[75]

> The emperor asked me, "Shaykh Mustafa, these scholars and jurists are devout and pious people who guide the people of my realms in their religious affairs, yet you openly refuse to pray behind them under their leadership. Why is that?" I answered him, "The Prophet is reported to have said that the man who seeks after the enjoyable things of this world is an impotent, false man, while the man who seeks after God alone is a real man. . . . Real men renounce the world to engage in regular prayers and remembrance of God at all times without letting anything else distract them. They listen to the explanation of the Qur'an and act according to its guidance. These are real men. All other men are impotent, false men. I ask the emperor to be just! Ask your court scholars to produce a commandment from the examples of the Prophet or the decisions of the jurists that require a real man to pray behind the leadership of an impotent man. To the contrary, many books contain eloquent arguments forbidding a eunuch from leading congregational prayers! For this very reason, I refused to recite my prayers behind the leadership of your court scholars, in the midst of a congregation led by an impotent pretender

> to manhood." The emperor burst out laughing and told me, "You have spoken the truth about them!" Then he turned to the scholars and said, "Shaykh Mustafa did not recite his prayers under your leadership because you are false men, as if you were impotent!"[76]

Present-day Mahdawi leaders narrate that ʿAli Muttaqi heard such a discourse about being a "real man," such that only a potent patriarchal man can lead communal prayers. Being at heart a dry and literalist scholar, ʿAli Muttaqi understood the preacher to be speaking of physical rather than spiritual impotence. He was filled with bitterness because he was actually physically impotent and could never achieve respect and leadership in the Mahdawi community. For this reason, say Mahdawi leaders, he turned against the community as its most bitter foe.[77]

This story is not corroborated by documentary evidence, but it may represent oral lore from the Mahdawi community dating back to the sixteenth century. Mahdawis in ʿAli Muttaqi's era generated such stories to refute their once-sympathetic critic. It was easy to dismiss an opponent with the accusation that he was a "false man" (*nā mard*)—in a patriarchal context, that term covers diverse meanings without specificity, including the descriptions of impotent, effeminate, cowardly, or lazy and the labels of hermaphrodite or eunuch. Yet, like all derogatory terms, it could be inverted. In Ahmedabad, there was a Chishti Sufi named Musa who embraced effeminacy so firmly that "she" dressed in women's clothes and became known as God's "Eternal Auspicious Wife" (Gj. Sadā Sohāg).[78]

When Ahmedabad's scholars criticized her, she retorted that because they harbored worldly ambitions they were not "real men," whereas she—who dressed and acted like a woman—was a "real man" because she cultivated inner virtue. When a drought plagued Gujarat, the ruler and scholars turned to her to lead them in prayer, and her supplications were answered with rain, securing her popular acclaim. Her tomb in Ahmedabad is a popular shrine for cisgender women who desire a blessed marriage and children.[79]

Among Muslims in Gujarat, masculinity was a contested term and a key component of social capital. Was ʿAli Muttaqi impotent or effeminate or made a eunuch? His biography relates that he married in Gujarat and sired a son. In addition, ʿAli Muttaqi recorded in an epistle that he had to thank God that he was created as a potent and masculine male, not like others who were created as effeminate men, impotent men, hermaphrodites, or eunuchs.[80] There are families in Mecca who claim to be descended from ʿAli Muttaqi up to the present.[81]

After arriving in Mecca, ʿAli Muttaqi researched whether Sayyid Muhammad Jawnpuri could be the promised Mahdi. He circulated a request for a judicial decision (*istiftāʾ*) about whether this was possible within the limits of scriptural sources:

> What decision do the most prominent scholars of the various schools of law and the most learned of the Muslims pronounce about a party of people who believe that a certain man (who was born in North India and died at the age of about forty years) is the Promised Mahdi of the End of Time and who declare that anyone who dies not believing in this deceased "supposed Mahdi" is therefore an infidel? Furthermore, what legal ruling should be applied to such people who deny that the Promised Mahdi will come [in the future]? I humbly ask for your fatwa in this matter, may God be content with you.[82]

The wording of this request reveals that ʿAli Muttaqi had already decided, while in the company of the hadith students of Ibn Hajar al-Haythami in Mecca, that Mahdawi doctrines were unacceptable. Al-Haythami wrote against the Mahdawis (although he used this term in a loose way to indicate all who questioned Sunni consensus, including the Shiʿa).[83] In his small treatise "A Concise Statement on the Signs of the Promised Mahdi," he notes that "there is a grave need for the Muslims to understand the correct signs of the Mahdi in these early days [of the tenth Islamic century]," when eschatological expectations were running high and impostors found fertile ground in the popular imagination.[84]

Al-Haythami gave ʿAli Muttaqi a treatise by al-Suyuti, titled "The Disclosure Open and Clear That This Muslim Community Will Not End at Its One-Thousandth Year."[85] The famous Egyptian hadith master refuted another scholar who claimed that the world would end at the year 1591 (AH 1000). The scholar circulated this pamphlet in 1495, at the advent of the tenth Islamic century, claiming that within the coming century the Mahdi would appear, Jesus would manifest, and Judgment Day would dawn; he based these claims on a hadith reporting that Muhammad would remain in his grave for only 1,000 years and wrote a fatwa declaring the alleged hadith authentic. Al-Suyuti noted that this fatwa circulated widely in the last years of the ninth Islamic century, inciting anxiety among the people such that those who refuted it were shouted down.[86] Al-Suyuti endeavored to prove the premise false by gathering the hadith about the advent of the Mahdi and signs of the End of Time into one book.[87] These two works, by the most esteemed hadith scholars of their generation, laid ʿAli Muttaqi's doubts to rest.

ʿAli Muttaqi's request for a fatwa was not a naive question but rather a strategy to critique and oppose the Mahdawi movement in Gujarat and wider South Asia. He sent his query to jurists of each school of law in Mecca and

Medina, so that his opponents could not evade their decisions by claiming that they represented only one section of the Sunni community. Al-Haythami was not just the leading hadith scholar but also an esteemed jurist of the Shafiʿī school; he provided the leading decision answering the query of ʿAli Muttaqi. He wrote,

> The doctrines of this sect are invalid and abominable, while their ignorance is clear and their heresy is admonishable. Their heresy poses the threat of absolute misguidance for others. Their doctrines are invalid since they contradict the clear statements of the hadith reports that are considered utterly reliable and widely confirmed [*al-aḥādīth al-mustayqana al-mutawātira*]. . . . Their obstinacy in following these doctrines and luring others to believe them, even after they were shown the authentic hadith, shows their ignorance of the Prophet's example and necessitates their refutation. . . . Furthermore, this doctrine leads them to denounce those scholars who oppose them and accuse them of being infidels. . . . One who calls a Muslim an infidel because of his adherence to his faith is himself an infidel who should be punished with exemplary punishment, if he does not repent and renounce these beliefs with a renewal of his submission to Islam. . . . Whoever misleads the Muslim community to accept invalid doctrines is an infidel. Because these sectarians act according to these criteria, they are to be considered disbelievers and rejected as renegades from the community of believers. Therefore, it is incumbent on the ruler—may God aid him with the justice of his sword in enforcing true religious doctrines and exterminating such heretics along with the infidels and corrupt sinners—to enforce those punishments that I have mentioned above upon these sectarians to nullify their rulings and erase their baseless claims. The leader should gradually intensify different kinds of punishment until they return to the truth and show sincere repentance. This is necessary and justified since they reject the *shariʿa* at its very source. This is infidelity and apostasy which requires them to be punished. They should be executed for repudiating the *shariʿa*, since this is nothing but an attempt to mislead the Islamic community. . . . That requires the ruler to restrain them with threats and to suppress them in any way the ruler deems appropriate to the gravity of their crimes, the awfulness of their hidden intentions, and the corruption of their doctrines. The ruler may choose between imprisonment, slapping, beating, or any other form punishment that will induce them to leave their foul practices.[88]

The other decisions—from the Mālikī, Ḥanafī, and Ḥanbalī schools of law—are more condensed than that of al-Haythami. The four decisions given in this fatwa range in tone from academic to polemic, while offering judgments skeptical of the Mahdawis' claims or harshly condemning them.[89] They move quickly from denouncing the Mahdawis' act of declaring other Muslims to be infidels to the need to punish them until they return to "the Sunni majority." The collection of these decisions, preceded by ʿAli Muttaqi's query, circulated in Gujarat and North India by 1543, exactly fifty years (according to the Islamic lunar calendar) before the millennium was due to occur.[90]

This fatwa was nonbinding. Its decisions could be used by scholars, Sufis, or nobles to petition rulers to punish Mahdawis but were not binding upon Mahdawis themselves. Mahdawi leaders proclaimed they did not adhere to decisions of the four Sunni schools, so ʿAli Muttaqi did not rely on *fiqh* (jurisprudence) but rather leveled a critique from the more basic foundation of hadith reports. If hadith reports describing the Mahdi could be proven to contradict facts and events in the life of Sayyid Muhammad Jawnpuri, ʿAli Muttaqi thought that he could oppose the movement at its source. He composed "The Ultimate Proof about the Signs of the Mahdi of the End of Time."[91] He appended to this text his query and the legal decisions it solicited, and he circulated the document in South Asia.

In this text, ʿAli Muttaqi refined a genre of hadith studies that had been growing for many generations and was focused on the question of the Mahdi. In such treatises, one can see scholars responding to increasing popular expectation of the Mahdi. This genre began with a standard "forty hadith" collection with reports pertaining to the Mahdi. Under pressure of public anxiety that the tenth Islamic century was about to commence, al-Suyuti expanded this text by adding other hadith reports; his more comprehensive collection was titled "Essence of Rose Distilled from Reports of the Mahdi."[92] Al-Haythami refined this genre in a different way: rather than create a more comprehensive collection, he wove the hadith reports into a narrative. His "Concise Statement on the Signs of the Promised Mahdi" records all the events that will transpire between the Mahdi and his eschatological opponent, the Dajjāl or "the Misleader," in a narrative that tells of future events.[93] ʿAli Muttaqi combined these two strategies to further refine the genre. He included more hadith reports and arranged them into a narrative that synthesized the discrete reports and portrayed the personality of the Mahdi.[94]

The titles of these works reveal the increasing sharpness of the rhetoric that underlies their composition. The earliest collections were simply samplers with generic titles, like "Forty Hadith" or "A String of Pearls," and had no ideological underpinnings. At the advent of the tenth century AH, however, al-Suyuti referred to his work as "a distillation," as if he were trying to squeeze the singular essence of the Mahdi's personality from the disparate hadith reports collected together, as one would distill perfume from individual rose petals. Al-Haythami's title is much sharper; his "Concise Statement" makes a clear discursive pronouncement about the Mahdi's required actions. Finally, ʿAli Muttaqi himself surpassed them all with his work titled "The Ultimate Proof." He intended his arrangement of hadith to be so comprehensive and so narratively convincing that it would be the single criterion against which any person who claimed to be the Mahdi must be judged.

ʿAli Muttaqi presented all the hadith reports that depict the characteristics of the Mahdi. He argued that that any claimant had to fit all these descriptions rather than merely some of them. His underlying assertion was that each hadith was valid, even if it seemingly contradicted other hadith reports: each contributed to building up a composite picture of the future Mahdi. This methodology is similar to the way earlier hadith scholars treated the biography of the Prophet and constructed narratives of the Prophet's night journey and ascension.[95] They took collections of discordant hadith and forged them into a single, integral narrative. ʿAli Muttaqi tried to depict the Mahdi as a miraculous and heroic figure, projected into the far future, larger than life; his intent was to repudiate any living person who claimed to be the Mahdi. He perceived that Mahdist movements were fueled by the belief that the world was either at a cataclysmic end (millennialism) or at a point of historical rupture marking a new dispensation (millenarianism). To refute these ideas, he concluded his hadith collection with the two short treatises of al-Suyuti and al-Haythami asserting that Islamic society was not facing an imminent rupture.

ʿAli Muttaqi hoped the readers of "The Ultimate Proof" would conclude that the world was not about to end, nor was Islamic society about to spiral back to its beginning, opening up new direct access to divine guidance. Therefore, there was no need to identify the Mahdi as a living person and build a social movement around him. However, ʿAli Muttaqi still needed to explain why a person of high spiritual caliber like Sayyid Muhammad Jawnpuri had insisted on just the opposite. ʿAli Muttaqi argued that the sayyid's claim to be the Mahdi was a natural expression of his sainthood: when saints reach a certain closeness with God, they perceive themselves to be unerringly guided by God directly, as if they were "the Mahdi" in the literal meaning of the word. Yet this is only a transient stage, he argued, like a type of spiritual euphoria: "Many Sufi masters in the past have claimed to be the Promised Mahdi of the

End of Time, and people believed them because of their lofty spiritual states, even though their claims contradicted the discrete signs of the Mahdi stated in hadith reports. There must a reason for this phenomenon. It can only be properly understood by one who knows the spiritual states of saints who have gained that incredible intimacy with God."[96] ʿAli Muttaqi pointed out famous Sufi masters in the past who had claimed to be the Mahdi, persisted in this state for some time, and then recanted.[97]

> I have investigated their belief and attribute it to the fact that they are unaware of the crucial difference between a Prophet and a saint in all its many dimensions. . . . They are confused about the fact that only a Prophet is protected from erring [*maʿṣūm*], while a saint enjoys no such protection. The saint is still capable of error and straying, as long as he does not pass beyond a certain boundary into persistent and willful sinfulness. This is why saints can still occasionally be guilty of major sins, and infidels can claim a measure of saintly power. A Prophet is preserved from this ambiguity by divine protection. If anyone objects that Sayyid Muhammad [Jawnpuri] was so saintly that he could not persist in asserting in error that he was the Mahdi, then I answer that acknowledging one's error and the subsequent regret over his mistake is an internal matter that arises in a person's heart and does not necessarily have outward signs. How can we know for sure that this great saintly sayyid persisted in his claim up until the very last breath before he died, without ever acknowledging his error in his heart? It is impossible for anyone, even his closest followers, to comprehend what might be in his heart and conscience [in his last moments of life].

ʿAli Muttaqi blamed the sayyid's eldest son, Sayyid Mahmud, for building a doctrine around the claim that his father was the Mahdi. "The party [built by his followers] can bring forth no evidence to prove their doctrine sound. However, it can be said that Sayyid Muhammad was a complete saint, in whose spiritual disclosures an error occurred; this is called 'an errant disclosure' and it can happen even in the most complete and virtuous of saints."[98] ʿAli Muttaqi relieved Sayyid Muhammad from blame for the movement that his followers built. This contrasts with his strategy in critiquing the Shattaris, in which ʿAli Muttaqi focused on the leader of the movement while remaining more or less silent about his many followers.

ʿAli Muttaqi argued that identifying the Mahdi with a living person (*tashkhīṣ al-mahdī*) was unnecessary, heretical, and harmful. He maintained that the Mahdawi movement was heretical in asserting that the Mahdi had already come in the form of a person who did not fit the hadith descriptions of the Mahdi. By doing this, he asserted, they denied the real Mahdi who would come in the future. He referred to a hadith report, which the Mahdawis themselves had publicized, that declared that a person who did not believe in the promised Mahdi was an infidel. ʿAli Muttaqi alleged that the Mahdawis were harmful in accusing other Muslims of being infidels (*takfir*): "It suffices to prove the inauthenticity of their beliefs and hollowness of their claims that the Mahdawis have killed some scholars [who opposed them]. It is as if this quality were enough to demonstrate that they have no proof for their beliefs and to establish their inability to garner any legitimacy for their claims."[99]

ʿAli Muttaqi sent "The Ultimate Proof" to Gujarat, hoping that it would circulate widely, not just among the Sunni scholars but among the Mahdawis as well. He believed that once the Mahdawi leaders read his collection of hadith, they would recant. In order to expand its circulation, he composed various abridgments, mentioning only major reports and omitting chains of transmission (*isnad*) for easier comprehension by nonspecialists.[100] His Mahdawi opponents claimed that his Arabic text had a limited audience in South Asia and that many Mahdawis could not read it themselves. In answer to this critique, ʿAli Muttaqi (or some of his followers) translated these abridged texts into Persian for even wider circulation.

"The Ultimate Proof" was not as ultimate as ʿAli Muttaqi had hoped. By publicizing the relevant hadith reports about the Mahdi, he expected the Mahdawis would admit that they were mistaken, desist from building a sectarian community, and rejoin the Sunni majority. Rather, educated Mahdawis read his collection of hadith reports through the eyes of their already established faith in Sayyid Muhammad as the Mahdi. They accepted those reports that coincided with his life story as valid but rejected some reports as inauthentic or not relating to the promised Mahdi, while others they interpreted as confirming Sayyid Muhammad's mission. Furthermore, ʿAli Muttaqi's protest led some Mahdawi scholars to specify verses from the Qur'an that they claimed indicated the Mahdi and confirmed him to be Sayyid Muhammad.[101] In these ways, Mahdawi scholars deflected ʿAli Muttaqi's critique.

This incited the Sufi scholar to further hone his critique of the Mahdawis. ʿAli Muttaqi composed "Refutation of Those Who Judge That the Promised Mahdi Has Already Come and Gone" in Mecca in 1557–58 (thirty-five years before the impending millennium).[102] He refuted Mahdawi doctrine directly, having already exonerated Sayyid Muhammad Jawnpuri from blame. He accused the Mahdawis of "inauthentic religious change" (*bidʿa*) in juridical terms, based on the teachings of Ahmad Zarruq.[103]

The innovations of the Mahdawis are the worst kind of forbidden innovation, for they are doctrinal. The rulings of the *shariʿa* cover both the principles which are matters of belief and doctrine, and the details which are matters of practice and daily transactions. A forbidden change in the realm of belief is more harmful than a forbidden change in the realm of practice or daily affairs. One can only recognize a forbidden innovation in the realm of beliefs if one is competent in the study of Prophetic hadith, [in this case] those hadith reports which discuss the advent of the Mahdi. For this reason, it has been said, "Learned struggle (*ijtihād*) against those who advocate inauthentic changes in religious affairs (*mubtadiʿīn*) is superior to armed struggle against the infidels (*jihād*)." This is because everyone recognizes infidels by appearance and behavior; it is easy to avoid them and reject their contentions. However, innovators appear to be Muslims, even sound Muslims or saintly ones. Only those with deep knowledge of the Qurʾan and the Prophet's example can recognize them for what they are. For this reason, the ignorant people and the common masses believe in this party of innovators because they display outward signs of piety and rectitude like canonical prayers, fasting and retreating from society. The common people do not perceive that their outward actions depend on their inward actions, which are their beliefs and principles. If their inward beliefs and principles are sound, then all their outward actions will also be sound. If their inward beliefs and actions are tainted by forbidden innovations in religion, then all their outward actions will be void and hollow. This has come down through a saying of the Prophet: "God accepts from the heretical innovator not a single prayer or fast, not an act of charity or pilgrimage, not a righteous struggle nor expenditure of wealth, not a just act. He is extracted from the bounds of Islam just like a stray hair is pulled out of a ball of dough in which it does not belong." In this same vein, it has also been related that the Prophet said, "God refuses to accept any good deed of the heretical innovator until he quits his heresy."[104]

ʿAli Muttaqi presented a metaphor to further clarify this point. One's actions are like bricks of a building, while one's doctrinal beliefs are like the building's architectural plan. The plan of the building is not evident to the casual observer, yet the soundness of the building depends on it.

The discipline of construction has two aspects: principles and practices. The principles are the things that architectural engineers know about

> planning to erect a building, calculating any deviation from the right plan, and other subtle arts known only to engineers. The practices are known to the bricklayer who actually sets stone upon stone. The pay of the bricklayer is a few dirhams a day for his work; but the engineer is paid an amount fit for princes because of the power of his knowledge of the principles of architecture. This is because the building as an external edifice is dependent upon the calculations of its total plan which constitutes its inner structure. These plans are the realm of the engineers and architects, who alone determine if the final building will be sound or faulty. But the ignorant and common people do not understand this distinction in relation to this sect.[105]

In this simple allegory, ʿAli Muttaqi declared that Mahdawi doctrines were based on invalid principles of theological interpretation and also claimed for himself the authority to judge them invalid. They were mere bricklayers, while he was an architectural engineer. As a specialist—a Sufi master and hadith scholar fused into one—he was an engineer of religious authenticity who was able to make the "subtle calculations" that declared whether a doctrine was authentic or void.

With this allegory, he also explained why the Mahdawi community attracted a mass following in Gujarat. Mahdawis appeared to perform religious obligations and cultivate virtues, leading people to admire them as saints, yet their outward rectitude was based on faulty principles. He claimed that their outward piety was not based on an authentic sainthood that would support and sustain the whole Muslim community; rather, it was a deceitful display to lure people into their distinct sectarian community that would weaken the Sunni community through schism. For them, belief that Sayyid Muhammad Jawnpuri was the Mahdi served as the sole criterion for judging a Muslim's faith and sincerity.

> One may object that there is a hadith saying, "Whoever says the Mahdi is not true has indeed made himself an infidel," which necessitates that whoever denies the Mahdi is an infidel. The answer to this objection is simple. This hadith has come down to us in a single chain of narration [*ḥadīth al-āḥād*] and is therefore very weak. It cannot lead to certainty, but rather only to probable opinion. One cannot use it to declare another Muslim to be an infidel if he denies a certain man is the Mahdi. This hadith points to the necessity of believing that the Mahdi will certainly appear, not to the necessity of acknowledging a certain specific person

> as the Mahdi. Even if we accept this hadith as valid, it is clear that the Mahdi who must be believed in is the authentic person who fits the descriptions given in the hadith reports that specify his characteristics. Most of these signs are not found in this person [Sayyid Muhammad]. . . . It is necessary to declare the Mahdawis to be infidels since they believe this person to be the Mahdi and that no real Mahdi will come after him.[106]

ʿAli Muttaqi indirectly condemned the Mahdawis to exemplary punishment (whether it be forced recanting, exile, or execution). He laid the blame for such extremism at the feet of the Mahdawis themselves, alleging that they were the first to denounce other Muslims as infidels and to have killed some scholars for opposing them.

In the end, ʿAli Muttaqi offered another colorful illustration from everyday life to deflate the doctrinal claims of the Mahdawis. He stated that they were reviving Islam with a false Mahdi and countered by asking how such a priceless goal could be purchased with such worthless means.

> I have found no better illustration of these Mahdawis than the example of a man who takes a louse and ties a thread around its leg. He takes it in his hand and goes up to another man in the market and says, "Hey, you want to buy an elephant?" The other man asks him the cost, and he specifies an exorbitant price worthy of an elephant. The other man agrees to buy the elephant, and insists that he present the beast before he purchases it. The man opens his hand as says, "Here it is!" The other man asks him how he could possibly consider this louse to be an elephant. The man says triumphantly, "Don't you see it has a long snout?" Just like him, these Mahdawis are foolish! They see one detail—that Sayyid Muhammad is a descendant of the Prophet and is named Muhammad—and thus they conclude that he is the Mahdi![107]

The parody is not absurd, for there was a trade in elephants. Brought in by ship from wider Asian trade ports and unloaded at Diu and Surat, elephants were sold to the sultans of Gujarat who rode them as signs of royal authority.

The sharpened nib of ʿAli Muttaqi's pen was connected to the well-honed blade of Gujarat's sultan. When ʿAli Muttaqi became the "Enforcer of the Shariʿa" in the court of Sultan Mahmud Shah III, he intended to suppress the Mahdawis. Historical sources do not tell what measures he took to translate his scholarly critique into state persecution, but Mahdawi sources record that "ʿAli Muttaqi's enmity against our Mahdawi brothers grew to such an extreme

King of Cambay, miniature painting by an anonymous Portuguese artist in 1540, depicting Sultan Mahmud III of Gujarat. (Biblioteca Casanatense in Rome, ms. 1889 c. 43.)

that he returned to Gujarat to oppose them personally." This opposition consisted of "baiting them with snares," meaning that he publicly denounced their claims and challenged them to debate with hadith reports. The Mahdawis concluded that ʿAli Muttaqi's snares "were dissolved by God, like salt dissolves in water, and he was not able to achieve his goals."[108]

The struggle continued. After his return to Mecca, ʿAli Muttaqi wrote a letter to Mahmud Shah III in 1554, urging him to execute some Mahdawis. It is not clear what events precipitated this letter, but the sultan executed twenty-one Mahdawi men.[109] Just four months later, Mahmud Shah III suddenly died in strange circumstances, as we will see at the end of this chapter. Mahdawis erupted in joy. In the tense atmosphere of the time, they pictured his death as divine vengeance for these unjust executions.

Rivalry: The Mahdawis Write Back

Mahdawi scholars responded to threats of violence with the same pen that ʿAli Muttaqi had unleashed against them. ʿAli Muttaqi's "Refutation of Those Who Judge That the Promised Mahdi Has Already Come and Gone" ignited a war of words. A Mahdawi scholar in Gujarat, Miyān ʿAbd al-Mālik Sajāwandī (d. 1573), faced ʿAli Muttaqi's accusations squarely in the arena of hadith.[110] Miyan Sajawandi became a Mahdawi at the hand of Shah Dilawar, the Mahdawi leader whom ʿAli Muttaqi had likely known in his youth. The two scholars faced off in a duel of words whose stakes were life or death for Mahdawis confronting state persecution.

Miyan Sajawandi composed a line-by-line refutation of ʿAli Muttaqi's treatise, launching an exhaustive and sharp-witted counter-critique against his nemesis. He addressed the questions of what counts as scripture, how it applies to juridical decisions, and who has the authority to decide. Foundational to his counter-critique was ʿAli Muttaqi's authority in hadith (just as the Shattaris had questioned his authority in sainthood). Since hadith reports could not clinch an argument either way, Miyan Sajawandi concentrated on the heart of the matter: ʿAli Muttaqi's competency to judge others with hadith reports in the first instance.

According to this strategy, Miyan Sajawandi questioned ʿAli Muttaqi's skill in Arabic, which was the key to holding authority to cite, authenticate, and interpret hadith. His refutation bristles with exclamations like, "I don't know whether this egregious construction is a copyist's error or whether the shaykh [ʿAli Muttaqi] cannot compose in Arabic!" ʿAli Muttaqi had repeatedly alleged that the Mahdawis were uneducated and insisted that Sayyid Muhammad was the Mahdi because they were untrained in Arabic grammar, scriptural studies, and jurisprudence. Miyan Sajawandi replied that there were many scholars among the Mahdawi community, though none of them boasted arrogantly of their abilities as ʿAli Muttaqi did.[111]

Miyan Sajawandi attacked ʿAli Muttaqi's methodology of using hadith, accusing him of warping scholarly principles in the name of orthodoxy. ʿAli Muttaqi insisted that the Mahdi, when he appeared, would fulfill the description of every hadith report that referred to him. This proposition, Miyan Sajawandi countered, showed gross disregard for the very basic principles of hadith. He claimed that hadith specialists distinguished those reports that were fully reliable, because they were related by uninterrupted and multiple chains of transmitters, from those that were doubtful, because they were related by only one chain of transmitters, weak due to a problem in the chain of transmission, or plainly forged. Addressing an issue, hadith experts relied on a few strong reports and discarded the others because they were weaker and contradicted those that were strong. Jurists were even more judicious in their use of hadith reports to apply to questions of legal, ritual, or doctrinal norms, argued Miyan Sajawandi.

> The authoritative jurist (*mujtahid*) who is qualified to make decisions from scriptural sources never upholds all the reports relating to a particular topic, since the reports contradict each other. He upholds only a few reports which he feels are strongest and most directly applicable, and he bases his decision on the scriptural principle of these limited hadiths. He discards the rest as weak and inauthentic, or interprets them in accord with the stronger and more applicable hadith reports. There is no juridical topic in which *mujtahids* agree on the strongest reports. They differ in specifying the characteristics of the Mahdi, just as they differed on all other topics. So how can a reasonable person imagine that all the hadith about the Mahdi are equally valid and add up to a holistic picture of who the Mahdi will be? Such a conclusion contradicts reason![112]

Having critiqued methodological presumptions, Miyan Sajawandi turned to reports themselves. He observed that reports referring to the Mahdi contradicted each other and concluded that they were therefore invalid except for the few foundational points that emerged from the confluence of their meaning: that there will be a Mahdi, his name will be Muhammad, he will be descended from the Prophet's lineage, and he will revive religion as taught by the Prophet. Since Sayyid Muhammad Jawnpuri fulfilled these basic points upon which all hadith reports concurred, it was irrelevant that other details in the vast genre of hadith did not accord with his life story, because reports with weak chains of transmission led only to opinion (*ẓann*) rather than certainty (*qaṭʿ*).

In a coup de grace, Miyan Sajawandi asserted that hadith alone—however they were evaluated and interpreted—could not provide sure guidance in religious matters. Rather, guidance would come only in the person of the Mahdi himself. The Mahdi's appearance would make plain which hadith were true or false; only the Mahdi's actions would distinguish between authentic religious custom and heretical innovation (*bidʿa*).[113] Earlier jurists gave approximate answers, full of doubts and equivocations, but the Mahdi would fix their mistakes and certify their guidance. As for hadith, Miyan Sajawandi concluded, most of them were of uncertain authenticity. The final decision about their authenticity would be deferred until the Mahdi appeared; after that event, hadith that applied to him could be judged as having truly come from the Prophet, while the others should be discarded as falsified or weak.[114] Hadith reports could not fully confirm him, nor could they be used to denounce those who believed in him.

At the crux of his argument, Miyan Sajawandi asserted that the Mahdi's mission was like the Prophet's mission. The Prophet Muhammad's mission was not confirmed by any hadith reports. One believed in the Mahdi on account of his virtues, just as early Muslims believed in the Prophet. The virtues embodied by the Mahdi would mark him as one who followed and perfected the Prophet Muhammad's spirit, and these eclipsed hadith in the power to convince and ignite faith, argued Sajawandi.

> Sayyid Muhammad Jawnpuri's virtues require us to believe in his divine mission, just as virtue is the single element that requires us to believe in the divine mission of the Prophet. Only a religious leader's virtues cause one to repose belief and faith in him. Virtue is the underlying principle in belief. We affirm that the Mahdi's virtue alone establishes him as the Mahdi, just as all people of insight insist that the Prophet Muhammad's virtues are enough to establish the truth of his claim to be a Prophet bearing revelation. . . . Muhammad's prophethood is proven by his virtue and his total sincerity in claiming this mission for himself. His virtue alone is absolute proof of his divine election for this role, which cannot be shaken by any other criteria which may support other opinions. Everyone who met Sayyid Muhammad described him as having the most praiseworthy virtues and the noblest human qualities; this was as plain as sunlight at noon. His discourse has spread to the far horizons. All manner of people flocked to him to become his followers: the brave and cowardly, the learned and ignorant, the pious and corrupt, the generous and stingy. This is the essential meaning of the hadith that the Mahdi "will fill the earth with justice and righteousness." It means that he will fill the hearts of every kind of person in the world with a sense of justice and righteousness that negates all worship of self and oppression of others.[115]

With this stirring sermon, Miyan Sajawandi sealed his argument. Beginning with the virtue of grammar, he questioned ʿAli Muttaqi's scholarly authority. Finishing with the grammar of virtue, he proclaimed that Sayyid Muhammad's message inspired his followers to righteousness. Hadith reports were irrelevant in establishing and confirming that Sayyid Muhammad was the promised Mahdi, and they were insufficiently authentic to justify punishing Mahdawis in what was purely a matter of faith.[116]

Miyan Sajawandi's counter-critique circulated widely in Gujarat. Shortly after its composition, it reached ʿAli Muttaqi in Mecca. He quickly wrote a short rebuttal, dated 1560 and composed in Persian in order to contain the potential damage of Miyan Sajawandi's exacting refutation. Writing in a popular vein, he cited Persian poetry to convey his contentions. He wrote this rebuttal for his disciples and allies in South Asia so that they could better face the Mahdawis in debate.

> There is a universal rule that for two people to argue, they must agree on a common standard of evidence. If they have two different standards of proof, then what use is arguing? What benefit can come from argument if the ultimate standard of proof for one party is the Qurʾan and the Prophet's example, while other party asserts "my standard of proof is the word of Sayyid Muhammad Jawnpuri and I am not a specialist in hadith which I don't understand and regard as unimportant," without admitting that the advent of the Mahdi is established for certain by these very hadith? It is utter foolishness to engage such an opponent in dispute! As the poet Saʿdi has said—
>
> If he disregards the Qurʾan and hadith in full
> the way to answer him is to not answer at all.[117]

Despite this disclaimer, ʿAli Muttaqi rebutted Miyan Sajawandi on several key points. He first reestablished his own authority as an expert. He upheld the authority of his own teachers; he refuted the Mahdawi assertion that the Mahdi would come when there are no authoritative scholars (*mujtahidūn*) who are learned and pious enough to make binding judgments. ʿAli Muttaqi claimed that al-Suyuti was a *mujtahid* living in the time of Sayyid Muhammad Jawnpuri and that Abuʾl-Hasan al-Bakri was a *mujtahid* after him (indirectly claiming that he himself, as a pupil of al-Bakri, was also a contemporary *mujtahid*). He charged that Miyan Sajawandi did not know these famous hadith scholars since he was a provincial scholar in Gujarat, quoting the Arabic proverb, "What does a little fish who lives in a well know about the big wide ocean?"[118]

ʿAli Muttaqi clarified that his claiming to be an authoritative scholar in hadith was no arrogant boast, for hadith was not like jurisprudence. Each generation of hadith scholars was more learned than the prior one and made more exacting pronouncements based on past researchers. In contrast, jurists were limited by the decisions of past jurists and could only follow their lead. Later hadith compilations were more authentic than earlier ones by the very nature of the discipline. He noted that al-Suyuti's vast hadith collection, *Jamʿ al-Jawāmiʿ*, was the most authentic book used in Arab and Persian lands in ʿAli Muttaqi's era, yet it was written only one generation earlier, even correcting some errors in the six canonical collections.[119]

Likewise, ʿAli Muttaqi claimed that his collection of reports about the Mahdi was the most comprehensive and accurate statement on the subject. Since he was a leading scholar of his generation, the Mahdawis were obliged to accept his research findings despite Miyan Sajawandi's allegation that he included weak or falsified hadith reports; instead, they rejected his conclusion and ridiculed his methods. For this reason, he rebutted Miyan Sajawandi's "partisan partiality" on the relevance of hadith. "Miyan Sajawandi says that the Mahdawis do not make original scholarship in hadith, but rather follow the example of earlier scholars who were experts in the field. He asserts that people should not criticize them for clinging to some reports while disregarding others, for in doing this they only follow the example of earlier experts."[120] In rebuttal, ʿAli Muttaqi alleged that the Mahdawis did not follow hadith in good faith—they followed the words attributed to Sayyid Muhammad rather than the example of the Prophet Muhammad. They adhered to those few reports that supported Sayyid Muhammad's claim and rejected those that did not support it. Rather than exerting effort to understand hadith, which would be praiseworthy even if they came to wrong conclusions, they arbitrarily dismissed reports that were valid along with the hadith scholars who validated them: "When an expert appears who has researched this field, published his findings, and circulated a legal decision that anyone who follows this fabricated Mahdi and declares his denouncers to be infidels are themselves infidels, they simply refuse to accept the word of the expert."[121] Confronting a stalemate between the two parties, ʿAli Muttaqi used a two-pronged strategy. On the one hand, he invited the Mahdawis to recant by outlining the benefits of abandoning their project to build a sectarian community; on the other hand, he threatened consequences in the voice of a jurist pronouncing legal decisions.

To keep open the door of reconciliation, ʿAli Muttaqi admitted that Sayyid Muhammad made his claim to be the Mahdi in good faith. He simply had not known all the hadith reports that laid out the criteria for the advent of the Mahdi. These hadith reports had not yet been collected into one text and published widely in South Asia. If he had read ʿAli Muttaqi's own collection of reports, he would have never made such a claim. However, his followers persisted in pressing his claim after his death and made it the central principle of their sectarian community. "It would not lower Sayyid Muhammad's reputation as a saint one bit if they recanted, nor would it lower their own. Rather all the Muslims would further respect him and learn from his virtuous example and practice his pious discipline. . . . Yet it is firmly prohibited to build a sect around him stubbornly and to bind themselves to doctrines about his being the Mahdi."[122] Despite this invitation to recant, the Mahdawis held fast to their convictions.

Their radical break with the conventional Sunni community caused ʿAli Muttaqi to issue an ominous warning. In his view, the basic issue was *takfir*. In declaring fellow Muslims to be infidels, the Mahdawis crossed a red line.

> They declare any Muslim who does not follow their fabricated Mahdi to be an infidel. In their view, all the Muslims of Arabia, Persia, and beyond are infidels! By this act, they reveal themselves to be infidels of the worst kind and have made themselves liable to punishment, even death. God leads astray whom God wills. How strange it is that this group of weavers and ruffians, along with those who follow such uneducated Muslims, think themselves divinely guided and declare the saints and scholars of Arabia and Persia to be infidels! Such a strange belief must have a cause. It is none other than this: they decided among themselves to disregard the hadith reports in bad faith and declared themselves to follow only the sayings of Sayyid Muhammad.[123]

Earlier, ʿAli Muttaqi declared that the Mahdawis were infidels for their belief, but in this passage he warns that they are liable for execution. The violence in his forthright legal declaration was in reaction to Miyan Sajawandi's implied threats in *Sirāj al-Abṣār*. Refuting ʿAli Muttaqi's accusation that the Mahdawis assassinated scholars who opposed them, Miyan Sajawandi said that Mahdawis did not sanction the killing of scholars in general, but only the killing of scholars like ʿAli Muttaqi who urged the execution of Mahdawis.[124]

A new round of fatwas reinforced the juridical tone of ʿAli Muttaqi's rebuttal. These were appended to the text and circulated with it.[125] It is not clear whether ʿAli Muttaqi himself requested more strident legal decisions against the Mahdawis.[126] The request asks for the decision of scholars and jurists about the signs of the Mahdi's advent and for a ruling against one who claimed that Sayyid Muhammad was this promised Mahdi. In the end, the jurist states,

> If the heretical innovator persists in dismissing the one who denounces him, and if he presses others to join his heretical and corrupt practices, and if many people are tempted in their ignorance to adopt his invalid beliefs, then there will be great disruption in religious life and terrible corruption in worship. In this case, it is legally incumbent upon whoever has political authority to remove this corruption by overpowering him and punishing him publicly in such a way that will prevent corruption. When this heretical innovator was called before the sultan, the ruler

> forbade this heresy and declared that it must stop. Yet the heretic did not stop and was not punished. Therefore, the ruler must order the means to stop him with exemplary public punishment with whatever the ruler might deem suitable, whether beating and imprisonment, until he displays the signs of sincere repentance. This should be combined with public announcement of his punishment and forbidding others from these heretical beliefs until the lands of Islam have been rid of him and other heretics like him.[127]

Whether this fatwa was penned by ʿAli Muttaqi or simply sent to the sultan under his guidance, it appears to bear his seal of approval, since it was appended to ʿAli Muttaqi's text. From Mecca, he could appeal to the sultan of Gujarat, but in reality, only puppet sultans ruled after the death of Mahmud Shah III while rival nobles plotted and fought.

The Mahdawis resisted accusations of corruption and civic disturbance. They did not accept being scapegoated for the unrest that wracked Gujarat. In self-defense, they pointed out their own pious actions and virtuous qualities. Miyan Sajawandi heckled ʿAli Muttaqi, saying that even he—the Mahdawis' greatest detractor—admitted that they "seemed outwardly" to be pious, ascetic, and saintly people who upheld the ritual norms of the *shariʿa*.

Convergence: Mahdawi and Shattari Commonalities

Resistance by the Mahdawis forced ʿAli Muttaqi and his allies in Gujarat to specify the ways that Mahdawi doctrine translated into social corruption, since on the surface their doctrine seemed conducive to admirable piety. In a final work attributed to ʿAli Muttaqi addressing the Mahdawis, he expanded his critique to note how the theological issues raised by the Mahdawis converged with those raised by the Shattaris. In ʿAli Muttaqi's perception, these two distinct Islamic movements shared heretical elements that necessitated his strong denunciation.

This final text is "An Admonition to the Heedless to Avoid the Evil Path of Those Led Astray and Those Who Pledge Allegiance to Follow Them So That They Might Return to the True Guide, Muhammad."[128] It is an assemblage of texts collected into one treatise, including letters that claim to represent firsthand accounts of the Mahdawis' "sinful activities" in the *daʾira*. It combines social analyses with theological objections to reveal the link between their doctrines and social practices. One writer claimed that Mahdawi men and women mixed freely in the *da'ira*, for they stated they had renounced family and considered each other as "brother and sister." Another wrote that they rejected wage-earning work as an indirect way of begging for handouts, alleging that Mahdawis forbade their followers from working, which contravened the teachings of the Prophet.[129] In a more theoretical vein, they contended that constant *dhikr* cannot lead to "the vision of God in the world," as claimed by the Mahdawis.[130]

ʿAli Muttaqi appears to have collected others' accounts and allegations into one treatise, authoring the final section himself and giving the collection a title.[131] The "admonition" of the title is directed to leaders of the Sunni community, warning them to restrain people under their authority from heresy and misguidance that was rampant in the land. Everyone should take up the Qur'anic obligation to *enjoin what is known to be good and forbid what is deemed evil* (Qur'an 3:111). ʿAli Muttaqi exhorted his fellow Muslims, especially their leaders, "My dear fellows, fix the ring of servanthood in your ear, tie the belt of humility around your waist, and accept in the depths of your hearts the presence of the Lord of all creation. Hold yourself back from infidelity and rebellion, then call back your followers and the followers of your followers [from trespassing outside the accepted religious custom], so that you might be included in the ranks of those who find ultimate felicity."[132] ʿAli Muttaqi did not target the Mahdawis in particular, unlike the other contributors to this text. Rather, he broadened his critique to address all those who stepped outside the *shariʿa*. The specific examples that he gives show that he considered the Mahdawis to be one group within the purview of this warning, one group in a general category. He kept his address wide-ranging to include the Shattari Sufis and others rather than to continue his early intensive argument directly with the Mahdawis.

ʿAli Muttaqi declared that he did not oppose these movements out of enmity or spite, despite the accusations of his opponents. He critiqued them over a principle that he believed was violated by the Shattari Sufis and the Mahdawi movement: no vertical dimension of authority could be claimed directly from the divine that marginalized the historic traces of the Prophet Muhammad's personage as contained in scripture, elaborated in legal norms, and embodied in Sufi lineages. ʿAli Muttaqi thought that such a transcendental assertion threatened the historically validated forms of Islamic legitimacy.[133] The leader of each movement maintained that his spiritual authority rested on a unique intimacy with God that completed the socially observable model of the Prophet Muhammad. Moreover, these leaders achieved this special intimacy through their personal experiences, either through direct vision of God or through ascension to the throne of God, not through religious learning or socially legitimized channels of authority.

ʿAli Muttaqi felt that both the Shattari Order and the Mahdawi movement, whose saintly leaders made such transcendent claims, would efface the centrality of the Prophet Muhammad. In his assessment, any outward elements of Islamic piety in these movements camouflaged an interior inauthenticity, since their pivotal claim to authority rested on the absolutely transcendental personal experiences of their leaders. In his view, if followers of these movements appeared "Islamic," they were more dangerous. "An Admonition to the Heedless" was sent as a warning to religious and political leaders in Gujarat to avoid heretical movements, in which he juxtaposed critiques of the Mahdawis and Shattari Sufis. "Reliable witnesses relate that everyone who enters the Mahdawi fold, even those who have been corrupt and sinful, claim to achieve the vision of God with their worldly eyes. They say, 'Yes, I have seen God with these very eyes! I have traveled up into the heavens and have witnessed this level and that level!'"[134] This passage ostensibly critiques the Mahdawi claim that Sayyid Muhammad witnessed God with his physical eyes through his practice of continuous *dhikr* and, in turn, that his closest followers claimed that Mahdawis could achieve it as well through pious concentration. Direct vision of God certainly transcended knowing about God through the scriptural traces left behind by the Prophet Muhammad. Mahdawi scholars such as Miyan Sajawandi upheld the legitimacy of Mahdawi interpretation of the Qur'an on the grounds that followers of Sayyid Muhammad experienced guidance directly from God, through such transcendent vision.[135] They claimed that this guidance was more insightful and binding than any knowledge provided by Arabic grammar, rhetoric, juridical reasoning, study of the Prophet's life, or the historical context of the original revelation. Therefore, ʿAli Muttaqi and his allies critiqued the claim that Sayyid Muhammad and his followers achieved such transcendent connection to God through *dhikr* and eyewitness experiences.

This prose passage slipped without interruption into a parallel critique of those who experienced such transcendent experiences through heavenly ascension. The Mahdawis did not claim to "have traveled up to the heavens and seen this level and that level." That was the rhetoric of the Shattari community that boasted of the efficacy of its practices based on Muhammad Ghawth's experience of ascension and his eyewitness account of the heavens and the primal archetypes of the divine names that gave rise to them. Muhammad Ghawth's ascension climaxed in a direct vision of God. Yet there is a clear doctrinal difference between the Mahdawi vision in the world as a result of intensive *dhikr* and the Shattari vision at the heavenly throne as a result of ascension. However, ʿAli Muttaqi stripped these claims of their distinctive outer narratives and juxtaposed them seamlessly. He even placed them in the mouth of a single anonymous "heretic," as if they were one and the same claim. The intent was to critique any such transcendent access to God that might bypass the person of the Prophet Muhammad, even as it claimed to recreate the Prophet's paradigmatic experience of intimacy with and guidance from God. The fact that both these experiences in their Mahdawi or Shattari manifestation were mediated through the quasi-prophetic figure of Khidr further linked these two movements in the eyes of critics.

There were actual relations between members of the two movements. Some Shattari masters defended the Mahdawis against those who would suppress them.[136] Most Sufis saw the Mahdawi movement in its early days as a Sufi movement of extreme renunciation that rejected not just "the world" of ambition but also "the world" of routine legitimacy and inherited social forms. Some Sufis sympathized with the Mahdawis while not taking part in their movement, though later Sufis increasingly denounced it along the lines of ʿAli Muttaqi's opinion, possibly as the result of his vocal critique.[137] Sufis may have been drawn to the movement in their youths but ended up in more moderate Sufi communities; examples include ʿAli Muttaqi himself, the Mughal historian Badaʾuni (who joined the Qadiri Order), and the poet of Sufi romances Mālik Muḥammad Jaysī (d. 1542, who joined the Chishti Order). Many Sufis who dabbled with the Mahdawi movement eventually ended up in the Shattari Order, such as the brother of Wajih al-Din ʿAlawi, who joined the Mahdawi movement but then left it to rejoin the routine social world and became a devoted follower of Muhammad Ghawth.[138] Shattaris affirmed that a transcendent saint would come who would act as the seal of sainthood (*khātam-e wilāya*); his spirit would be in direct contact with Muhammad, who acted as the seal of Prophethood (*khātam-e nubuwwa*). The Shattaris asserted that this supreme saint would be called "the Mahdi" and would be the paramount leader of all Sufi orders.[139]

The perceived convergence of these two movements explains why the critiques launched by ʿAli Muttaqi were so intense, even to the point of sanctioning violence. He aimed to draw clear limits to the authority of sainthood in order to revive the *shariʿa*, anchored by the person of the scholarly saint, as documented in the second satchel. He desired to intensify saintly authority by yoking it tightly to the *shariʿa* and limiting its outward form to the social role of scholars like hadith masters; he claimed to embody this form of special authority himself and founded a reformist Sufi community that aspired to imitate him, as explained in the third satchel. The Shattari Sufis up until the death of Muhammad Ghawth, in contrast, aimed to intensify saintly authority by diffusing its relationship to the *shariʿa* and linking it to other discourses that were equally popular in South Asia, such as existential philosophy, yogic asceticism, astrology, and epic poetry. Shattari Sufis therefore worked directly against the outer dimension of ʿAli Muttaqi's reform program, which sought to revive and reinforce the *shariʿa*. This led to their direct confrontation; however, once the Shattaris adopted a more *shariʿa*-oriented rhetoric, the confrontation subsided.

As the Shattari Sufis worked against the outer dimension of ʿAli Muttaqi's reform program, the Mahdawis worked against the inner dimensions of it. The Mahdawis aimed at reviving the *shariʿa* around the person of a divinely guided leader, the Mahdi, who would eclipse all routine sources of authority and thereby return the Muslim community to its original state of guidance, as if the Prophet had never died. To achieve this, they denounced Sufis, hadith scholars, and jurists as corrupt and inauthentic. They directly contradicted ʿAli Muttaqi's project to revive the *shariʿa* around the figure of the scholar-saint, whose personal sanctity would unite the various discrete traces of the Prophet Muhammad's authority that were preserved in scriptural studies, legal decisions, and Sufi devotion. ʿAli Muttaqi and the Mahdawis ultimately had the same goal but adopted opposing means to achieve it. ʿAli Muttaqi could not allow them to undermine the continued authority of saints in Islamic society, upon which his reform project ultimately depended. This is why their clash was so vitriolic. In contradistinction to the Shattaris, the Mahdawi movement accepted no compromise and persisted to challenge the very notion that saints would carry the spiritual authority of the Prophet Muhammad through the vacillations of Islamic history.

ʿAli Muttaqi held that both of these movements led their followers to relegate the hadith-based pattern of the Prophet to the dustbin of irrelevant data. This was an especially potent danger on the brink of the second Islamic millennium, when the ideas circulated among Muslims that the world would come to an end or would continue under a new revelatory dispensation in the second thousand years. In such an expected dispensation, the Prophet Muhammad, whose traces are found in scripture, might be replaced by his eternal spiritual presence, known by the allegorical name Aḥmad or Maḥmūd.[140] Therefore, religious guidance—which had been previously available through the *shariʿa*—might be replaced by guidance directly from the divine source. Accordingly, the scholars who read and interpreted authoritative texts would be sidelined by those religious leaders who could claim a direct vertical connection to the source of prophecy.

The leaders of the Shattari and Mahdawi movements made bids for transcendental vertical authority. They upheld their spiritual experiences as persuasive to others by emphasizing the vertical dimension to their religious authority while denigrating horizontal dimensions. The forces that conferred horizontal authority, like Islamic law or Sufi orders, ultimately traced their origin and justification to the traces of the Prophet Muhammad's work in the world (his scripture, his pattern of behavior, his method for spiritual training). In contrast, the vertical dimension of authority relied on identification with the Prophet's "spirit" rather than on explicitly following his emulatable actions as preserved in tradition. True to his reformist agenda, ʿAli Muttaqi critiqued these movements by strategically using hadith reports. In this way, he opposed each movement and, at the same time, aimed to revive the Prophet's historical legacy. He bolstered hadith-based opposition with sociological critiques that claimed to reveal the internal politics of their building social movements based on their personal claim to sanctity.

Dissolution: Severing Connections to Gujarat

ʿAli Muttaqi encountered intractable obstacles as he endeavored to be the "Enforcer of the Shariʿa" in Gujarat. He denounced Muhammad Ghawth, but the Shattari order thrived in Gujarat as well as in Bihar and South India; the Shattaris produced lasting masterpieces of literature and profound esoteric devotions and helped spread Islam in Southeast Asia through poetry, music, shadow-puppet dramas, and syncretic mystical practices. ʿAli Muttaqi persecuted the followers of Sayyid Muhammad Jawnpuri, but the Mahdawis persisted in Gujarat and the Deccan; the Mahdawis created strong communities with ardent devotion, communal cooperation, commitment to Islamic education, and an almost Protestant work ethic, all of which continue today. ʿAli Muttaqi's experiment as "Enforcer" was a historic failure.

ʿAli Muttaqi conceived of himself as a reformist scholar-saint occupying political office. He was more concerned with the purity of his pious comportment than with the political effectiveness of his demeanor, and this exacerbated the problems he faced. Although he enjoyed a special intimacy with the sultan, he had nothing but distain for most of the nobles and "people of worldly ambition." He disliked courtiers and considered their presence around him to be contaminating. He barred them from his office and dealt with them only through the mediation of his followers. These disciples who functioned as his staff sat with the ministers of state and observed how they came to decisions, what rituals they observed in state protocol, and for what projects they requested treasury funds. They would then relate all these observations back to ʿAli Muttaqi in his office. He reviewed the legality and probity of each action against the criteria of the *shariʿa*. He needed a staff of jurists to assist him, since the amount of material to be reviewed was hefty and the disjunction between legal judgments and governmental regulations was wide. ʿAli Muttaqi isolated himself from the courtiers to reduce the possibility of corruption and intrigue. Yet, such a cumbersome administrative procedure slowed the distribution of funds from the royal treasury and, if the historical chronicles are to be believed, actually threatened to bring state machinery to a grinding halt.[141]

As illustrated by the opening vignette, the nobles at court soon resorted to bribery and intrigue to reclaim their powers of running the state. The follower whom ʿAli Muttaqi had entrusted to run the reform proceedings did not prove sterling in his honesty. Courtiers quickly exploited this follower's greed to have him manipulate decisions in their favor. The story is told in relation to silver cups. At first, ʿAli Muttaqi and his staff outlawed the practice of drinking from silver cups in court as a violation of the *shariʿa*. However, his delegate slowly eroded that decision by allowing exceptions without the shaykh's knowledge. Eventually, silver cups were back in court protocol, and the delegate had begun to collect silver (in the form of cups or coins) in exchange for exceptions. When the ministers of state realized that ʿAli Muttaqi's reforms were stalling good governance and were tainted by ethical improprieties, they decided to derail the experiment for good. One minister engineered for a woman to give the delegate her jewelry on behalf of her husband, with witnesses hidden from sight. Then the woman lodged a complaint with top court officials, accusing ʿAli Muttaqi's followers of accepting the jewelry as a bribe. The sultan came to know of the incident, interviewed the woman, and found that the delegate had no alibi for possessing women's jewelry.

At ʿAli Muttaqi's next audience, the sultan did not look him in the face, suspecting that the corruption of his personnel implicated the saint himself. When ʿAli Muttaqi realized what had happened, he picked up his staff and strode out of court. Without returning to his quarters, he walked out of the city toward the nearest port, searching for a ship bound for Khōkha (a port in Yemen, en route to Mecca). Such a forceful resignation made the sultan acknowledge the saint's innocence. With regret, he sent a party of his closest nobles to catch up to the saint and to persuade him to return. ʿAli Muttaqi took this as an opportunity to deliver a sermon on the nature of worldly trials, based on a sermon by ʿAlī ibn Abī Ṭālib (d. 661, cousin of the Prophet Muhammad and fourth caliph).

> In the presence of ʿAli, a man once cursed this world as a worthless place. ʿAli rebuked him, "This world is the place of sincerity for one who fulfills their duties to it, and the place of liberation for the one who understands it. This world is a place of sufficiency for those who take their provision from it. This world is the place where the revelations of God have come down. It is the place of worship for all the Prophets and the place of trade for all the saints who have earned in it divine compassion and acquired through it the gardens of paradise. Who are you to curse this world? . . . The happiness of this world resembles the salvific happiness to come, and its trials resemble the damning trials to come, to instill you, who curse this world, with longing and with horror. Do you indulge vain hope that the world was made to serve you? How could the world be worthy of blame whether it oppresses your fathers with trials or gives your mothers repose in luxury?"[142]

ʿAli Muttaqi later recalled these thoughts in his text "On the True Nature of the World."[143] He argues that one should neither accept the world on its own deceptive terms nor reject it absolutely in a show of ascetic confrontation. The world is a place of trials. One must be always on guard against worldly ambitions and temptations without missing an opportunity to turn its forces toward benevolence and actions that benefit yourself and others. This notion is a practical translation of the Shadhili teaching "The basic good is to follow the truth, not to constantly oppose your ego in an absolute confrontation; if the self desires to follow the truth, then that is a double blessing, like mixing sugar into milk."[144] It is a call to minimize one's reliance on other people and worldly means while maximizing one's reliance on divine provision, whether evident in the form of sustenance and blessing or hidden in the form of trials and travails.

ʿAli Muttaqi's speech was an exhortation to the nobles to uphold ethics in their fulfillment of worldly duty, and it was also an exoneration from the accusations against him of worldly ambition.

> While all the nobles. gathered around him to listen, Sultan Mahmud Shah III rode up. He requested the blessing of ʿAli Muttaqi's remaining among them in Gujarat, so that the sultan might treat the world in ways that would secure his place in the next world with the fortune of his company. ʿAli Muttaqi replied, "God has graced Mecca with being the

> land from which prayers are answered. God is more likely to answer my prayers on your behalf from Mecca. That would be more beneficial to you than my presence here. I have said to you before that the world and religion are like two wives of one man who will never coexist peaceably. My heart was possessed with the idea that I might forge the two in accord one with the other, and I hoped to show that this was possible with my experiment [at court]. I thought it over carefully, and decided to embark on the journey from Mecca to stay with you all, in hopes that you could fulfill that possibility that I envisioned for you. Now that I have spent some time among you, I have seen that the divine has not ordained for you [this benefit], and I have been disappointed by those who have failed to overcome temptations and trials. Now I know by experience and experiment that the two can never be in accord, just like two wives. I have gotten what I came for. Now the time has come for me to return to the House of God [the Kaʿba in Mecca] to spend the rest of my days living in its shelter."[145]

ʿAli Muttaqi left one of his followers, named ʿAbd al-Ṣamad, in Ahmedabad to represent him and to pronounce blessings and prayers on his behalf. "I advise you to entrust God with all your affairs and to carry out the orders of the *shariʿa* and to honor those people who study it and keep it firm. I advise you to sit with the righteous saints, for a man is counted along with those he loves, even if he is not like them." With these words, reaffirming the basic principles of his social reform program even as its details lay in shards at his feet, he left Gujarat and headed to Mecca, never to return to his homeland.

Historical chronicles preserve the image of a self-composed ʿAli Muttaqi leaving Gujarat after having asserted the rightness of his cause. Yet the collapse of his reform program was a major blow. ʿAli Muttaqi may have been planning to settle in Gujarat had the program been a success. Human weakness had seemingly laid waste to a cherished hope: that his authority established in Mecca would serve as the spiritual foundation of Islamic society in Gujarat. He appeared resigned to live out his remaining days in Mecca, but the sea journey back to Mecca must have been a time of introspection and self-assessment for him. He wrote a short treatise that reflected this mood, titled "A Reminder of Blessings and Divine Gifts to Have Patience and Give Thanks for Being in Need and in Affliction." In contrast to his other writings, which are pervaded by a tone of advice and exhortation to others, this is a work of very personal reflection. It seems as if he were writing primarily as a form of stock-taking and reassurance, for the work comprises a long list of those divine favors that he enjoyed, even if anxiety weighed on his mind: "The blessings which I mention here are such that, if one recalls them to mind often, so that they reign over his heart, then all the calamities and afflictions one faces will fade in importance in his sight. In reality, one can never enumerate the extent of divine blessings and subtle gifts in all their details. As the Qur'an says, *If you try to count the blessings given by God you can never come to their end* [Qur'an 16:18]."[146]

Despite admitting the never-ending blessings of God, ʿAli Muttaqi persisted in compiling a list: it reads like a desperate bid for reassurance during a grave trial, as if he were trying to justify himself to himself. He acknowledged that being in existence was a great blessing; the alternative was to be complete void. Then he listed being animate and sentient as a human, rather than being a rock or a plant or an animal. Breathing, too, was a great gift; inhaling and exhaling were actually separate blessings—"imagine being given one but not the other!" He gave thanks for being a Muslim rather than an infidel or heretic, followed closely by thanks for being created a man rather than a woman. Furthermore, he acknowledged that he was created a potent male rather than one of the many types whose masculinity was questionable. He ended this exercise by giving thanks that he was in total poverty and that fate had forced him to live in Mecca, close to God's own house: "Most people do not know the power of this blessing. Who could fully understand it except one who has lived in Mecca and then left it and been separated from it? Having returned, such a person envisions all his poverty and afflictions and compares them with being once again in Mecca. Who would complain except a fool or an ignoramus?"[147] This comment reads like a justification against those courtiers in Gujarat who drove him out of court. In reality, he argued, they had secured for him the highest blessing: to live out the rest of his earthly life at the center of the world, in the shadow of the Kaʿba.

After ʿAli Muttaqi's dramatic departure, Sultan Mahmud Shah III prospered for a while. With the support of his prime minister, Asaf Khan, the sultan reformed the administration in Ahmedabad and strengthened the military. He patronized religious scholars, venerated local Sufis, and wooed the support of Sayyids, inducing all kinds of religious notables to back his rule. The historian Ulughkhani depicts the sultan as a great patron of celebrations for the Prophet's Birth (Mawlid al-Nabī) after these authorities showed their support of his rule. He filled the night with Qur'an recitation, hadith recital, and narration of the Prophet's birth, along with Sufi devotional singing. Yet he also drank wine, smoked opium, and consumed "snake-blood" (a drug like hashish). For these kingly indulgences, he came to rely on a young male slave, Burhān al-Dīn Sharrābī, "the Wine-Pourer." The young man was ambitious and soon became the sultan's confidant, perhaps even his lover. Asaf Khan recommended that the sultan dismiss him, warning that his young wine-bearer would ruin him, but Mahmud Shah III persisted in his intimate relationship. In 1554, only five years after ʿAli Muttaqi left, the wine-pourer drugged and stabbed the twenty-eight-year-old sultan and engineered a palace coup during the festivities of Mawlid al-Nabi.[148]

The coup lasted only a day, but it left deep political scars. The rebellious wine-pourer was killed and his body tossed to the pigs and dogs. But no act of vengeance could bring back the sultan who had restored the semblance of strong central rule in Gujarat over his sixteen years on the throne: he was murdered along with the ablest of his ministers and left no son to perpetuate the Muzaffar-Shahi dynasty. This final blow to the sultanate in Gujarat came not from millennial movements like the Mahdawis or from adventurous Sufi orders like the Shattaris or from rival empires like the Mughals—rather, it came due to greed, lust, and ambition within the sultan's own household. Gujarat plummeted again into rivalry among nobles and civil strife for the next two decades.[149] One minister, Mubārak Sayyid, a scion of the Bukhari family of Suhrawardi Sufis, had helped Mahmud Shah III secure the throne and now tried to keep the peace and protect the later puppet sultans; his magnificent tomb at Mahmudabad stands as a last monument to the Sultan-Sufi cooperation through which Gujarat flourished.[150] But he could not rescue the dynasty from impending ruin. Ulughkhani opines that unity disappeared from among the nobles after Sultan Mahmud Shah III's assassination and also that the overall quality of the nobility declined precipitously.[151]

People are only as righteous as their rulers
  While on land and sea spreads corruption
Witness the crimes people set their hands to commit
  Giving the rulers a taste of their own medicine

The political disaster that darkened Gujarat spread a much wider foreboding shadow. In the fateful year of 1554, three major rulers died unexpectedly: Mahmud Shah III of Gujarat, Salīm Shāh Sūrī of North India, and Nizām Shāh of Ahmednagar (the Deccan kingdom on Gujarat's southern border). In memorial, they were lauded as "India's Three Khusros" or heroic princes. Their deaths left a power vacuum that set the stage for Humayun, the Mughal ruler in exile, to return from Safavid Iran.[152] Once Mughal forces took control of Delhi and Agra, nothing could prevent their eventual expansion into Gujarat.

Within twenty years of Mahmud Shah III's death, Gujarat's independence dissolved until it became just another province of the Mughal Empire.

Through these radical political changes, 'Ali Muttaqi lived out his twilight years in Mecca. As he aged and weakened, his followers strove to preserve his legacy, perpetuate his Sufi training method, and expand his hadith-based reform program both in Arabia where they were based and also back in South Asia. As they emptied his "death satchel" to prepare to bury him, they began to fill a larger satchel to contain his legacy. Their work would perpetuate his legacy. That satchel is waiting to be opened now.

FIFTH SATCHEL

ʿAli Muttaqi's Legacy

Approaching the Kaʿba never ceased to awe him, even though he came almost daily since arriving in Mecca from India. As he sat down next to his shaykh in the midst of a vast study circle in the shadow of the black shrine, he regained his composure. He recalled how, when he first stepped foot in the holy city almost three years ago, he was overwhelmed. Yet after circling the Kaʿba and visiting the Prophet's tomb in Medina, his ardor cooled and his reason returned. He began to study hadith with ʿAbd al-Wahhab Muttaqi, to whom he now bowed low in respectful greetings before sitting in the study circle.

Learning traditions about the Prophet's actions and attitudes, in the very place where the Prophet was born and raised, filled his heart with wonder. Gradually, he found that his teacher was not merely a master of hadith but also a spiritual mentor and guide. He quickly became the shaykh's strongest disciple, even though he was new to the circle of scholarly devotees in Mecca. As he sat in the gathering next to his teacher, the other students gazed at him with respect or mouthed greetings silently, so as not to interrupt the teachings.

As the culmination of his Sufi training, Shaykh ʿAbd al-Wahhab Muttaqi sent him into a secluded retreat for forty days, checking in on him every Friday after leaving home to offer congregational prayers at the Kaʿba's sanctuary. Removing him from seclusion, ʿAbd al-Wahhab pronounced, "Praise be to God, your spiritual state is ripened as it should be." His disciple returned the next day to the hadith study circles, as if his life would continue in Mecca as it had been. He took his place sitting beside the shaykh at the Maqam Hanafi overlooking the Kaʿba, one of hundreds of students and disciples who came to learn the Prophet's sayings and deeds with all their detailed chains of narration and subtleties of authentication.

That day, the shaykh began discussing a report from the hadith collection titled *Sahih Muslim*: "A dead man leaves behind three things as a legacy: family, wealth and good deeds. Of these, two things return while one remains: family and wealth eventually return to God but one's deeds remain as one's legacy in the world."[1] Shaykh ʿAbd al-Wahhab paused as tears filled his eyes. "I have no family and no wealth, and my good deeds are few! What will be my legacy?" He turned to his disciple, saying, "You, ʿAbd al-Haqq, you will be my legacy! Go back to your home now, for your wife and children are waiting anxiously for you, and they will be relieved to see you again. Get ready to return to India."

The disciple, ʿAbd al-Haqq, was startled to hear this command. His heart sank, but regaining his composure, he replied, "I intended to remain here in this holy land to learn from you, but if you send me from here then I desire to go to Baghdad to visit the tomb of Shaykh ʿAbd al-Qadir Jilani!" Shaykh ʿAbd al-Wahhab responded to his favorite student and closest disciple, "You cannot remain here any longer, and there is no possibility for you to go anywhere other than your own place of origin! The *shariʿa* can be practiced anywhere, and ʿAbd al-Qadir Jilani is with you wherever you reside. Keep firm your love for him, faith in him, and concentration on him. Resolve in your heart to follow his teachings wherever you are. He would never be content with you if you leave your mother, your wife, and your young children in a state of anxiety and need! Besides, you told me that your mother gave you permission to visit Mecca and Medina after you promised her to not go to any third place, so how can you go elsewhere?"

The disciple humbly averred, "But I made the intention in my heart to visit Baghdad and it is on the way back to India, so in reality it does not count as a third locale." His shaykh replied, "That is true enough, if you could simply stay there for a short time as if it were stopping in the midst of an ongoing journey. But is it possible for you to stop in Baghdad without doing a forty-day retreat there? If you stay for that long, your desire to remain there for an extended time will grow uncontrollably—it will be impossible for you to pull away. Your journey to Baghdad will become extended. Your family will suffer ruin while waiting for you."

Desperate to stay in his Sufi master's circle, ʿAbd al-Haqq implored, "Please turn your spiritual attention to this issue, and then tell me whatever is best for me." The shaykh replied sternly, "Inshallah, it is always good for you to do *istikhara*, to make a special prayer for divine guidance, but it is already clear that what is best for you is to return right now to your own place and family!"[2] ʿAbd al-Haqq rose in bewilderment—leaving his books on the ground where he had been sitting at his privileged place next to the shaykh—and headed out of the study circle on unsteady feet. All the students watched him, some with sympathy and some with jealousy, as he walked slowly, with uncertainty, out of the sanctuary.

ʿAbd al-Haqq later recorded these events in the biography of his Sufi masters, ʿAli Muttaqi and his successor, ʿAbd al-Wahhab Muttaqi. The former had sojourned to study in Mecca and settled there, after twice attempting to return as a reformer to Gujarat. The latter had traveled to study in Mecca and settled there for good, after returning to India only to face assassination attempts. Their new and zealous follower ʿAbd al-Haqq wished to stay on in Mecca to follow in their footsteps and felt anxious about his prospects in returning to India. Yet in his formal account, ʿAbd al-Haqq carefully edited out emotions of uncertainty, disappointment, and doubt.

> During the time when I was living in Mecca and serving Shaykh ʿAbd al-Wahhab Muttaqi, I used to occasionally visit the tomb of Shaykh ʿAli Muttaqi. One day, while sitting by his noble tomb, I presented the troubled state of my heart and humbly requested that he grant me insight for a solution to my anxieties. That night while sleeping, I saw in a dream Shaykh ʿAli Muttaqi on a seat of authority at the Maqām Ḥanafī [a place in the courtyard of the Haram to the right side of the Kaʿba when approached from the Bāb al-Salām and Maqām Ibrāhīm].[3] I stood in his august presence and said, "I, a poor mendicant, am a follower of your successor and representative, Shaykh ʿAbd al-Wahhab; for his sake, please accept my humble request . . ." Then he turned to me with kind consolation, and I said to him exactly what I had been thinking while sitting at the side of his grave earlier that day. He replied, "Your request is granted, if God wills—just keep your thoughts concentrated and you'll attain what you seek. Go in peace and safety!"[4]

ʿAli Muttaqi left behind a vivid legacy after he died. Indeed, some of his followers continued to experience his guidance in visions and dreams long after he was buried. His followers, admirers, and detractors shaped his legacy through worldly activities in succeeding generations. This chapter is a satchel containing elements of the personas and activities of his followers as they pursued his principles of reformist Sufism in their own changed surroundings. Its contents even include ʿAli Muttaqi's own "death satchel," which was finally unpacked by his followers upon his demise.

As the hadith report quoted above explains, "In this world, we leave behind our deeds, our pious efforts and charitable activities." ʿAli Muttaqi lived with an acute awareness of this hadith and its consequences, and he strove to shape the world through reformist Sufism and hadith scholarship to leave an active legacy. After ʿAli Muttaqi died, his followers and disciples extended his reform project and built a community around him as their guiding saint, thereby reacting to new local environments and political developments. We can document the legacy of ʿAli Muttaqi through the activities of his major disciples. Three figures were important in transmitting ʿAli Muttaqi's legacy back to South Asia: ʿAbd al-Wahhab Muttaqi, Muhammad ibn Tahir Patani, and ʿAbd al-Haqq Muhaddith Dihlawi. Hagiographic and historical records preserve the stories of these three figures in detail.[5] The life of ʿAbd al-Wahhab Muttaqi was already discussed in the third satchel as he embodied the teachings of ʿAli Muttaqi; he lived in such self-abnegation that it is as if his life were an extension of his master's very life. The latter two will be documented in this chapter because they returned to South Asia and died there.

ʿAli Muttaqi's disciples endeavored to transpose his reformist Sufi community to South Asia. In Gujarat, the reform project was mired in social conflict and violence with the Mahdawi movement and fell into disarray as Gujarat's independent polity was subsumed by the Mughal Empire under Akbar. In this new political and cultural climate, his later followers transported the legacy of ʿAli Muttaqi to Delhi, the heart of the Mughal polity that he had abhorred. The youngest Muttaqi disciple, ʿAbd al-Haqq (whose story is recounted above), refashioned the important elements of this reform program into a form more suitable to the new environment—in returning to India he became known as Shaykh ʿAbd al-Haqq, the Hadith Master of Delhi. This entailed abandoning allegiance to the triple *tariqa* that had been the distinctive marker of this reformist community, making ʿAli Muttaqi's reform project more broadly effective and more subtly hidden. That moment marks the historical dissolution of this distinctive community.

Threshold: ʿAli Muttaqi's Death

When ʿAli Muttaqi left Gujarat for good, it seems that divine protection was lifted from its sultanate. Mahmud Shah III and his realm were exposed to grave danger, first from within and then from outside. After the sultan's death in a lust-driven coup, ʿAli Muttaqi's personal connection to Gujarat dissolved.

In Mecca, he entered the twilight of his life. After Mahmud Shah III died and ʿAli Muttaqi's political ties to Gujarat were severed, the Sufi scholar lived in Mecca for thirteen more years. His khanqah hosted visiting pilgrims from South Asia, his Sufi followers, and countless students of hadith. He continuously worked on his huge hadith book *Kanz al-ʿUmmāl*: until his dying breath, he kept revising his magnum opus, taking hadith reports from al-Suyuti's *Jamʿ al-Jawāmiʿ* and organizing them into legal subject categories in order to facilitate their use in juridical decisions and devotional reforms. Yet he grew so weak in this last chapter of life, from prior ascetic rigors and fasting, that his followers had to carry him to the mosque for Friday communal prayers.

In his old age, ʿAli Muttaqi established his community and built its institutions in Mecca. Thus, he no longer needed to rely on the remnants of his past in Gujarat and the Deccan. To expunge memories of uncertainty, he revised his own past in a series of acts of repression, dismissal, and disguise. He suppressed the memory of his own search for authenticity once he had found a version that made sense. He dismissed his youthful quest for inspiration through the annals of Chishti masters. And he repressed his prior admiration for the Mahdawis. These acts of repression were the aftershocks of his experiences of spiritual rebirth and social reconstruction in Mecca.

The last year of his life held bizarre events and ironic reversals that can only be understood as a "return of the repressed" (a concept from psychoanalysis that Freud discussed in *Moses and Monotheism*). After several severe illnesses, ʿAli Muttaqi displayed some uncharacteristic behavior that inverted his normal comportment. In temporary fits, he experienced poetic ecstasies and feelings of cosmic, oceanic unity, akin to what he had dismissed regarding the Chishti masters of his youth and what he had critiqued in the Shattari Sufis during his mature years. During one such fit, ʿAli Muttaqi requested his successor, ʿAbd al-Wahhab, to recite for him a Persian couplet by Amir Khusro that is sung in Qawwali.[6] "Never will I see a vision finer than your face's luminous beauty / I know no sun or moon as radiant, as lovely no human or fairy." His biographer, ʿAbd al-Haqq, recalls the whole incident that followed this return to repressed elements of his childhood environment.

> When ʿAli Muttaqi heard these words, a strange state overwhelmed him. He called out, "Recite it again—recite it again and again!" ʿAbd al-Wahhab repeated it several times, and ʿAli Muttaqi responded with expressions of loving ecstasy and heaved passionate sighs. In these last days, he was so weak that he could hardly chew his food, so he requested his servant to knead the food to make it soft. While this ecstatic state still possessed him, the servant brought his meal and ʿAli Muttaqi watched him knead

the rice and gravy into a smooth paste. At the vision of this union of opposites and mingling of discrete substances, he called out for the servant to "knead it harder—keep kneading until all becomes one and there exists no duality or separation!" Transported by this domestic scene of existential love, he uttered a poetic couplet of his own inspiration.[7]

Listen to the poetry told of the divine beauty's essence:
Life of bride and groom mingles like sweet rice and milk.

It is next to impossible to translate this couplet into English, for it speaks on three levels at once. The first level is about a simple dish in which rice is kneaded until soft and mixed with sweetened milk. Yet this domestic imagery leaps into higher, theological registers. This dish is *dūdh-bhāt*, a dish presented to newly married couples as their first symbolic meal together, suggesting their imminent sexual intimacy. Yet the subject of the couplet is also *param*, the divine absolute essence. The convention of Indic devotional poetry is that the poet is like a bride offering herself to the groom, who represents the divine beloved. In this way, a simple observation of softened rice evokes sensuous spirituality of love integrated with a philosophical message of existential union between God and the created world.

The couplet itself is common enough, for South Asian saints peppered their teachings with such poems and often uttered by them in trancelike states of selfless union with the divine beloved. Yet, it is surprising that ʿAli Muttaqi abandoned himself to such a state, for he habitually rejected poetry as an expression of sainthood and advocated silence about the metaphors of love and experiences of union that inspired them. He once even had a poet forcibly removed from his khanqah in Mecca when his metaphors became too exaggerated![8] ʿAli Muttaqi momentarily inverted his lifelong rejection of practices that characterized the Chishti and Shattari communities. Sparked by this couplet, his ecstatic state persisted while he spoke out in more expressions of love and passion. ʿAbd al-Wahhab had to stay by his side day and night to care for him.

This illness in the last months of his life displays a more dramatic moment of the "return of the repressed." ʿAli Muttaqi became possessed by the intuition that he was himself the Mahdi, the exact claim for which he had so thoroughly critiqued Sayyid Muhammad Jawnpuri. He acted upon this intuition with a zeal that totally surprised his colleagues and followers, who had thought him ill enough to die. One of his students, Qadi Hamid Muhaddith, related this story in detail, for he was present with him at the onset of this strange spiritual state.[9]

A serious illness inflicted Shaykh ʿAli Muttaqi. It was so intense that all thought he had neared the end of his life and that there was little hope of living on. Everyone was awaiting news of the shaykh's death and were making preparations to attend his funeral.

Suddenly at dawn, he exhibited signs of an intoxicated spiritual state. He summoned a follower and asked, "Do you bear witness that I am sincere in what I now declare?" The follower attested to this. Then Shaykh ʿAli Muttaqi declared, "I am the Mahdi of the End of Time. Declare that you believe me and accept this." Then he requested the presence of ʿAbd al-Qādir al-Fākihī, one of the greatest scholars and jurists of Mecca who was eloquent, intelligent, and from a renowned scholarly family. He was a devoted follower of ʿAli Muttaqi, a firm lover of his, and his disciple. . . . The shaykh said "ʿAbd al-Qadir, bear witness that I am sincere in what I now say." He agreed and then the shaykh said again, "I declare that I am the Promised and Expected Mahdi!" ʿAbd al-Qadir bore witness to his declaration.

Shaykh ʿAli Muttaqi stood up as if he were not weak at all, though he had been so sick only moments before that he had been unable to stand and it appeared that no life remained in him except his last dying breath. Now, his power of motion had returned to the point that he stood up and went to take a full bath with cold water [a full ablution since he felt he was no longer sick]. He put on white clothes, placed his notebook on his head, took up his staff in his hand, and went out toward the Kaʿba. He moved so swiftly that it was as if he were flying; nobody was able to keep up with him.

He entered the sacred enclosure on Friday morning when a huge crowd had gathered inside. Before this throng, he declared three times with a loud voice, "I am the Promised Mahdi!" Everyone was stunned that Shaykh ʿAli Muttaqi, so pious and scrupulous, should make so bold a claim. Asaf Khan, the prime minister of Gujarat, was present at the time, having been expecting the shaykh's funeral. He said secretly to his aids that the shaykh must be in a fever and ordered some trusted people to take him aside and keep him safely in an isolated corner, away from the crowds. However, ʿAli Muttaqi shook himself free of his would-be protectors. He rushed over to Abu'l-Hasan al-Bakri, who was shocked that, at the very moment when all the people were awaiting his death, the shaykh was here in the sacred enclosure. He wondered from where this bodily vigor had come and thought that today, the shaykh has returned from the dead.

Passion, wherever it turns its face, in truth
transforms an old man into vigorous youth

Shaykh Abu'l-Hasan al-Bakri rose to greet him, as was his custom in the circle of hadith studies, indicating that ʿAli Muttaqi should sit on his own raised seat. [Normally he would decline] but today, he ascended and sat there, saying, "As for today, yes, I will sit here above you all, for today is my day. Today is my day of inerrant guidance [*ʿiṣma*] and absolute authority. Today I have been granted the most exalted position."

Tumult has knocked on my heart's door today
a lover's insanity inhabits my mind today
lowly beggars don't have an inkling of the fact
that the Lord of the World is with me today!

ʿAli Muttaqi asked Abu'l-Hasan al-Bakri to bear witness that he was the Mahdi, and he immediately agreed. Then he turned to his son, Muhammad al-Bakri, and asked him to do the same, but he hesitated. Abu'l-Hasan quickly said, "My son, don't hesitate a moment but bear witness to the sincerity of his claim, for the man is in a trance-like state and is not conscious of his actions!"

I don't say "I'm the Truth"—my heart-friend says it.
How could I not say it when my dear Lover says it![10]

Shaykh ʿAli Muttaqi said, "Now, all that is left is to spread this claim among the people in order to get acknowledgment in accordance with the Word of God!" However, Abu'l-Hasan gestured quietly to his servants to shut the door of the house and to not let ʿAli Muttaqi out. He apprehended this plot and slipped out as if he were flying, saying, "I am going before the Pasha who governs on behalf of the Ottoman sultan to lay this claim before him!" ʿAli Muttaqi headed off directly toward the home of the Pasha, even though he had never before seen where that house actually was located.

On the way, he passed by his own home. He entered his cell and, falling on the bed, he slept until midnight, completely unaware of the world around him. Then he rose after midnight and called his servant asking, "Do you know anything of what happened with me this day?" The servant replied, "You yourself know better what happened." ʿAli Muttaqi said, "I repent of everything I have said and done—I retract it all." Over and over he repented of God and begged forgiveness. When news of this reached Abu'l-Hasan al-Bakri, he came running barefoot to the shaykh's home. He thanked God that ʿAli Muttaqi had been saved from this deadly trap. He was overcome with joy that ʿAli Muttaqi was now safe.[11]

ʿAli Muttaqi never explained this bizarre incident of spiritual ambition, but it caused much confusion among his followers. His successor, ʿAbd al-Wahhab, glossed over the incident, refusing to acknowledge that it happened as he responded to questions from his closest disciples.

In narrating these events as presented above, ʿAbd al-Haqq also hesitated. He interrupted the narrative with many poetic couplets, which serve to deflect the reader's attention from the spiritual claim that ʿAli Muttaqi was making toward the fact that he was in a state of uncontrollable intoxication. ʿAbd al-Haqq carefully noted that ʿAli Muttaqi had a seemingly supernatural strength during the day when he thought himself to be the Mahdi; thus, the narrator subtly framed the whole event as an example of possession by spiritual state that was both beyond ʿAli Muttaqi's rational faculty to control and beyond his accountability to bear.[12]

These strange experiences, in which the states he denounced in others overwhelmed him from within himself, were ephemeral. They lasted a few hours or days, and he dismissed them as trivial. These states (Ar. *aḥwāl*, singular *ḥāl*) neither proved his sainthood nor called it into question. In fact, these experiences only served to prove ʿAli Muttaqi's fundamental point, that an authentic saint tempered by religious studies may experience such spiritual intoxication but will disregard it, refuse to rely on or publicize it, and eventually move beyond it.

Even in the throes of illness and uncontrollable spiritual seizures, ʿAli Muttaqi asserted his unflinching opinion that Sufi practices must be tempered by knowledge of the religious disciplines. The strange experiences of the forcible return of what he had repressed did not call his opinions into question. Rather, these experiences of trance and ecstasy showed his increasing self-confidence. Late in his life, ʿAli Muttaqi could indulge in expressions that, earlier in his life, would have shaken his emerging sense of being a saint in a reformist Sufi community. He was not afraid of being accused of what he critiqued in others, as we have seen while unpacking the previous chapter's satchel of conflict, denunciation, and persecution. His followers excused these outbursts of elderly passion, even as they recorded them in his biography. They were already looking toward preserving his legacy as ʿAli Muttaqi approached his death, packing his spiritual baggage for the final journey beyond this world toward the furthest shore. His whole life, he had been carrying a little "death satchel" around his neck instead of the customary Sufi cloak; his satchel contained a Qurʾan, a shroud, and all he needed for burial, as a constant reminder of imminent death. Now, his followers would have to carry him, bearing not just the weight of his body but also the burden of memories that they had to record on paper.

ʿAli Muttaqi died on November 4, 1567 (2 Jumādā ʾl-Awwal, AH 975), a quarter century before the advent of the new millennium that he worked so hard to downplay.[13] He was buried at Jannat al-Muʿallā, the most prestigious cemetery in Mecca, where the Prophet's wife, Khadīja, and many of his ancestors are buried. His tomb was near that of the famous Sufi Fuḍayl ibn ʿIyāḍ (d. 803, who is included in the Chishti Order's lineage), so it was likely destroyed along with those of the Prophet's family when Saudi kings ordered the demolition of cemeteries in 1925.

This event reminds us how delicate legacies are, even those that appear solid and durable like a stone tomb. The shaykh's legacy on paper was also fragile. His earliest biographies have been lost, though we know of their titles. The most authoritative biography of ʿAli Muttaqi was written by his successor, ʿAbd al-Wahhab Muttaqi, titled "Ittiḥāf al-Taqī fi Manāqib ʿAlī al-Muttaqī," or "Gift of the God-Fearing about the Virtues of ʿAli Muttaqi." This early record has not survived as a manuscript, though ʿAbd al-Haqq copied some narratives from it into his existing books. The second lost biography is "al-Qawl al-Naqī fi Faḍl ʿAlī Muttaqī," or "The Pure Statement on the Excellence of ʿAli Muttaqi" by ʿAbd al-Qadir al-Fakihi, a jurist and hadith scholar in Mecca who was a close follower. ʿAli Muttaqi's death and the disappearance of sources about him did not dissolve his reformist project, since his successors lived on, gaining in strength and influence.

Critique: Muhammad ibn Tahir Patani in Gujarat

ʿAli Muttaqi had opposed the Mahdawi movement by writing a series of interlinked texts documented in the previous chapter. In addition to these penned polemics, he trained his disciples to carry on the work of reform and critique back in South Asia. The most renowned of these students was Shaykh Muhammad ibn Tahir Patani (d. 1578), whose career formed an extension of ʿAli Muttaqi's own. Muhammad ibn Tahir channeled his teacher's textual war of words against the Mahdawi movement into a violent struggle for power. He hailed from the old Gujarati capital of Patan from a wealthy Bohra family that traded goods (mainly cloth and paper) through Gujarat's ports.[14] He pursued studies in the Qurʾan, hadith, and law. At age fifteen, he graduated and began to teach under the patronage of his former master, Shaykh Muṫhiya (also known as Mullā Muṫh).[15] Like ʿAli Muttaqi, Muhammad ibn Tahir left Gujarat during the political turmoil of Humayun's invasion and the subsequent collapse of the sultanate of Gujarat. He arrived in Mecca in 1537 and settled down for training in hadith studies. At first, he sat in the company of teachers who were mostly Qadiris from Yemen.[16] Perhaps at their recommendation, he shifted to the more famous circle of hadith study under Ibn Hajar al-Haythami and Abu'l-Hasan al-Bakri.

There, he met ʿAli Muttaqi, and chose him to be his teacher in outer learning and his master in spiritual discipline. ʿAli Muttaqi recognized Muhammad ibn Tahir's talent with hadith studies and cultivated him as his special follower. The biographical sources use Sufi terminology to describe this outpouring (*fayḍ*) of spiritual insight and personal sanctity from master to disciple. In his own writings, Muhammad ibn Tahir describes ʿAli Muttaqi as "the most virtuous man of his times, and the greatest man in his sincere sainthood [*wilaya*]." This indicates that Muhammad ibn Tahir regarded him not only as his teacher but also as his Sufi master.[17]

ʿAli Muttaqi prepared his follower to return to Gujarat as the main exponent of his program of reform there. So Muhammad ibn Tahir returned to Patan and took up teaching religious sciences at a madrasa. In accord with ʿAli Muttaqi's method, he would subtly teach Sufi devotion from within his lessons on hadith and jurisprudence with the slogan *Dil bi yār o dast bi kār*—"Keep your heart busy with God as you keep your hands busy with work." Even as he would discourse orally to his students, his hands would be busy preparing ink and paper for his researches and copying out drafts. He spent his family fortune to recruit students from distant primary schools, asking Qur'an teachers to send him their brightest students, to whom he gave full stipends.[18] In his farewell address, ʿAli Muttaqi ordered him to remain in constant research correcting hadith reports and publishing them far and wide. In answer, Muhammad ibn Tahir composed many works on hadith and attempted to weed out weak reports from the body of generally accepted hadith.[19]

Muhammad ibn Tahir's erudition earned him the title Mālik al-Muḥaddithīn, "King of the Hadith Scholars," in Gujarat.[20] ʿAli Muttaqi trained him as a reformer in general and specifically as an opponent of the Mahdawis. In Mecca, Muhammad ibn Tahir may have witnessed the interaction between ʿAli Muttaqi and one of his own distant family members, a Mahdawi who had come for pilgrimage. Instead of hosting him, as was the custom, ʿAli Muttaqi sent him a bit of money as a token of respect for their undeniable blood relation, saying he could come to ʿAli Muttaqi's home if he desired to "have his beliefs set right." The relative, evidently terrified by such treatment, never showed up. ʿAli Muttaqi outspokenly wondered whether the man would go to Medina to pay respects to the tomb of the Prophet after completing his pilgrimage to Mecca, or whether his Mahdawi allegiance to Sayyid Muhammad completely eclipsed his devotion to the Prophet.[21] ʿAli Muttaqi needed an expert in hadith studies to act as his exponent in Gujarat, and Muhammad ibn Tahir did so with zeal. He had personal reasons as well as ideological reasons to oppose the Mahdawi movement, for members of his Bohra community were joining the Mahdawis.[22] He critiqued the Mahdawis through the study of hadith reports, opening a new front in this textual war.

Muhammad ibn Tahir excelled in documenting forged and false hadith reports that had circulated since the second or third Islamic century, even those that had become popularly respected as the Prophet Muhammad's own words. His book on inauthentic hadith reports included a whole chapter on the Mahdi, declaring invalid many of the reports upon which numbers of Muslims, including the Mahdawis, based their speculations. He judged the famous report "God sends to the Islamic community at the inception of each new century a leader who will revive and renew the community's religion" to be falsely ascribed to the Prophet and baseless. He noted, "Many people believe that the reviver [*mujaddid*] of the tenth century will be the Mahdi or Jesus, and nowadays every sect claims that its own leader is the Mahdi, but God knows the truth that the Mahdi must be accepted by all the scholars and authorities in general [and cannot be some sectarian figure]."[23] He further judged that another hadith was forged, one that the Mahdawis used to highlight that Sayyid Muhammad was a juridical authority above the established legal methods and their founders: "There will be at the end of time a man who is my follower and vice-regent [*khalifa*] who surpasses even Abū Bakr and ʿUmar."[24] ʿAli Muttaqi had tried to prove that the Mahdawis did not follow authentic hadith reports in their totality; Muhammad ibn Tahir attempted to show that they based their doctrines on unreliable and invalid individual hadith reports.

Muhammad ibn Tahir likely served as the channel through whom ʿAli Muttaqi's anti-Mahdawi treatises were copied and circulated. In addition, historical sources record Muhammad ibn Tahir's own activities in critique of the Mahdawis.

> He used to openly contradict their [Mahdawis'] doctrinal beliefs while engaging them in disputations and debates, urging them to recant their doctrines and give up their misguided beliefs and hypocritical

> dissimulation. This was his constant project, and he prevailed through many conflicts with them and defeated them in debates in many large gatherings, exposing their disgraceful actions and baseless tales. He proved their doctrines to be void and refuted what they held up as proof, revealing it as invalid. He went to extremes to denounce them and warned them of punishment if they persisted. He accused them of infidelity and having stepped outside the boundaries of Islam. He wanted to uproot this heresy from its very source, striving with all possible means.[25]

Mahdawi sources blame "the scholars of Patan" for their partisan opposition, without naming Muhammad ibn Tahir. Scholars from Patan had raised the stakes of the conflict to violent heights by requesting legal decisions from Mecca to justify executing Mahdawis as heretics.[26] This was at a time of increasing Mahdawi activity, as the government of Gujarat weakened with the assassination of Sultan Mahmud Shah III. Court intrigue and open conflict between nobles meant that Mahdawis were no longer the object of state persecution and were freer to openly proselytize.

Muhammad ibn Tahir wrote "Naṣīḥat al-Wulāt," or "Advice to the Rulers," warning of the need to suppress the Mahdawi movement and sent it to Shēr Khān Fulādī, the governor of Patan (and possibly to the governors of other Gujarati cities as well). Under his influence, the governor of Patan reportedly took action against the Mahdawis. However, Muhammad ibn Tahir did not have such success when he traveled to the capital. He found the political situation chaotic under the last sultan of Gujarat, the pretender Muẓaffar Shah III (ruled nominally 1561–73). The regent, Iʿtimad Khan, controlled the sultan while other nobles vied for influence. As this power struggle verged toward civil war, the Mahdawis gained political leverage. In the capital, Muhammad ibn Tahir was attacked by a Mahdawi partisan who wounded him with a sword, and he returned to Patan in frustration. There is further evidence that the Mahdawis openly exercised power in the capital. When ʿAli Muttaqi's successor, ʿAbd al-Wahhab Muttaqi, returned to Ahmedabad in 1567 (just after ʿAli Muttaqi's death) to visit his family, a group of Mahdawis overran his home with the intent to kill him. He escaped by climbing over the compound wall and fleeing the city, returning quickly to Mecca.[27]

This situation caused Muhammad ibn Tahir to adopt a new political strategy. His teacher, ʿAli Muttaqi, supported the Muzaffar-Shahi dynasty and pinned his hopes of reform in Gujarat upon its strength, seeing the Mughals as the main threat to this program. However, by the time Muhammad ibn Tahir returned to Gujarat, the sultanate was weak and its nobles had conceded precious ports to the Portuguese in exchange for help against their political rivals. After the Mughal ruler Akbar consolidated power, he conquered Gujarat in 1573. Muhammad ibn Tahir took this opportunity to ally with the Mughals, in hope that Akbar's invasion might be leveraged to assert his program of reform.

When Akbar's armies crossed into Gujarat, they first conquered the northern city of Patan before moving south to take the port of Surat and then the capital at Ahmedabad. At Patan, Islamic scholars and Sufis pledged allegiance to Mughal rule, followed quickly by scholars at Ahmedabad and Khambhat. When the Mughal army camped at Patan, Muhammad ibn Tahir met Akbar and informed him that Mahdawis posed a grave threat to religious rectitude and social stability. He urged Akbar to suppress them. Most likely, the emperor answered him in the affirmative and promised to pursue this course of action, for at this early stage in his career, Akbar justified his rule with reference to upholding the *shariʿa*. He had not yet decided to humble Islamic scholars and elevate his own personality to the status of a divinely enlightened ruler who was independent of juridical authority. As an invader, Akbar would have relied for legitimacy and recognition upon scholars and saints in the area he conquered. Rumors abounded that Akbar was poised to attack the Mahdawi *da'iras* in Gujarat and drive them out of the province. The Mahdawis prepared for the assault; however, it never came.

Akbar was personally uninterested in persecuting Mahdawis. One of his court scholars, Shaykh Mubārak Nāgōrī (d. 1593), had Mahdawi sympathies, and Akbar grew to rely on his brilliant sons Abū'l-Faḍl and Fayḍī (a philosopher and a poet, respectively, who grew up liberally beyond strict Mahdawi loyalties) as his leading courtiers. However, in 1573 Akbar appointed his foster-brother, Mirzā ʿAzīz Kōkā (d. 1624), to be governor of Gujarat. Later that year, the governor executed the policies urged by Muhammad ibn Tahir and ordered a military attack against the *da'ira* at Mōrbī, which Miyan Mustafa's father had founded; the father was killed in the assault along with many of his followers, while the son, Miyan Mustafa Gujarati, was arrested and taken captive to Ahmedabad.[28] Akbar did make a show of "upholding orthodoxy," as he called Miyan Mustafa, the most erudite Mahdawi in the locale of Patan, to justify his Mahdawi beliefs.[29] After questioning in court, he was released without punishment.

Muhammad ibn Tahir's political strategy seemed to work while Mirza ʿAziz Koka governed Gujarat from 1573 till 1579. Mahdawis were driven into hiding, and "most of the traces of this heretical innovation were wiped out."[30] However, the position of governor under Mughal rule rotated regularly. Within a few years, the position was given to ʿAbd al-Raḥīm Khān-e Khānān (d. 1627, the son of Akbar's former regent, the Shiʿi general Bayrām Khān). Under ʿAbd al-Rahim's governorship, the Mahdawis increased in visibility. One chronicler accused the new governor of "offering the Mahdawis protection," while others alleged that he "was in league with the heretical innovators" and actively encouraged their activities.[31] Since he came from a Shiʿi family, the new governor probably advocated the protection of minority communities. Muhammad ibn Tahir decided to petition Akbar to replace the governor. But while traveling to Agra to meet Akbar in 1578, a band of "heretical extremists" assassinated him on the road between Ujjain and Sarangpur (Sārangpūr, both towns in Malwa).[32]

The assassination of Muhammad ibn Tahir lends credence to ʿAli Muttaqi's accusation that the Mahdawis and Shattaris were allied. Wajih al-Din ʿAlawi, the primary successor to Muhammad Ghawth in Gujarat, provides dramatic evidence that some Shattari masters allied with the Mahdawis. When Muhammad ibn Tahir came from Patan to Ahmedabad, Wajih al-Din tried to dissuade him from confronting the Mahdawis; the Shattari master delivered to him a subtle discourse on ultimate reality.

> My dear brother, the true saint recognizes the world's nature. The world was created in an orderly arrangement and everything has its purpose; this is so that all the names of God can manifest in the world, both the beauteous names and the mighty names. On the order of your Lord, each name manifests itself and in its particular form with its own effects and powers. The real meaning of the "straight path" [*ṣirāṭ-e mustaqīm*] is that each being expresses its own nature as a manifestation of the divine names. All appearances of contradiction and deviation are only manifestations of the divine names as they manifest here in the world. From this point of view, every Moses should come to some sort of peaceful reconciliation with his Pharaoh. . . . Therefore, my dear brother, there is no need for this political maneuvering and crafty showmanship! Stay engrossed in God and don't meddle in what other people are doing! These are times to keep silent and stay at home.[33]

Wajih al-Din insisted that the true saint should perceive no enemies, for conflict and contradiction are only illusory appearances in the world that belie an underlying unity. To oppose others with force is to give in to worldly illusion and lose grasp of the divine unity that sustains everyone, the seemingly orthodox as well as the apparently heretical. Wajih al-Din made this philosophical argument for ethical relativism, which he saw as the essential principle of Islamic spirituality that seeks to apprehend divine unity.

Muhammad ibn Tahir, however, did not buy the argument. He continued to oppose the Mahdawis, raising the stakes by pledging to take his case to Akbar. The famous biographer of Sufis, Muḥammad Ghawthī Shaṭṭārī, judges that Muhammad ibn Tahir disregarded this advice because he was "too engrossed in political partisanship."[34] But Ghawthi himself was subtly partisan: he was a student and disciple of Wajih al-Din. It was not political hardheadedness that led Muhammad ibn Tahir to disregard it but rather his commitment to ʿAli Muttaqi's ideal of reformed Sufi training that would revive the *shariʿa*. Such a revival necessitated limitation of "authentic sainthood" and strong critique of those judged to have transgressed its borders. On principle, he could not accept Wajih al-Din's proposed truce. Even if he believed that the universe was really nothing but the manifestation of the divine names, he did not accept the proposal that insight about the oneness of being could form the authentic basis for Islamic social ethics. Rather, he argued that social ethics must be based on the behavior of the Prophet Muhammad, as focused into definite legal boundaries.

Wajih al-Din was the pivotal figure who defused reform efforts of the Muttaqi community by presenting them as unjustified persecutions, as we observed in the fourth satchel. In response to the persecution of Shaykh Muhammad Ghawth, Wajih al-Din wrote a scholarly treatise against the practice of declaring others to be non-Muslims and liable to state punishment (*takfir*). He used juridical terms and hadith reports to justify his argument, claiming that what Sufis or saints pronounce in a state of spiritual intoxication (*sukr*) should not make them liable for censure or punishment. Specifically, he defended certain statements in Muhammad Ghawth's ascension narrative against censure, concluding that "nobody who recites the attestation to faith [*kalima*] and turns toward Mecca for prayer [*qibla*] should be called an infidel or unbeliever."[35]

Wajih al-Din presented the same argument to protect Mahdawis from persecution. When a fatwa circulated in Gujarat declaring the Mahdawis to be unbelievers and liable to be executed, some scholars in Ahmedabad pressed Wajih al-Din to sign it. He refused and denounced their efforts, repeating his mantra that nobody who recites the attestation to faith should be called an infidel. Even if someone does just one thing in accord with the *shariʿa*, he should always be protected as a Muslim. Wajih al-Din appeared to be trying to save Muhammad ibn Tahir's life by urging him to quit critiquing the Mahdawis;

however, he profited by Muhammad ibn Tahir's demise, for he was left as the leading hadith scholar of Gujarat.

Muhammad ibn Tahir was killed while on the road to Agra to petition Akbar. He assumed that the Mughal emperor would act upon his advice to champion Sunni Islam and would trust hadith scholars and jurists, like himself, to define what were the bounds of orthodoxy. He expected that the Mughal emperor would behave like the sultans of Gujarat, who periodically acted upon the advice and rulings of ʿAli Muttaqi to suppress the Mahdawis and others who were perceived to threaten Sunni orthodoxy. When Akbar was younger, this assumption might have held. He came to the throne at age twelve but ruled under a regent, Bayram Khan (d. 1561), a Shiʿi Turkoman from Iran and able general who loyally supported Humayun and secured him aid from the Safavid ruler of Iran, Shah Tahmasp, to survive exile and reconquer South Asia. Akbar grew up under Bayram Khan's care and considered him a stepfather, passing all governing authority to him.

By the age of eighteen, however, Akbar began to chafe at the regency. After a military confrontation, Akbar dictated that Bayram Khan should leave South Asia to make the Hajj. The deposed regent traveled with his family toward the ports of Gujarat to secure the sea passage, but upon reaching the city of Patan he was assassinated. Mughal sources blame his death on an Afghan soldier who wanted revenge for a military defeat he had suffered when Bayram Khan secured Mughal rule. However, it is telling that Akbar did not send a detachment of guards to protect the family on their long journey.

For a period after Bayram Khan's death, Akbar ruled as a typical Sunni ruler, paying homage to Sufis and allowing religious scholars at court to determine *shariʿa* rulings. Akbar drew close to Chishti saints, both living and dead, whose patronage shored up his legitimacy in the public eye and whose blessings facilitated the birth of his sons. He instituted a yearly pilgrimage to the dargah of Khwaja Muʿin al-Din Chishti, who was perceived to be the guarantor over South Asia's sovereignty.

As Akbar successful conquered Gujarat and Bengal, both coastal regions with ports rich in trade and industry, he increasingly centralized power. He promoted himself as a divinely appointed, just ruler and began to undermine the authority of traditional scholars. Even if Muhammad ibn Tahir had survived to get an audience with Akbar, his petition would likely have fallen on deaf ears. One year after Muhammad ibn Tahir was killed, in 1579, Akbar circulated the document known as the *maḥḍar*; it called upon religious scholars and many Sufi leaders to affirm with their signatures that "a just ruler is more favored by God than a paradigmatic jurist [*mujtahid*]," which would place the emperor above even the founders of the four Sunni legal schools as well as any later jurist who upheld them.[36]

Akbar forced religious authorities in his realm, which now included Gujarat, to sign away their power to give or withhold legitimacy over his rule. Many scholars and jurists who previously wielded power and prestige in court were subsequently denounced, humiliated, and exiled. Even before this formal declaration, Akbar distanced himself from living Sufi masters and in compensation exaggerated his devotion to the long-dead saint Muʿin al-Din Chishti. The Shattari Sufis also lost the influence they once enjoyed. When Shaykh Muhammad Ghawth returned to Gwalior from his years of exile in Gujarat, Akbar did not invite him to court. Akbar refused to take initiation with Shaykh Muhammad Ghawth, as his father Humayun had done. After a few years, Muhammad Ghawth requested an audience with Akbar at court, and the chief court scholar roused some powerful nobles to ridicule him about his ascension experience and threatened him with persecution.[37] Yet when Muhammad Ghawth died in Gwalior, Akbar had a grand mausoleum built for him: it was the first Mughal-built dargah and the first to use *jali* (carved lattice of stone), a technique common in dargahs during the sultanate of Gujarat, which became increasingly incorporated into the Mughal architectural style.

When the young Mughal dynasty was struggling to win ascendancy, its survival depended on gaining popular recognition through alliances with Sufis like Muhammad Ghawth and other Shattaris. But by the time Akbar ruled as a mature emperor, administration was strong, authority was centralized, and relentless conquest enriched his coffers. He ceased to depend upon Sufis or scholars to convey legitimacy and consolidate sovereignty. Rather, he began to elevate his own authority and rein in their power with his innovated concept of "sacred kingship," in which the just ruler drew on higher inspiration than Sufis or scholars. Some historians, like Azfar Moin, misread Akbar's religious innovation and assert that the ruler was claiming "sainthood" for himself. Others correct this misreading, such as Corrine Lefevre, who observes that Akbar elevated reason and millennial election, forces that made him, the divinely illumined emperor, more just and authoritative than jurists, scholars, or saints.[38] There are different modes of sacred power in the Islamic tradition, but sainthood should not be used as an umbrella term to cover all of them. Akbar articulated "sacred kingship," but this does not mean he claimed to be a saint or referred to himself as the Mahdi. His claim to absolute political authority based on divine appointment signaled the maturation of a new imperium at the advent of the new millennium. This was the environment in which the next phase of ʿAli Muttaqi's legacy took shape, embodied in ʿAbd al-Haqq Muhaddith Dihlawi.[39]

Rebuilding: ʿAbd al-Haqq Muhaddith Dihlawi

When Gujarat was absorbed as a Mughal province, ʿAli Muttaqi's reform project seemed overturned in South Asia. ʿAli Muttaqi's primary Sufi successor, ʿAbd al-Wahhab Muttaqi, had tried to return but was attacked by Mahdawi partisans and fled Gujarat for good. His primary hadith student, Muhammad ibn Tahir, had returned from Mecca to Gujarat but was assassinated. For a decade after Muhammad ibn Tahir's death, his colleague ʿAbd al-Wahhab Muttaqi stayed in Mecca, quietly tending the foundation of training Sufi hadith scholars while keeping aloof from South Asian politics. Then ʿAbd al-Haqq Muhaddith Dihlawi arrived in Mecca a few years before the millennium. ʿAbd al-Wahhab Muttaqi carefully cultivated him to take this foundation back to Delhi and rebuild their reform project in the heart of the Mughal Empire.[40]

ʿAbd al-Haqq is mentioned often in this book as a biographer of ʿAli Muttaqi and his followers. Yet he was also famous as a hadith scholar and is often credited with reviving Islamic scholarship in South Asia. In his mature years in Delhi (for forty years, until his death in 1642), he articulated this revival with the aim of social reform to gently undermine some of the Mughal cultural synthesis and religious experimentation of Akbar's reign. His moderate approach sought to avoid extreme rhetoric and the ideological stridency of movements like the Mahdawis or the Naqshbandis led by Ahmad Sirhindi. ʿAbd al-Haqq's endeavor to reform society, through revival of the study of scriptural sciences and moderation of Sufi practice, matured after training in Mecca under Shaykh ʿAbd al-Wahhab Muttaqi.

The memory of ʿAbd al-Haqq is best preserved for modern audiences by Khaliq Ahmad Nizami, his biographer in Urdu. Nizami describes ʿAbd al-Haqq as the reviver of the *sharīʿa* at the height of the Mughal Empire, emphasizing his role over and against the more popularly acknowledged revivalist, Shaykh Ahmad Sirhindi. Despite Nizami's heroic portrait, ʿAbd al-Haqq's journey to becoming a profound and prolific Sufi scholar was full of dead ends, disasters, and disappointments. It was no foregone conclusion that he would become a reformist Sufi and politically influential scholar. As a young man, ʿAbd al-Haqq left Delhi to make the Hajj; in the process, he tarried in Gujarat and studied in Mecca, transforming his approach to both *sharīʿa* and Sufism. His pilgrimage sojourn lasted only three years, but its impact on his life was immeasurable because it gave him the chance to join the Muttaqi community.

ʿAbd al-Haqq began his Sufi training under his father, Shaykh Sayf al-Dīn.[41] His father was famous in Delhi as a poet who expressed mystical themes of self-obliteration through immersion in the divine presence. Sayf al-Din initiated his son into the Qadiri Order in 1559, when he was only nine years old. His early Sufi orientation was ecstatic and philosophical, emphasizing poetic eloquence and passionate longing over scholarly acumen. In old age, ʿAbd al-Haqq's father ordered him to take initiation from another Qadiri preceptor, Shaykh Mūsā Jīlānī, whom he met in 1577 when ʿAbd al-Haqq was twenty-seven years old and already an accomplished scholar.[42] His Qadiri training focused on immersion in love mysticism with the goal of subverting the bonds of reason and freeing the heart.[43] ʿAbd al-Haqq writes of his life during that time:

> I was engaged, night and day, in trying to gain the great profit of divine union. Sometimes I would stay awake for many nights so that a flash of that divine beauty might light up my consciousness. Sometimes I would spend many days as if in a dream of my imagination so that I might find some sign of divine union.
>
> If you promise to meet me while I am awake
> then I forbid myself from sleeping even a peep
> If you reveal a glimmer of your beauty in my dreams
> till judgment day I won't lift my head from sleep
>
> I remained in this practice until the obstructing veil of my reason and the desire for self-knowledge were lifted from me. This act was the result of divine blessing and generosity alone, that raised me up, helpless in myself, and brought me to the threshold of God's House [the Kaʿba in Mecca].[44]

ʿAbd al-Haqq saw his second initiation as an intensification of the first with his father. His father was a Qadiri Sufi, but Shaykh Musa was a direct descendant of ʿAbd al-Qadir Jilani, the founder of the order. ʿAbd al-Haqq praised him as the physical embodiment of ʿAbd al-Qadir and reported that "Shaykh Musa loved me to the furthest extent possible and accepted me as his son, and gave me leave to be his vice-regent."[45] Under his care, ʿAbd al-Haqq experienced ecstasy, alienation from his ego, and longing for union with divine beauty by breaking the bonds of his reason. These were all standard stages of love mysticism, which did not erase allegiance to *shariʿa* norms but also did not normally lead to reification of *shariʿa* through revivalist strategies.[46] In ʿAbd al-Haqq's early life under Qadiri preceptors, scholarly discipline and mystical devotion had their own spheres of activity and their own religious legitimacy.

After his second initiation, ʿAbd al-Haqq stayed in Delhi for some time, for he was thirty-two years old and married with children.[47] Shortly after his father died in 1582, ʿAbd al-Haqq moved to Fatehpur Sikri, the new Mughal palace-city a short distance from Agra, where his new shaykh, Musa Jilani, had connections in Akbar's court. Shaykh Musa had sought Akbar's aid in a conflict of succession, and Akbar persuaded him to settle at Fatehpur Sikri with a noble rank. Shaykh Musa introduced ʿAbd al-Haqq to court as an educated gentleman, budding scholar, and avid poet; he befriended leading personalities there like Faydi (the court poet, d. 1595), ʿAbd al-Qadir Bada'uni (a court historian, d. 1605) and Niẓām al-Dīn Aḥmad Bakhshī (a high administrator and historian, d. 1621).

ʿAbd al-Haqq came to Fatehpur Sikri seeking royal patronage or a teaching position. He may have spent five years there, but, unlike his Sufi master, ʿAbd al-Haqq could not turn the Mughal court to his own advantage. In *Akhbār al-Akhyār*, ʿAbd al-Haqq makes elliptical and literary references to this period, as if he were scarred by his experience. He uses deliberately double-sided expressions that could describe both his Sufi exercises and his liminal social status. "I was sitting in isolation, separated from home and relatives. My heart bore great hopes, yet I neither performed favors for others nor harmed them. I never allowed the dust of other's footsteps to settle on my heart. My conscience was clear of the need to keep the company of this particular person or that person; no, even more than this I had grown tired of mentioning the names Zayd and ʿUmar from grammar lessons and books of composition."[48] When ʿAbd al-Haqq claims that his conscience was "clear of the need" to sit with this person or that person, he unintentionally reveals that he was both tempted and compelled to find patronage, support, and allies at court. Courtiers vied with each other over who could claim this brilliant young scholar in their circle of debate, discussion, plotting, and planning. This is the direction pointed out by the metaphor of "Zayd and ʿUmar," who are the stock characters of classical Arabic grammar exercises (like "Jack and John" in English). "Zayd and ʿUmar" could be a cipher for the two leading personalities at court, the brothers Abu'l-Fadl and Faydi, the ideologues responsible for promoting Akbar as a universal and enlightened monarch who was above the conventional *shariʿa*. ʿAbd al-Haqq was engaged as a teacher of Arabic as well as religious sciences in court circles, so that even common lessons involving "Zayd and ʿUmar" entangled him in exhausting court intrigues.

ʿAbd al-Haqq mentions that he had turned to the council of others and relied on their guidance during this time, a move that gave way in his conscience to temptation, doubts, and even moments of disbelief.

> I am made joyful by those times, like in my youth and my student days, when I pass through the straits and snares which cause the foot to slip and the eyes to stray. In those times, divine help extended from beyond the veil of the unseen from that place I know, so that the overwhelming power of God leads me, without my own choosing, from the doubts and weak misgivings that are dropped into the workshop of the ego and the tempter, and leads me to sit in the tranquil haven of alienation and aloneness. By these means, the Lord turned my seeking aid from others into another direction, toward seeking the Lord alone. For a time, due to the rebellion of my reason and the turbidity of my vain ambition, I did not even have that basic belief in divine unity that is the primary condition for any Sufi seeker. My heart was not inscribed with the desired orientation toward sincerity and righteousness. In the end, after no good came from taking council with other people and following their advice, there remained no way out for me except to pass the reins of choice back to the true One. Since my reason could not untie the knots that held me down, there was no way forward except through letting go of reason and embracing a holy madness.
>
> You must leave aside calculated rationality
> and lay hold of what seems like insanity.[49]

In this delicately phrased text, ʿAbd a-Haqq does not accuse others of disbelief and heresy at court but rather confesses that he himself was found guilty of disbelief, for he turned to others for material aid and social advancement rather than relying on God alone.

An "unofficial" autobiographical fragment that ʿAbd al-Haqq included in one of his later letters sheds light on his experience at court. He found a modicum of success at court, for the emperor Akbar raised his position and provided for his material needs. However, success led only to dissatisfaction: he suspected that various factions at court sought to manipulate him and use his fame to increase their own power and achieve their own designs. In this letter, written by ʿAbd al-Haqq just after he returned to Delhi from Mecca, he reveals some candid details of his experience at court.

> I am a man who grew up since my youngest days accustomed to exertions of learning and worship. I never got accustomed to the company of worldly people and the demands of socializing with them. Once I had acquired, by the grace of God, reasonable experience with socializing and satisfied my needs and aims by engaging with society, some powerful people in the government prevailed upon me to present myself for service before the worldly rules. I met the sultan of the age [Akbar] and he provided for me, took care of my needs, and raised my position. They sought to increase their following through using me and to gain command of wealth and power through manipulating me, but God protected me and did not leave me to their designs. God evoked in the heart of his servant an overwhelming attraction and passion for God and led him out of India to this holy place [Mecca].[50]

The historian Bada'uni claimed that ʿAbd al-Haqq left court in protest against the emperor's heretical experiments.[51] Yet in reality, Akbar's new policies were in place before ʿAbd al-Haqq came to court: the *maḥḍar* was decreed that Akbar's judgment was more authoritative than that of Muslim jurists, and a forum for debates among scholars of differing sects and religions (*ʿibādat-khāna*) was established. Why would ʿAbd al-Haqq take a position teaching at court in 1582 if he saw these ongoing innovations as heretical? In 1584, while still at court, he began to compile his first major work, *Akhbār al-Akhyār*, yet this hagiography offers no evidence of disgust at contemporary heresies in South Asia.

ʿAbd al-Haqq became a reformist Sufi dedicated to reviving the *shariʿa* only after meeting Shaykh ʿAbd al-Wahhab Muttaqi in Mecca. ʿAbd al-Haqq was not disgusted by others at court, only at himself for having come there. He was perplexed not by the spread of heresy but by his own worldly ambition to gain fame as a religious scholar. In the intense internal reaction that overwhelmed him, he abandoned the court, his teaching position, and even all pretense of being a Sufi master. This was a precarious passage, even a dangerous one. Throughout his early life, ʿAbd al-Haqq's loyalty to the ideals of Sufism and its practice did not conflict with his aspiration to become a scholar and teacher. As he began to teach, attain renown, and accrue symbolic capital, he experienced an internal backlash; he questioned all that he was engaged in, including his pursuit of knowledge.

ʿAbd al-Haqq justified his devastating internal critique and subsequent renunciation as the effect of *jadhba*, overpowering attraction to God that draws one out of one's own reason. Its manifestations were only shades different from the signs of insanity. His bout of "holy madness" was a socially acceptable means to escape from the Mughal court. ʿAbd al-Haqq left Fatehpur Sikri and claims to have wandered, disregarding work and human contact, until he ended up in Mecca.

> After I found some peace of mind and the agitation of doubts and temptations subsided, doubts which ultimately cause disappointment and despair, then I ceased to struggle with any kind of work and shut my eyes to the presence of others around me. I sat on the threshold of my own heart, waiting to see what might happen and what door might open before me. Under the ruling of the phrase "Those who allow God to act on their behalf will never be disappointed and those who turn to God in trials will find release," the empowerer of the helpless and the guide of the wandering called me toward the divine presence. God placed the chain of longing and love around the neck of this homeless wanderer, and pulled him toward his own abode. And this undeserving one reached that most sought after goal, the place of the beloved, Mecca and Medina.[52]

Despite what he says, ʿAbd al-Haqq did not go directly to Mecca; he did not have the material means to go and his journey meandered.

In his state of *jadhba* he wandered to Delhi, where his family had remained when he moved to court. As he renounced all ambitions at court, ʿAbd al-Haqq also renounced the model of Shaykh Musa, who was still alive. He regressed to the more comforting model of his first Sufi master, his dead father; he explained his renunciation as his faithfully upholding his father's advice and embodying the very spirit of his guidance. "From my very earliest days, I have observed the advice of my father, who used to tell me, 'Be careful that you don't become a dry and hard-hearted scholar [*mullā*].' Thus, every breath that I draw in love and passion increases my tenderheartedness, and each step I take is on the path of distancing my need from others and evoking sympathy to their needs from myself. . . . I am hopeful that with each breath, I can follow his footsteps and that I succeed in the real task of desisting from the business of the self."[53] ʿAbd al-Haqq sorely missed the warm and sheltered atmosphere of his father's circle in Delhi, so he drifted back there with vague hopes of rediscovering this lost equipoise.

Yet when it was not to be found, the last strands of reason beyond the cords of ambition snapped: his state of *jadhba* reached its fullest extent. This "madness" allowed him to leave his family and children behind and to wander to Gujarat without funds to get to Mecca. He had fallen into the perplexed state we may call a "nervous breakdown" or "midlife crisis." The advice of colleagues and plans of his reason led him to a dead end; only the waves of insane attraction to God could carry him on a sojourn to the other side. ʿAbd al-Haqq roamed overland from Delhi to Gujarat for one year, heading toward the port of Surat that commanded the overseas routes to Arabia.

How did ʿAbd al-Haqq travel in his state of "madness" and without funds? He found in the Shattari Order a powerful network that connected inland Delhi to the Gujarati coasts, for Shaykh Muhammad Ghawth had survived persecution and, over the next sixteen years, built a strong following in Gujarat. As ʿAbd al-Haqq traveled to Gujarat, he found himself supported by Shattari Sufis in this network. In Mandu, he stayed with the Sufi biographer Muhammad Ghawthi Shattari. In Ahmedabad, he kept company with Shaykh Wajih al-Din ʿAlawi.[54] Furthermore, ʿAbd al-Haqq enjoyed support from Mughal nobility and administrators in his travels. In Malwa, he was hosted by the Mughal governor, Mirza Aziz Koka. In Ahmedabad, he was welcomed by Nizam al-Din Ahmad Bakhshi, the Sufi-minded and philosophical noble who was provincial treasurer and prior acquaintance from the Mughal court.[55] His good relations with Shattari Sufis further demonstrate that ʿAbd al-Haqq did not advocate a reformist agenda at this stage in his life; his friendship with Mughal officials shows that he was not protesting Akbar's policies.

His powerful friend Nizam al-Din Ahmad Bakhshi secured for ʿAbd al-Haqq a sea passage to Mecca.[56] By then, the sailing season to Arabia had already ended, and he had to wait for up to ten months for seasonal winds to change.[57] He waited in Ahmedabad, spending time with Wajih al-Din, from whom he learned Qadiri litanies and prayers. By acquiring *dhikr* techniques from him, ʿAbd al-Haqq treated him as a *shaykh al-istifāda*, a Sufi master who granted him litanies and techniques without giving him initiation as a disciple. If ʿAbd al-Haqq were searching for a new Sufi initiation to provide him with a new foundation and allow him to rebuild his life, Wajih al-Din would be a choice dear to his heart; this Gujarati shaykh compounded an outer *shariʿa* rectitude and acumen in the discipline of hadith with an inner attachment to ecstatic experience and existential philosophy. At this point in his life, ʿAbd al-Haqq did not consider philosophy to be an obstacle to authentic Islamic piety, nor did he view hadith studies as a method of tempering the speculative, poetic, and musical currents of Sufi devotion. If he had taken a new Sufi master in Gujarat from among the Qadiri and Shattari networks that he traveled through, then he might never have evolved into a reformist Sufi and reviver of *shariʿa* disciplines.

Many Sufis who made the Hajj and stayed in Mecca for intense scholarly training never became reformers. Many, even after extended residence in

Arabia, never wavered in their devotion to existential philosophy as the primary intellectual and aesthetic articulation of Sufi practice.[58] ʿAbd al-Haqq's reformist ideas, therefore, cannot be explained simply by his going on the Hajj and staying three years in Mecca. His reformist ideas developed because there he met Shaykh ʿAbd al-Wahhab Muttaqi, who combined initiation and scholarly training in a unique way.

Initiation into the triple *tariqa* opened a devotional and ideological world for ʿAbd al-Haqq that was much wider than the options he had explored in South Asia. Examining the content of this teaching—how it both challenged and disciplined him—makes clear that ʿAbd al-Haqq became a reformer and revivalist because he was first and foremost an interregional, multilingual Sufi scholar, which attracted him to the Muttaqi method. His connection with ʿAbd al-Wahhab Muttaqi allowed ʿAbd al-Haqq to return to Delhi, reoriented and strengthened to build his mature career.[59] Indeed, it forced him to do so against his will.

At first, ʿAbd al-Haqq had intended only to find hadith experts in Mecca and to master their scholarly discipline. Yet, in hindsight, he records that he also harbored an unarticulated hope of finding another Sufi guide.

> After I came to Mecca and Medina, I fulfilled my primary goal: I was blessed by visiting the tomb of the Prophet, witnessing the beauty of the Kaʿba, and performing the rites of the Hajj. These are the peak experiences of anyone's life! But I also had a secondary goal, which was to study the hadith of the Prophet, which brings one closer to his spirit, in the very place where he had lived. Here I might mention a further blessing, the realization of which was completely outside of my planning or control—that was to find one of the special people who dwell here in Mecca, who are so intimate to the Prophet in their own souls. I could barely hope that I might meet one such as this, so that he might perceive my plight or my eyes might be illuminated by the sight of him, for either event would be a great bliss. If I might get the chance to speak with one such as this or serve him, this would be the key to attain salvation that would lay the foundation upon which I could build my whole life in the future. Sufi masters say that one hour of sitting with love and affection in the presence of one who has reached the ultimate goal and one who is chosen by the Prophet, that single hour would be the apex of one's whole life. . . . And if I could stay in his company and training for an extended time so that [absorbing the illumination of his sainthood] could reach its full effect, filling me with the reflection of the brilliant

manifestations of divine beauty and keeping my gaze from straying to the multiplicity of the created world, then this would indeed fulfill the promise of the Qur'an: *light upon light, God guides to the light whomever God wills* [Qur'an 24:35]. For many years, a prayer has been on my tongue and in my heart, to ask for just this. As Shaykh ʿAbd al-Qadir Jilani has instructed, I prayed, "Oh Lord, guide me to one from among those who are intimate with you, who may guide me to your presence and may teach me the way to reach you."[60]

As he explained, ʿAbd al-Haqq first performed the pilgrimage and then studied in Mecca with some unspecified masters of hadith. Through them, he met ʿAbd al-Wahhab Muttaqi. Toward the end of his first year in Mecca, he began to study the hadith collection titled "The Niche for Lamps" (*Mishkāt al-Maṣābiḥ*) under the tutelage of ʿAbd al-Wahhab.[61] ʿAbd al-Haqq may not have recognized ʿAbd al-Wahhab as a Sufi master, for it was his method to simply teach what each student came to learn from him. Only slowly did the shaykh focus his inner attention upon the soul of the student and subtly achieve spiritual direction as well, rather than demanding up-front allegiance with dramatic rituals of renunciation and submission.[62]

Within a year, ʿAbd al-Haqq recognized him as the spiritual guide for whom he had been secretly longing and became a disciple (*murīd*). ʿAbd al-Haqq's record of his interaction with his new shaykh shows that he was extremely willful, assertive, and questioning with his master, in contrast to ʿAbd al-Wahhab's almost complete self-abnegation under ʿAli Muttaqi. Despite this, ʿAbd al-Wahhab carefully cultivated ʿAbd al-Haqq to return to Delhi to spread the Muttaqi reform project. This was against ʿAbd al-Haqq's own will and natural inclination. This initiation was going to be a monumental challenge for ʿAbd al-Haqq, from the very first moment that he requested formal initiation.

I told Shaykh ʿAbd al-Wahhab, "When I arrived in the Hijaz and was made joyful after visiting the tomb of the Prophet, then I came into your circle of students and followers and was ennobled with your company. There appeared in my heart a little of the light of faith that refuted whatever might have remained in my heart of greed for worldly gain and hopes of attaining worldly recognition. Now, I desire only to course the path that you teach along with your followers and enter into the company of the spiritual seekers who are devoted to you." The shaykh remained silent for a while with his head bowed. Then he raised his head and said, "Praise be to God! Nothing could be better than that one choose to halt the natural course of his life and commit himself to sitting in the corner of

> isolation and anonymity, for this is the highest level of achieving divine acceptance." Then he added, "Following my path is a very difficult task! Attaining firm footing in it takes long struggle. The basic principle is that you must participate in the lives of others and mix with them constantly, sharing with them in what is good and avoiding in them what is evil."[63]

How striking this challenge must have been. ʿAbd al-Haqq had just finished baring his heart to ʿAbd al-Wahhab Muttaqi by admitting that before his experience at court, he "never had socialized with people and thus suffered despair at their hands." Then his master replied that he would not be allowed to stay in Mecca and Medina, leading a simple and scholarly life in detachment from the political and social confusion back home.

For over two years, ʿAbd al-Wahhab challenged ʿAbd al-Haqq and cleverly diverted him from his intellectual and ideological inclinations. For example, consider how he wavered in choosing a legal school to follow. Like most South Asian Muslims, ʿAbd al-Haqq was raised with the Hanafi legal school. In sailing to Mecca, he passed beyond the zone where the Hanafi legal school predominated and entered a zone of Shafiʿi dominance. In most coastal regions around the Indian Ocean, Muslims follow the Shafiʿi school. Hanafi visitors to Mecca found themselves to be often beset by zealous Shafiʿis who were convinced that their own legal method was the purest and most elegant; they accused others, especially the Hanafis, of basing their decisions on personal opinion (*ẓann*) and reasonable speculation (*rāʾī*) rather than on that squarely proven by the Prophetic hadith.

ʿAbd al-Haqq was initially convinced by these arguments. As a hadith scholar, he was eager to follow a juridical method that ideologically based itself on Prophetic reports, and most of the great hadith scholars in Mecca were Shafiʿis from Egypt. But when ʿAbd al-Haqq admitted to ʿAbd al-Wahhab that he wanted to change allegiance to the Shafiʿi school, the shaykh defended the Hanafi school and its founder, Abū Ḥanīfa (d. 767).[64] ʿAbd al-Wahhab claimed that although the Shafiʿis were ideologically articulate in stressing the importance of hadith in legal reasoning, the Hanafis actually made more important contributions to hadith literature than did the Shafiʿis. Since the Hanafi school organized first, its books contain the earliest record of hadith and include some reports not found in decisions of the Shafiʿi jurists.[65]

With these creative arguments, ʿAbd al-Wahhab Muttaqi dissuaded his disciple from rashly changing his legal school. Becoming a Shafiʿi would have been a serious obstacle to ʿAbd al-Haqq's return as an effective teacher and reformer in South Asia, where the Hanafi school predominated.[66] By discouraging his disciple from becoming a Shafiʿi, ʿAbd al-Wahhab subverted his explicit policy that everyone should choose for themselves which legal method to follow rather than be a partisan of the method into which they were born. That the shaykh blatantly disregarded his own policy reveals just how crucial he considered it that ʿAbd al-Haqq remain a Hanafi so that he could viably return to South Asia as a reformer.

ʿAbd al-Wahhab also confronted his disciple over his extreme partisanship in regard to the Qadiri Order. ʿAbd al-Haqq's partisanship was investigated in the third satchel to illustrate how fusing three orders into one was critical for the Muttaqi community's reform efforts. This chapter revisits the issue, to show how the leader of the triple *tariqa* changed ʿAbd al-Haqq's viewpoint on the matter and moderated his partisanship.

> Shaykh ʿAbd al-Wahhab gave me legitimate certification in the books of the Sufis and their methods and initiation into these orders: the Qadiri, Shadhili, Madyani. . . . But this lowly one abridges these initiations and just calls himself "Qadiri" and is content with the nobility of this single order. I used to be excessively and zealously devoted to ʿAbd al-Qadir Jilani. I used to never look to other masters or even mention their names, so absorbed was I in turning toward Shaykh ʿAbd al-Qadir, for he is always present for those who turn their attention toward him. Shaykh ʿAbd al-Wahhab [Muttaqi] had told me, "You are certainly from among Shaykh ʿAbd al-Qadir's disciples and servants. However, it is the duty of one who seeks the truth to learn from every beneficial source and also to teach whoever can learn from you [regardless of their lineage]. Never close upon yourself the door of seeking or bar the way of learning from others. From whatever source you may draw benefit, you may ascribe the blessing to the presence of your shaykh [ʿAbd al-Qadir]."[67]

ʿAbd al-Wahhab conflicted many times with his disciple, who was too eager to learn any new litany or ritual with a Qadiri pedigree. He often stressed that "one should never believe that absolute perfection lies in one place and one place only; whoever claims this will induce others to denounce him and weaken his own belief."[68] ʿAbd al-Wahhab argued that one could have a constant spiritual orientation to Shaykh ʿAbd al-Qadir without that preventing one from taking initiation into other orders, for the method of each was beneficial.[69] ʿAbd al-Wahhab was also a Qadiri, but his method was moderate compared with the other Qadiri masters whom ʿAbd al-Haqq met and admired, for it was tempered by being fused into the triple *tariqa*.

ʿAbd al-Wahhab moderated his disciple's admiration for the intellectual elegance of existential philosophy and overtly emotional ecstasy in intoxicated states. He subtly turned ʿAbd al-Haqq's attention away from the texts of Ibn ʿArabi and ʿAbd al-Karim al-Jili. He never prevented him from reading these books, but when ʿAbd al-Haqq was leaving to return to Delhi, the shaykh forbade him to speak openly with others about the secrets and subtleties of existential unity. Soon after he had arrived in Delhi, ʿAbd al-Haqq received a letter from a Qadiri shaykh from Arabia that was loaded with reason-dazzling expressions about *wahdat al-wujud*. In his response, ʿAbd al-Haqq wrote that he admired them but was forbidden to speak of the philosophy of oneness.[70]

ʿAbd al-Wahhab spent two intense years cultivating his disciple in this path of Sufism that was moderated from within (by having several orders fused together) and tempered from without (by being joined with hadith studies). Yet his disciple was still recalcitrant and headstrong, insisting on staying in Mecca or else going to Baghdad to stay at the tomb of ʿAbd al-Qadir Jilani, as depicted in the vignette that opens this chapter. The shaykh had to abandon his normally subtle arguments and strategic silences: he directly commanded ʿAbd al-Haqq to return straight to Delhi. ʿAbd al-Wahhab also ordered him to keep isolated from the worldly people who had devastated him before at the Mughal court. Further, he urged his disciple to be flexible, visit other Sufis and scholars, and maintain contacts with society. ʿAbd al-Haqq still had not fully acknowledged the role for which ʿAbd al-Wahhab had primed him, still longing to avoid the responsibilities of his mature life, which was now beginning to dawn as he prepared to sail back to South Asia.

Capital: Reform in the Mughal Heartland

ʿAbd al-Haqq returned in 1592, a few months into the beginning of the new Islamic millennium. By this time, the Mughal rulers had endowed several cities with the privilege of being their capitals. Delhi had long been the imperial center of the sultanate of Delhi in its successive ruling dynasties; its last dynasty, the Lodis, invested Agra as their new capital just before the Mughals conquered them. The Mughals construct forts and palaces at Delhi and Agra while also building other capitals. ʿAbd al-Haqq had worked at Fatehpur Sikri, which housed the court from 1571 until 1585; by the time he returned to South Asia, the capital had shifted again to Lahore. In reality, the Mughal capital was wherever the peripatetic emperor's body stood, whether in urban centers or in mobile army encampments.

While the political capital moved with the emperor, according to the shifting tides of military strategy and political expediency, Delhi retained its central position in the Mughal heartland. It had social capital even if the political center moved periodically outside it. It was favored by both Sufi and scholarly families who sought stability outside the tumultuous life of court. Settling in Delhi, ʿAbd al-Haqq built a khanqah, training those whom he initiated into his Sufi lineages, which also served as a madrasa for teaching Islamic sciences.[71] In the Mughal capital, he sought to unpack the symbolic capital of his sojourn in Arabia, his innovative Sufi connections, and his hadith expertise.

For thirteen years, while Emperor Akbar reigned (until his death in 1605 at Agra), Shaykh ʿAbd al-Haqq kept a low profile. However, when Akbar was succeeded by Jahangir, the shaykh tried to spread his reformist ideals among Mughal nobility and even to the new emperor himself. ʿAbd al-Haqq drew from his overseas experience with the Muttaqi community to convert his symbolic capital into social clout. He aimed to alter the course of Islamic society under the Mughal ruler, noting in one of his letters, "This prayer in Arabic has come down to us from the greatest Shaykhs: 'Oh God, keep sound our ruler and his community, our shepherd and his flock, and unite their hearts in doing good.'"[72] He would eventually try to guide the new emperor's boat to safety through the seas of justice and benevolence. However, those political seas would be tumultuous.

During his initial period of quiet and calm, ʿAbd al-Haqq circulated works he had begun in Mecca, instigated by ʿAbd al-Wahhab Muttaqi. He gained renown as a hadith expert and turned his skills to practical use in writing Persian commentaries on the major collections of hadith, in the hopes that other scholars and Sufis would integrate the meanings of the reports into their own juridical, devotional, and literary work. In addition to hadith texts, he authored extensive translations of Arabic works into Persian, mainly from books on Sufism.[73] ʿAbd al-Haqq would often rework an Arabic text with a fuller commentary in Persian, perhaps with a direct translation of the text into Persian.

His most complete theoretical work is a dual composition of this nature. ʿAbd al-Haqq first wrote a Persian treatise entitled *Maraj al-Baḥrayn fī Jamʿ bayn al-Ṭarīqayn*, or "The Meeting of Two Oceans and the Joining of Two Paths."[74] He explained that the book aimed to join the two paths of jurisprudence and mysticism. One could think of this as uniting the dual aspects of religious life: "joining righteous comportment [*shariʿa*] to refined character [*ṭariqa*], or outer manifestation [*ẓāhir*] to inner potential [*bāṭin*], or appearance [*ṣūrat*] to essence [*maʿnā*], or covering [*qashr*] to core [*lubb*], or religious knowledge [*ʿilm*] to spiritual state [*ḥal*], or sobriety [*ṣaḥw*] to intoxication [*sukr*], or ritual exactness [*madhhab*] to spiritual acumen [*mashrab*], or reason [*ʿaql*] to passion [*ʿishq*]."[75] In this work, he argues that Sufism is an integral part of Islam, one that is fully compatible with jurisprudence and scriptural scholarship; in fact, the disciplines of jurisprudence and scriptural studies are not complete without Sufism. In its medieval elaboration, ʿAbd al-Haqq explains, Sufism had become separated from jurisprudence—partly because of Sufi masters who were not educated enough and partly because of jurists and hadith scholars who were jealous of Sufi masters and their spiritual accomplishment. In the natural growth of religious disciplines of knowledge, Sufism and jurisprudence had evolved into separate branches with specialized terminology and distinct regimes of training. Thus separate, each was incomplete. They needed to be rejoined in order to revive authentic Islam.[76]

In order to achieve this revival, ʿAbd al-Haqq advocated the Muttaqi method. In this, his primary intellectual source was the text of Zarruq, *Qawāʿid al-Taṣawwuf*, or "Principles of Sufism," which was unknown in South Asia.[77] He rendered Zarruq's ideas in Persian in thirteen chapters, each entitled a *qaʿida*, a principle or rule, in imitation of Zarruq's original text.[78] ʿAbd al-Haqq claimed that Zarruq was among "the greatest contemporary scholars and grandest Sufi masters of North Africa, as all the shaykhs of the Arab lands concur. I quote extensively from his book, *Qawāʿid al-Ṭarīqa fī'l-Jamʿ bayn al-Sharīʿa wa'l-Ḥaqīqa*.[79] Because all the people of truth and masters of realization speak the same message, quoting the words of one of them is the same as quoting from many of them."[80] *ʿAbd al-Haqq* was careful to disguise the innovative quality of Zarruq's writing, presenting his book as the distillation of five centuries of Sufi theoretical prose that began with Junayd (d. 910). After citing Junayd as the architect of sober Sufi discourse of intellectual Sufism attentive to the *shariʿa*, he launches into his exposition of Zarruq's ideals. "Because the expressions in this book [*Qawāʿid al-Taṣawwuf*] are subtle and eloquent, I took the liberty of explaining them in more words and paragraphs, but I have not added meanings beyond the original intent of Shaykh Zarruq's discourse. If I am accompanied by divine favor, I will write these meanings out more fully in another book, as time allows and by God's will."[81] This promise he fulfilled; he turned to composing an Arabic text that presented the same ideas in a fuller and more detailed way.

This fuller Arabic explanation is titled "Achieving Acquaintance for Insight into the Equivalence of Sufism and Jurisprudence" ("Taḥṣīl al-Taʿarruf fī Maʿrifat al-Fiqh wa'l-Taṣawwuf"). It has never been published or translated: it lies in manuscript form at the Reza Library archives at Rampur. Because it gives a much fuller treatment of the subject than the Persian text that has been published with an Urdu translation for modern readers, this book offers the following translated excerpts from manuscript sources. In its ornamental introduction, he elucidates his purpose by presenting Sufi saints and legal scholars as parallel authorities who, though diverged in the past, must rejoin in the present.

> In the name of God, the merciful, the compassionate. Praise be to God who for all sufficed, and peace be upon the servants whom God purified, especially upon their chief and leader, Muhammad the specially selected. Peace be also upon his family and companions, the most special followers of the religion of surety, those who take refuge on the bench of the brethren of purity. Peace be upon the saints of this community, the revivers of the true religion and exemplars of the folk of divinity. Peace be also upon its scholars, the preservers of *shariʿa* ordinances, and upon all those who follow their blessed guidance.
>
> This book is by a weak one who is impoverished depending on his God, the powerful One beyond need, namely ʿAbd al-Haqq Dihlawi, the son of Sayf al-Din, belonging to the Qadiri Order and the Hanafi School of law. This book is entitled "Achieving Acquaintance for Insight into the Equivalence of Sufism and Jurisprudence." It documents the spiritual states of the Sufis and jurists. It comprises two parts: the first part is on Sufism and the second part is on jurisprudence. For the first part, I extracted statements from the writings of the realized sages who join together these two paths, may God be merciful with them.
>
> You should know that Sufis offer different definitions of Sufism, but all of them center upon this one core meaning: refining one's moral character and purifying one's inner life, taking on virtues of perfection and adopting qualities of God the transcendent, perseverance in the way of truth and preserving the rights of others, focusing the heart on God alone and dismissing all that is other than God, passing away from lowly human qualities and achieving faith in religion, renouncing worldly ambition by fleeing vanity and choosing anonymity, taking on the duties of piety and pursuing the love of divinity. Once, Junayd was asked about Sufism. He answered, "It is purifying the heart from reliance upon people, severing base qualities, quelling the lowly human character, avoiding egoistic claims, embracing the descent of spiritual qualities, depending upon disciplines of divine knowledge, implementing the first principle for eternity, advising the entire community, staying faithful to God in reality, following the Prophet—upon him be peace and blessings—in his custom, and doing all such things that increase in people blessings."[82]

ʿAbd al-Haqq begins his discourse by quoting Junayd, just as he did in "The Meeting of Two Oceans." He starts with Junayd because he is the undisputed founder of Sufi theoretical prose. ʿAbd al-Haqq then moves quickly to discuss Shaykh Zarruq, as if there were not five centuries of Sufi experiment, expansion, and exposition between the two learned writers. In his view, Junayd began the intellectual exposition of Sufism, while Zarruq summed it up.

According to ʿAbd al-Haqq, just as Junayd's clarity began the evolution of Sufism as an Islamic discipline of knowledge (as he coined the term, "Knowledge of Hearts" as a cipher for Sufism), Zarruq's concision would end the diverse proliferation of Sufi paths by uniting them with hadith and jurisprudence.

> In his book "Principles of Sufism," the learned shaykh and moderate sage Ahmad Zarruq writes that "Sufism has been delimited and institutionalized and explained in thousands of ways but all of them center upon sincerity in turning attention toward God. The varieties express different aspects of that [sincerity]."[83] This sentence is the general summary, and all Sufi sayings that come subsequently express its details. Sufis have individually expressed the details in accord with what each has earned in knowledge, practice, state, and realization. Whoever has been granted a bit of sincerity in focusing on God thus has been granted a bit of Sufism. The Sufism of each person is the sincerity of that person's turning attention toward God.[84] But sincerity is conditioned by being pleasing to God—meaning with right faith—and in ways that satisfy God—meaning with proper worship—for that which is conditioned is not acceptable without its condition. . . . Nobody can be a Sufi without jurisprudence [*fiqh*], because divine orders can be known only through jurisprudence. Nor is jurisprudence sound with Sufism, for action cannot be carried out without sincerity in turning towards God. There is neither jurisprudence nor Sufism without faith, because both of them are only sound when based on firm faith. One must join them together as integral, just as souls are integral to bodies.[85]

ʿAbd al-Haqq admired Zarruq's "Usuli approach" to Sufi practice, which was the chosen method of the Muttaqi community. Usuli scholars endeavored to explain the principles upon which practices were based and to check that all behaviors drew nourishment from deep scriptural roots. ʿAbd al-Haqq paraphrased Zarruq's principles, simplifying their rarefied prose and providing compelling examples and explanations for his new South Asian audience.

> Jurisprudence is based on the root foundation of submission [*islām*] and theology is based on faith [*iman*]. The root foundation of being a Sufi is

the station of virtue [*iḥsan*] as explained by the Prophet Muhammad, who said, "Doing what is beautiful is worshipping God as if you see God, and if you cannot see God then know that God is seeing you." Sufi practice is one part of the religion that the Prophet explicated to Gabriel, so his companions might learn of its totality.[86] It is related that the Prophet's companion Mālik ibn Anas [d. 795] said: "One who follows the Sufi path while neglecting jurisprudence is a heretic, while one who learns jurisprudence while neglecting the Sufi path commits transgression. However, one who conjoins both has attained to realization of the Truth."[87]

Before ʿAbd al-Haqq, many Sufi scholars from South Asia sought to translate theoretical works written in Arabic for the Persian reading world. The difference is that ʿAbd al-Haqq projected the engagement with Arabic learning as part of a wider strategy to limit Sufi devotion within the parameters of hadith and jurisprudence. That strategy was central to the Muttaqi method, and its foundation was the previous scholarship of Ahmad Zarruq.

ʿAbd al-Haqq pursued this strategy not just in formal books but also in the less formal medium of letters. He preserved them in a volume of his collected letters, or *Maktūbāt*. This volume includes sixty-eight letters written to specific recipients, including Sufis, legal scholars, and Mughal nobles. They were given formal titles and a short prose introduction when collected and published by his eldest son, Muḥammad Nūr al-Ḥaqq (d. 1663), to whom the majority of them were addressed.

This poor humble one, ʿAbd al-Haqq son of Sayf al-Din, has a number of letters which he wrote according to the demands of the time and the needs of his audience. Some were addressed to his inner circle and close companions among the Sufis [*ahl-e sulūk o irādat*], while others were sent to nobles and rulers who are pious [*umarāʾ o mulūk az ahl-e saʿādat*]. Others were sent by others to give me advice, which are nearer and dearer to me than all the others. I have been ordered to speak only about affairs of religious scholarship and communal welfare that will further promote and revive Islamic custom [*tarwīj o tajdīd-e sharīʿat*] while preserving the beliefs and commands of the Prophet's example [*sunna*]. I am commanded to not step beyond the circle of moderation [*iʿtidāl*] and the bounds of precaution [*iḥtiyāṭ*]. I was told not to employ the metaphors of existential philosophers [*wujūdiyya*] or the interpretations of spiritualist adventurers [*bāṭiniyya*]. My Sufi master advised this poor fellow: "Do not speak of cosmic realities and existential subtleties but rather explain to the people knowledge that will improve their behavior and help them desist from sins. Never give precedence to spiritual discipline over legal discipline, just as you should never rely on legal correctness to the exclusion of spiritual refinement." In accord with this advice, this weak one has, in most all of his writings and compositions, relayed quotes from the esteemed Sufi masters and made reference to the leading scholars, namely those who join the two paths [*jāmiʿ al-ṭarīqayn*] and harmonize the two groups, meaning the Sufis and scholars.[88]

ʿAbd al-Haqq's letters provide crucial evidence about his intention and authority after moving back to South Asia, as guided by the Muttaqi method. He relayed quotes from those Sufi masters who "joined the two paths" of scriptural knowledge and mystical discipline. Of course, Zarruq and his own Muttaqi masters were the paragons of this method, and he quoted from them liberally throughout his letters.

After establishing his own madrasa, ʿAbd al-Haqq took a further initiation in the Naqshbandi Order from Khwāja Muḥammad Bāqī Bi'llāh (d. 1603). ʿAbd al-Haqq already had two initiations in the Qadiri Order, one as family inheritance and one from his youth. As he matured, he took initiation with the Muttaqi community in the triple *tariqa* that fused the Qadiri, Shadhili, and Madyani Orders; with it, he additionally received initiation in the Chishti Order that Shaykh ʿAbd al-Wahhab Muttaqi carried from his youthful wanderings.[89] Despite his initiation into the multiple orders, the Naqshbandi Order was newly ascendant in Mughal domains. Initiation in it was a valued addition as ʿAbd al-Haqq sought to root his authority in the Mughal capital, to guide its nobility, and to shape its scholars. From the time of Babur, Mughal rulers had ancestral connections to the Naqshbandi Order from their origins in Central Asia because the order's founder, Bahā' al-Dīn Naqshband, was buried in Bukhara.

Like most Naqshbandis of this era, Khwaja Baqi Bi'llah was born in Central Asia (in Kabul). In his youth, he studied hadith and scripture, determined to become a jurist. Once an ecstatic Sufi (*majdhūb*) recited to him a line of poetry disparaging Hanafi jurists and their dry scholarship.[90] "Will you ever find God in *Kanz* or *Hidāya* or some legal book? / There is no better tome than the heart—it's just there! Take a look!" This verse stirred his imagination, and he set off on a journey to learn from Sufi masters, which took him eventually to Delhi. Historian of South Asian Sufism Khaliq Ahmad Nizami notes his surprising combination of "the sternness of an Usuli scholar and the gentleness of a Sufi sage."[91] Though born three generations after the great Naqshbandi systematizer ʿUbaydallāh Aḥrār (d. 1490), Baqi Bi'llah was known as "Sultan of the Naqshbandis" in South Asia.[92] As Baqi Bi'llah's fame spread in Delhi, ʿAbd al-Haqq took initiation with him after a dream vision of Shaykh ʿAbd al-Qadir Jilani urged him to do so.[93] As a Naqshbandi, ʿAbd al-Haqq forged strategic alliances with the forces of reform and social activism that were rising in Delhi at that time; in these Naqshbandi networks, he circulated the ideals of the Muttaqi community without labeling them as such.

ʿAbd al-Haqq's compilation of letters is one of his most important and intimate writings. He ordered them collected and penned a short introduction to them. The first six letters, those he deemed most important, were addressed to Baqi Bi'llah. They offer his critiques of various religious movements that flourished in the time of Akbar, thus giving himself the reputation of an avid reformer that was to make him so renowned during his later years in Delhi and after his death.[94]

The first letter is written to Baqi Bi'llah and ʿAbd al-Haqq and titled "Sulūk Ṭarīq al-Falāḥ ʿind Faqd al-Tarbiya bi'l-Istilāḥ," or "Traveling the Path of Felicitous Renown When Lacking Sufi Training as It Is Customarily Known." This letter is based on the famous saying of Zarruq's master Shaykh Ahmad ibn ʿUqba al-Hadrami (discussed in the second satchel) stating that Sufi training as it had existed in former times was no longer valid and instead must be fused with learning scriptural knowledge. This letter communicates the ideals of Zarruq's short treatise on the death of self-will and ʿAli Muttaqi's elaboration upon it. The second letter, titled "Uṣūl al-Ṭarīqa li-Kashf al-Ḥaqīqa," or "Sufism's Sources' Exposure for Spiritual Reality's Disclosure," deals with Zarruq's *Uṣūl al-Ṭarīqa*. The third letter is titled "Tabyīn al-Ṭurūq li-Ahl al-Irāda bi-Iltizām Waẓā'if al-Khayr wa'l-ʿIbāda," or "Exposition of the Paths for the Folk with Sufi Initiation with Admonition for Disciplines of Worship and Devotion," which plays off the title of ʿAli Muttaqi's first treatise, "Tabyīn al-Turūq ilā 'llāh," or "Exposition of the Paths to God." Through these letters, ʿAbd al-Haqq continued the project of ʿAli Muttaqi to transfer Zarruq's critical assessment of Sufism to a South Asian audience that had never encountered him directly.

It is an open question just how ʿAbd al-Haqq and Baqi Bi'llah interacted, and in what ways they influenced each other's conceptions of reform. His letters to the Naqshbandi master offer critiques of various religious movements of his era. A prime example is the fifth letter, addressed to Baqi Bi'llah, which ʿAbd al-Haqq titled "Taḥṣīl al-Kamāl al-Abadī bi'l-Ikhtiyār al-Faqr al-Muḥammadī," or "Achieving the Completion of Eternity by Choosing the Muhammadan Poverty." ʿAbd al-Wahhab had introduced ʿAbd al-Haqq to the book that is the topic of this letter, "Al-Faqr al-Muḥammadī" ("Muhammadan Poverty"), and had critically considered it with him.[95] Discussing this book gave ʿAbd al-Haqq the vehicle to express his dissatisfaction with many elements of religious life in Delhi under Mughal rule.

Yet ʿAbd al-Haqq's initiation with Baqi Bi'llah obscured the sources of his reformist program. Many scholars assume that Baqi Bi'llah—and thus the Naqshbandi Order as a whole—conveyed to ʿAbd al-Haqq the ideals of Sufi reform through revival of *shariʿa*. However, ʿAbd al-Haqq had by this time already taken initiation into the triple *tariqa*, absorbed its ideals, and learned its methods from ʿAbd al-Wahhab Muttaqi. His initiation with Baqi Bi'llah was more like an alliance of like-minded reformers than an initiation of an inferior disciple to a superior master. Both tone and content of their correspondence affirm this, demonstrating that ʿAbd al-Haqq conveyed as much about reform to the Naqshbandi master as he accepted from him. Many of his letters to Baqi Bi'llah introduce ideas or actual texts of Ahmad Zarruq and ʿAli Muttaqi.

After Akbar died in 1605, ʿAbd al-Haqq adopted a more assertive position. He took initiative to contact and advise nobles who were close to the new Mughal emperor. He first wrote a letter to Shaykh Farīd Bukhārī (d. 1615), who held the position of royal treasurer (*mīr bakhshī*) and then governor of Ahmedabad and later governor of Punjab. Shaykh Farid helped Akbar's son Prince Salīm to take the throne under the name Jahangir. For his support, Shaykh Farid was granted the title Murtaḍā Khān and enjoyed the trust of the new emperor. He was sympathetic to Sufis but like many nobles was addicted to alcohol. ʿAbd al Haqq intended the letter to reach the new emperor through Shaykh Farid.[96] This letter reveals his sly eloquence and cautious approach to reform. A full translation of it is included in the digital version of this work, in appendix E.

ʿAbd al Haqq catches his nobleman's attention with a hair-raising tale about a hunter who becomes the hunted, as a man—chased by a tiger—leaps down a dry well to escape only to find himself suspended above a deadly serpent by grabbing desperately at a straw that mice are steadily chewing. The mice represent time, the tiger is this world, and the serpent is damnation in the next world. Death hunts down each person regardless of his or her station or power in this world; it spurs us on to face the spiritual challenge of purifying the heart before it is too late. ʿAbd al-Haqq explains this challenge through nobility's common obsession, sexual pleasure. "The spirit is by nature sacred and holy, but it is brought low by its relationship to the body and by its mingling with the ego; it is made passionately attached to the ego and, getting mixed, it goes astray. The relationship of the spirit to the ego is exactly like the relationship of a man with his wife, and their interpenetration produces a subtle energy center [*laṭīfa*] called the heart."

His ethical and theological discourse decried the arrogance of rulers who thought themselves divine, above death, or beyond the Prophet's example. ʿAbd al-Haqq treaded on dangerous territory, for Emperor Akbar's mature rule boldly departed from prior Islamic norms of governance and appealed to more universal norms of divine kingship. Akbar had taken as his advisor a radical Mahdawi intellectual, Shaykh Mubarak, and had elevated his two sons, Abu'l-Fadl and Faydi, as powerful courtiers. They led him to downplay the authority of Sunni scholars in the court and to declare himself to be a just ruler who was divinely guided to decide matters of religion as well as state.

In an effort to integrate Rajput warriors and Iranian Shiʿi nobility into his administration, Akbar had integrated elements of Hindu and Zoroastrian ritual into court life. While he never claimed to be a "prophet" per se, Akbar appealed to religious ideals far beyond the bounds of Sunni orthodoxy in his bold claims to authority as a universal emperor. ʿAbd al-Haqq did not name Akbar in his letter yet critiqued rulers who claimed divine guidance as a kind of intoxication with worldly power.

No ruler can claim to excel the Prophet, argued ʿAbd al-Haqq. Rather, a spiritual quest is required for all people, including nobles and rulers, who are not exempt from the challenge to walk humbly and purify their souls under the guidance of a prophet. ʿAbd al-Haqq employed hadith reports to compare worldly life to the sleep of neglect and spiritual torpor: "People are sleeping and only upon dying do they wake."[97] One can wake up only by dying to the ego, which means living by the guidance of the Prophet. ʿAbd al-Haqq wrote in rhyming prose, "The human being is captive to countless trials and tribulations. About their details we obsessively think, and into worrying about them we inevitably sink, until they scatter our energies to the brink. For this reason, the Prophet Muhammad said in a hadith, 'If you knew what I know, you would laugh less and weep more.'"[98]

This was the greater jihad of spiritual striving, which was manifest in all kinds of renunciation and acts of justice. In this way, ʿAbd al-Haqq presented Sufism to appeal to nobles and rulers and ended his letter with subtle allusions to the Muttaqi method based on the writings of Zarruq. Like ʿAli Muttaqi before him, he argued that there was a style of Sufism to suit people of each class and profession. Thus, nobles and rulers were not exempted from following the *shariʿa*, and they could perfect their spiritual life while still pursuing their worldly duties with the proper discipline (*adab*) and spiritual principle (*qaʿida*).

This letter must have been received by Shaykh Farid with approval, for there followed an intricate correspondence. We do not have the letters that the Mughal noble sent to ʿAbd al-Haqq, but we do have several that the Sufi scholar sent to him. These include a letter explaining the four types of people, with the most blessed category being nobles who rule justly and piously. With these letters, ʿAbd al-Haqq probed to see if Shaykh Farid would serve as his channel of communication with the new Mughal emperor, Akbar's rebellious son Jahangir.

As ʿAbd al-Haqq contemplated approaching the Mughal emperor directly, he stood squarely in the footsteps of ʿAli Muttaqi. It was up to him to embody the Muttaqi method in a new and challenging environment. This chapter unpacked the satchel containing elements of the personas and activities of ʿAli Muttaqi's followers as they upheld his legacy in South Asia, from where it had been ejected. ʿAli Muttaqi was dead, but ʿAbd al-Haqq faced a final challenge to put into practice his principles of moderation, justice, and reform. The way that ʿAbd al-Haqq did this would obscure the memory of ʿAli Muttaqi even as it perpetuated his mission, and it would place ʿAbd al-Haqq's own life in peril.

ʿAli Muttaqi's Memory

"Approach the august throne!" The mace-bearer's voice echoed through the pillared vaults of the *divan-e khass*, the emperor's hall of private audience. Before stepping forward, the shaykh bowed low three times, touching the earth with his right hand and raising its dust over his head. Keeping his gaze on the carpeted floor, he walked slowly forward past rows of courtiers standing at attention, arms crossed, until he saw the steps before him that led up to the throne. He raised his eyes only until he could see the emperor's gold-embroidered slippers. Then he smiled and said calmly, "Peace be with you, oh Light of the Faith and Justice of the World."

Emperor Jahangir looked down from his high seat while the shaykh waited patiently for a reply, eyes still lowered. Finally, the mace-bearer standing beside the throne broke the deafening silence. "Surely you know the proper *adab* to approach the throne?" The shaykh answered, "Yes, I have heard that courtiers prostrate. Forgive me, but I am not of the court. Rather, I pay respect to our majestic emperor as the noble companions greeted our holy Prophet." The emperor laughed quietly, "So you would compare me to the Prophet himself?" The shaykh replied, "Your majesty, there is no greater honor for me than to greet you as our Prophet taught us, since you strive to do justice just as the Prophet modeled for us." The emperor pronounced loudly, "He is exempted from prostrating to the throne because he does not come asking for worldly favors." Jahangir lowered his voice and said quietly, "Then, peace be upon you. You are unusually bold for a scholar." The shaykh took a step forward to reply, "My masters have taught me that one who has already died to himself has nothing to fear from others."

From beyond a curtain that hung behind the emperor's throne, a voice called out, interrupting him. "Must he not present a gift to the emperor, or is he allowed to be stingy?" asked the queen. Jahangir turned his head slightly, acknowledging the presence of Nurjahan behind him. He spoke loudly to the court, "Yes, of course he must present a gift! Wasn't it also the custom of our Prophet to never visit a house empty-handed?" The shaykh said, "I have heard that his majesty is fond of beautiful things." Jahangir raised an eyebrow. "I already own the most exquisitely crafted objects that this world can produce. What could you give me that I don't already possess?"

The shaykh drew out from his robe a small book, bound in leather, saying, "My humble offering to your majesty." Jahangir motioned for the mace-bearer to bring the book to him. The emperor flipped through the pages and mused, "Only words and no pictures?" The shaykh said, "Your majesty's love for artwork and illuminated books is world-famous, yet this book contains something more valuable. Its words portray the saints: it does not picture their forms, but it evokes their personas and their teachings. They blessed the rule of your ancestors, and now, by their support, your majesty adorns the throne. I entitled it *Akhbar al-Akhyar* or 'Reports of the Pious.'"

Queen Nurjahan's voice emerged again from behind the curtain. "This Sufi says that he has documented the lives of saints! Ask him whose saints are in his book? Did he begin with the righteous Imams, or did he exclude them?" Jahangir shut the book with one hand and smiled threateningly. "Answer our queen! Are the twelve Imams counted in your book or not?" The shaykh replied, "My book begins with ʿAbd al-Qadir Jilani, the master of spiritual masters . . ." The queen retorted, "You see, this Sufi is partisan against our Imams, the rightly guided descendants of the Prophet!" The shaykh continued unflustered, " . . . but Shaykh ʿAbd al-Qadir was a Sayyid, descended on his father's side from honorable Hasan, whom some call the second Imam, and descended on his mother's side from noble Husain, whom some call the third Imam. So he is a descendant of the Prophet, through the Imams. He met Muʿin al-Din Chishti in Baghdad and encouraged him in his career that led him to settle in Ajmer, blessing the lands that your majesty now rules. My book preserves their lofty sayings, pious deeds, and ardent love for God through only the most reliable reports, sifted and sorted to present the truth of their teachings. Please accept this modest gift from your humble servant! Now, I beg that you dismiss me and allow me to return to my khanqah, where I pray daily that the emperor live long to enforce justice in our land."

The shaykh bowed again, waiting to be dismissed. He felt the emperor hesitate, as he heard whispering from beyond the curtain that hung behind the throne. Then Jahangir spoke. "Your visit pleases us, as does your gift. So, accept from me a gift in return—the annual tax revenue from a village not far from Delhi, which will be assigned to your name in perpetuity." The shaykh replied, "Your excellency is kind, but it is not the custom of this impoverished one to accept money from anyone, no matter how good their intentions. God has told us, *Take provision on your journey but know that the best provision is sincere piety.* I humbly entreat your highness to forgo this kindness and allow me to leave empty-handed."

In his royal memoir, the emperor Jahangir records how this meeting occurred at the Mughal court: "Shaykh ʿAbd al-Haqq Dihlawi is one of the virtuous people and is among the masters of salvation. Arriving at court, he had the opportunity to serve me. He presented me a book of his, consisting of the lives of Sufi masters of India, for which he took great pains."[1] The shaykh came to court to present the emperor with a copy of his masterpiece, *Akhbār al-Akhyār fī Asrār al-Abrār,* or "Reports of the Pious and Secrets of the Devout." It is a memorial (*tadhkira*) that collects and retells the biographies of leading Sufis who were active in South Asia. The book begins with ʿAbd al-Qadir Jilani, who, though he never came to South Asia, blessed and encouraged Muʿin al-Din Chishti, who brought Sufism to that region, and includes biographies of ʿAbd al-Haqq's own mentors, ʿAli Muttaqi and ʿAbd al-Wahhab Muttaqi. At the end of the collection, ʿAbd al-Haqq appended his own concise biography for posterity.

The emperor did not record what he thought of his gift, but ʿAbd al-Haqq's persona impressed him. Jahangir continued in his record, "For a long time, he has lived in isolation in Delhi, in a condition of poverty and complete trust in God. His company was not without liveliness. After presenting him with some kindness, I bid him farewell."[2] The kindness that Jahangir showed him was an offer of a land-grant (*jāgīr*) that would provide revenue from a village to the southwest of Delhi. The shaykh demurred, but the emperor insisted and forced him to accept it before giving him permission to leave.[3]

This ominous "kindness" highlights how dangerous it was to go to court. Presenting gifts to the emperor might allow a Sufi reformer access to the most powerful men with tremendous potential for benefit, but it also involved one in intrigues, jealousies, and competitions that could lead to great harm. Meeting Jahangir face to face—and meeting his queen from behind a curtain—exposed ʿAbd al-Haqq to grave threats. This satchel is filled with danger caused by rivalry with his fellow Naqshbandi and famous Sufi reformer Ahmad Sirhindi, who was suspected by Mughal rulers of challenging their sovereignty. His theological sparring with Sirhindi, preserved in a remarkable private letter, threatened ʿAbd al-Haqq later in life with banishment or imprisonment. As we unpack this satchel, we reach the conclusion of this book, and readers, with all the provisions they need on deck, can set sail.

Justice: Enlightening Advice for Emperors

In the previous chapter, we observed how ʿAbd al-Haqq carefully cultivated certain highly placed nobles in the Mughal court. One of these nobles, Shaykh Farid, was especially instrumental in helping Jahangir to ascend the throne when Akbar died in 1605. As the new emperor's trusted companion, Shaykh Farid was perfectly positioned to convey ʿAli Muttaqi's reformist ideals to Jahangir. When the noble agreed to act as a conduit, ʿAbd al-Haqq wrote a short letter to the new emperor. In it, he expanded upon how a just ruler should behave under the guidance of *shariʿa*. He carefully counseled Jahangir to reverse Akbar's policies and worldview. He had to be clever and careful in addressing the emperor. When Jahangir was a prince rebelling against his father, he had promised support to Naqshbandi Sufis and Islamic scholars; yet when he mounted the throne, Jahangir showed no real interest in the *shariʿa*. Yet new rulers need legitimacy, and the approval of Sunni scholars was a traditional key to winning popular acclaim.

ʿAbd al-Haqq hoped that the advent of a new emperor would give him the opportunity to put ʿAli Muttaqi's memory into a practical program. He composed for Jahangir a book of political advice based on hadith reports and Qur'anic verses, in the well-established genre of "mirror for princes" literature. This short book fully expressed ʿAbd al-Haqq's approach to reform, so this study translates its introduction and opening chapter.[4]

> It is proper respect [*adab*] that when one enters the presence of kings and the court of sultans, one's tongue must first announce their praise and salutation. One must salute them with adulation and compliments due to the pomp and might of their station. Only after offering this can one stand ready to serve and obey them, fastening the hands of respect before the waist of servitude and devoted submission. Only then can one offer a present that is suitable to the grandeur of the royal court.
>
> As for the exalted presence in which I now stand, any praise or salutation is too small, and recounting its glory is not possible at all. What words of praise could anyone offer to that person whom the mighty creator elevated to be emperor of the world and made ruler of all humanity?

> What station is loftier than that of an emperor? What words are suitable to praise his virtue and glorify his position, oh Lord? If I praise his quality of justice [*ʿadl*] and righteousness [*dīndārī*] by saying "righteous and just emperor," then one short phrase includes all good qualities, every kind of praise, and each cause of salvation in this world and the hereafter. It is just like a hadith that recounts the words of the Prophet—may peace and blessings be upon him—who said, "A moment of justice surpasses seventy years of worship." For me, sitting for one moment in the presence of an emperor who is just and rules with equity and compassion is better than offering supererogatory worship for seventy years. What could be of loftier virtue or higher station than to be called "the shadow of God on earth" or "the successor to the Prophet"?[5]

ʿAbd al-Haqq first praises the new emperor, Jahangir, as the ruler chosen by God. He then quotes common titles of praise for the Islamic ruler in Sunni discourse. Mughal rulers inherited this discourse from many centuries of Islamic rule in South Asia, from the inception of the Delhi sultanate in the twelfth century. Previous Sultans had, at least in theory, claimed to rule as delegates of the Sunni *khalifa* in Baghdad, even after he ceased to be an active force.

The Mughals dispensed with such niceties when Akbar arrogated the title *khalifa* to himself without being appointed by any higher Sunni authority. He did not recognize the Ottoman ruler who claimed the same title; rather, he increasingly fashioned his own imperial authority through universal and multireligious symbols unbounded by Sunni standards. ʿAbd al-Haqq tried to persuade the new Mughal emperor to reverse course.

> Because a just emperor is the real vice-regent to the Prophet Muhammad, he must act as the Prophet acted. The meaning of "vice-regent" is just this. The wisdom behind God's establishing emperors and empowering rulers is that they enforce the *shariʿa* of the Prophets—may God grant peace and blessings upon them all. Prophets are sent by the Lord to give news of the eternal unseen world and establish religious order. Rulers enable this by applying coercive force [*zōr-e bāzū*] and establishing just law [*qānūn-e ʿadālat*]. All members of the community take part in this to assist the rulers in spreading religion. The scholars spread knowledge and expound the *shariʿa*. The Sufis establish rituals of worship and devotion. The soldiers carry out raids and wars. Other craftspeople and experts in professions—like farming, weaving, building, and trading—help make religion firm by pursuing their expertise through which the world remains and existence stays productive.

> Above them all, the emperor commands and dominates. He establishes justice and equity, ensuring that everything in this great chain of being works in harmonious order. In this way, the emperor's existence is related to the components of the world and members of humanity just like the soul is related to the body. It is said that the mover of the body and that which keeps its components in harmony is the soul. The body is sound only as long as the soul is sound as its foundation. The body gets corrupted if the soul is absent.[6]

As ʿAbd al-Haqq argued that each class and every profession contributed to building an Islamic society, he echoed ʿAli Muttaqi's series of five epistles on "soul training" for each class. Each had its own *adab*, or way of respectful behavior, and its own *suluk*, or devotional path of spiritual training. However, in writing for the emperor, ʿAbd al-Haqq emphasized that the ruler was the key to the health of the whole.

At this point in his introduction, ʿAbd al-Haqq ventured into delicate territory. Akbar had just died, and Jahangir, his mature son of thirty-eight years, took over after bouts of rebellion, intense family rivalry, and fragile reconciliation. Yet the Sufi scholar boldly asserted that every thoughtful person must imagine a time when the reigning emperor dies—a calamity, for sure, but also an opportunity.

> May God be praised that, at the very foundation and initiation of this great reign and mighty rule, the lights of the dawn of salvation and guidance are shining clearly, marking the traces of the principles and laws of justice and security both inner and outer. Rational men must think and for a moment ponder about how long the emperor will reign and what disorder will come when he leaves the world. Considering this, all the people of this country, from east to west, tremble in fear and slip into the whirlpool of perplexity, imagining that it is like the calamitous day of judgment. By the perfection of divine power and by the dominion of royal authority, not an atom moves out of its proper place, no person deviates from the circle of just action, and the entire world remains firmly established upon the fulcrum of security and stability.
>
> This is strong proof and clear evidence that the overwhelming power and dynastic might of the emperor is a divine bestowal, from beyond the boundaries of worldly cause and effect, from outside the routine means of acquisition. To present a gift that is deserving of his royalty and suitable for the emperor's fortune-granting sight is really not possible—not even imaginable! Whatever one might present would be merely like a

drop of water to the ocean or like a speck of dust to the sun. Only the scholars and Sufis can present a worthy gift as they offer prayers and petitions at the court for the preservation of his rule. They can relate to those at court the speech of God, reports of God's Prophet, sayings of the great religious leaders, and the character of just rulers of the past. These treasures of the hereafter and fortunes of salvation are gifted to those admitted to the exalted assembly of the court.

With this introduction, this humble servant presents himself with his head prostrate in the dust. For a long time, I have been away from the company of the people of this realm. I traversed the wild expanses, laying my head to rest in the wasteland of exile until I came to the holy land of the House of God, that residence of spirits and focal point of divine manifestation in the world—namely, to Mecca, may God increase its greatness and nobility. Then, with an indication from the unseen world, I returned to my homeland, to this plot of purity, Delhi, which is the home of the servants of this path and the residence of those close to the royal court. I have spent my life sitting in isolation with my sight fixed upon God, petitioning for the wellness and wise rule of your exalted dynasty and your noble family, while staying engrossed in praying for the Muslims at large. I present some words from hadith attributed to the Prophet, may God bless him and grant him peace, and reports from his noble companions and followers, along with stories preserved from the great rulers of the past, all of which convey the means to good and righteousness in this world and the hereafter. I translate them [into Persian] and relate them as a way to give thanks to God for divine blessings and wish well to this dynasty, as do all the Muslims.[7]

With this humble introduction, ʿAbd al-Haqq delves to the heart of the matter. He praises the new emperor and offers his book of ethical advice as a gift. The title of the book echoes the new regnal title of the emperor: "Epistle for an Enlightened Ruler."

The light in the "Enlightened Ruler" is not from sun, fire, or reason, all sources that Akbar had drawn from to elevate himself as a divinely guided king. Rather, ʿAbd al-Haqq asserts that the light is from the Prophet Muhammad's example as expounded by Sunni scholars. He avers that he would never offer the emperor advice except that some nobles indicated that he desired guidance from the corpus of hadith reports; he implies the mediation of Shaykh Farid but does not spell out his name.

I present this book as a gift to the court of the emperor, the refuge of religion, the greatest sultan, the noblest ruler, wearer of the crown of perfection and light, occupant of the exalted throne of suzerainty and might, generous as the sea, courageous as the sky, enjoyer of fortunate reign, spreader of justice, nurturer of the people, conqueror of the world, dawning-place of the gracious lights of divinity, setting-place of the noble glow of the shadow of God on earth, the protector of the religion from Mecca, Nūr al-Dīn Muḥammad Jahāngīr, the Mughal emperor and pious warrior—may God make his reign last forever in divine contentment and guide his boat through the seas of justice and equity.

Because it is a gift to the emperor whose name means World-Ruler and Light of the Faith, I entitle this book "Epistle for an Enlightened Ruler" [*Risāla-ye Nūriyya-ye Sulṭāniyya*]. It was indicated to this humble servant that the emperor of Islam intimated to one of his friends at court that hadith reports from the Prophet addressing just rule should be written down along with their sources and chains of narration. After diligent search and persistent inquiry, I composed this book in which I recorded hadith reports and sent it as a gift to the court. I make this bold gesture only because of an indication from the unseen and to obey the divine that is worthy of worship. For this reason alone, Sufis approach the door of the exalted royal court: namely, to pronounce advice for you and pray for your welfare. Otherwise, how could one like me stand the majesty of this place and the awesomeness of this court? My prime purpose and essential duty is to pray: "Oh God majestic and exalted, keep all the people—especially the community of Islam—in the shade of his great reign and magnificent rule, safe and secure in the shadow of his protective aid, with welfare and peace of mind preserved from all afflictions and sins, for the sake of the Prophet and his pure family and great followers." Now, I begin the intended book.

I start with the name of God, who is the creator of the world and all that is in it. I bear witness that Muhammad is God's prophet and messenger. God is the possessor of dominion, who has made justice to be the essence of generosity and the beauty of existentiality. God made justice to be the element that ensures the continuation of this world and its spiritual existence and to be the cause of the harmonious order in the production house of the cosmos. God granted the salvation of doing justice to good sultans and noble emperors, especially to the rulers of India who manifest the rulings of Islam, spreading the light of faith and

> dispelling the darkness of infidelity, making the world more enlightened and pure, for *those are the ones who rule with truth and justice.*[8]

After the personal introduction, ʿAbd al-Haqq begins his discourse in earnest. A just ruler is part of the salvific plan of the cosmos; he joins this world to the hereafter, manifesting divine qualities of power, harmony, and order in this ephemeral and chaotic world.

In ʿAbd al-Haqq's exposition, the bifurcation between two realms—the seen and the unseen—is bridged by both prophets and just rulers who follow them. He expands on his classification of people into four classes, which he had sent to Shaykh Farid in letters. He gives more details about the most blessed of these four classes, those who rule in the world with justice, which earns them the hereafter.

> God, the creator of the cosmos and the fashioner of humanity, has made two realms: this world, which is ephemeral and phenomenal, and the hereafter, which is eternal and spiritual. For each realm, God made a perfection and happiness that is suitable to it, and to humanity God granted authority [*sulṭanat*] and dominion [*dawlat*]. To some people, God grants authority and dominion in both this world and the hereafter. To others, God withholds authority and dominion in both this world and the hereafter. And to others, God grants authority and dominion in only one but not the other—either in this world or the hereafter. The authority to grant or withhold is God's, for *God does whatever God wills* [Qur'an 14:27] and *God gives to whomever God wills* [Qur'an 3:26].
>
> So according to this division, there are four kinds of people. Those who have power and dominion in this world and the hereafter are the just emperors. In this world, they have pomp and power, ability and command, while in the hereafter they earn eternal reward through their justice, mercy, care for their subjects, obedience to divine commands, kindness, and compassion to the servants of God. They join [*jāmiʿ*] the blessings of both this world and the hereafter, earning perfection both inner and outer. They were created as actual members of the human species but bear the special responsibility of exerting leadership and power, which disciplines their character and regulates their political life; the work of the world and the order of human needs cannot be solved without their presence.
>
> If everyone would renounce the world, sit in isolation, and worship in quiet devotion, the ways and means of the world would fall out of balance! The structure of the world and life in it would veer toward ruin.

> Thus, the masters of political fortune [*arbāb-e dawlat*] must remain engrossed in worldly affairs and their management, while training their spiritual life informally [*bī-ṭarīqat sulūk*] in such a way that does not damage their worldly responsibilities, while they conduct themselves such that they earn fortune and authority in the hereafter as well, doing nothing that would alienate them from that higher goal. With the emperors especially, in whose power rests the affairs of all people and the harmonious ordering of the cosmos in general, they must enforce and promote their power and rule in such a way that it becomes the very means to achieve authority in the realm of the hereafter. The emperor must become one who joins both realms [*jāmiʿ-ye dawlatayn*] and attains happiness in both realms [*saʿādat-e dārayn*]. *That is divine bounty that God gives to whomever God wills, and God possesses great bounty* [Qur'an 62:4].[9]

With this Qur'anic verse, ʿAbd al-Haqq concludes his introductory chapter. He sets up a parallelism between his reformist program for Sufism and his strategy for political reform. The Muttaqi method for reform of Sufism elevates a kind of scholarly saint as a *jamiʿ* who "joins" spiritual training with scriptural knowledge. Similarly, his political program requires an emperor who rules with justice, as defined by *shariʿa*, who "joins" secular power to religious ethics.

His introduction to "Epistle for an Enlightened Ruler" explains this scheme in general. He gives details in five chapters, quoting copiously from hadith reports and narratives about the *salaf*, or pious early Muslims. His chapters follow this plan: Section 1 explains the various essential pillars of political rule, namely supplying the treasury, raising the army, maintaining coordination in the army, and enforcing justice by desisting from oppression and coercion against the common people. Section 2 explains how the pillars of rule are acquired. Section 3 describes some respectful manners (*adab*) through which rulers treat their subjects for the perfection and beautification of virtue. Section 4 discusses some moral points, knowledge of which promotes the affairs of state. And section 5 relates some stories about Islamic rulers of earlier times who displayed forbearance, clemency, generosity, charity, justice, strength, and bravery.

This book reached Jahangir, but we do not know if he read it.[10] He certainly did not follow its advice. As his rule progressed, the emperor earned a reputation for rage and cruelty tempered only by his keen observation of birds, beasts, and flowers, along with refinement in court aesthetics, painting, and architecture. Yet the channel of communication was open for ʿAbd al-Haqq to the highest echelons of the Mughal administration. He subsequently collected forty hadith reports about good government and translated them into Persian, titled "Tarjamat al-Aḥādīth al-Arbaʿīn fī Naṣīḥat al-Mulūk wa'l-Salāṭīn" ("Translating Forty Prophetic Reports on Advice to Rulers and Royal Courts").[11] This short book was for Jahangir's son Prince Khurram (later Shāhjahān, ruled 1628–58). The ambitious prince was sent to conquer the Deccan south of Khandesh, and his successes vaunted him to the position of heir apparent. Perhaps ʿAbd al-Haqq hoped that the father's failings would translate into the son's success.

Jahangir showed little inclination to follow ʿAbd al-Haqq's ethical advice. After six years as emperor, he married Nurjahan, a strong-willed woman from an Iranian Shiʿi family who would become his favored queen.[12] She swiftly took control, elevating members of her family to authoritative positions and ruling as partner to her husband. She conspired to sideline Prince Khurram in favor of his stepbrother Shahriyar (the son of one of Jahangir's concubines) whom she married to her daughter. Queen Nurjahan's manipulations drove a wedge between son and father, and Prince Khurram was pushed into open rebellion.

As his queen's authority expanded, Jahangir's authority receded. He slumped into alcoholism and drug addiction. In the fourteenth year of his reign, ʿAbd al-Haqq met Jahangir at court and perceived with his own eyes that the emperor did not fit his ideals. That encounter with the emperor—outwardly ruler of the most powerful empire in the world but inwardly riven with conflicts—would force ʿAbd al-Haqq to make one last journey. It was a journey that involved controversies about the millennium that persisted even after the Mahdawi movement had died down. It was a journey that almost cost him his life.

Moderation: Sparring with Ahmad Sirhindi

Toward the end of his reign, Emperor Jahangir ordered ʿAbd al-Haqq into exile. Exactly what angered the emperor remains a mystery, one partially resolved here. In 1619, the emperor summoned the elderly ʿAbd al-Haqq to Srinagar, where the court spent summers, to answer for unstated misdeeds. He had previously ordered the shaykh's son Nur al-Haqq to be banished from Delhi to provincial Kabul. Together, the shaykh and his son traveled as far as Lahore, where they were racked with anxiety as their paths diverged—the younger to banishment and the elder likely to imprisonment. In Lahore, ʿAbd al-Haqq met a fellow Qadiri Sufi with close ties to Mughal nobility, Shaykh

Miyān Mīr (d. 1635). ʿAbd al-Haqq complained of having to leave country and family behind, but Miyan Mir assured him that he had nothing to fear from Jahangir. As ʿAbd al-Haqq he set off for Srinagar, news arrived that Jahangir had died. Both father and son returned to Delhi together, with the threat of danger averted.

What caused this close brush with royal displeasure? It was a controversy over moderation (*iʿtidal*), an ideal at the heart of the Muttaqi reform project. ʿAbd al-Haqq's own writings do not explain why Jahangir got angry with him, but other Mughal sources shed light on the matter. The eldest grandchild of Jahangir, Prince Dara Shikoh (d. 1659), was at court in Kashmir and took a keen interest in Sufism. He and his sister Jahānārā were Qadiri disciples of Miyan Mir, and both authored biographies of important Sufi masters. Dara Shikoh wrote, "During the time that Emperor Jahangir was in Kashmir, some people said untrue things about Shaykh ʿAbd al-Haqq Dihlawi—who was the leading hadith scholar of his age—and Mirzā Ḥusām al-Dīn—who was an accomplished disciple of the fiery and charismatic Shaykh Ahmad Sirhindi. They were both called to face the Emperor."[13]

Who were the "some people" who slandered ʿAbd al-Haqq? Scholar Khaliq Ahmad Nizami speculates that Queen Nurjahan circulated false accusations because she disliked the shaykh.[14] It is true that Nurjahan was from a Shiʿi family that had grown immensely influential as Jahangir's competence faded and that ʿAbd al-Haqq had authored a book about the twelve Imams from a Sunni perspective, which might have contradicted some points of Shiʿi dogma.[15] It is also true that ʿAbd al-Haqq was accused of some wrongdoing along with a disciple of Ahmad Sirhindi, who took a strident stance against Shiʿism. Nizami suggests that both ran afoul of Queen Nurjahan, who slandered them and urged the emperor to punish them.

Yet Nizami offers no textual proof of this theory. There was no love lost between Dara Shikoh and Nurjahan, his grandfather's wife who schemed to get her relatives on the throne in place of Dara Shikoh's own father. If Nurjahan had slandered ʿAbd al-Haqq, there would be no reason for Dara Shikoh—himself a Qadiri Sufi—to hide that unflattering fact by vaguely saying "some people said untrue things." If both ʿAbd al-Haqq and Ahmad Sirhindi's disciple were accused of anti-Shiʿi statements, they most likely would have traveled to Kashmir together to face the emperor. However, ʿAbd al-Haqq traveled with his son and was anxious of traveling alone after Lahore when they had to part ways.

It appears that ʿAbd al-Haqq and the Sufi disciple of Sirhindi remained separate during the journey: this suggests an alternative theory. It could be that

ʿAbd al-Haqq and Sirhindi's disciple were disputants rather than comrades. Jahangir may have heard exaggerated reports about rivaling Sufi masters and called them to court to answer and clarify their disputes. Jahangir had jailed Ahmad Sirhindi previously, due to allegations that he claimed to be the Mahdi, a claim that the emperor saw as a political challenge. Those allegations against Sirhindi originated with ʿAbd al-Haqq, for he wrote a letter to Sirhindi accusing him of various kinds of exaggeration and self-aggrandizement.

Both ʿAbd al-Haqq and Ahmad Sirhindi were disciples of Khwaja Baqi Bi'llah in the Naqshbandi Order. Both sent letters to Jahangir urging him to support the *shariʿa* as a proper Sunni ruler. Yet ʿAbd al-Haqq carefully distinguished his own style of reform from that of his colleagues who followed Sirhindi. ʿAbd al-Haqq's approach emphasized scholarly acumen and political moderation; in contrast, Sirhindi was charismatic and brash in his theology. ʿAbd al-Haqq advocated reform that spread through a Sufi community, with the saint as the prime agent of reform; as such, the figure of the saint was also the central subject of reformist limitation. He conflicted with Sirhindi over the latter's claims to transcendent spiritual authority. His critiques of Sirhindi were much like those that ʿAli Muttaqi had launched against the Mahdawis and Shattaris two generations earlier.

Ahmad Sirhindi absorbed the fiery piety of the Mahdawi movement, as implied by his title Mujaddid-e Alf-e Thānī or "Renewer of the Second Millennium." The Mahdawi movement had by then cooled significantly, for the Islamic millennium passed in 1591 just before ʿAbd al-Haqq returned to Delhi. Mahdawi partisans altered their dogma to reflect the new reality—they built a solid community around the slogan that "the promised Mahdi has come and gone" in lieu of the expectation that the world would end or radically transform with the millennium. Like the Mahdawi hero Sayyid Muhammad Jawnpuri, Ahmad Sirhindi similarly claimed to be not just a saint who achieved that status through allegiance to and initiation from earlier saints. Rather, he asserted that he inherited authority from the Prophet himself because he shared the Prophet's nature and substance. He called himself the heir to the source of Prophetic inspiration as opposed to one who simply followed the *sunna* in outward obedience to the Prophet's example, for although the office of prophecy came to an end, the perfect followers of the prophets had a share in the perfections of prophecy.[16] He observed that the system of disciple and saintly master was becoming irrelevant. What was once the inner training ground for spirituality was now merely external trappings; he located the source of his attaining sainthood beyond contemporary saints.

In Sirhindi's metaphysical schema, he was suffused with the Prophet's essence. In his speculation, Muhammad had not just one individuation (*taʿayyun*) but two, which coexisted during his lifetime. These were a bodily human individuation (*ḥaqīqat-e muḥammadī*) and a spiritual individuation (*ḥaqīqat-e aḥmadī*). Since the death of Muhammad, the bodily manifestation grew steadily more elevated, subtle, and freed from worldly affairs; this was in accord with the nobility of the "Essence of Muhammad." Yet its steady diffusion left the Muslim community in dire need of continual guidance. This need was fulfilled by the "Essence of Aḥmad," which was the renewing spirit of divinity that served as mediator between the source of revelation and the Muslim community.[17] Sirhindi took seriously a famous *ḥadīth qudsī*, a report in which the Prophet declares what God says, but not through revelation; in this report, God says, "I am *Aḥmad* without the *m*." This means that God is *Aḥad*, absolutely one, but manifest uniquely in the form of *Aḥmad*.[18] "Aḥmad" was one of the many honorific praise-names of the Prophet Muhammad. Sirhindi speculated that the *m* stood for Muhammad's human form, which lingered with his body at his tomb in Medina; his body faded with time but his spiritual essence in the form of Ahmad persisted and actually grew stronger as the body-in-history receded. Through that spiritual essence, the absolutely single God—signified by the divine name al-Aḥad—continued to manifest guidance to the community of believers.

Between the embodied Muhammad and the noncorporeal God was the spiritual essence of Ahmad. Sirhindi speculated that after a thousand years, the bodily manifestation of Muhammad would fade in importance while the spiritual manifestation of Ahmad would persist, energizing the next thousand years of the "second millennium" that began in 1591 (AH 1000). His wordplay on the term "Ahmad" hinted that Ahmad Sirhindi himself was the new personal locus (or bodily individuation) of the Prophetic spirit, which had passed beyond its previous individuation in the Prophet of Mecca and Medina, namely Muhammad.

Sirhindi explained his saintly qualifications by claiming to hold a direct allegiance to God, transcending any allegiance he may have had to a human master or a Sufi lineage. Although he admitted that Khwaja Baqi Bi'llah was his master in the Naqshbandi Order, he effaced this relationship by claiming to be the disciple of God.

> I am both a disciple who desires God [*murīd allāh*] and one desired by God [*murād allāh*]. The chain of my discipleship [*irāda*] is connected with

> God without any mediation. My hand is a substitute for the hand of God. I am a disciple of Muhammad connected with him through many intermediaries: in the Naqshbandi Order, there are twenty-one intermediaries in between; in the Qadiri Order, there are twenty-five; and in the Chishti Order, there are twenty-seven. However, my relationship with God as a disciple is not subject to any mediation. Hence, I am both the disciple of the Prophet Muhammad and his co-disciple [*ham-pīrah*]. Though I am a parasite [*tufaylī*] at the table of this wealth, sitting near the Prophet, yet I have not come uninvited. Though I am a follower, I am not without a share of genuineness. . . . Though I take initiation without human intermediary [*uwaysī*], I have an omnipresent and all-seeing instructor [*murabbī-ye ḥāḍir o nāẓir*]. Though in the Naqshbandi community my instructor is ʿAbd al-Bāqī [Khwaja Baqi Bi'llah], yet the one who has undertaken my instruction is the everlasting One [al-Bāqī]. . . . I am a divine disciple.[19]

Sirhindi veered alarmingly close to equating himself with the Prophet. He claimed to re-embody the Prophet's presence, bringing the Prophet's spiritual guidance back in the realm of human affairs.

ʿAbd al-Haqq challenged Sirhindi's self-aggrandizing speculations. He charged that Sirhindi's position showed intense disrespect for the Prophet and disparaged the Sufi masters from whom he gained training and authority. ʿAbd al-Haqq sent a letter to Sirhindi, repeating what the latter had claimed in his writings and what others reported from hearing him preach. ʿAbd al-Haqq cited his own son Nur al-Haqq as a source of information since he had sat in Sirhindi's assemblies. His letter to Sirhindi is a model of tough-love critique and subtle Sufi analysis. He pointed out the contradictions of Sirhindi's claim to be follower who enjoyed authority unmediated by the leader he followed.

> These words are written with the goal of investigating the case, discovering the truth, preventing any suffering, and settling matters of controversy that divide this body [the Naqshbandi Order in South Asia]. I intended to write whatever is required to settle my conscience. Its first principle is to give you good advice, wish you well, and discover the truth of your state; as the Prophet said, "Religion consists of good advice." I do this after several sittings during which I made a special prayer for guidance [*istikhāra*] before setting pen to paper, asking for deliverance from the evil of selfishness and turning to God alone for support. Only having done all this do I write to you. I hope that any shortcomings will be forgiven and any right doings will be rewarded.
>
> I hold a very high opinion of you, O Shaykh. My love for you is not less

> than anyone else's! But it is just as [the great Sufi scholar] Hujwīrī wrote in *Kashf al-Maḥjūb* about Manṣūr Ḥallāj: "God be praised, as a person he is dear to my heart, yet his spiritual teachings are in no way acceptable!" Thus, this humble writer says, "You are dear to me, yet what you say about the Prophet (upon him be peace and blessings) has no worth, even if what you say about other Sufi masters must be endured, however painful. It is beyond my patience's capacity to bear hearing these words from you." . . . Considering the reputation that you have developed, I pray, "Oh God, this man is making public claims to have spiritual perfection! If he is sincere in these claims, please show me proof of his sincerity, give me insight into his actual spiritual rank, and let me witness his miraculous deeds so that any confusion or ambiguity may be removed. If he is not sincere, then bring him to justice and prevent him from persisting with such claims."[20]

ʿAbd al-Haqq compares Sirhindi's discourse with the "intoxicated" speech that Sufis had used in the past to express spiritual states of union. The most famous of these is Hallaj (d. 922), who was executed for ecstatic preaching in public as he declared, "I am the Truth." ʿAbd al-Haqq mentions Junayd, the paragon of sobriety (*sahw*), who disavowed Hallaj when the latter had cited him as a teacher. Pointedly, ʿAbd al-Haqq also cites Bayazid Bistami, an important early Sufi whom the Naqshbandis claimed in their lineage. Bistami was a paragon of ecstasy (*sukr*), yet ʿAbd al-Haqq states that he recanted his ecstatic boasts at the end of his life, as Sirhindi should do now.[21]

In examining Sirhindi's state of mind while making extravagant claims, ʿAbd al-Haqq cites Sirhindi's famous *Maktūbāt*, his book of letters. In it, Sirhindi states that he does not speak from spiritual intoxication or ecstatic union but rather from considered sobriety in his full faculties. For this reason, ʿAbd al-Haqq analyzes these statements with theological rigor.

> Adversity is caused by speech that reveals the secrets of existential unity and proclaims spiritual boasts [*shaṭḥiyāt*], for it diverges from the words' evident meaning and is not understood by common people. Such speech is called "obscure imaginings" [*mawhūmāt mubhamāt*]. There are many examples from previous Sufis. Yet none has ever witnessed the type of speech that has come [from you] about the saints and, most especially, the Prophet Muhammad, as you make false claims of equality and identity. . . . The evident meaning of your speech is disrespect and insult [*bē-adabī o gustākhī*] to the Prophet, and there is no interpreting them away from their evident meaning.[22]

ʿAbd al-Haqq asserts that all good qualities, virtues, and spiritual states come from following the Prophet and in no other way.[23] He takes exception to Sirhindi's claim to surpass the status of other saints, though he took initiation from them and especially from Khwaja Baqi Bi'llah. ʿAbd al-Haqq takes special umbrage at Sirhindi's assertion that he gets spiritual guidance from God directly without even the mediation of the Prophet.

> Glory be to God, what confusion and delusion is this? . . . He is the Prophet of God, so how can any claim equality with him? There has been discussion over whether or not the saints are superior to the prophets—upon them be peace. That needs no repetition here. Yet it bears repeating that you claim to need no mediation from the Prophet Muhammad. None has claimed this before! Muhammad is the beloved of the Lord of all creation and the purpose of this world and religion itself, yet you call him "a veil" [*parda*] and "a separation" [*ḥijāb*]. Yet many realized sages have explained that they witness God only as reflected in Muhammad! May our souls be sacrificed for such a "veil." Glory be to God, it is hardly an incapacity to be veiled or separated from God by the Prophet Muhammad. What perfection could be greater than this, that one witnesses the perfection of God in the perfection of Muhammad? For this purpose, God created Muhammad, that the divine essence should be seen in his beauty and perfection. God allowed Muhammad to enter the intimate chamber of spiritual reality, to display union with the divine essence and attributes so that all would know that whatever exists, exists with him and through him.[24] A sage has said, "The light of God does not illuminate any human heart except through the reflection of Muhammad's secret for he is the divine light [*al-nūr al-muṭlaq*]." The veils that separate us from God are veils of darkness, veils of spirit, veils of ego, and veils of materiality—these are properly understood as veils and separation. But when you call the essence of Muhammad a veil which you claim to throw off from between yourself and God, you utter something that one should never say!
>
> On the day of judgment, Muhammad will appear in person before us, God willing, or even before that in the intermediate realm after death. If I should leave this world before you, the first complaint about you that I will lay before Muhammad will be this. God alone knows best if he may even appear to me before I die in a spiritual vision, for that is possible. It is my discipline and habit, like that of all those belonging to our Naqshbandi Order, to concentrate upon God's essence by contemplating

> the noble beauty of the Prophet Muhammad. By contemplating his noble presence, one gradually achieves union with the divine essence [*dhāt-e ḥaqq*], meaning total absorption and conscientious presence, which is how our order defines "union with God." . . . When I survey all the sages, mystics, saints, and lovers of God, I see that they all affirm—by word and state—the practice of seeking favor [*tawassul*] from the Prophet, humbly begging [*gadāgīrī*] and asking his help [*istimdād*]. They show no attitude toward the Prophet except obedience [*bandagī*], submission [*niyāz*], humbleness [*shikastagī*], servitude [*ghulāmī*], and doggish loyalty [*sagī*]. Facing him in this way, I cannot elucidate the doors of spiritual insight that have opened for them such that, in facing him, they witness God. Considering this, I cannot account for your discourse. It is evident that you have been deceived, but I cannot say who has deceived you. God alone knows best. . . . Without belaboring the point, you may simply say that all spiritual outpouring and opening—from beginning to end, inwardly and outwardly, both before achieving union and after it, for seekers and masters, for lovers and beloveds—all of it comes from adhering, following, and beseeching mediation with that noble presence, the Prophet Muhammad. Nothing else need be said. Nothing more can be said.[25]

ʿAbd al-Haqq alleges that Sirhindi disparages other Sufi masters, even his own Naqshbandi master, Khwaja Baqi Bi'llah. The issue is whether saints can ascend into God's presence, based on the Prophet's model but effacing the Prophet's efficacy. This first line of analysis mirrors ʿAli Muttaqi's critique of the Shattaris and Shaykh Muhammad Ghawth in particular. Second, ʿAbd al-Haqq asserts that Sirhindi belittles the Prophet, misunderstanding his cosmic existential being and therefore falling in the error of imagining equality with him. This second line of analysis mirrors ʿAli Muttaqi's critique of the Mahdawis and their claims about Sayyid Muhammad Jawnpuri.

ʿAbd al-Haqq asks how Sirhindi can claim spiritual ascension (*miʿrāj*) that supersedes the presence of the Prophet. He explains that ritual prayer is a means of ascension—according to a hadith report—yet after every prayer one pronounces blessings and greetings and praise on the Prophet Muhammad. So, the ascension of every believer culminates with offering praise and blessings upon the Prophet, who enables any spiritual ascension of his followers and can never be surpassed.[26]

> How can it be said that a spiritual seeker always travels the path as a servant of the Prophet, moving forward by adhering to him and following him, and yet when he approaches the court of divinity he moves ahead

> of the Prophet and goes into the inner chamber leaving the Prophet behind? How could he enter without following, leaving aside the Prophet's mediation? How could he go in and sit on the throne of intimacy and union and be crowned by divine presence all alone? How could he then say, "You and I are now equals—I came as your servant but now that I am here your authority of mediation no longer remains. Although I am your servant and follower originally and I arrived here only by your mediation, now you have no presence or mediation here."[27]

This claim, says ʿAbd al-Haqq, degrades the status of the Prophet. Accepting mediation is a sign of vulnerability and humility, while offering mediation is a sign of authority and superiority. It may be possible for one to surpass one's Sufi master, but it is unthinkable that one could claim equivalence with the Prophet. That is not just moral fault—and he describes it as disrespectful, insulting, and arrogant—but also a metaphysical error.

The Prophet, explains ʿAbd al-Haqq, is not just a person but rather a spiritual presence. The prophetic reality (*ḥaqīqat-e muḥammadiyya*) is present in all levels of the cosmos, in which it functions as the "spiritual reality of realities" (*ḥaqīqat-e ḥaqāʾiq*) and the existential light and energizes all being.[28] In this exposition, he follows the formulation of Muhammad ibn Fadlallah Burhanpuri in his *al-Tuḥfa al-Mursala ilā Rūḥ al-Nabī* ("Gift Sent to the Prophet's Spirit"), which became popular in Chishti, Shattari, and Qadiri Orders after its composition in 1590.[29]

This text was so prominent that it helped fuel conversion to Islam of many in Indonesia, as the text and its ideas spread from the Deccan to Gujarat to Mecca and from there to the wider Indian Ocean world.[30] ʿAbd al-Haqq employs the cosmological arguments of Burhanpuri, who calls Muhammad "the reality of realities."

> How can you say that the spiritual seeker's reality achieves union with the reality of the Prophet, which is the reality of realities? That has no meaning and saying that leads you far from the station of respect [*adab*] and justice [*inṣāf*]. This is evident insult and disgraceful vanity that is clearly against reason. It is impossible for two things to be united when one of them is partial [*juzʾ*] and the other is universal (*kull*), without the partial becoming universal or the universal becoming partial, so this idea is obviously null and void.[31]

ʿAbd al-Haqq accuses Sirhindi of overstepping the proper bounds of a Muslim saint. He notes that the saying "Scholars of my community are like Prophets of the Israelite community" circulated as a hadith, but he disparages it as "not authentic [*ṣaḥīḥ*]," in contrast to "Scholars are the inheritance of the Prophets."[32] He claims that his son Nur al-Haqq heard Sirhindi say in his preaching that "sainthood is superior to prophethood."[33] This claim, ʿAbd al-Haqq says, transgresses basic Sunni beliefs and, in being quoted, shows Sirhindi's lack of mastery (*tanāquṣ*).

ʿAbd al-Haqq says that human beings are always vulnerable to error and slippage. Only prophets are granted protection from error (*ʿiṣma*).[34] Sirhindi should acknowledge that he has erred, especially in his claim to have surpassed their own teacher, Khwaja Baqi Biʾllah.

> As for what you have written, that our Khwaja—may God keep his heart sacred—"decided to give me, in the beginning of my training with him, special training to become one whom God desires [*murād*] [rather than a routine disciple who desires God (*murid*)]." Our honorable Khwaja persevered with you to a great extent—many people are aware of this, most of all this humble writer. If our Khwaja were still alive today, it is certain that he would be angry at hearing what you wrote. Nobody would be pleased with it, and I hope that you, deep inside, are not content with it. God alone knows best. . . . I admit that you may have received special guidance in the beginning of your training, but it is weak-minded corruption to claim that this special guidance "to become one whom God desires" results in your becoming his equal, such that his mediation is no longer required for you, for this makes you disrespect his honor, the Prophet Muhammad.[35]

With this scolding observation, ʿAbd al-Haqq moves to his second line of analysis. In boasting to have surpassed the mediation of his own Sufi master, Sirhindi also claims to have moved beyond mediation of the Prophet Muhammad. ʿAbd al-Haqq compares Sirhindi's discourse to that of the Mahdawis, who also veered close to claiming equivalence of their leader, Sayyid Muhammad Jawnpuri, to the Prophet, and that Jawnpuri had come to renew the Prophet's legacy for the coming millennium.

> Any claim to equality with the prophets and especially to the leader of prophets, Muhammad—may peace and blessin gs be upon him—is void of truth [*bāṭil*]. Splitting hairs over distinctions between "servant and master" or "original and derivative" is likewise void of truth and full of vanity. There is no need to discuss it further. Discourse of this type is heard from some Mahdawi leaders whose sect, consensus of opinion has

it, controverts the norm. In the creed of Sayyid Muhammad Jawnpuri, which is the origin and growth and location and station of their misguidance [*ḍalālat*], it is claimed that every perfection that the Prophet Muhammad possessed—may God bless and grant him peace—was also possessed by Sayyid Muhammad Jawnpuri. They say that the only difference is that the former had them originally [*bi-aṣālat*] and the latter received them as a result of following the Prophet. This is the very essence of their claim. Likewise, the Shiʿa say that the twelve Imams—may God be content with them—are equal to the Prophet except that they are his pupils and he is their teacher. In any case, a true servant recognizes the rights over him exercised by his benefactor and treats the master in every moment with obedience and submissiveness, never for an instant making claims of equality.[36]

ʿAbd al-Haqq then turns to a parable to make his point, as he did in the letter to Shaykh Farid Bukhari. An apt story can express a subtle point more forcefully than intellectual argument.

This is the parable of a servant and his master to whom he makes an insulting claim of equality. The servant accompanies his master to the court of the ruler. They enter the court's assembly. The noble master goes and sits at his place close to the sultan, and the servant follows him to the same place to stand by him. Seeing himself in this royal assembly with his master in the presence of the sultan, the servant feels proud and haughty. Because of his impotence and lack of awareness, which is the sad condition of all servants, he loses hold over himself and begins to imagine that he is equal to his master and partakes in his master's authority.

The servant says, "I am a servant of the ruler and am intimate with him!" He does not realize the first principle in training on the path of intimacy and union: that is, that he arrives in the sultan's court only by mediation and by following his master. His master is his intermediary [*wāsiṭa*]. The intimacy and union he now enjoys is mediated by this intermediary. However, because of his pride and lack of awareness and thoughtlessness, the existence of intermediaries has fallen from his gaze. He has fallen into the prison of disavowing his benefactor [*kufrān-e niʿmat*].

If you consider carefully the soundness of this story, oh Shaykh, then you should reassess the meaning of your discourse that I am refuting. You have said, "I was created for the purpose of uniting the perfections

> of Abraham and Muhammad." What does this mean and what is its consequence? The answer is found in my story about the servant and his master. What you have said is in no way sound except for asserting a difference between the original and the follower. Any claim to equality and equivalence by servants and followers is unacceptable and unsuitable to the utmost extent.[37]

This letter to Sirhindi is full of subtle Sufi theology, but it is really about the content and style of Sunni reformist movements. In the era of the Muttaqi community, reform was driven by Sufi communities, and they argued over its contours and limitations through their own technical vocabulary.

ʿAbd al-Haqq's poignant letter did not cause Sirhindi to alter his charismatic claims. We have no letter that Sirhindi wrote in response. ʿAbd al-Haqq considered this to be a message between fellow disciples and equal Sufi masters, so he did not include it in his collection of letters. Instead, it was preserved in a massive seventeenth-century collection of Sufi biographies that contains rare texts, letters, and fatwas that, without being included there, would have been lost to history.[38] ʿAbd al-Haqq later wrote to jurists in Mecca, whom he had known while a member of the Muttaqi community there, seeking a legal decision against a man like Sirhindi who claimed to embody the perfection of Muhammad. This critique helped to suppress the teachings of Sirhindi for a time by Mughal imperial decree.[39]

ʿAbd al-Haqq's critique of Sirhindi was the last pronouncement of the Muttaqi reform movement as a distinct Sufi community. It displayed the common elements that linked it to the critiques launched by ʿAli Muttaqi before him. They all concentrated on the nature of sainthood, delineating who could assert its status, under what terms, and with what social effects. They tried to limit who could claim to embody the ideals of sainthood in Islamic societies and to live their lives as exemplars of their own extremely limited and limiting paradigm of what a saint should be like. Soon this paradigm, along with the Sufi community that upheld it, would dissolve into obscurity.

ʿAbd al-Haqq disengaged the ideals and techniques of reform from the community of ʿAli Muttaqi, which had cultivated them. He hoped to spread these ideals in a diffused way, through his own disciples and students at his madrasa and also through Sufi communities that held allegiance to the Naqshbandi Order. This strategy had the unintended effect of obscuring important aspects of ʿAbd al-Haqq's personality, as posterity remembers him as merely a Naqshbandi. For instance, Muḥammad Ṣādiq Hamadānī (d. circa 1614), a

Dargah of ʿAbd al-Haqq Muhaddith Dihlawi near Shamsi Talab at Mehrauli in Delhi.

disciple of Khwaja Baqi Biʾllah who memorialized Sufis of Delhi, wrote a biography of ʿAbd al-Haqq. In it, Hamadani quotes ʿAbd al-Haqq as saying, "The Sufi initiation that I received from Khwaja Baqi Biʾllah is superior to the initiations that I received previously from great masters, just like the spirit is superior to the body."[40] This ascribed quote cannot be accurate: it contradicts the content of ʿAbd al-Haqq's writings in books and letters, in which he conveys the Muttaqi method and praises his Sufi masters in Mecca. But posthumously, ʿAbd al-Haqq's reputation as a Naqshbandi prevailed, partly through memorialization by Hamadani and other Naqshbandi authors. This obscured the personality and reputation of ʿAli Muttaqi, who also became known to later generations as "Naqshbandi" by association, even though he never took initiation into that order. In retrospect, the distinctive history of his claim to be a scholar-saint and leader of a reformist Sufi community were erased. His successes were absorbed into the later fame of the Naqshbandi community as the preeminent force of reform and revival in Mughal dominions.

Because ʿAbd al-Haqq was misremembered as a Naqshbandi, so were the Muttaqi masters who taught him. The hagiographer Ghawthi noted that people in South Asia knew ʿAli Muttaqi as a "Naqshbandi."[41] They, along with

Ghawthi, misrecognized ʿAli Muttaqi as a Naqshbandi for two reasons. First, ʿAli Muttaqi's followers did not preserve his teachings in a discrete Sufi community beyond a few generations. Second, his teachings, along with those of Zarruq, spread beyond the boundaries of a single Sufi community that owed allegiance to him as a founding saint. Reform became the project of other communities centered on different patterns of saintly authority. The substance of reform would be woven into the fabric of other movements, some Sufi and some anti-Sufi, in later times.

Setting Sail: Sufi Journeys, Saintly Lives, and Islamic Reform

Piety is provision for the journey from this world to the next: this maxim guided the life of ʿAli Muttaqi. It comes from a sermon by ʿUmar ibn ʿAbd al-ʿAzīz (d. 720), the Umayyad ruler who was the only pious member of Islam's earliest power-hungry dynasty. He is credited with ordering the first compilation of hadith books and was a cherished hero of ʿAli Muttaqi. ʿAli Muttaqi believed that piety was the best provision from this world to the next, and also from one phase of life to the next. He left his hometown of Burhanpur with this idea, rooted in the Qur'an and reinforced by hadith reports and pious sermons, firmly in his mind and heart. He settled in Ahmedabad to spread this idea among the Sufi communities, hadith scholars, jurists, and rulers. He sailed to Mecca from Gujarat with this idea foremost in his mind. It allowed him to embrace a tenuous future in exile and later allowed him to return to Gujarat empowered as a reformer in scholarship, in communal relations, and in court.

ʿAli Muttaqi's goals were to organize his own reformist Sufi community, argue against the Mahdawis and oppose the Shattaris, and reform the political order of the sultanate of Gujarat. He did not succeed in organizing a durable Sufi community; after ʿAbd al-Haqq died, there was no identifiable "Muttaqi method" in any Sufi order, let alone a new movement called the "Muttaqi Order." ʿAli Muttaqi's reputation was distorted such that he is not remembered as a Sufi but rather as a hadith scholar. This distortion stems largely from Wajih al-Din Alawi's counter-critique of ʿAli Muttaqi charging that he was not an authentic saint; the Shattari scholar defended his own masters, and these charges stuck, shaping ʿAli Muttaqi's image for posterity. He often appears as an acerbic scholar and ascetic renunciant, but not necessarily as a saint.

ʿAli Muttaqi's broader mission was to integrate hadith studies into Sufi training. He succeeded, as many Shattaris took refuge in hadith scholarship. Muhammad Ghawth's boldly transcendent and outspokenly ecstatic style of Sufi devotion did not persist even as his lineage thrived. The persecution in

Ahmedabad drove the next generation of Shattari Sufis toward a more *shariʿa*-oriented framework, as noted by Carl Ernst.[42] Ironically, this is exactly what ʿAli Muttaqi desired as the outcome of his critique in the first place, though he could not have predicted the means and modality of the change.

In succeeding generations, ʿAli Muttaqi's followers integrated hadith study into Sufism. In South Asia, ʿAbd al-Haqq's initiation into the Naqshbandi Order accelerated this process, for in the eighteenth century, many Naqshbandis became renowned hadith scholars in South Asia—so much so that most current scholarship identifies the reformist current of Sufism exclusively with the Naqshbandi Sufi order.[43] To posterity, ʿAbd al-Haqq and his Muttaqi teachers are commonly remembered as Naqshbandis, even though their affiliations were more complex. For example, today in Burhanpur there is an institution named the ʿAli Muttaqi Madrasa, and it is run by Naqshbandi scholars who teach Qur'an and hadith. When I met the rector there and asked about ʿAli Muttaqi's legacy, they referred to him with veneration as "the author of *Kanz al-ʿUmmāl*," his most enduring book of hadith. If they also teach Sufism, they do not discuss it openly.

Remembered as a Naqshbandi, ʿAbd al-Haqq Muhaddith Dihlawi looms large in South Asian Islamic cultural history but is often severed from his actual reformist Sufi community. He is pivotal in any assessment of shifts in Islamic discourse toward the *shariʿa* or between rival Sufi orders during the early modern period, such as the most recent assessment of Islamic reform in the early modern period by Ahmad Dallal. Dallal aptly describes how Sufism spread by the sixteenth century in both elite philosophical forms and in vernacular popular forms: "The emergence of a popular reformed Sufism . . . consciously partook in all aspects of Islamic intellectual life . . . [and] affirmed its conformity with the Qur'an and Sunna as the ultimate sources of its legitimacy and underscored compliance with the formal obligations of the law as the indispensable prerequisite for deeper forms of Sufi religiosity."[44] Dallal is speaking of eighteenth-century Sufi reformers, but the movement that he describes has roots in the fifteenth century and grew throughout the sixteenth century with the Muttaqi community; then, spurred by millennial anxieties, it blossomed in the seventeenth century with the activities of ʿAbd al-Haqq.

But ʿAbd al-Haqq did not arise *ex nihilo*, nor did he synthesize elements of Sufism and Islamic scholarship that were current in Delhi where he grew up. Rather, he adopted his ideals from the Muttaqi community. This community was actively engaged in Islamic reform, in the interstices between Gujarat and Mecca, long before the term "reform" gained wide currency and scholarly recognition. Reformist discourse is usually dated to the late Mughal period,

The ʿAli Muttaqi Madrasa in Burhanpur.

after Aurangzeb (ruled 1658–1707). He began his career as governor of Gujarat and then the Deccan, with his base at Burhanpur, from where he built his resources of power to seize the throne. He oversaw the widest expansion of the Mughal realm to cover almost all of modern South Asia, but by the time he died in 1707 Mughal power had already begun to recede due to internal uprisings and external pressure from European trade that was veering toward colonial occupation.

As Mughal authority wavered, the empire's reliance on Sufi exemplars and syncretic religiosity had come under question. Scholars forged popular movements to reform Islamic mores and reestablish a new balance of religious and political power in a mood of urgent crisis. However, the Muttaqi community reveals that the quest for reform began in the long sixteenth century, as the sultanate of Gujarat toppled under expansionist pressure from the early Mughal Empire. These political forces drove ʿAli Muttaqi into exile and gave him access to reform recourses in Arabia and North Africa.[45] The new political reality of the Mughal imperium, fed by millennial expectations and syncretic creativity, fueled his spiritual quest and textual project to reform Islamic discourse in order to fuse Sufi ideals and scriptural studies in hadith.

ʿAli Muttaqi's personality, writings, and disciples shaped several centuries of reform movements in South Asia, giving rise to forces that have become dominant in reaction to colonial occupation. Rapprochement between Sufi *adab* and hadith study was an enduring feature in South Asia and gained momentum during the eighteenth century as Mughal suzerainty shrank and crumbled. ʿAbd al-Haqq Muhaddith Dihlawi passed his ideals to Shāh ʿAbd al-Raḥīm (d. 1719), a disciple of Khwāja Khurd (the son of Khwaja Baqi Bi'llah), who was educated at ʿAbd al-Haqq's madrasa. He later established his own institution, the Madrasa Raḥīmiyya (at Kotla Firuz Shah).[46] There, he trained his son Shāh Walī'llāh (d. 1762), who perpetuated ʿAbd al-Haqq's ideals.[47]

Shah Wali'llah thus built upon the foundation set by ʿAli Muttaqi, who integrated Sufism and hadith; two generations later, ʿAbd al-Haqq tightened this fusion and integrated into it jurisprudence through his intricate textual engagement with Zarruq. Then Shah Wali'llah widened this fusion by added into it elements of the Hellenic disciplines of ethics and philosophy, as they had been adopted and adapted by Islamic civilization. Modern scholars have exaggerated the importance of Ahmad Sirhindi, picturing him as the reviver of the *shariʿa* in South Asia who influenced modernity. They have portrayed Shah Wali'llah as a genius but a dead-ender whose synthesis of hadith, jurisprudence, Sufism, ethics, and philosophy was too complex and "medieval" to influence modernity. Current scholarship on the influential Deobandi reform movement and its emphasis on hadith studies elucidates its Sufi origins. This book demonstrates how the fusion of forces that fed the Deobandi movement had its roots in the Muttaqi community three centuries earlier.

It is easier to write the history of a broad movement than to write a nuanced account of a complex life. This study offers a portrait of ʿAli Muttaqi's passage through life, with as much nuance as archival sources and literary traces can reveal. It details the Sufi precedents of his childhood, social aspirations of his youth, spiritual quest of his maturity, and political disappointment of his old age. It extends beyond him into the life of his admirers and followers, who expanded the scope of his reform project nurtured within Sufi ideals. It aims to reveal the texture of his thought through translation from rare documents and to expose his interpersonal relations with those whom he trusted and those who betrayed him. With this nuanced portrait now before us, we can describe how ʿAli Muttaqi's obscured legacy developed in modern South Asia and how he might critique its modern manifestations.

In modern times, ʿAli Muttaqi's revival of hadith in South Asia led in two directions, neither of which would be acceptable to him. The first direction saw the hadith revival giving rise to anti-Sufi reformist movements, like the Wahhabis and the Ahl-e Hadith. The second direction saw Sufi scholars focused on jurisprudence and hadith to form the Deoband Academy and its pan–South Asian reform movement. All these movements reacted strongly to British colonialism in the nineteenth century as they tried to articulate a counter-modernism, which took on Islamic fundamentalist modalities in the twentieth century.

These modern reform movements seem to be successful; indeed, they deeply shape Muslim communities in South Asia today as they spread globally, not through seafaring but through digital media. They were fueled by the hadith studies that ʿAli Muttaqi so advocated, yet they lack something basic that ʿAli Muttaqi cherished: moderation (*iʿtidal*), just balance (*ʿadl*), and refinement (*adab*). As the centerpiece of his reformist Sufism, he studied and taught "The Book of Wisdom Sayings" of Ibn ʿAtaʾallah, which includes this aphorism: "A seeker's ignorance results in his display of bad *adab*, while punishment may be delayed for him such that he might say, 'If this were bad *adab* then divine aid would cease and alienation would increase.' In fact, divine aid does cease in ways of which he is unaware, for, if not, he would not persist in bad *adab* without a care—he dwells in alienation and never realizes, for God leaves him to that which he devises."[48] Despite their worldly success, reform movements without good *adab*—*adab* that comes only through Sufism—is a sign of alienation and impending disaster.

Ideology is no replacement for *adab*, for only in face-to-face interactions is refinement, virtue, and respect displayed. This is ʿAli Muttaqi's real message to us in the twenty-first century and reason enough to rummage through the dusty shelves of archives to search for the contents of his satchels. If we imagine making a journey toward God, it can only be a Hajj to the heart. It is in bringing knowledge, contentment, and care to the hearts of those around us that we find the way, through twisted paths and stormy seas, to the heart that is in each of us.

APPENDIX A

Sultans of Gujarat in the Muzaffar-Shahi Dynasty, 1407–1584

Muzaffar Shah, ruled 1391–1407 (as Zafar Khan, governor of Gujarat province on behalf of the Tughlaq dynasty of Delhi sultans) and ruled as sultan of Gujarat from 1407 to 1411 from his capital at Patan.

Ahmad Shah I, ruled 1411–42 (grandson of Muzaffar Shah) from new capital at Ahmedabad.

Muhammad Shah II, ruled 1442–51 (elder son of Ahmad Shah I).

Ahmad Shah II (also known as Qutb al-Din Ahmad Shah), ruled 1451–58 (son of Muhammad Shah II); his uncle Dawud Shah (younger son of Ahmad Shah I) succeeded him but was deposed after a few days.

Mahmud Shah Begra, ruled 1458–1511 (son of Muhammad Shah II and Sindhi princess Bibi Mughli) from his new capital of Champaner (formally dubbed Muhammadabad).

Muzaffar Shah II, ruled 1511–26 (eldest son of Mahmud Shah Begra).

Sikandar Shah, ruled 1526 (eldest son of Muzaffar Shah II) but murdered after a few weeks of rule.

Mahmud Shah II, ruled 1526 (son of Muzaffar Shah II) for only a few weeks as a boy.

Bahadur Shah, ruled 1527–37 (formerly known as Qutb al-Din Khan; son of Muzaffar Shah II) from his capital at Ahmedabad; his rule was interrupted by Mughal invasion in 1532, and the Portuguese murdered him at Diu.

Miran Muhammad Faruqi, claimed to rule in 1538 (Bahadur Shah's nephew and the sultan of Khandesh) but died before reaching Ahmedabad.

Mahmud Shah III, ruled 1538–54 (son of Bahadur Shah's brother Latif Khan) as a boy governed by regents; when mature, he built a new capital at Mahmudabad and was later murdered, leaving no heir.

Ahmad Shah III, ruled 1554–61 (a distant descendant of Ahmad Shah I) in name only while nobles divided Gujarat into spheres of influence.

Muzaffar Shah III, ruled 1561–73 (claimed to be the posthumously born son of Mahmud Shah III); imprisoned by Emperor Akbar at Agra until he briefly reasserted rule in 1584; and captured by Mughal forces but committed suicide, ending the Muzaffar-Shahi dynasty.

APPENDIX B

Sufi Lineages of ʿAli Muttaqi and ʿAbd al-Haqq Muhaddith Dihlawi

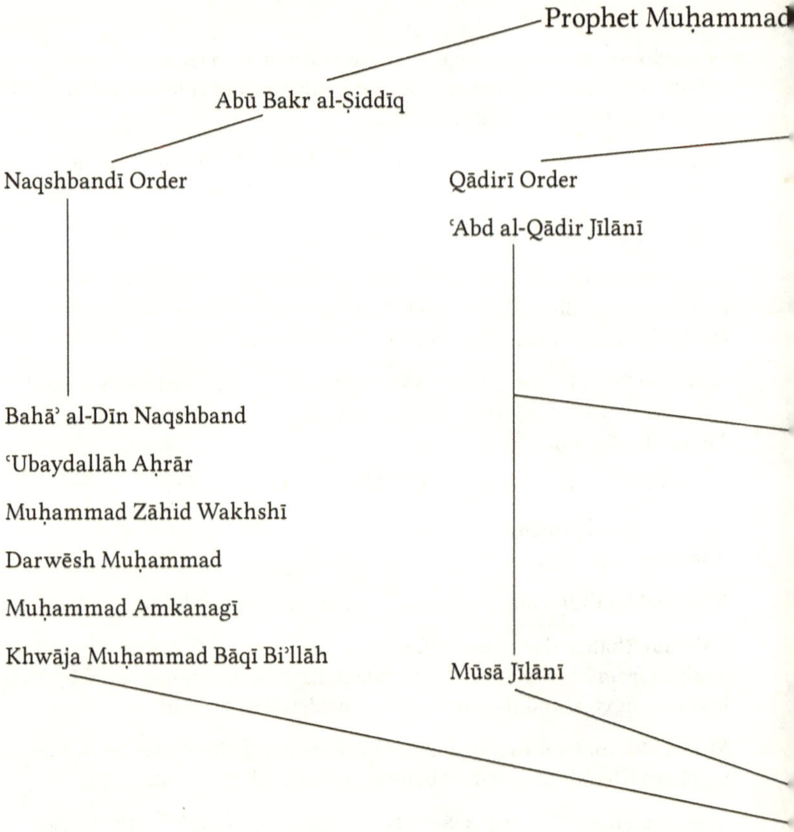

Chart of the Sufi initiatory chains (*silsila*) of ʿAli Muttaqi and ʿAbd al-Haqq Muhaddith Dihlawi. Their initiations in the triple *ṭariqa* are recorded in the notebook of texts by ʿAli Muttaqi that was compiled by an anonymous disciple of ʿAbd al-Haqq, who himself recorded an account of his lineages in *Zād al-Muttaqīn*.

Source: Anonymous disciple of ʿAbd al-Haqq Muhaddith Dihlawi, "Risāla-ye Khirqa." For the initiations of Ahmad Zarruq, see Kugle, *Rebel between Spirit and Law*, 128.

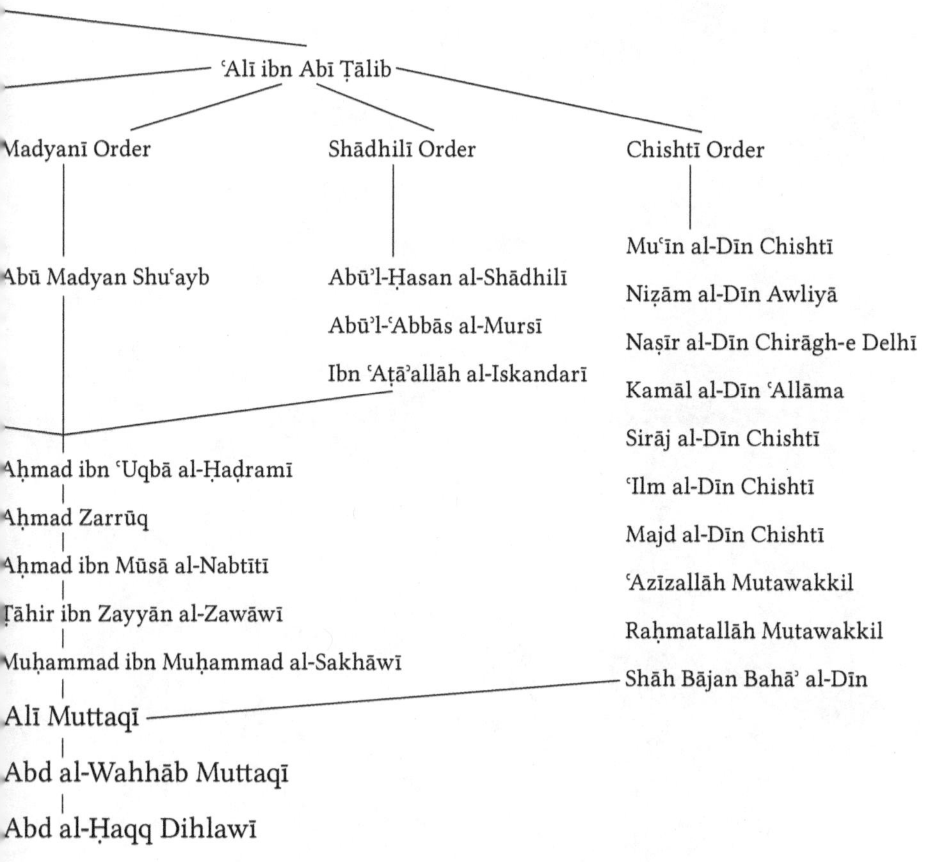

ʿAlī ibn Abī Ṭālib
Madyanī Order
Shādhilī Order
Chishtī Order
Abū Madyan Shuʿayb
Abū'l-Ḥasan al-Shādhilī
Abū'l-ʿAbbās al-Mursī
Ibn ʿAṭā'allāh al-Iskandarī
Muʿīn al-Dīn Chishtī
Niẓām al-Dīn Awliyā
Naṣīr al-Dīn Chirāgh-e Delhī
Kamāl al-Dīn ʿAllāma
Sirāj al-Dīn Chishtī
ʿIlm al-Dīn Chishtī
Majd al-Dīn Chishtī
ʿAzīzallāh Mutawakkil
Raḥmatallāh Mutawakkil
Shāh Bājan Bahā' al-Dīn
Aḥmad ibn ʿUqbā al-Ḥaḍramī
Aḥmad Zarrūq
Aḥmad ibn Mūsā al-Nabtītī
Ṭāhir ibn Zayyān al-Zawāwī
Muḥammad ibn Muḥammad al-Sakhāwī
Alī Muttaqī
Abd al-Wahhāb Muttaqī
Abd al-Ḥaqq Dihlawī

ABBREVIATIONS USED IN THE NOTES AND BIBLIOGRAPHY

APR	Arabic and Persian Research Institute Library in Tonk (Rajasthan, India)
Azad	Abul Kalam Azad Library, Aligarh Muslim University (Uttar Pradesh, India)
BJI	B. J. Institute of Learning and Research (Shaykh Qazi Collection of Manuscripts formerly in the Wajih al-Din ʿAlawi Madrasa) in Ahmedabad (Gujarat, India)
BL	British Library in London
DK	Deutsches Kulturbesitz in Berlin
GB	Ganj Bakhsh Library (Iranian Cultural Institute) in Islamabad (Punjab, Pakistan)
GC	Garrett Collection at Princeton University
KB	Khuda Bakhsh Library (formerly Bankipore Oriental Public Library) in Patna (Bihar, India)
OML	Oriental Manuscript Library in Hyderabad Deccan (Telangana, India)
PU	Punjab University Library in Lahore (Punjab, Pakistan)
RL	Reza Library in Rampur (Uttar Pradesh, India)
SJ	Salar Jung Library in Hyderabad Deccan (Telangana, India)

NOTES

Introduction

1. The Hindavi couplet is sung in Qawwali: Khusrō, daryā prēm kā ulṫī wā kī dħār / jō utrā sō ḋūb gayā jō ḋūbā sō pār."

2. Mojaddedi, *Rumi*, 174–75.

3. Dihlawī, "Zād al-Muttaqīn," 30b–31b. All translations are from this British Museum manuscript. Other copies are found at Rampur 407 (acquisition no. P/19); and Hyderabad OML 1523 (farsi tasawwuf). In this book, this author is named ʿAbd al-Haqq and is listed in the bibliography under "Dihlawī, ʿAbd al-Ḥaqq Muḥaddith."

4. Eaton, *Social History of the Deccan*, 3–4.

5. Sheikh, *Forging a Region*.

6. Balachandran, *Narrative Pasts*, 8.

7. Blake, *Time in Early Modern Islam*, 146.

8. Fleischer, "Mediterranean Apocalypse," 27–29.

9. "Speaking the End Times: Prophecy and Messianism in Eurasia," special issue, *Journal of Economic and Social History of the Orient* 6, no. 1–2 (2018): 1–71.

10. Fleischer, "Mediterranean Apocalypse," 26 and 50–51.

11. M. Alam, *Languages of Political Islam*.

12. Green, *Bombay Islam*, 8–19; Moin, *Millennial Sovereign*, 99–100.

13. Knight, *Muhammad's Body*.

14. Dihlawī, *Zād al-Muttaqīn*, a rare book recently translated into Urdu but never analyzed in English, provides the gripping account of ʿAbd al-Haqq's shipwreck.

First Satchel

1. The quatrain in Persian is inscribed on the doorway of Muʿīn al-Dīn Chishtī's *dargah* and is sung in Qawwali.

2. Parwēz, *Shāh Bājan*, 139, cites this Persian couplet by Hafiz: "Shab-e tārīk o bīm mawj o girdāb chunān ḥā'il / Kujā dānand ḥāl-e mā bigusārān-e sāḥil-hā." See Eaton, *Social History of the Deccan*, 61.

3. Kāshānī, *Aḥsan al-Aqwāl*, 65, cites this quatrain in Persian by an unknown poet: "Gar dard dehī dawā na-khwāham / dar ʿishq-e tū juz balā na-khwāham // Gar kushta shawam bi-rāh-e ʿishq-at / har giz ze tū khūn bahā na-khwāham.

4. Parwēz, *Shāh Bājan*, 140–41. Translation by author with Dr. Oudesh Rani Bawa.

5. Schimmel, *Mystical Dimensions of Islam*, 3–12.

6. Ernst, *Introduction to Sufism*, 18–31.

7. Ernst and Lawrence, *Sufi Martyrs of Love*, 36–38.

8. Scott Kugle, "Nizam al-Din Awliya," in Meri, *Medieval Islamic Civilization*, 563–65.

9. Lawrence, *Morals for the Heart*, 198.

10. Lawrence, 202, describes the hadith circles where Nizam al-Din Awliya studied.

11. Lawrence, 201–2.

12. Ernst, *Eternal Garden*, 119.

13. Bukhārī, *Ṣaḥīḥ al-Bukhārī*, 3:1303 (Kitāb al-Riqāq, chapter 3, report 6492).

14. Ernst, *Eternal Garden*, 120–26.

15. Ernst, 229–32. After 1382, Khandesh became an independent kingdom. Its ruler, Nāṣir Khān Fārūqī, captured Asīrgaṛh fortress in 1431 and established a new capital, Burhanpur, between the fort and the Tapti River, and a subsidiary settlement on the opposite bank, Zaynābād (after Shaykh Zayn al-Dīn Shirāzī, successor to Burhan al-Din Gharib).

16. ʿAli Muttaqi's full name is ʿAlī ibn Ḥusām al-Dīn ibn ʿAbd al-Mālik ibn Qāḍī Khān al-Hindī al-Muttaqī, as recorded in the most authoritative hagiographic source, Dihlawī, *Zād al-Muttaqīn*. Later sources render his name as ʿAlī Nūr al-Dīn ibn Ḥusām al-Dīn or ʿAlī ʿAlāʾ al-Dīn ibn Ḥusām al-Dīn. The key elements (ʿAli son of Husam al-Din known as Muttaqi) identify the author as a single person, distinguished from ʿAlī Muttaqī Khurd "the Lesser" (a Sufi in Ahmedabad during the same period who is known for living on discarded vegetables rather than being a scholarly author); see ʿAli Khān, *Mirʾāt-e Aḥmadī Supplement*, 73 and 83.

17. Ernst, *Eternal Garden*, 118–32 and 147–54.

18. Kugle, *When Sun Meets Moon*, 108–11; see also Bawa, "Role of Sufis and Saints."

19. In addition to Parwēz, Shah Bajan's biography is found in modern Urdu sources: Mutālā, *Mashāʾikh-e Aḥmadābād*, 2:36–42; and B. Khān, *Tārīkh-e Awliyā*, 71–92.

20. Shāh Bājan Chishtī, "Khazāʾin-e Raḥmatallāh," is primarily a hagiography of Raḥmatallāh Mutawakkil and his father. For Shah Bajan's poetry in Persian, see Kugle, "Burhan al-Din Gharib," 96.

21. Scott Kugle, "Making Passion Popular: Sung Poetry in Urdu," in S. Alam, *Cultural Fusion of Sufi Islam*, 103–6; other translations are in Shamsur Rahman Faruqi, "Long History of Urdu Literature, Part 1," in Pollock, *Literary Cultures in History*, 821–23; and Sheikh, *Forging a Region*, 209–12.

22. B. Khān, *Tārīkh-e Awliyā*, 71–92; Parwēz, *Shāh Bājan*, 87.

23. B. Khān, *Tārīkh-e Awliyā*, 86; Parwēz, *Shāh Bājan*, 149.

24. Ernst and Lawrence, *Sufi Martyrs of Love*, 34–46.

25. Hodgson, *Venture of Islam*, 1:445.

26. Hodgson, 2:484–93 and 501–3.

27. Biagi, *Collection of Sufi Rules*, xxiv–xxxiii.

28. M. Alam, *Languages of Political Islam*, 12–13.

29. Metcalf, *Moral Conduct and Authority*, 4.

30. Farishta, *History*, 4:143.

31. Farishta, 4:103. Malwa broke from the Delhi sultanate in 1405, when the governor's son took the title Hōshang Shāh Ghōrī (perhaps after poisoning his father).

32. Farishta, 4:144.

33. ʿAlī Muttaqī, "al-Jawāhir al-Thamīna" (MSS Hyderabad OML).

34. Shah Bajan's Sufi masters were Rahmatallah Mutawakkil and his father, ʿAzizallah. See Ghawthī, *Gulzār-e Abrār*, 204; Anonymous, "Baḥr-e Zakhkhār" (MSS Hyderabad OML), 262–64; and Malkāpūrī, *Maḥbūb Dhūʾl-Minan fī Tadhkira Awliyā-ye Dakkan*, 1:330 and 551–53. He took initiation with Rahmatullah first in Ahmedabad and later settled in Burhanpur where ʿAzizallah's reputation was stronger; therefore, hagiographies relate Shah Bajan to the latter rather than the former. Yet in Shāh Bājan Chishtī, "Khazāʾin-e Raḥmatallāh," Shah Bajan states that his master was Rahmatallah, as explained in Mutālā, *Mashāʾikh-e Aḥmadābād*, 2:38.

35. Anonymous, "Baḥr-e Zakhkhār" (MSS Hyderabad OML), 262–64.

36. Mutālā, *Mashā'ikh-e Aḥmadābād*, 1:364–5.

37. Moin, *Millennial Sovereign*, 155–61.

38. Dihlawī, *Zād al-Muttaqīn*, 7b. This is the definitive biography of ʿAli Muttaqi and ʿAbd al-Wahhab Muttaqi, completed in 1594–95 (some twenty-eight years after ʿAli Muttaqi died), as the author heard accounts from ʿAli Muttaqi's followers in Mecca and benefited from two prior biographies that are no longer extant.

39. ʿAli Muttaqi recommended that those who did not have a shaykh experiment with the "death of self-will" and wrote a short book, "Risālat-e Ḍurūriyāt dar Bāb-e Mubtadī-ye Ṭarīqat" (MSS Lahore PU), recommending nine things to be observed while searching for a shaykh. Four practices in the outer life are hunger, wakefulness, silence, and isolation. Five principles in the inner life are sincerity, reliance on God alone, patience, determination, and certainty.

40. Steinfels, *Knowledge before Action*.

41. The Qadiri Order was active after the Sayyid family of Bandagī Muḥammad Ghawth Qādirī settled at Ūch in 1482.

42. *Kharāj* is a tax on agricultural produce from lands conquered by Muslim rulers, in contrast to lands owned privately by Muslims. Husam al-Din Muttaqi insisted on paying *kharaj* to protest predatory taxation and illegal seizure of crops by Muslim rulers from lands owned by Muslim cultivators. He refused land grants that rulers granted to scholars and Sufis, which were exempt from *kharaj*. Expenditure from *kharaj* was restricted to projects benefiting the Muslim community rather than aggrandizing the rulers or enlarging the treasury.

43. Ḥusām al-Dīn Muttaqī, "Ādāb al-Mā'ida," details the Prophet's table manners as preserved in hadith: what to eat, how to eat, and how to limit how much one eats.

44. Ḥasanī, *Nuzhat al-Khawāṭir*, 4:76.

45. Balkhī, "ʿAyn al-ʿIlm wa Zayn al-Ḥilm" (MSS Hyderabad SJ). A commentary was also composed by ʿAli Muttaqi's student ʿAlī ibn Sulṭān al-Qārī al-Harawī (d. 1605, known as Mulla ʿAlī Qārī), "Tibyān al-Ṭurūq li-Ahl al-Ḥilm Mukhtaṣar ʿAyn al-ʿIlm" (MSS Hyderabad SJ). On Mulla ʿAli Qari, see Patrick Franke, "The Ego of the Mullah," in Elger and Köse, *Many Ways of Speaking about the Self*, 185–200; and Dihlawī, *Zād al-Muttaqīn*, 15b.

46. Dihlawī, *Zād al-Muttaqīn*, 7b.

47. Husam al-Din Muttaqi, "Ḥifẓ al-Īmān" (MSS Islamabad GB), likely was a collaboration between Husam al-Din and ʿAli Muttaqi. Attribution should go to Husam al-Din as a teacher advising his pupil; ʿAli Muttaqi asserted that his first composition was "Tabyīn al-Ṭurūq," written after he left Multan.

48. Ḥ. Muttaqī, "Ḥifẓ al-Īmān," 78.

49. Ḥ. Muttaqī, 81.

50. Dihlawī, *Zād al-Muttaqīn*, 60a.

51. Lawrence, *Morals for the Heart*, 186.

52. Ḥasanī,, *Nuzhat al-Khawāṭir*, 4:76.

53. Dihlawī, *Zād al-Muttaqīn*, 8a–8b.

54. Shaw, *Paradox of Intention*, 61–74.

55. Kugle, *Book of Illumination*, 121.

56. Dihlawī, "Miftāḥ al-Futūḥ" (MSS Hyderabad OML), fourth discourse.

57. Dihlawī, fourth discourse.

58. ʿAlī Muttaqī, "Malfūẓāt-e Shaykh ʿAlī Muttaqī" (MSS Hyderabad OML).

59. After ʿAbd al-Qadir Jilani, Sufi masters elaborated on the death of self-will, especially those remembered as "founders" of Sufi orders such as al-Shadhili and Najm al-Dīn Kubrā (d. 1221, founder of the Kubrawi Order).

60. ʿAbd al-Haqq calls this a Qadiri practice adapted by ʿAli Muttaqi for new purposes. Earlier, some Sufis used a "little bag" (*kinf* or *kunayf*), as mentioned in Lawrence, *Morals for the Heart*, 204, to minimize possessions.

61. Dihlawī, *Zād al-Muttaqīn*, 21b–22a.

62. Dihlawī, 37a–37b.

63. Tirmidhī, *Ṭabāʿi al-Nufūs*, 83–101.

64. Biagi, *Collection of Sufi Rules*, xxxii–xxxiii.

65. Tirmidhī, *Tabāʿi al-Nufūs*, 22–23.

66. ʿAlī Muttaqī, "Tabyīn al-Ṭurūq," is preserved in Dihlawī, *Zād al-Muttaqīn*, 41a–45b, and also as an independent text (MSS Lahore PU).

67. Zargar, "Ten Principles," 113.

68. ʿAli Muttaqi's text has been translated online by Dar al-Ulum Deoband; see https://www.deoband.org/2015/11/tasawwuf/shariah-and-tariqah-tasawwuf/explanation-of-the-paths-to-reach-allah/ (accessed August 21, 2019).

69. ʿAlī Muttaqī, "Tabyīn al-Ṭurūq."

70. Tirmidhī, *Ṭabāʿi al-Nufūs*, 83–84.

71. ʿAlī Muttaqī, "Asrār al-ʿĀrifīn wa Sayr al-Ṭālibīn."

72. Dihlawī, *Zād al-Muttaqīn*, 9a.

73. Sheikh, *Forging a Region*, 16–19.

74. Sheikh, 164, notes Bahāʾ al-Dīn Zakariyā Suhrawardi's role in Gujarati conversion narratives; one of his descendants, Makhdūm-e Jahānīyān, reportedly converted the father and uncle of the first sultan of Gujarat, Muẓaffar Shāh.

75. Campbell, *History of Gujarát*, 671n26, lists Gujarat's twelve main ports from north to south, including Diu, Bharoch, Khambhat, Surat, and Mahim.

76. ʿAlī Khān, *Mirʾāt-e Aḥmadī Supplement*, 24–36 and 96–97, recounts how Muzaffar Shah was given a dagger belonging to Makhdum-e Jahaniyan, predicting his rule as sultan of Gujarat. Sheikh, *Forging a Region*, 205–6, notes how Sultan Ahmad wrote an Arabic ode praising Qutb-e ʿAlam; see also Ho, *Graves of Tarim*, 108–9.

77. Chishti Sufis like Shaykh Sirāj al-Dīn settled in Patan but were overshadowed by Suhrawardis who settled in Ahmedabad under the sultanate of Gujarat. ʿAlī Khān, *Mirʾāt-e Ahmadī Supplement*, 64, notes how Shāh Bārikallāh Chishtī, designated by Nizam al-Din Awliya to settle at Ahmedabad, humbly granted popular acclaim to Suhrawardis like Shah-e ʿAlam, giving rise to the proverb, "The Chishtis baked and the Bukharis ate."

78. ʿAlī Khān, *Mirʾāt-e Ahmadī Supplement*, 2–4. See also Balachandran, *Narrative Pasts*.

79. Sheikh, *Forging a Region*, 172–75.

80. Sheikh, 82–83.

81. Farishta, *History*, 4:47.

82. Blecher, *Said the Prophet of God*, 143–46.

83. The Suhrawardi leader, Shah-e ʿAlam, predicted this.

84. Farishta, *History*, 4:58–59. Sultan Muzaffar II, being deferential to Sufis and scholars (he copied the Qurʾan in his own calligraphic hand to send to Mecca as gifts), favored Bahadur but refused to raise his rank to equal the older brothers. Before his

death, the sultan recalled Bahadur, who was with Ibrahim Lodi's army opposing the Mughals, back to Gujarat.

85. Farishta, *History*, 4:60. Sikandar marched to battle without stopping at Vatva, home of the Bukhari Sayyids and Suhrawardi Sufis (considered the spiritual patrons of Ahmedabad). He abused their leader who had predicted the ascendancy of Bahadur. Oral lore recounts that Sikandar dreamed that a Bukhari Sayyid warned him to renounce the throne.

86. Other nobles resented this minister's regency and entreated Bahadur to return to Gujarat and replace the boy-puppet; the minister incited the Mughals to intercept Bahadur, but Prince Bahadur eluded them.

87. Dihlawī, *Akhbār al-Akhyār*, 279; Ghawthī, *Gulzār-e Abrār*, 504. Most Sindhi scholars who fled to Gujarat and the Deccan joined the Shattari community.

88. Dihlawī, *Akhbār al-Akhyār*, 279.

89. ʿAli Muttaqi dreamed that the Prophet Muhammad specified Miyan Ghiyath as "the best man of his age," after Muhammad ibn Tahir Patani and ʿAli Muttaqi himself.

90. Dihlawī, *Zād al-Muttaqīn*, 9b. ʿAli Muttaqi discusses how a child is the primary benefit of marriage in his treatise on Sufi training for married men, "Jarr al-Thaqīl fī Sulūk al-Maʿīl" (MSS Lahore PU).

91. Dihlawī, *Zād al-Muttaqīn*, 10a.

92. Ulūghkhānī, *Ẓafar al-Wālih*, 257 and 333, provides a biography of Asaf Khan; see also Ḥasanī, *Nuzhat al-Khawāṭir*, 4:162.

Second Satchel

1. Dihlawī, *Zād al-Muttaqīn*, 10b–11a. The companion of ʿAli Muttaqi was Qaḍi ʿAbdallah Sindhi, whose son Qadi Hamid Muhaddith told the story to ʿAbd al-Haqq Dihlawi.

2. Farishta, *History*, 4:62–69, 184–87. Bahadur Shah's paternal aunt married into the Faruqī dynasty that ruled Khandesh. One generation later Bahadur Shah's sister married the next sultan of Khandesh, ʿĀdil Khān II. Bahadur Shah was the uncle of the sultan of Khandesh when their son Mīrān Muḥammad Khān became ruler (ruled 1520–35). Bahadur Shah's brother Chānd Khān fled to Malwa after unsuccessfully challenging Bahadur Shah, who, allied through family ties with the ruler of Khandesh, leveraged this alliance to take over Malwa using the presence of his renegade brother there as a cause of war.

3. Farishta, *History*, 4:74.

4. Chaube, *History of the Gujarat Kingdom*, 252.

5. Currim and Michell, *Dargahs*, 94–103.

6. Farishta, *History*, 4:19.

7. Commissariat, *History of Gujarat*, 88–89.

8. Farishta, *History*, 4:43–44; Commissariat, *History of Gujarat*, 204.

9. Mamluk sultans of Egypt appointed a naval commander, Amīr Ḥusayn Mushrif al-Kurdī, to fortify Jedda and attack the Portuguese at Diu. Ottomans conquered Egypt in 1505–6 and continued this policy to protect the Indian Ocean trade; see Özbaran, *Ottoman Response to Portuguese Expansion*.

10. Sheikh, *Forging a Region*, 44–45.

11. Casale, *Ottoman Age of Exploration*, 32.

12. Quoted in Mehrdad Shokoohy and Natalie Shokoohy, "The Karao Jami Masjid of Diu," *South Asian Studies* 16 (2000): 57; see also Alam and Subrahmanyam, *Writing the Mughal World*, 42–50.

13. Casale, *Ottoman Age of Exploration*, 26–29.

14. Ulūghkhānī, *Ẓafar al-Wālih*, 218.

15. Casale, *Ottoman Age of Exploration*, 46–48.

16. Farishta, *History*, 4:69.

17. Chaube, *History of the Gujarat Kingdom*, 257.

18. Ulūghkhānī, *Ẓafar al-Wālih*, 237.

19. Ulūghkhānī, 257.

20. Sheikh, *Forging a Region*, 207. Ibn Suwayda had a copy of *Fatḥ al-Bārī* (Ibn Ḥajar al-ʿAsqalani's commentary on the hadith collection *Ṣaḥīḥ al-Bukhārī*) brought to Gujarat in 1514; the friend of Ibn Suwayda's who presented it to the sultan was appointed governor of Bharoch.

21. Ulūghkhānī, *Ẓafar al-Wālih*, 117–18; Ishaq, *India's Contribution to the Study of Hadith Literature*, 93–94.

22. Brown, *Hadith*, 58–63.

23. Dihlawī, *Zād al-Muttaqīn*, 13a. Al-Haythami was an orphan raised by a pupil of the famous legal scholar Shams al-Dīn Muḥammad ibn ʿAbd al-Raḥmān al-Sakhāwī; at age fifteen, he studied at al-Azhar with Abu'l-Hasan al-Bakri and Nāṣir al-Dīn al-Laqānī (an Egyptian follower of Ahmad Zarruq); he died in 1566 according to Anonymous, "Tarjamat Ibn Ḥajar al-Haythamī" (MSS Patna KB), folios 265–73.

24. Dihlawī, *Zād al-Muttaqīn*, 12a. ʿAli Muttaqi considered himself to be one generation removed from al-Suyuti and to have assumed his mantle of authority (after al-Haythami) by authoring his magnum opus, *Kanz al-ʿUmmāl fī Sunan al-Aqwāl wa'l-Afʿāl.* ʿAli Muttaqi began a condensed version of it, "Minhāj al-ʿUmmāl," which was completed by ʿAbd al-Wahhab Muttaqi, that exists only in manuscript.

25. ʿAlī Muttaqī, "al-Aḥādīth al-Mutawātira al-Ma'khūdha min Risālat al-Suyūṭī" (MSS Aligarh); see also his "Mukhtaṣar Qaṭf al-Azhār" (MSS Tonk APR).

26. ʿAlī Muttaqī, "Kitāb Wāsiṭat al-Wuṣūl al-Musāmma bi-Sharḥ al-Fuṣūl li-Jāmiʿ fī al-Furūʿ wa'l-Uṣūl" (MSS Patna KB).

27. ʿAlī Muttaqī, "Chehel Ḥadīth" (MSS Aligarh).

28. ʿAlī Muttaqī, "Maṭlaʿ al-Ghāya fī Ikhtiṣār an-Nihāya" (MSS Berlin DK).

29. ʿAlī Muttaqī, "Shamā'il al-Nabī" (MSS Aligarh).

30. ʿAydarusī, *al-Nūr al-Sāfir*, 134, 155, and 194, documents how the coffee trade grew over the Indian Ocean during the sixteenth century.

31. Ho, *Graves of Tarim*, 117, translates the title as "The Traveling Light" while noting that it could also be "The Light Unveiled." His first option is incorrect.

32. Dihlawī, *Zād al-Muttaqīn*, 29b. ʿAli Muttaqi's comment caused a public row, but Muhammad al-Bakri later apologized to ʿAli Muttaqi, admitting that he deviated from the ethics exemplified by his father and ʿAli Muttaqi.

33. Dihlawī, 20a. ʿAli Muttaqi suspected that Ottoman stipends came from illegal sources (like taxes imposed beyond *shariʿa* boundaries), showing continuity with Husam al-Din Muttaqi's ascetic teachings.

34. Dihlawī, "Anwār al-Jaliyya fī Aḥwāl Mashāyikh al-Shādhiliyya," likely included information about al-Sakhawi; this rare Persian hagiography about Shadhili Sufis is untraceable, as cited in Niẓāmī, *Ḥayāt-e Shaykh ʿAbd al-Ḥaqq*, 204.

35. Kugle, *Rebel between Spirit and Law*; see also Ali Fahmi Khushaim, *Zarruq the Sufi*.
36. Kugle, *Rebel between Spirit and Law*, 117–18.
37. Zarrūq, *Qawāʿid al-Taṣawwuf*, principle 26.
38. Dihlawī, *Zād al-Muttaqīn*, 21b and 75b.
39. Haythamī, "Kaff al-Raʿāʿ ʿan Muḥarramāt al-Lahw waʾl-Samāʿ" (MSS Istanbul). After initiation, he wrote about Sufism in line with ʿAli Muttaqi's reformist project; see Haythamī, "Taʿarruf fī al-Aṣlayn waʾl-Taṣawwuf" (MSS Patna KB).
40. ʿAlī Muttaqī, "Tajrīb al-Wāfī fī al-Ḥibr al-Ṣāfī" (MSS Aligarh).
41. ʿAlī Muttaqī, "Ghāyat al-Kamāl" (MSS Princeton GC), 1–7.
42. Dihlawī, *Zād al-Muttaqīn*, 16a, describes how ʿAli Muttaqi corrected hadith books on his deathbed.
43. ʿAlī Muttaqī, "Ghāyat al-Kamāl," 9.
44. ʿAlī Muttaqī, 7–8.
45. ʿAlī Muttaqī, 9–11.
46. Zarrūq, "Sulūk al-Ṭarīq idhā fuqida al-Rafīq" (MSS Ahmedabad); see Kugle, "Death before Death" and *Rebel between Spirit and Law*, 112–13.
47. ʿAlī Muttaqī, "Hidāyat Rabbī ʿinda Faqd al-Murabbī" (MSS Ahmedabad).
48. Zarrūq quotes his teacher in the conclusion of *Qawāʿid al-Taṣawwuf*.
49. Danner, *Book of Wisdom*.
50. ʿAlī Muttaqī, "Dhikr al-Mawt li-Tadarruk al-Fawt" (MSS Aligarh).
51. Shaw, *Paradox of Intention*, 4–5.
52. ʿAlī Muttaqī, "Ghāyat al-Kamāl," 12–14. He wrote a treatise on the spirituality of scholarly work, "Riqq al-Marqūm fī Ghāyat al-ʿUlūm" (MSS Aligarh).
53. ʿAlī Muttaqī, "ʿUrwat al-Salaf" (MSS Princeton Yehuda), quotes Zarrūq, *Qawāʿid al-Taṣawwuf*, principle 4.
54. ʿAlī Muttaqī, "ʿUrwat al-Salaf."
55. ʿAlī Muttaqī, "ʿUrwat al-Salaf."
56. Kugle, *Rebel between Spirit and Law*, 51–52.
57. Kugle, 134–36.
58. ʿAlī Muttaqī, "Sharḥ Qawāʿid al-Ṭarīqa" (MSS Berlin DK), is a commentary on Zarrūq, *Qawāʿid al-Taṣawwuf*.
59. ʿAlī Muttaqī, "Ḍābiṭa li-Uṣūl al-Ṭarīqa" (MSS Rampur RL).
60. ʿAlī Muttaqī, "ʿUrwat al-Salaf."
61. ʿAlī Muttaqī, "Zād at-Ṭālibīn" (MSS Patna KB).
62. ʿAlī Muttaqī, "Ḍābiṭa li-Uṣūl al-Ṭarīqa."
63. Dihlawī, *Zād al-Muttaqīn*, 65b.
64. Dihlawī, 65b–66a.
65. Dihlawī, 14b–15a.
66. Dihlawī, 15b.
67. ʿAlī Muttaqī, "Al-Nahj al-Atamm fī Tabwīb al-Ḥikam" (MSS Rampur RL); see also his "Taʿlīq ʿalā Sharḥ al-Ḥikam al-Khāmis ʿĀshar" (MSS Berlin DK) and "Tabwīb Sharḥ al-Ḥikam li-Ibn ʿAbbād al-Rundī" (MSS Istanbul).
68. ʿAlī Muttaqī, "al-Mawāhib al-ʿAliyya fī Jamʿ al-Ḥikam al-Qurʾāniyya waʾl-Ḥadīthiyya" (MSS Istanbul).
69. ʿAlī Muttaqī, "al-Ḥikam al-ʿIrfāniyya fī Maʿānī Irshādiyya wa Ishārāt Qurʾāniyya" (MSS Hyderabad SJ). The first saying quotes Qurʾan 2:269; the second quotes Qurʾan 25:7; the third quotes Qurʾan 27:88.

70. Kugle, *Book of Illumination.*

71. ʿAlī Muttaqī, "al-Tawaṣṣul fī'l-Yaqīn wa'l-Tawakkul" (MSS Aligarh); see also "Kifāyat-e Ahl-e Yaqīn fī Ṭarīq al-Mutawakkilīn" (MSS Tonk APR). Both are Persian translations from *The Book of Illumination*, written at different times to popularize this text with Sufis in South Asia who did not know Arabic. He also wrote a treatise on the same theme, "Tabyīn al-Rāfa fī-mā li'llāh min al-Ḍiyāfa" (MSS Aligarh).

72. ʿAlī Muttaqī, "al-Kibrīt al-Aḥmar fī'l-Kīmiyā' al-Akbar" (MSS Aligarh).

73. Ulūghkhānī, *Ẓafar al-Wālih*, 237. Sultan Bahadur of Gujarat offered Sher Shah Suri money to rebel quickly to compel Mughal forces to abandon their siege of Gujarati forces at Chittor.

74. Pearson, *Indian Ocean*, 121–23.

75. Chaube, *History of the Gujarat Kingdom*, 268; see also Ulūghkhānī, *Ẓafar al-Wālih*, 116.

76. Ghawthī, *Gulzār-e Abrār*, 504. One Sufi, Sayyid ʿAṭā' Muḥammad, after fleeing Humayun's invasion with Bahadur Shah's army, was captured by the Portuguese off the Arabian Sea coast; he continued to Mecca after escaping or being ransomed.

77. Alam and Subrahmanyam, "View from Mecca," details the stay of Asaf Khan and the sultan's family in Mecca.

78. Maʿbarī, *Tuḥfat al-Mujāhidīn*; see also Pearson, *Indian Ocean*, 124–25.

79. Casale, *Ottoman Age of Exploration*, 59.

80. Ulūghkhānī, *Ẓafar al-Wālih*, 252.

81. In Arabic, Persian, and Urdu, letters are associated with numbers (*abjad*) so that a phrase encodes an event's date.

82. Ulūghkhānī, *Ẓafar al-Wālih*, 264; Casale, *Ottoman Age of Exploration*, 60–63.

Third Satchel

1. Qur'an 2:153.

2. Dihlawī, *Zād al-Muttaqīn*, 32a–32b; and *Akhbār al-Akhyār*, 264.

3. Ulūghkhānī, *Ẓafar al-Wālih*, 315–16; see also ʿAlī Khān, *Mir'āt-e Aḥmadī Supplement*, 74.

4. Lawrence, "Early Indo-Muslim Saints and Conversion."

5. Faruqi, "Music, Musicians and Muslim Law."

6. ʿAlī Muttaqī, "Sharḥ Qawāʿid al-Ṭarīqa," addresses legality of *samāʿ* and its legal limits. Dihlawī, *Zād al-Muttaqīn*, 16b, recorded oral teachings of ʿAli Muttaqi that reduced the possibilities of *samāʿ* to discrete categories with detailed specifications, conditions, and restrictions "in accord with how the earliest Sufi masters treated the subject."

7. Dihlawī, *Zād al-Muttaqīn*, 19a, recorded that ʿAli Muttaqi thought it best to give people money to buy supplies to cook at their own homes, and if that were not possible, then to give uncooked foodstuffs or send cooked food. The worst way to host people was to invite them to one's own home to eat in the host's presence, since that involved vanity and display.

8. *Shāhid-bāzī* or "playing the witness" involved gazing at "the witness," usually a young man, as the locus for manifestation of divine beauty in the world.

9. Like ʿAli Muttaqi, other Sufis wrote against *shahid-bazi* in Burhanpur, such as Muḥammad ibn Faḍlallāh; see Scott Kugle, "Sufi Attitudes toward Homosexuality," in Aquil and Curley, *Literary and Religious Practices*: 31–60. In Gujarat, the Shattaris were particularly known for *shahid-bazi.*

10. ʿAlī Muttaqī, "Tanbīh al-Aḥibba" (MSS Delhi).

11. Dihlawī, *Zād al-Muttaqīn*, 57a–b.

12. Dihlawī, 53b, quotes ʿAbd al-Wahhab Muttaqi but reflects ʿAli Muttaqi. Jurists in Yemen similarly warned against Ibn ʿArabi's texts, see Knysh, *Ibn ʿArabi*, 245.

13. Dihlawī, *Zād al-Muttaqīn*, 54b and 56a. The Muttaqi community allowed one to read any text (even those that "seemed to be apparently against the outer form of the Islamic faith") if one eschewed any partisanship or did not suffer negative effects. ʿAbd al-Wahhab repudiated one of his students who burned Ibn ʿArabi's *Fuṣūṣ al-Ḥikam* after he returned to Bihar from Mecca and became a religious official.

14. Dihlawī, *Zād al-Muttaqīn*, 16b. This textual ambivalence is preserved in ʿAli Muttaqi's compilation of Sufi quotations, "al-Jawāhir al-Thamīna" (which ʿAbd al-Haqq cites by its alternate title, "Ḥikam-e Kabīr").

15. Dihlawī, *Zād al-Muttaqīn*, 55a. Like ʿAli Muttaqi, ʿAbd al-Wahhab censored his discussions depending upon his audience, in accord with the Prophet Muhammad's saying, "Speak to each according to their power of reason." He silenced his students in Urdu if they discussed metaphysics of *wahdat al-wujud* in front of Arab jurists who might object. Dihlawī, 52b, records how ʿAbd al-Wahhab conditionally allowed ʿAbd al-Haqq to read Ibn ʿArabi's *Futūḥāt Makkiyya*, saying, "If you have the ability to follow what it says, buy it and read it, for it is a book containing subtle knowledge of many different disciplines—but I lay this condition upon you, that you pass over any passage that is difficult to comprehend or ambiguous in meaning, without dwelling on it and becoming stuck."

16. ʿAlī Muttaqī, "Risālat-e Ḍurūriyāt," attempted to veil Ibn ʿArabi's ideas while quoting his name for the simplest building blocks of dogma. He asserted that he culled from *Futūḥāt Makkiyya* nine basic strategies for building faith and purifying the soul, to be practiced before one has yet found a Sufi teacher. His "Khulāṣat al-Ḥaqāʾiq fīʾl-Ḥikam waʾl-Raqāʾiq" (MSS Berlin DK) may involve the same strategy. ʿAli Muttaqi is reputed to have composed a commentary on the book of Shaykh Najm al-Dīn Dāyā, "Baḥr al-Ḥaqāʾiq," which interprets the Qurʾan in the light of existential cosmology; this commentary might employ the same dissimulating strategy, but no copy of it is known to exist today.

17. Dihlawī, *Zād al-Muttaqīn*, 47a–b.

18. Dihlawī, 45a–103b, offers the most intimate portrait of ʿAbd al-Wahhab.

19. Many Sufi masters recommended obliteration in one's shaykh as the only means to reach ethical selflessness, and later reformers, especially Naqshbandis, adopted this technique; see Annemarie Schimmel, "The Golden Chain of the Sincere Muhammadans," in Lawrence, *Rose and the Rock*, 104–34.

20. Dihlawī, *Zād al-Muttaqīn*, 59–60.

21. Dihlawī, 95–96.

22. Dihlawī, 86a–86b, records how ʿAbd al-Wahhab—in a vision—entered paradise and was invited into a heavenly mansion. Not recognizing the man who invited him, he refused to enter; the man told him, "Although outwardly we are not acquainted, inwardly we are united in essence as if we were one being," and he realized it was Abuʾl-Abbas al-Mursi.

23. Dihlawī, 98b–104b, recorded ʿAbd al-Wahhab Muttaqi's experiences with magic, alchemy, manipulation of jinn, and other kinds of demonic powers.

24. Dihlawī, 95a.

25. ʿAbd al-Wahhāb Muttaqī, "Bishārat al-Ḥabīb fī Faḍl al-Gharīb" (MSS Rampur RL).

No comprehensive list of his writings exists; four texts survive in manuscript about hadith, Qur'anic interpretation, and devotion. See the bibliography in this book for the most complete list of his works.

26. Dihlawī, *Kitāb al-Makātib wa'l-Rasā'il*, 283. ʿAbd al-Wahhab Muttaqi repeated this advice in Dihlawī, *Zād al-Muttaqīn*, 64b.

27. Dihlawī, *Zād al-Muttaqīn*, 62b.

28. Dihlawī, 63a–64b.

29. Like ʿAbd al-Haqq, ʿAbd al-Wahhab Muttaqi had Qadiri contacts before joining the Muttaqi community in Mecca yet refused to take initiation from any Sufi master until he met ʿAli Muttaqi. In his youthful travels, he met Makhdūm Jīū Qādirī at Bidar and recalled that this Qadiri master was similar to ʿAli Muttaqi in piety, scrupulousness, and rectitude. At that time, ʿAbd al-Wahhab demured from entrusting him with initiation, due to the same partisanship that he later critiqued in ʿAbd al-Haqq; see Dihlawī, *Akhbār al-Akhyār*, 279; and G. Lāhōrī, *Khazīnat al-Aṣfiyā'*, 126.

30. ʿAbd al-Haqq mentions how *Fuṣūṣ al-Ḥikam, al-Futūḥāt al-Makkiyya, al-Insān al- Kāmil* and commentaries on them circulated through Sufi communities in Mecca, though ʿAbd al-Wahhab Muttaqi regarded them with extreme caution.

31. Dihlawī, "Miftāḥ al-Futūḥ."

32. ʿAlī Muttaqī, "Jarr al-Thaqīl fī Sulūk al-Maʿīl."

33. Shaikh, *Sufi Narratives of Intimacy*, 45–60.

34. Kugle, *Rebel between Spirit and Law*, 47.

35. Homerin, *Aisha al-Baʿuniyya*.

36. ʿAlī Muttaqī, "ʿUnwān fī Sulūk al-Niswān" (MSS Ahmedabad).

37. ʿAlī Muttaqī, "Sulūk al-Rijāl" (MSS Khayrpur). The author has not been able to access this manuscript, but ʿAli Muttaqi's other works display his opinions about "real men."

38. ʿAlī Muttaqī, "Malfūẓāt-e Shaykh ʿAlī Muttaqī."

39. ʿAlī Muttaqī, "Taʿrīf al-Ṣirāṭ fī Sulūk al-Ghazāt" (MSS Lahore PU).

40. Ulūghkhānī, *Ẓafar al-Wālih*, 287; Dihlawī, *Zād al-Muttaqīn*, 22b–23a. Asaf Khan was in close contact with ʿAli Muttaqi in Mecca and saw him as the axial saint of his time.

41. ʿAli Muttaqi discouraged formation of a Sufi community for slave soldiers, for this could lead to exaggerated partisan identification with the soldier corps itself, inducing them to infringe on the sultan's political authority and resulting in coups and court factions.

42. ʿAlī Muttaqī, "al-Ratba al-Fākhira" (MSS Rampur RL), 1.

43. ʿAli Muttaqi criticized those who fashioned transcendent justification for absolute rule; soon after his death, the emperor Akbar did this by raising the status of a "just ruler" to the level of a paradigmatic jurist, thereby subjugating jurists and scriptural scholars as a class. See Nizami, *Akbar and Religion*, 127–29.

44. ʿAlī Muttaqī, "al-Ratba al-Fākhira," 1.

45. Influenced by the Mahdawi movement, many nobles and military leaders in Gujarat renounced their positions of power. Ministers prevented Sultan Mahmud Begra from visiting Sayyid Muhammad Jawnpuri and hearing him preach for fear that the sultan might renounce his worldly position.

46. ʿAlī Muttaqī, "al-Ratba al-Fākhira," 2.

47. Meisami, *Sea of Precious Virtues*; Alvi, *Advice on the Art of Governance*.

48. Moin, *Millennial Sovereign*, 138–46.

49. ʿAlī Muttaqī, "al-Burhān al-Jalī fī Maʿrifat al-Walī" (MSS Aligarh), expands the prior work of Suyūṭī, "al-Qawl al-Jalī fī Ḥadīth al-Walī" (MSS Patna KB). Suyuti gathered hadith reports that characterized the saint (*wali*); ʿAli Muttaqi used these reports to outline the criteria for judging a saint to be sincere or not.

50. Culled from Zarruq's work are principles 162 (on displaying miracles), 167 (on spiritual poverty and saintly authority), 164 (on the saints' getting what they pray for), and 147 (on miracles, magic, and *istidrāj*).

51. ʿAli Muttaqi claims to represent an old and respected Sufi tradition rather than an innovative system. In another instance, he traces this fourfold division of obstacles to the Sufi theologian al-Muḥāsibī (d. 857).

52. ʿAlī Muttaqī, "Ghāyat al-Maʿmūl."

53. ʿAlī Muttaqī, "Ghāyat al-Maʿmūl."

54. ʿAlī Muttaqī, "Ghāyat al-Maʿmūl." He developed the idea of graded levels of *taqwa* in other works, including "al-Burhān al-Aqwā."

55. ʿAlī Muttaqī, "Niʿam al-Miʿyār."

56. Dihlawī, *Zād al-Muttaqīn*, 19b, notes that ʿAli Muttaqi gave gifts to those who displeased or disappointed him, so those who received gifts would beg his forgiveness.

57. ʿAlī Muttaqī, "Tanbīh al-Aḥibba."

58. ʿAlī Muttaqī, "Malfūẓāt-e Shaykh ʿAlī Muttaqī."

59. Ulūghkhānī, *Ẓafar al-Wālih*, 264–72.

60. The Mughal prince, Muḥammad Zaman Mirza (who married a daughter of Babur and served as a general in Babur's army), challenged Humayun; he was imprisoned but escaped to Gujarat, where he ingratiated himself to Bahadur Shah's mother, who reputedly adopted him. Bahadur Shah sheltered him, provoking Humayun to invade Gujarat.

61. Miran Muhammad Faruqi, ruler of Khandesh, was Bahadur Shah's nephew; his accession as sultan of Gujarat would have united the two realms to repel Mughal incursion southward.

62. Sultan Mahmud Shah III built Mahmudabad (now known as Mehmedabad), a town south of Kheda, halfway between Ahmedabad and Khambhat; see Burton-Page, *Indian Islamic Architecture*, 93. It should not be confused with Sultan Mahmud Begra's prior renaming of Champaner as "Muhammadabad."

63. Bahmani rulers built Firozabad then shifted farther to Bidar to escape their intrigue-prone capital of Gulbarga; see Eaton, *Social History of the Deccan*, 63–67. Several decades after Mahmud Shah III, the same pattern was followed by Akbar, who built Fatehpur Sikri in 1571 as a palace city thirty-six kilometers away from Agra.

64. Farishta, *History*, 4:89.

65. Farishta, 4:91.

66. The chronology of ʿAli Muttaqi's visits to Gujarat places his first return in 1540 (AH 946–47). This contradicts Ghawthī, *Gulzār-e Abrār*, who claims ʿAli Muttaqi left Ahmedabad in 1546 (AH 953), traveled to Mandu to see his mother, and from there went to Mecca, where he lived till his death, but does not mention his initial flight from Gujarat in 1535 (AH 943) when Bahadur Shah was defeated; Bilgrāmī, *Maʾāthir al-Kirām*, 192, follows Ghawthi's doubtful chronology. But ʿAli Muttaqi could not have gone to Mandu and then to Mecca in 1546 because that year the Portuguese attacked Diu and burned towns along the Gujarat coast in retaliation for Gujarati resistance

to their siege; also, travel to Mandu was not possible for the period from 1540 to 1547 (AH 947–53) due to Sher Shah Suri's threat to invade Gujarat from there. These inconsistencies discount Ghawthi's chronology.

67. Ulūghkhānī, *Ẓafar al-Wālih*, 315.

68. Ulūghkhānī, 315.

69. Dihlawī, *Zād al-Muttaqīn*, 32a, emphasizes the importance of a saint instructing the ruler how to obey the *shariʿa*, rather than emphasizing the sultan's anxieties. This narrative is highly charged, as seen in South Asian Sufi lore that tells that the young Hasan Basri requested ʿAlī ibn Abī Ṭālib show him how to make ablutions, and this lesson served as a channel for blessings from the elder to the younger; see Kirmānī, *Siyar al-Awliyā*, 32.

70. Dihlawī, *Zād al-Muttaqīn*, 11b.

71. Farishta, *History*, 4:89.

72. Ulūghkhānī, *Ẓafar al-Wālih*, 266–68.

73. Sighting approaching Portuguese ships, Khudawand Khan sailed to Surat with the Gujarati forces, deserting the Ottoman forces who immediately returned to Yemen, abandoning Turkish cannons on shore.

74. Ulūghkhānī, *Ẓafar al-Wālih*, 312. Royal patronage was critical to the economic life of Mecca. Its scholars and notables depended half the year on patronage from the Ottoman sultan that arrived overland with the Hajj caravan, and half the year on patronage from Sultan Mahmud Shah III that arrived by ship. It is not clear whether the personal grant entrusted to ʿAli Muttaqi was the same as the grant known as the Waẓīfa Maḥmūdiyya that Sultan Mahmud Shah sent to the inhabitants of Mecca collectively. It may be that ʿAli Muttaqi was given a personal stipend for administering and distributing the larger collective grant.

75. Shaʿrānī, *al-Ṭabaqāt al-Kubrā*, 185. Shaʿrani visited this complex in 1540–41 (AH 947), which supports the contention that ʿAli Muttaqi's first return to Gujarat was completed by that year, just at the time that Sultan Mahmud Shah III gained political independence.

76. Dihlawī, *Zād al-Muttaqīn*, 25a. Later in his life, ʿAli Muttaqi accepted funds from an Ottoman governor of Mecca to build a hospice known as "Ribāṭ al-Muttaqī."

77. Ulūghkhānī, *Ẓafar al-Wālih*, 274–75. Mahmud Shah III laid siege to the Portuguese at Diu. When the Portuguese fleet sailed from Goa to break the siege, the young sultan ordered a new Gujarati fleet equipped with cannons to be built at the port of Bharoch. He also built a fortress at Nawanagar (on the opposite side of the Saurashtra Peninsula from the Portuguese fort at Diu) so that these two fortified ports could restrict Portuguese access to Diu.

78. Ulūghkhānī, 287.

79. ʿAli Muttaqi took as his model for this government intervention the hadith scholar Ibn Suwayda. Sultan Mahmud Begra appointed this leading hadith scholar in Gujarat as "chief of the Revenue Officers" to oversee tax collection and fund disbursal.

Fourth Satchel

1. Ulughkhani's Iranian family settled in South Asia, though he was born in Mecca and was raised speaking Arabic. Ulughkhani held administrative posts in Mecca (distributing Mughal charity to pilgrims), Gujarat, and Khandesh; known as Ḥājjī Dabīr,

the "Royal Scribe returned from Mecca," he wrote a history of Gujarat up until 1605 when Akbar died.

2. Ulūghkhānī, *Ẓafar al-Wālih*, 315–18.

3. Dihlawī, *Zād al-Muttaqīn*, 27b–28a.

4. Devin DeWeese, "Spiritual Practice and Corporate Identity in Medieval Sufi Communities of Iran, Central Asia, and India: The Khalvatī/ʿIshqī/Shaṭṭārī Continuum," in Lindquist, *Religion and Identity in South Asia and Beyond*, 251–300.

5. ʿAlī Muttaqī, "Tanbīh al-Aḥibba."

6. Michael Brand, "The Sultanate of Malwa," in Lambah and Patel, *Architecture of the Indian Sultanates*, 88–90; about *pietra dura* on Nurjahan's building, see Findly, *Nur Jahan*, 230–38.

7. Kugle, "Heaven's Witness," gives a fuller account of Shattari support of Mughal conquests.

8. Ernst, *Refractions of Islam in India*, chaps. 8, 10, and 12.

9. Kugle, *Sufis and Saints' Bodies*, 136–60, offers translation of his ascension narrative.

10. Moin, *Millennial Sovereign*, 97.

11. Gwāliyarī, *Awrād-e Ghawthiyya*, 105, on his seventh *mukāshifa*. Muhammad Ghawth and all his eight brothers were Shattari disciples of Ḥājjī Ḥamīd Ẓuhūr al-Ḥaqq. Even though Shaykh Bahlul was older, Muhammad Ghawth meet their shaykh first and then his brothers took initiation; see Faḍlallāh Shaṭṭārī, "Manāqib-e Ghawthiyya."

12. Ghawthī, *Gulzār-e Abrār*, 234. One Suhrawardi, Mawlānā Jalāl al-Dīn Ṫhaṫṫawī (who was Humayun's teacher in rational sciences and chief scholar, Ṣadr al-Ṣudūr), and one Naqshbandi, Mawlānā Muḥammad Farghalī, were forced to join the Shattari Order.

13. Moin, *Millennial Sovereign*, 98–99, recounts the rivalry between a Naqshbandi, Khwāja Nūra (grandson of the famous Khwāja Aḥrār), and the Shattari Sufis advising Humayun.

14. Ghawthī, *Gulzār-e Abrār*, 234–35; Abū'l-Faḍl, *Akbar Nama*, 3:1080; Moin, *Millennial Sovereign*, 101–2.

15. Chishtī, "Mukhbir al-Awliyāʾ," 628b–629a (MSS Ahmedabad); see Kugle, *Sufis and Saints' Bodies*, 162–63.

16. Kugle, *Sufis and Saints' Bodies*, 163–79.

17. Gwāliyarī, *Awrād-e Ghawthiyya*, 107, reporting his tenth *mukashifa*.

18. Wajih al-Din ʿAlawi was born in 1504 in Champaner to a family of jurists, and he established the leading madrasa of Ahmedabad.

19. ʿAlawī Gujarātī, "Silsila-ye Ṭarīqat-e Shāh Wajīh al-Dīn" (MSS Ahmedabad).

20. ʿAlī Muttaqī, "Tanbīh al-Ghāfilīn," 50a (MSS Rampur RL).

21. The text says Muḥammad Khaffāf, a scribal error that must refer to Shaykh Muḥammad ibn Khafif, a Syrian Sufi who is credited for introducing Sufism to Shiraz.

22. ʿAlī Muttaqī, "Tanbīh al-Ghāfilīn," 50a–50b. ʿAli Muttaqi quotes this whole story from ʿAbd al-Raḥmān Jāmī, *Nafaḥāt al-Uns*.

23. Karamustafa, *Sufism*, 58–59.

24. Nicholson, *Kitab al-Lumaʿ*, 117; the narrative translated above is on page 428 of the Arabic text. Sahl Tustarī (d. 896) was an important Sufi, theologian, and Qurʾan commentator from the province adjoining Shiraz.

25. Chishtī, "Mukhbir al-Awliyāʾ," 648b; see Kugle, *Sufis and Saints' Bodies*, 143–48 and 166.

26. Gwāliyarī, *Awrād-e Ghawthiyya*, 103.

27. Moin, *Millennial Sovereign*, 99.

28. Dihlawī, *Zād al-Muttaqīn*, 46b. This son grew up to be ʿAbd al-Wahhab Muttaqi. Bahāʾ al-Dīn Shaṭṭārī, "Risāla-ye Shaṭṭāriyya," 16–23, discusses such invocatory techniques, Yogic techniques of concentration, and powers of enchantment (*sīmīyā*).

29. Dihlawī, *Zād al-Muttaqīn*, 61a. See also Faḍlallāh Shaṭṭārī, "Manāqib-e Ghawthiyya," 89–90 and 112.

30. ʿAlī Muttaqī, "Tanbīh al-Ghāfilīn," 43b–50b.

31. ʿAlī Muttaqī, "Malfūẓāt-e Shaykh ʿAlī Muttaqī," 4.

32. ʿAlī Muttaqī, *Al-Nahj al-Atamm fī Tabwīb al-Ḥikam*, 81, citing Qurʾan 7:182.

33. Lawrence, *Morals for the Heart*, 98.

34. ʿAlī Muttaqī, "Tanbīh al-Ghāfilīn," 48a.

35. ʿAlī Muttaqī, 47b, cites Abū ʿAbdallāh ibn ʿUmar al-Suhrawardī, "Aʿlām al-Hudā wa ʿAqīdat Arbāb al-Ghinā."

36. Zargar, "Ten Principles," 109.

37. ʿAlī Muttaqī, "Tanbīh al-Ghāfilīn," 41b–43b.

38. ʿAlawī Gujarātī, "Malfūẓāt-e Wajīh al-Dīn," 13.

39. Chishtī, "Mukhbir al-Awliyāʾ," 629a, records that a Sufi in Ahmedabad questioned Muhammad Ghawth's competence and legitimacy because he quoted the Qurʾan with grammatical mistakes.

40. ʿAlawī Gujarātī, "Malfūẓāt-e Wajīh al-Dīn," 9; see also Kugle, *Sufis and Saints' Bodies*, 170–74.

41. ʿAlawī Gujarātī, "Malfūẓāt-e Wajīh al-Dīn," 8.

42. ʿAlawī Gujarātī, 11.

43. ʿAlawī Gujarātī, 8–9.

44. ʿAlawī Gujarātī, 13.

45. Burton-Page, *Indian Islamic Architecture*, 94.

46. Moin, *Millennial Sovereign*, 97.

47. Qadri, "Mughal Relations with the Shattari Sufis," 79–114.

48. Moin, *Millennial Sovereign*, 104.

49. The Hindi film *Tansen* (directed by Jayant Desai in 1943) portrays Muhammad Ghawth as a venal and scheming ascetic who exploits the singer's talents.

50. Moin, *Millennial Sovereign*, 109.

51. Behl, *Madhumalati*, introduction.

52. Behl, *Love's Subtle Magic*, 219–63.

53. Moin, *Millennial Sovereign*, 108 and 136.

54. I translate *ajsam* as "materialism," which literally means "solid bodies" or "material substances" but implies worldly authorities and self-worship.

55. Qamaruddin, *Mahdawi Movement*, 46, quotes from Badāʾūnī, *Najāt al-Rashīd*, 38. Sayyid Muhammad's aim of removing differences between various legal methods did not lead to a "Madhhab Mahdawiyya." Rather, after Sayyid Muhammad's death, Mahdawi leaders identified themselves as Ḥanafī, like Shaykh ʿAlāʾī did while debating with Shafiʿī scholars.

56. Gujarātī, *Majālis-e Khamsa*, 39. Miyān Muṣṭafā Gujarātī (d. 1578) was a Mahdawi leader who was imprisoned by Akbar. Under court interrogation, he called Sayyid Muhammad Jawnpuri the "promised Mahdi" and the "seal of Muhammadan sainthood" rather than merely a saint and declared that those who did not accept his claim were infidels, even the emperor himself.

57. Chishtī, "Mukhbir al-Awliyā'," 618b, records that Sayyid Muhammad Jawnpuri was a disciple of Shaykh Jalāl al-Ḥaqq, but Mahdawi records say that he was a disciple of Shaykh Dāniyāl Chishtī.

58. Qamaruddin, *Mahdawi Movement*, 32–33.

59. ʿAydarusī, *al-Nūr al-Sāfir*, 41, records that a comet sighting seemed to support the Mahdi's claims.

60. Chishtī, "Mukhbir al-Awliyā'," 619a.

61. Chishtī, 619b. This generated the rumor that Sultan Mahmud Begra was joining the Mahdawis. It spread so much that ʿAlī Khān, the author of *Mir'āt-e Aḥmadī*, counts the sultan as one of Sayyid Muhammad's followers.

62. Chishtī, "Mukhbir al-Awliyā'," 620a.

63. Chishtī, 622b–623a, cites *Mir'āt-e Aḥmadī* to report persecution against Sayyid Muhammad Jawnpuri.

64. Chishtī, 622b, varies the story, claiming that Sayyid Muhammad Jawnpuri reprimanded the inquisitorial scholar, Muhammad Taj Ganj-e Shakari.

65. Chishtī, "Mukhbir al-Awliyā'," 622b–623a. Shaykh Ji Bukhari was the nephew of Qutb-e ʿAlam, a most prominent saint of Ahmedabad. In the interview, he asked questions phrased in Qur'anic verses and Sayyid Muhammad Jawnpuri answered in Qur'anic verses, for three rounds of questions and answers.

66. Chishtī, 622b–623a.

67. ʿAlī Muttaqī, "al-Burhān fī ʿAlāmāt al-Mahdī" (MSS Hyderabad OML), 4.

68. Interview with Mahdawi leaders at the Anjuman-e Mahdawiyya (Chanchalguda, Hyderabad Deccan, May 1998); their oral tradition about ʿAli Muttaqi explains his later hostility to the Mahdawi movement in terms of betrayal and grudge.

69. Chishtī, "Mukhbir al-Awliyā'," 623a.

70. Chishtī, 623b–624a.

71. Chishtī, 624a. Sayyid Mahmud's children fled Gujarat and took refuge in the Deccan where former Afghan governors of the Lodi dynasty were ruling, such as in Ahmednagar. There is confusion about the date of these events. Chishtī, "Mukhbir al-Awliyā'," cites ʿAlī Khān, *Mir'āt-e Aḥmadi* to claim that this transpired in the final days of sultan Mahmud Begra's reign in 1511. Qamaruddin, *Mahdawi Movement*, 105–6 mentions the year of his incarceration as 1513.

72. Darryl Maclean, "The Sociology of Political Engagement: The Mahdaviyah and the State," in Eaton, *India's Islamic Traditions*, 150–68. Mahdawi sources like Sayyid Ghulāb Ṣāḥib, *Tārīkh-e Palanpūr*, claim that literalist scholars provoked the sultan to murder Sayyid Khundamir; however, it is not clear that the governor of Patan, who led the attack, acted on the orders of the sultan. Qamaruddin, *Mahdawi Movement*, 110, records that Mahdawis assassinated two Sunni scholars who had incited violence against two Mahdawis; Sayyid Khundamir publicly affirmed this as legal revenge, provoking a government assault.

73. ʿAlī Muttaqī, *al-Burhān fī ʿAlāmāt al-Mahdī*, 4.

74. In Sufi discourse, the term "real man" (*rajul*) means a spiritually realized person of virtue.

75. Darryl Maclean, "Real Men and False Men at the Court of Akbar," in Lawrence and Gilmartin, *Beyond Turk and Hindu*, 199–215.

76. Gujarātī, *Majālis-e Khamsa*, Session Five.

77. Interview with Mahdawi leaders of the Anjuman-e Mahdawiyya.

78. Anjum, "Perpetually Wedded Wife of God."

79. Kugle, *Sufis and Saints' Bodies*, 209.

80. ʿAlī Muttaqī, "Tidhkār al-Niʿam wa'l-ʿAṭāyā" (MSS Istanbul).

81. Telephone interview, ʿAlī Zayn al-ʿAbidīn, descendant of ʿAli Muttaqi (Mecca, January 1999).

82. ʿAlī Muttaqī, *al-Burhān fī ʿAlāmāt al-Mahdī*, 30a.

83. Tashrīfallāhī, *Muqaddima-ye Sirāj al-Abṣār*, 710–29, notes that al-Haythami discussed the Mahdi while denouncing the Shiʿa in *al-Sawāṭiʿ al-Muḥriqa*.

84. Haythamī, "al-Qawl al-Mukhtaṣar fī ʿAlāmāt al-Mahdī al-Muntaẓar," recorded in ʿAlī Muttaqī, *al-Burhān fī ʿAlāmāt al-Mahdī*, 79–87. This text also exits as an independent treatise (MSS Rampur RL and Patna KB).

85. Suyūṭī, *al-Kashf fī Mujāwazat hādhihi al-Ummat al-Alf*, cited in ʿAlī Muttaqī, *al-Burhān fī ʿAlāmāt al-Mahdī*, 68–79.

86. ʿAlī Muttaqī, *al-Burhān fī ʿAlāmāt al-Mahdī*, 77–78; see also Moin, *Millennial Sovereign*, 159–60.

87. Suyuti refuted this fatwa to dispel anxiety about the approaching millennium, declaring this alleged hadith to be inauthentic; he gathered valid reports in which the Prophet declared the world to last 7,000 years, such that the world must exist beyond the year AH 1000.

88. This fatwa is appended to ʿAlī Muttaqī, "al-Burhān fī ʿAlamāt al-Mahdī" (MSS Tonk APR).

89. The other jurists who offered their decisions were Aḥmad Abū'l-Sarūr ibn Ḍiyā' (Hanafi), Muḥammad ibn Muḥammad al-Khaṭṭāb (Maliki) and Yaḥya Muḥammad (Hanbali), and Ibn Ḥajar al-Haythamī (Shafiʿi), whose legal reasoning is most clear and detailed.

90. Gujarātī, *Majālis-e Khamsa*, mentions that the fatwas circulated in Gujarat thirty years before his inquisition in 1573–74.

91. ʿAlī Muttaqī, *al-Burhān fī ʿAlāmāt al-Mahdī*, exists in many archives and has been printed in Kuwait.

92. Suyūṭī, *al-ʿArf al-Wardī fī Akhbār al-Mahdī*.

93. Haythamī, "al-Qawl al-Mukhtaṣar fī ʿAlāmāt al-Mahdī al-Muntaẓar."

94. ʿAli Muttaqi built upon *al-ʿArf al-Wardī* (composed before 1505) by adding other hadith that the original compiler had neglected, drawn from Jalāl al-Dīn Suyūṭī, *Jamʿ al-Jawāmiʿ*, and Yūsuf ibn Yaḥya al-Maqdisī, *ʿIqd al-Durar fī Akhbār al-Mahdī al-Muntaẓar*.

95. Colby, *Narrating Muhammad's Night Journey*.

96. ʿAlī Muttaqī, "al-Burhān fī ʿAlāmāt al-Mahdī" (MSS Hyderabad OML), introduction.

97. Chishtī, "Mukhbir al-Awliyā'," 618b–623b. Later Sufis built upon this critique leveled by ʿAli Muttaqi. They identified "thinking oneself to be the Mahdi" as a stage (*maqām*) of the spiritual path that is far from the final goal. They opined that Sayyid Muhammad Jawnpuri got "stuck at this one stage" and argued that his Sufi master died before he made any claim to be the Mahdi, such that, had his master still been alive, he would have guided Sayyid Muhammad to recant this claim and move on to higher levels of spiritual realization.

98. Chishtī, "Mukhbir al-Awliyā'," 622b, cites ʿAlī Muttaqī, "Risālat al-Radd" (MSS Rampur RL).

99. ʿAlī Muttaqī, "al-Burhān fī ʿAlāmāt al-Mahdī" (MSS Hyderabad OML), introduction.

100. This abridgment in Arabic circulated under the title "ʿAlāmāt al-Mahdī Ṣāḥib al-Zamān" (MSS Hyderabad OML). The hadith reports are organized into four

chapters, as compared to the thirteen chapters of *al-Burhān fī ʿAlāmāt al-Mahdī*. A further redaction was circulated as "Talkhīṣ al-Bayān," which was translated into Persian under various titles: "Ḥashar Nāma" (MSS Rampur RL), "ʿAlāmāt-e Mahdī-ye Mawʿūd" (MSS Islamabad GB), and "ʿAlāmāt-e Imām al-Mahdī" (MSS Lahore PU). It is not clear whether ʿAli Muttaqi himself is responsible for these further abridgments and translations or whether some followers wrote them to more widely circulate his arguments.

101. In his oral teachings, Sayyid Muhammad Jawnpuri claimed that eighteen verses of the Qurʾan predicted his advent as the Mahdi; see Gujarātī, *Jawāhir al-Taṣdīq*.

102. ʿAlī Muttaqī, "Risālat al-Radd."

103. Kugle, *Rebel between Spirit and Law*, 166–73.

104. Sajāwandī, *Sirāj al-Abṣār*, 36.

105. Sajāwandī, 48.

106. Sajāwandī, 132–48.

107. Sajāwandī, 66.

108. Sajāwandī, 234.

109. Sajāwandī, 234. ʿAli Muttaqi composed "Risālat al-Radd" in 1557–58 to justify state persecution of the Mahdawis and encourage nobles in Gujarat to be vigilant against them after Mahmud Shah III's sudden death.

110. Tashrīfallāhī, *Muqaddima-ye Sirāj al-Abṣār*, 715. After Shah Dilawar died, Miyan Sajawandi studied under Sayyid Shihāb al-Dīn and wrote *Sirāj al-Abṣār* between 1556 and 1561 at his request.

111. Sajāwandī, *Sirāj al-Abṣār*, 50.

112. Sajāwandī, 158.

113. Sajāwandī, 160.

114. Sajāwandī, 146.

115. Sajāwandī, 168–70.

116. Sajawandi's arguments in defense of the Mahdawi community under threat of persecution were amplified by Gujarātī, *Majālis-e Khamsa*, Session One.

117. ʿAlī Muttaqī, "Jawāb Risālat ʿAbd al-Mālik" (MSS Rampur RL), 1.

118. ʿAlī Muttaqī, 2.

119. ʿAlī Muttaqī, 6. Since ʿAli Muttaqi corrected and reorganized Suyuti's *Jamʿ al-Jawāmiʿ*, he wore the mantle of authoritative research in hadith studies by expanding al-Suyuti's projects.

120. ʿAlī Muttaqī, "Jawāb Risālat ʿAbd al-Mālik," 4.

121. ʿAlī Muttaqī, 5.

122. ʿAlī Muttaqī, 3–4.

123. ʿAlī Muttaqī, 8–9. Weavers were low-caste workers who converted en masse to Islam; ʿAli Muttaqi uses "weaver" as a pejorative for superficial and unrefined Muslims. "Ruffians" refers to displaced Afghan soldiers who joined the Mahdawi community as Lodi rule disintegrated.

124. Sajāwandī, *Sirāj al-Abṣār*, 62.

125. Anonymous, "Taʿlīq-e Maktūbī-ye Shaykh ʿAlī Muttaqī" (MSS Rampur RL), 8–11.

126. The anonymous author of this fatwa in "Taʿlīq-e Maktūbī-ye Shaykh ʿAlī Muttaqī" renders Sayyid Muhammad Jawnpuri's name differently from the way ʿAli Muttaqi did, so it is doubtful that the latter authored it. In *al-Burhān fī ʿAlāmāt al-Mahdī* and "Risālat al-Radd," ʿAli Muttaqi writes "Sayyid Muḥammad ibn Sayyid Khān," but this fatwa calls him "Sayyid Muḥammad ibn Yūsuf Hindī." Chishtī, "Mukhbir al-Awliyāʾ," 618a–624a, reveals that Sunni detractors claimed Sayyid Muhammad

Jawnpuri's father was not ʿAbdallāh (and titled Sayyid Khan) but rather Yusuf, implying that he did not fulfill the basic criterion of the Mahdi, whose name should be Muhammad and whose father's name should be ʿAbdallah, mirroring the Prophet's own names.

127. Anonymous, "Taʿlīq-e Maktūbī-ye Shaykh ʿAlī Muttaqī," 10–11.

128. ʿAlī Muttaqī, "Tanbīh al-Ghāfilīn," 11–49. The text is not ascribed to ʿAli Muttaqi, although the manuscript catalog lists him as the author. The text is a patchwork of sources with different levels of fluency in Persian in addition to some sections in Arabic. The final and longest section (pages 24–49) was authored by ʿAli Muttaqi, judging from the prose style, quotations from other scholarly works, and the theological subtleties that contrast with the preceding sections.

129. ʿAlī Muttaqī, 16.

130. ʿAlī Muttaqī, 16, argues that it is the heart that engages in continuous *dhikr* rather than the tongue or eyes, as proved by the Prophet Ayūb (Job), whose eyes were eaten by worms but whose heart was still remembering God.

131. Tashrīfallāhī, *Muqaddima-ye Sirāj al-Abṣār*, 726–29.

132. ʿAlī Muttaqī, "Tanbīh al-Ghāfilīn," 25.

133. Ernst, *Refractions of Islam in India*, 76–96.

134. ʿAlī Muttaqī, "Tanbīh al-Ghāfilīn," 15.

135. Sajāwandī, *Sirāj al-Abṣār*, 122.

136. Shattari Sufis allied with the Mahdawis against persecution since they themselves had, for a brief period, been under the threat of persecution by the very same class of scholarly Sufis.

137. Sufi sympathizers were persecuted as suspected Mahdawis in North India, such as Shaykh Mubārak (the father of Abū'l-Faḍl and Fayḍī), instigated by ʿAbdallāh Sulṭānpūrī (chief court scholar under the Lodi, Mughal, and Suri regimes), a literalist scholar who opposed Sufis as well as "heretical" movements to gain power at court; he did not distinguish between "authentic sainthood" and "illegitimate heresy," as did the project to which ʿAli Muttaqi dedicated his life.

138. ʿAlawī Ḥusaynī, "Miṣbāḥ al-ʿĀlam" (MSS Ahmedabad BJI), 69.

139. Khwāfī, "Thamarāt al-Ḥayāt min Kalām Shaykh Burhān al-Dīn" (MSS Hyderabad OML), 134, authored by a disciple of Shaykh ʿĪsā Shaṭṭārī of Burhanpur.

140. Nizami, *Akbar and Religion*, 56–61, notes how the Nuqṭawī movement spread among courtiers in Akbar's reign. They held that the physical manifestation of Muhammad ascended by the year 1591 (AH 1000) into a new spiritual form, initiating a new spiritual dispensation, heralded by their leader, named Maḥmūd. Both the Mahdawi movement and the personal aspirations of Akbar were similarly obsessed with the new millennium; see also Moin, *Millennial Sovereign*, 164–69.

141. Ulūghkhānī, *Ẓafar al-Wālih*, reflects the worldview of courtiers and their exaggerated fears of how a saint as governor would stall the administration; he was loyalty to the nobles who continued in power under Mughal administration, rather than to the sultans of Gujarat who patronized and elevated the status of Sufi scholars like ʿAli Muttaqi.

142. Ulūghkhānī, *Ẓafar al-Wālih*, 317–18. ʿAlī Muttaqī composed "al-ʿIbārāt al-Faṣīḥa fī'l-Wāʿiẓ wa'l-Naṣīḥa" on advice and sermons that move listeners to renounce worldly ambition.

143. ʿAlī Muttaqī, "Risāla dar Maʿrifat-e Dunyā"; his Arabic text with similar con-

tent is "Al-Ghāya al-Quṣwā fī Maʿrifat al-Dunyā," published in Urdu translation as *Maʿrifat-e Dunyā*, trans. ʿAbd al-Qādir Pāṭanī (Lucknow: Mashhur Enterprises, 2013).

144. Dihlawī, *Zād al-Muttaqīn*, 68b.

145. Ulūghkhānī, *Ẓafar al-Wālih*, 315–19.

146. ʿAlī Muttaqī, "Tidhkār al-Niʿam wa'l-ʿAṭāyā." Similar arguments are presented in ʿAlī Muttaqī, "al-Raghā'ib fī'l-Ṣabr ʿalā al-Maṣā'ib."

147. ʿAlī Muttaqī, "Tidhkār al-Niʿam wa'l-ʿAṭāyā."

148. Farishta, *History*, 4:89–91. The rebellious wine-pourer assassinated ministers as well, including Asaf Khan, his brother Khudawand Khan (mentioned in the Third Satchel chapter), and Faḍl Khān, but the coup failed. ʿAlī Khān, *Mir'āt-e Aḥmadī*, as translated by Bayley, *The Local Muhammad Dynasties of Gujarat*, 445–53, emphasizes the wine-pourer's low caste and homosexuality to denounce the coup.

149. Nobles placed a distant boy relative of Ahmad Shah I on the throne and began to divide the kingdom between themselves. When the puppet sultan was assassinated, one noble installed on the throne "a long-lost son of Mahmud Shah III." This pretender, titled Muzaffar Shah III, was a puppet sultan who—despite his questionable legitimacy—ruled in name for twelve years until the Mughal conquest in 1573; he escaped from Mughal jail after a decade, tried unsuccessfully to retake Gujarat, then committed suicide.

150. ʿAlī Khān, *Mir'āt-e Aḥmadī*, as translated by Bayley, 415–20 and 453–55.

151. Ulūghkhānī, *Ẓafar al-Wālih*, 295.

152. Farishta, *History*, 4:92.

Fifth Satchel

1. Muslim ibn al-Ḥajjāj, *Saḥīḥ Muslim*, 2:1246 (Kitāb al-Zuhd wa'l-Rāqa'iq, report number 7613).

2. Dihlawī, *Zād al-Muttaqīn*, 110b–111b.

3. Wasserstein and Ayalon, *Mamluks and Ottomans*, 171–72.

4. Dihlawī, *Zād al-Muttaqīn*, 33a–33b.

5. *Zād al-Muttaqīn* provides short biographies of approximately thirty members of the Muttaqi community who came from South Asia, Egypt, or North Africa to Mecca and perpetuated ʿAli Muttaqi's reformist community as teachers, scholars, or Sufi masters.

6. Niẓāmī, *Surūd-e Rūḥānī*, 84. The ghazal begins with "Ay chehra-ye zēbā-ye tō rashk-e butān-e ādharī."

7. Dihlawī, *Zād al-Muttaqīn*, 38b–39a. The couplet is in Gujarī: "Dohrā sun sahelī param kī bātā / yūñ milī rahī jīwan dūdh bhātā."

8. Dihlawī, 26b.

9. Hamid Muhaddith was the son of Qaḍi ʿAbdallah Sindhi, a close follower of ʿAli Muttaqi. ʿAbd al-Haqq heard and recorded many eyewitness accounts about ʿAli Muttaqi.

10. ʿAbd al-Haqq's narration is commonly interrupted by poetic couplets and quatrains; this particular couplet refers to Ḥallāj, who declared, "I am the Truth!" and made public an ecstatic claim that might better be kept hidden.

11. Dihlawī, *Zād al-Muttaqīn*, 33b–36b. During this spiritual state, ʿAli Muttaqi displayed his only miracle by restoring the infertility of ʿAbd al-Qādir al-Fākhihī's wife, publicly claiming, "I may provide her with a son."

12. ʿAbd al-Haqq frames this incident as the cause of ʿAli Muttaqi's refutation of the Mahdawis.

13. Dihlawī, *Zād al-Muttaqīn*, 37a.

14. ʿAydarusī, *al-Nūr al-Sāfir*, 36, reports that Muhammad ibn Tahir was born in 1507–8 (AH 913); see also ʿAbd al-Wahhāb ibn Aḥmad, *Tadhkirat Muḥammmad ibn Ṭāhir*; and Khānum, "Muḥammad ibn Tāhir Patanī."

15. Hanif, *Islamic Concept of Crime and Justice*, 283–84. Muhammad ibn Tahir was from the Sunni Bohra group that broke from the Ismaʿili community in 1538 and adopted Hanafi law. He adopted the nickname "Ṣiddīqī" to display his Sunni allegiance to Abū Bakr al-Ṣiddīq (in contrast to Shiʿa who called themselves "Ḥaydarī" to display allegiance to ʿAli), causing some confusion as to whether he was genealogically descended from Abu Bakr and not Bohra at all; see Bilgrāmī, *Maʾāthir al-Kirām*, 194–96.

16. M. Lāhōrī, *Ḥadāʾiq al-Ḥafaniyya*, 385–87; see also Dockrat, *Between Orthodoxy and Mysticism*, 30–31. Muhammad ibn Tahir took initiation into the Qadiri order from Sayyid ʿAbdallāh ʿAydarusī in Aden before he met ʿAli Muttaqi.

17. Ghawthī, *Gulzār-e Abrār*, 322–24, cites Muhammad ibn Tahir Pātanī, *Majmaʿ Biḥār al-Anwār*.

18. ʿAydarusī, *al-Nūr al-Sāfir*, 362.

19. Muhammad ibn Tahir wrote thirty-one books; three of them addressing forgeries and false hadith reports have been published.

20. ʿAydarusī, *al-Nūr al-Sāfir*, 361.

21. Dihlawī, *Zād al-Muttaqīn*, 27a–27b; ʿAlī Muttaqī, "Tanbīh al-Ghāfilīn," 15–16. A standard critique of Mahdawis is that they visit Sayyid Muhammad's tomb while ignoring the Prophet's tomb in Medina and visit only the tombs of Mahdawi leaders rather than those of Sunni Sufis.

22. Many Bohras joined the Mahdawi movement, such as Mustafa Gujarati's family. Some sources conflate these two communities: Ghawthī, *Gulzār-e Abrār*, writes that Muhammad ibn Tahir Patani "opposed the Bohras," but in fact he rather opposed the Bohras who joined the Mahdawis. ʿAydarusī, *al-Nūr al-Sāfir*, is more exact, stating that he rejected the Mahdawis as heretics and opposed the Bohras as Shiʿa.

23. Pātanī, *Tadhkirat al-Mawḍūʿāt*, 91.

24. Pātanī, 221–23.

25. ʿAydarusī, *al-Nūr al-Sāfir*, 361.

26. Gujarātī, *Majālis-e Khamsa*, Session One; he may be referring to the fatwas preserved as Anonymous, "Taʿlīq-e Maktūbī-ye Shaykh ʿAlī Muttaqī."

27. Dihlawī, *Zād al-Muttaqīn*, 80 b.

28. Badāʾūnī, *Muntakhab al-Tawārīkh*, 3:83–85. Akbar summoned Mustafa Gujarati to court at Ajmer at the instigation of some nobles and court scholars. Later, Akbar brought him to Fatehpur Sikri, where he participated in debates for almost two years, five sittings of which are recorded as *Majālis-e Khamsa*. In 1577, he was permitted to return to Gujarat but died en route, his health broken due to prolonged captivity.

29. Gujarati, *Makātib*, 68.

30. Bilgrāmī, *Maʾāthir al-Kirām*, 194–96.

31. Bilgrāmī, *Maʾāthir al-Kirām*; Ghawthī, *Gulzār-e Abrār*, 323.

32. ʿAydarusī, *al-Nūr al-Sāfir*, 361, specifies that Muhammad ibn Tahir died at "the hands of these two sects, the murderous Mahdawis and the slanderous Shiʿa Bohras." The culprits were likely Bohra converts to the Mahdawi movement whom Muhammad ibn Tahir had targeted for critique.

33. Ghawthī, *Gulzār-e Abrār*, 324. Reflecting Ibn Arabi's teachings in *Fuṣūṣ al-Ḥikam*, Wajih al-Din ʿAlawi gave Patani a discourse insisting on the plurality in creation and in the Muslim community.

34. Ghawthī, 324.

35. Wajīh al-Dīn ʿAlawī Gujarātī, "Risala-ye Mas'ala-ye Takfīr" (MSS Ahmedabad: Pir Mohammed Shah Dargah), as cited in Ahmad, *History of the Shattari Silsila*, 285.

36. Akbar's innovation in religious ideology was inspired by many sources—cataloged by Nizami, *Akbar and Religion*, 42–77—including the Mahdawi movement (through Shaykh Mubarak and his sons, Abu'l-Fadl and Faydi).

37. Ernst, *Refractions of Islam in India*, 84–85.

38. Corinne Lefevre, "Mughal Early-Modernity and Royal Adab," in Mayeur-Jaouen, *Adab and Modernity*, 67–68.

39. Nizami, *Akbar and Religion*, 175–78, notes the international implications of Akbar's absolutism in circulating the *maḥḍar*, most notably asserting his authority as caliph, which challenged Ottoman rule; on millennial speculation in Akbar's court, see Moin, *Millennial Sovereign*, 132–39.

40. Kugle, "Accidental Revivalist," provides detail about ʿAbd al-Haqq's youth in Delhi, his interactions with Akbar's court, and his decision to join ʿAbd al-Wahhab Muttaqi.

41. Dihlawī, *Akhbār al-Akhyār*, 243.

42. Dihlawī, 316–17, discusses Musa Jilani in his autobiographic sketch to avoid mentioning the inheritance controversy that led the shaykh to seek Akbar's support and stay in Agra with a royal *mansab* rank of 500.

43. Jīlānī, "Adhkār-e Qādiriyya" (MSS Calcutta), folios 45–125, is an exposition of prayers, meditations, and recitations used by Qadiri Sufis.

44. Dihlawī, *Akhbār al-Akhyār*, 317.

45. Niẓāmī, *Ḥayāt*, 132, quotes ʿAbd al-Haqq's "Waṣiyat-Nāma," which details his Sufi initiations; it is preserved in Bukhārī, *Mir'at al-Ḥaqā'iq*, 89–91, but no longer exists as an independent manuscript. However, a manuscript containing similar information exists as "Risāla-ye Khirqa."

46. Rizvi, *Muslim Revivalist Movements*, 156, recounts how Shaykh Musa Jilani scrupulously performed prayers, even delivering the call to prayer in Akbar's court; however, this does not imply that Shaykh Musa was a "revivalist."

47. Niẓāmī, *Ḥayāt*, 257. ʿAbd al-Haqq's eldest son and successor, Nūr al-Ḥaqq, was born in 1575.

48. Dihlawī, *Akhbār al-Akhyār*, 313–14.

49. Dihlawī, 314.

50. Dihlawī, *Kitāb al-Makātib wa'l-Rasā'il*, 279, from letter number 75. Niẓāmī, *Ḥayāt*, 92, quotes this letter as a biographical source, and Rizvi, *Muslim Revivalist Movements*, 155, mistakenly claims that this letter was addressed to ʿAbd al-Wahhab Muttaqi. The addressee is unnamed but was likely ʿAlī ibn ʿĪssā al-Ḥalabī al-Shāfiʿī al-Qādirī, an advocate of "the oneness of being" whom ʿAbd al-Haqq mentions as a notable Qadiri he had met in Medina, in *Zād al-Muttaqīn*, 63b.

51. Badā'ūnī, *Muntakhab al-Tawārīkh*, 3:113; Niẓāmī, *Ḥayāt*, 92. Rizvi, *Muslim Revivalist Movements*, 156, claims that ʿAbd al-Haqq left the Mughal court because he found its liberality and catholicity "irreconcilable to his sense of orthodoxy and his hide-bound prejudices." There is nothing in the sources to justify Rizvi's opinion.

52. Dihlawī, *Akhbār al-Akhyār*, 314, finished his "autobiographic statement" in 1590

with this episode; he took up the narrative of his own life again in the introduction to *Zād al-Muttaqīn*, completed in 1594, which details his arrival to Mecca.

53. Dihlawī, *Akhbār al-Akhyār*, 314.

54. Ghawthī, *Gulzār-e Abrār*, 405–10.

55. Hamadānī, *Kalimāt al-Ṣādiqīn*, 241–58.

56. Ghawthī, *Gulzār-e Abrār*, 599.

57. Pearson, *Pious Passengers*, 149–50. The season for sailing out of Surat to Arabia was March–April, before the monsoons made navigation westward across the Arabian Sea difficult.

58. Shāh Ṣibghatallāh (d. 1607) was a student of Wajih al-Din ʿAlawi who took Shattari initiation; a contemporary of ʿAbd al-Haqq, he moved from Bharoch to Medina from where his successors spread the Shattari Order to Indonesia. See Ghawthī, *Gulzār-e Abrār*, 576; and Anonymous, "Malfūẓāt-e Shāh Ṣibghatallāh."

59. Dihlawī, *Zād al-Muttaqīn*, 59b.

60. Dihlawī, 4b–5b.

61. Dihlawī, 6a; Blecher, *Said the Prophet of God*, 178.

62. Dihlawī, *Zād al-Muttaqīn*, 66a–66b.

63. Dihlawī, *Kitāb al-Makātib wa'l-Rasā'il*, 279. ʿAbd al-Haqq refers to Qur'an 3:17 to require of others what is known to be good while forbidding others from what is uncertain and harmful.

64. Dihlawī, *Zād al-Muttaqīn*, 72b–73a.

65. Dihlawī, 72b.ʿAbd al-Wahhab Muttaqi argued that a Hanafi text by Ibn Humām, commenting on the *Hidāya*, makes use of hadith reports as methodically as Shafiʿi texts.

66. Dihlawī, "Taḥṣīl al-Taʿarruf," 150, calls himself "a Hanbalo-Hanafi," a neologism describing how his attention to hadith harmonized with his juridical affiliation. His insights formed the basis for "Shāh Walī'llāh's attempts to harmonize Hanafi jurisprudence and hadith; see Dallal, *Islam without Europe*, 272–74.

67. Dihlawī, *Kitāb al-Makātib wa'l-Rasā'il*, 283, justifies why he took a further fourth initiation into the Naqshbandi lineage with Khwāja Muḥammad Bāqī Bi'llah once he returned to Delhi; see also Dihlawī, *Zād al-Muttaqīn*, 64b.

68. Dihlawī, *Zād al-Muttaqīn*, 62b.

69. Dihlawī, 63a–64b.

70. Dihlawī, *Kitāb al-Makātib wa'l-Rasā'il*, 272.

71. Dihlawī, 279.

72. Dihlawī, 85.

73. Examples include *Miftāḥ al-Ghayb* (from ʿAbd al-Qadir Jilani's *Futūḥ al-Ghayb*) and *Zubdat al-Asrār* (from al-Yafiʿi's *Bahjat al-Asrār*).

74. Not to be confused with the later Sufi text by Dara Shikoh; see Gandhi, *Emperor Who Never Was*.

75. Dihlawī, *Maraj al-Baḥrayn*, 17. According to Niẓāmī, *Ḥayāt*, 185, a manuscript of the text corrected by ʿAbd al-Haqq himself exists at the Khuda Bakhsh Library.

76. Kugle, *Rebel between Spirit and Law*, 131–34.

77. Kugle, 134–47.

78. Dihlawī, *Maraj al-Baḥrayn*, 56–73.

79. ʿAbd al-Haqq calls it *Qawāʿid al-Ṭarīqa fī'l-Jamʿ bayn al-Sharīʿa wa'l-Ḥaqīqa*, but he quotes from Zarrūq, *Qawāʿid al-Taṣawwuf*.

80. Dihlawī, *Maraj al-Baḥrayn*, 56–57.
81. Dihlawī, 73.
82. Dihlawī, "Taḥṣīl al-Taʿarruf," 2–3.
83. Zarrūq, *Qawāʿid al-Taṣawwuf*, 7. Qaʿida 2.
84. Zarrūq, 8. Qaʿida 3.
85. Dihlawī, "Taḥṣīl al-Taʿarruf," 3–4, quoting Zarrūq, *Qawāʿid al-Taṣawwuf*, 8. Qaʿida 4.
86. Zarrūq, *Qawāʿid al-Taṣawwuf*, 9. Qaʿida 5, quoting the hadith of Gabriel. See Kugle, *Rebel between Spirit and Law*, 11–12.
87. Zarrūq, *Qawāʿid al-Taṣawwuf*, 8. Qaʿida 4.
88. Dihlawī, *Kitāb al-Makātib wa'l-Rasā'il*, 2–3. On the similarity of this use of the term *jāmiʿ* for scholar-saints, see Kugle, *Rebel between Spirit and Law*, 112, 132, 151, and 164.
89. Rizvi, *Muslim Revivalist Movements*, 159, mistakenly reads the Madyanī as the Madīnī Order (there is no such order). ʿAbd al-Haqq received a Chishti initiation as a residual blessing from ʿAbd al-Wahhab but never practiced Chishti rituals.
90. Niẓāmī, *Ḥayāt*, 138.
91. Niẓāmī, 138.
92. Hamadānī, *Kalimāt al-Ṣādiqīn*, 199–202, claims that Baqi Bi'llah took Sufi training directly from visionary experiences with the long-deceased Khwaja ʿUbaydallah Ahrar.
93. Hamadānī, 186.
94. Niẓāmī, *Ḥayāt*, 139.
95. Dihlawī, *Zād al-Muttaqīn*, 65a.
96. Niẓāmī, *Ḥayāt*, 145–46; summarized in Rizvi, *Muslim Revivalist Movements*, 162–63.
97. It is debated whether this is a Prophetic hadith or a statement of ʿAli ibn Abi Talib; Ibn Arabi cites it as a hadith, as do most Sufis after him; see Austin, *Bezels of Wisdom*, 121.
98. Bukhārī, *Ṣaḥīḥ al-Bukhārī*, 3:1315–16 (Kitāb al-Riqāq, chapter 27, report 6564).

Sixth Satchel

1. Niẓāmī, *Ḥayāt*, 146, quotes from *Tuzuk-e Jahāngīrī*.
2. Niẓāmī, 146.
3. Niẓāmī, 148.
4. The translated passages here supplement passages offered in Lefevre, "Mughal Early-Modernity and Royal Adab," in Mayeur-Jaouen, *Adab and Modernity*, 76–86.
5. Dihlawī, *Risāla-ye Nūriyya*, 23–24.
6. Dihlawī, 24–25.
7. Dihlawī, 25–26.
8. Dihlawī, 26–28.
9. Dihlawī, 28–29.
10. ʿAbd al-Haqq's advice went unheeded, for another book of advice was sent to Jahangir later in his reign; see Alvi, *Advice on the Art of Governance*.
11. Niẓāmī, *Ḥayāt*, 146.
12. Findly, *Nur Jahan*, 204–12, documents Nurjahan's Shiʿi allegiance and animosity

toward reform-oriented Sufis; he describes her opposition to Sirhindi, which applies equally to Shaykh ʿAbd al-Haqq.

13. Niẓāmī, *Ḥayāt*, 148, quoting Dārā Shikōh, *Sakīnat al-Awliyāʾ*, 140.

14. Niẓāmī, 149.

15. Niẓāmī, 204, discussing Dihlawī, "Aḥwāl A'imma Ithnā ʿAshar Khulāṣat Awlād Sayyid al-Bashar."

16. Friedmann, *Shaykh Aḥmad Sirhindi*, 15–19. Sirhindi describes those who inherit prophetic perfection as *al-wārith al-ākhidh ʿan al-aṣl*, adopted from Ibn ʿArabī, *Fuṣūṣ al-Ḥikam*, 64.

17. In Sirhindi's speculation, the empowerment of *Aḥmad* by the singular divinity, *Aḥad*, allows the Prophet Muhammad to remain in loving union with God.

18. Schimmel, *And Muhammad Is His Messenger*, 116–17.

19. Friedmann, *Shaykh Ahmad Sirhindi*, 27–28.

20. Niẓāmī, *Ḥayāt*, 343–44.

21. Niẓāmī, 339.

22. Niẓāmī, 342.

23. Niẓāmī, 335.

24. Schimmel, *And Muhammad Is His Messenger*, 131.

25. Niẓāmī, *Ḥayāt*, 334–35.

26. Niẓāmī, 333.

27. Niẓāmī, 330.

28. Niẓāmī, 328–29.

29. Martin van Bruinissen, "The Impact of Kurdish ʿUlama on Indonesian Islam," *Les annales de l'autre islam* 5 (1998): 83–106.

30. Riddell, *Islam and the Malay-Indonesian World*, 110–16, documents how Shams al-Din Sumatrani (d. 1630) received Burhanpuri's text and its "seven grades of being" suffused with the spirit of the Prophet Muhammad; see also Johns, *Gift Addressed to the Spirit of the Prophet*. Burhānpūrī, *al-Tuḥfa al-Mursala ilā Rūḥ al-Nabī*, 14–15. The seventh level of emanation of the divine is the level of the human being, in which all the other levels of being make their most complete manifestation; the perfect human being is the Prophet Muhammad, who embodies the principle of reflectivity in which divine and material, the universal and particular, are joined.

31. Niẓāmī, *Ḥayāt*, 321.

32. Niẓāmī, 321.

33. Niẓāmī, 332.

34. Niẓāmī, 320.

35. Niẓāmī, 320–21.

36. Niẓāmī, 317–18.

37. Niẓāmī, 318–19.

38. Niẓāmī, 312, transmitted this letter from Khwēshgī, "Maʿārij al-Wilāya," from a copy of the manuscript in his private collection.

39. Friedmann, *Shaykh Ahmad Sirhindi*, 96. The royal order is preserved in "Maʿārij al-Wilāya."

40. Hamadānī, *Kalimāt al-Ṣādiqīn*, 186.

41. Ghawthī, *Gulzār-e Abrār*, 402.

42. Ernst, *Refractions of Islam in India*, 86–93.

43. Muzaffar Alam, "The Mughals, the Sufi Shaikhs and the Formation of the Akbari Dispensation," *Modern Asian Studies* 43, no. 1 (2009): 135–74.

44. Dallal, *Islam without Europe*, 96.

45. Scott Kugle, "Usuli Sufis: Ahmad Zarruq and His South Asian Disciples," in Geoffroy, *La Voie Soufie des Shadhilis*, 181–204.

46. Dallal, *Islam without Europe*, 245–48.

47. Hermansen, *Conclusive Argument from God*, xxiii–xxvi.

48. ʿAlī Muttaqī, *Al-Nahj al-Atamm fī Tabwīb al-Ḥikam*, 81.

BIBLIOGRAPHY

Alphabetization in the bibliography is by the author's name, giving priority to the *nisba* (epithet of ascription or affiliation) or *kunya* (teknonym) for Islamic names. The bibliography includes all of ʿAli Muttaqi's known compositions in extant manuscript sources and corrects errors found in Brockelmann, *Geschichte der arabischen Litteratur.* The title of ʿAli Muttaqi's works are given in English translation as well as the original Arabic or Persian. Unpublished manuscripts are listed with location, archive or library institution, and manuscript number (followed by language and genre when those labels are integral to the archive's catalog system).

Works in Islamicate Languages (Including Unpublished Manuscripts)

ʿAbd al-Wahhāb ibn Aḥmad. *Tadhkirat Muḥammmad ibn Ṭāhir.* Delhi: n.p., 1954.

ʿAlawī Gujarātī, Wajīh al-Dīn. "Malfūẓāt-e Wajīh al-Dīn Gujarātī." MSS Hyderabad Deccan: OML 547 farsi tasawwuf; and Calcutta: ASB Society Collection.

———. "Silsila-ye Ṭarīqat-e Shāh Wajīh al-Dīn." MSS Ahmedabad: Pir Mohammadshah Dargah 1363.

ʿAlawī Ḥusaynī, Sayyid ʿAbd al-Mālik. "Miṣbāḥ al-ʿĀlam." MSS Ahmedabad: BJI 293.

Anonymous. "Baḥr-e Zakhkhār." MSS Hyderabad Deccan: OML 238 farsi tazkira.

Anonymous. "Malfūẓāt-e Shāh Ṣibghatallāh." MSS Hyderabad Deccan: OML, 1460 farsi tasawwuf.

Anonymous. "Taʿlīq-e Maktūbī-ye Shaykh ʿAlī Muttaqī." MSS Rampur: RL 1975 arabic.

Anonymous. "Tarjamat Ibn Ḥajar al-Haythamī." MSS Patna: KB 2632, folios 265–73.

Anonymous disciple of ʿAbd al-Ḥaqq Muḥaddith Dihlawī. "Risāla-ye Khirqa." MSS Rampur: RL 992 farsi.

ʿAydarusī, ʿAbd al-Qādir. *al-Nūr al-Sāfir ʿan Akhbār al-Qarn al-ʿĀshir.* Baghdad: Maṭbaʿ al-Furāṭ, 1934.

Badāʾūnī, ʿAbd al-Qādir. *Najāt al-Rashīd.* Lahore: Punjab University Idāra-ye Taḥqīqāt, 1972.

Balkhī, Muḥammad ibn ʿUthmān. "ʿAyn al-ʿIlm wa Zayn al-Ḥilm." MSS Hyderabad Deccan: SJ 29, 30, 31, 32, and 59 tasawwuf.

Barakat ʿAlī, Munshī. *Mirʾat al-Ḥaqāʾiq Ḥayāt-e Shaykh ʿAbd al-Ḥaqq Muḥadith Dihlavī.* Rampur: Maṭbaʿ-ye ʿAzīz, AH 1322.

Bilgrāmī, ʿAli Azād. *Maʾāthir al-Kirām.* Agra: Maṭbaʿ Mufīd-e ʿĀmm, 1910.

Bukhārī, Muḥammad. *Ṣaḥīḥ al-Bukhārī.* Lichtenstein: Thesaurus Islamicus Foundation, 2000.

Bukhārī, Munshī Barakat Alī. *Mirʾat al-Ḥaqāʾiq: Ḥayāt-e Shaykh ʿAbd al-Haqq Muḥaddith Dihlavī.* Rampur: Maṭbaʿ ʿAzīz, n.d.

Burhānpūrī, Muḥammad ibn Faḍlallāh. "Taḥdhīr al-Ṭālibīn ʿan Ruʾiyat al-Amrad liʾl-Wuṣūl ilā ʾllah." MSS Hyderabad Deccan: SJ 29 arabic tasawwuf folios 112–17.
——. *al-Tuḥfa al-Mursala ilā Rūḥ al-Nabī*. Lithograph, n.p.: Maṭbaʿ Kabīr-e Dakkan, n.d.
Chishtī, Rashīd al-Dīn Lālā. "Mukhbir al-Awliyāʾ." MSS Ahmedabad: Nāṣir Bāgh Dargāh.
Dārā Shikōh. *Sakīnat al-Awliyāʾ*. Urdu translation by Maqbūl Bēg Badakhshānī. Delhi: Arshad Press, n.d.
Dihlawī, ʿAbd al-Ḥaqq Muḥaddith. *Akhbār al-Akhyār fī Asrār al-Abrār*. Lithograph. Delhi: n.p., AH 1308.
——. *Kitāb al-Makātib waʾl-Rasāʾil ilā Arbāb al-Kamāl waʾl-Faḍāʾil*. Lithograph. Delhi: Maṭbaʿ-ye Mujtabāʾī, 1867.
——. *Maraj al-Baḥrayn fī Jamʿ bayn al-Ṭarīqayn*. Delhi: ʿAbd al-Ḥaqq Muḥaddith Akademi, 1991; first published Karachi: Muḥammad Aʿlā, 1968; reprint with Urdu translation, 2014.
——. "Miftāḥ al-Futūḥ." Lahore: Maṭbaʿ-ye Hūp, 1865. MSS Hyderabad Deccan: OML 1771 farsi tasawwuf.
——. *Risāla-ye Nūriyya-ye Sulṭāniyya*. Edited by Muḥammad Salīm Akhtar. Islamabad: Iran Pakistan Institute of Persian Studies, 1985.
——. "Taḥṣīl al-Taʿarruf fī Maʿifat al-Fiqh waʾl-Taṣawwuf." MSS Rampur: RL 1347 arabic.
——. "Zād al-Muttaqīn fī Sulūk Ṭarīq al-Yaqīn." MSS London: BL or 217.
——. *Zād al-Muttaqīn, Urdū Tarjama*. Translated by Masʿūd Anwar ʿAlawī Kākorwī. Private printing, 2009.
——. *Zubdat al-Asrār wa Zubdat al-Āthār*. Jazira: Maṭbaʿ Bookselling Company, 1316, Hijri.
Fārūqī, Aḥmad ibn Muḥammad. "Khulāṣat al-Wajīh." MSS Ahmedabad: BJI 291.
Ghawthī, Muḥammad Shaṭṭārī. *Gulzār-e Abrār*. Urdu translation by Faḍl Aḥmad Jewarī. Agra: Maṭbaʿ-ye Mufīd-e ʿĀmm, AH 1326.
Gujarātī, Muṣṭafā. *Jawāhir al-Taṣdīq*. Hyderabad Deccan: Dār al-Ishāʿāt, 1409 AH.
——. *Majālis-e Khamsa*. Mushirabad Deccan: n.p., AH 1367.
——. *Makātib*. Hyderabad Deccan: Jamiyat-i Mahdaviyah, 1957.
Gwāliyarī, Muḥammad Ghawth. *Awrād-e Ghawthiyya*. Raichur, Karnataka: Maṭbaʿ-e Ṣibghatallāhī, AH 1313.
Hamadānī, Muḥammad Ṣādiq. *Kalimāt al-Ṣādiqīn*. Urdu translation by Laṭīfallāh. Karachi: Idāra-ye Nashr al-Maʿārif, 1995.
Ḥasanī, ʿAbd al-Ḥayy. *Nuzhat al-Khawāṭir wa Bahjat al-Masāmiʿ wa al-Nawāẓir*. 10 vols. Hyderabad Deccan: Dāʾirat al-Maʿārif, 1988.
Haythamī, Aḥmad Ibn Ḥajar. "Kaff al-Raʿāʿ ʿan Muḥarramāt al-Lahw waʾl-Samāʿ." MSS Istanbul: Wali al-Din Library 794.
——. "al-Qawl al-Mukhtaṣar fī ʿAlāmāt al-Mahdī al-Muntaẓar." MSS Rampur: RL 1805 arabic; and Patna: KB catalog, vol. 26.
——. "Taʿarruf fī al-Aṣlayn waʾl-Taṣawwuf." MSS Patna: KB 2632.
Ibn ʿArabī, Muḥammad ibn ʿAlī al-Ḥātimī. *Fuṣūṣ al-Ḥikam*. Edited by ʿAfīfī. Cairo: Dār Iḥyāʾ al-Kutub al-ʿArabiyya, 1946.
Jāmī, ʿAbd al-Raḥmān. *Nafaḥāt al-Uns min ḥaḍarāt al-quds*. Tehran: ʿIlmī Publishers, 1996.

Jīlānī, Shaykh Jalāl al-Dīn Mūsā. "Adhkār-e Qādiriyya." MSS Calcutta: Asiatic Society Collection 1261 farsi tasawwuf.
Kāshānī, Ḥammād al-Dīn. *Aḥsan al-Aqwāl*. Urdu translation by Muḥammad ʿAbd al-Majīd. Miraj: Ganj Bakhsh Publications, 1987.
Khān, ʿAlī Muḥammad Bahādur (also known as Mirzā Muḥammad Ḥasanī). *Mir'āt-e Aḥmadī Supplement*. Translated by Nawwāb ʿAlī. Baroda: Gaekwad's Oriental Series, 1928.
——. *Mir'āt-e Aḥmadī*. Bombay: Fatḥ al-Karīm, 1889. Partially translated into English as Edward Clive Bayley, *The Local Muhammad Dynasties of Gujarat*. 1886. New Delhi: S. Chand and Company, 1970).
Khān, Bashīr Muḥammad. *Tārīkh-e Awliyā-ye Kirām-e Burhānpūr*. Pune: Sihr Art Press, 1997.
Khānum, ʿĀbida. "Muḥammad ibn Tāhir Patanī: Ḥayātuhu wa taṣānīfuhu." MA thesis, Punjab University, Department of Arabic, 1970.
Khwāfī, ʿAbd al-Dā'im. "Thamarāt al-Ḥayāt min Kalām Shaykh Burhān al-Dīn." MSS Hyderabad Deccan: OML 484 farsi tasawwuf.
Khwēshgī, ʿAbdallāh. "Maʿārij al-Wilāya." MSS Lahore: PU H-25/7765.
Kirmānī, Muḥammad ibn Mubārak (known as "Amīr Khurd"). *Siyar al-Awliyā*. Delhi: Matbaʿ Muhibb-i Hind, AH 1302.
Lāhōrī, Ghulām Sarwar. *Khazīnat al-Aṣfiyā'*. Lucknow: Nawal Kishore, n.d.
Lāhōrī, Muḥammad Ṣāḥib. *Ḥadā'iq al-Ḥafaniyya*. Lucknow: Nawal Kishore, n.d.
Malkāpūrī, Muḥammad ʿAbd al-Jabbār Khān. *Maḥbūb Dhū'l-Minan fī Tadhkira Awliyā-ye Dakkan*. Hyderabad: Hasan Press, AH 1331.
Muslim ibn al-Ḥajjāj. *Saḥīḥ Muslim*. Lichtenstein: Thesaurus Islamicus Foundation, 2000.
Mutālā, Muḥammad Yūsuf. *Mashā'ikh-e Aḥmadābād*. Meerut: Maktaba Maḥmūdiyya, 1993.
Muttaqī, ʿAbd al-Wahhāb ibn Walī'llāh Mañdwī. "Bishārat al-Ḥabīb fī Faḍl al-Gharīb." MSS Rampur: RL 993 arabic.
——. "Ḥabl al-Matīn fī Taqwīyat al-Yaqīn." MSS Hyderabad Deccan: OML 1550 farsi taswwuf.
——. "Mafātīḥ al-Ghuyūb fī Maʿrifat Khawāṭir al-Qulūb." MSS Rampur: RL 993 arabic.
——. "Tafsīr al-Ḥikam wa Shu'ūn al-Munazzalāt." MSS London: BL India Office Collection 1152.
Muttaqī, ʿAlī ibn Ḥusām al-Dīn. "al-Aḥādīth al-Mutawātira al-Ma'khūdha min Risālat al-Suyūṭī" [Abridged collection of authentic hadith reports extracted from a writing by al-Suyūṭī]. MSS Aligarh: Azad, Sulayman Collection 28/17 hadith arabic.
——. "ʿAlāmāt al-Mahdī Ṣāḥib al-Zamān" [Signs of the Mahdi, the master of time]. MSS Hyderabad Deccan: OML 608 arabic hadith. This is an abridgment of ʿAlī Muttaqī, *al-Burhān fī Alāmāt al-Mahdī*; it is unclear whether ʿAli Muttaqi or one of his followers composed this text.
——. "Aqrab al-Ṭurūq ilā 'llah" [The closest of ways to reaching God]. MSS Rampur: RL 787 farsi suluk, folios 294–96; and Istanbul: Suleymaniye, Darul Mesnevi 111, folios 60–63. This small treatise is bound in a collection of other works by Sayyid ʿAlī al-Hamadhānī in the RL collection, and its catalog attributes authorship to

him, written in the margins by a cataloger. The text comments on the saying by Najm al-Din Kubra that "the ways to God are as manifold as the breaths of all creation" and is more likely attributed to ʿAli Muttaqi. Monzawi Catalogue, 3:1284, entry 2280 notes copies in private collections in Quetta and Lahore.

Muttaqī, ʿAlī ibn Ḥusām al-Dīn. "Asrār al-ʿĀrifīn wa Sayr al-Ṭālibīn" [Secret of the knowers on the journey of seekers]. MSS Patna: KB catalog, vol. 13, no. 957.

——. "al-Burhān al-Aqwā fī Sharaf al-Taqwā" [The strongest proof on the nobility of awe and fear of God]. MSS at Aligarh: Azad, Subhanallah Collection shamil 297.7/51 tasawwuf farsi.

——. "al-Burhān al-Jalī fī Maʿrifat al-Walī" [The clear proof about recognizing the saint]. MSS Aligarh: Azad, Subhanallah Collection shamil 297.7/51 tasawwuf farsi.

——. *al-Burhān fī ʿAlāmāt al-Mahdī Ākhir al-Zamān* [The ultimate proof about the signs of the Mahdi of the end of time]. Kuwait: Dhāt al-Salāsil, 1988. MSS Hyderabad Deccan: OML 968 arabic hadith; SJ A & K 18 arabic; Osmania, 297.49 arabic; Tonk, Rajasthan: APR 903; Rampur: RL 933; London: BL India Office 1031, 2; and Princeton: GC 504 [1, no. 3].

——. "Chehel Ḥadīth" [A collection of forty sayings of the Prophet]. MSS Aligarh: Azad, Sulayman Collection 27/16 hadith.

——. "Ḍābiṭa li-Uṣūl al-Ṭarīqa" [Fixing the meaning of Zarrūq's "Foundations of the Path"]. MSS Rampur: RL 3083 arabic; and Aligarh: Azad, Subhanallah Collection 297.7/51 farsi tasawwuf.

——. "Dhikr al-Mawt li-Tadarruk al-Fawt" [Reminders of death for gradually passing away]. MSS Aligarh: Azad, Subhanallah Collection 297.7/51 farsi tasawwuf.

——. "al-Fikr fīʾl-Jahr biʾl-Dhikr" [Thoughts on recitation performed aloud]. MSS Lahore: PU 3923/871, folios 191–92. There is no clear ascription in the introduction of the text, but it exists in a collection of ʿAli Muttaqi's other works, and ʿAbd al-Ḥaqq Dihlawī,, *Zād al-Muttaqīn* mentions that ʿAli Muttaqi wrote about reciting *dhikr* aloud.

——. "al-Ghāya al-Quṣwā fī Maʿrifat al-Dunyā" [The extreme remoteness on the nature of the world's lowliness]. MSS Aligarh: Azad, Subhanallah Collection 297.7/51 farsi tasawwuf. This Arabic treatise is similar to the Persian work "Risāla dar Maʿrifat-e Dunyā."

——. "Ghāyat al-Kamāl fī Bayān Afḍal al-Aʿmāl" [The ultimate perfection about the best of all meritorious actions]. MSS Princeton: GC SII 519, no. 15. This work is known by the alternative title "Minhāj al-Matāh al-ʿAlīm fī Faḍl al-Taʿallum waʾl-Taʿlīm."

——. "Ghāyat al-Maʿmūl fīʾl-Sulūk waʾl-Wuṣūl" [The greatest hope in soul training and arriving to God]. MSS Lahore: PU 4862/1842. This text exists only in excerpt, titled "Qāʿida Mukhtaṣara fīʾl-Sulūk ilā ʾllah" [The basic principle for striving toward Allah] in the Punjab University catalog, though it bears the full title in the text itself.

——. "Hidāyat Rabbī ʿinda Faqd al-Murabbī" [My Lord's guidance if one has no master for training]. MSS Ahmedabad: Pir Mohammadshah Dargah 70 dhayl; and Cairo: al-Azhar ʿayn 5446 tasawwuf.

——. "al-Ḥikam al-ʿIrfāniyya fī Maʿānī Irshādiyya wa Ishārāt Qurʾāniyya" [Wisdom of spiritual insight containing principles of guidance in Qurʾanic phrasing]. MSS Hyderabad Deccan: SJ 42 arabic taṣawwuf; and Istanbul: Sūleymaniye, Çelebi Abdullah Effendi 384 folios 81–92, and Bagdati Vehbi Effendi 757 folios 1–50.

——. "al-ʿIbārāt al-Faṣīḥa fī'l-Wāʿiẓ wa'l-Naṣīḥa" [Eloquent expressions of admonition and advice]. MSS Aligarh: Azad, Aftab Collection 20/9 farsi.
——. "Jarr al-Thaqīl fī Sulūk al-Maʿīl" [Bearing the heavy burden on soul training of men considering marriage]. MSS Lahore: PU 4950/1937 folios 22–29; Islamabad: GB 3745; and Khayrpur: Madrasa-ye Rashidiyya, Pir Goteh Collection.
——. "Jawāb Risālat ʿAbd al-Mālik" [Answer to a treatise by ʿAbd al-Mālik Sajāwandī]. MSS Rampur: RL 1975 arabic.
——. "al-Jawāhir al-Thamīna" [The precious jewels]. MSS Calcutta: ASB Society Collection 1254 farsi; Hyderabad Deccan: OML 231 farsi taṣawwuf; Rampur: RL 3085 folios 118–25; and Islamabad: GB 8911. This work is also known by the title "Jawāmiʿ al-Kilam fī Mawāʿiẓ wa'l-Ḥikam."
——. *Kanz al-ʿUmmāl fī Sunan al-Aqwāl wa'l-Afʿāl* [Treasury of good works on the words and actions of the Prophet Muhammad]. 2nd ed. Hyderabad: Dā'ira-ye Maʿārif-e ʿUthmāniyya, 1995. A condensed version of this text was printed under the same title in Beirut: *Dār Iḥyā' al-Turāth al-ʿArabī.*
——. "Khulāṣat al-Ḥaqā'iq fī'l-Ḥikam wa'l-Raqā'iq" [Essence of cosmic realities on wisdom sayings and spiritual subtleties]. MSS Berlin: DK, Oct 1074.
——. "al-Kibrīt al-Aḥmar fī'l-Kīmiyā' al-Akbar" [The red sulfur of the greater spiritual alchemy]. MSS Aligarh: Azad, Subhanallah Collection 297.7/51.
——. "Kifāyat-e Ahl-e Yaqīn fī Ṭarīq al-Mutawakkilīn" [Sufficiency for the faithful folk on the way of those who rely upon God alone]. MSS Tonk, Rajasthan: APR 3775 part 6; and Aligarh: Azad, Habibganj Collection 24, part 5. This is a Persian translation of parts of Ibn ʿAṭā'allāh, *Kitāb al-Tanwīr.*
——. "Kitāb Wāsiṭat al-Wuṣūl al-Mūsāmma bi-Sharḥ al-Fuṣūl li-Jāmiʿ fī al-Furūʿ wa'l-Uṣūl" [A text leading to union, titled "Commentary on the Chapters That Gather the Branching Elaborations with the Root Principles"]. MSS Patna: KB catalog, vol. 5, no. 225. This text is a commentary on "Jāmiʿ al-Uṣūl ilā Aḥādīth al-Rusūl" (a collection of hadith reports culled from the six canonical collections, gathered into a single text by Majd al-Dīn Abū al-Saʿāda al-Jarzī).
——. "Maktūbāt-e Ghawthiyya" [Eighteen letters of the greatest succor, Shaykh ʿAbd al-Qādir Jīlānī]. MSS Hyderabad Deccan: SJ 471 and 1059 farsi A.Nm, and 36 farsi tasawwuf; and Patna: KB catalog, vol. 16, no. 1385.
——. "Malfūẓāt-e Shaykh ʿAlī Muttaqī" [Oral teachings of Shaykh ʿAli Muttaqi]. MSS Hyderabad Deccan: OML 852 farsi tasawwuf.
——. "al-Maqṣad al-Asnā fī Sharḥ Asmā' Allah al-Husnā" [The noblest goal in explicating the beautiful names of God]. MSS Aligarh: Azad, Habibganj Collection 21, part 24.
——. "Maṭlaʿ al-Ghāya fī Ikhtiṣār an-Nihāya" [The furthest overview in abridgment of "The Final Word"]. MSS Berlin: DK 1662. This is an abridgment of Ibn al-Athīr, *al-Nihāya fī Gharīb al-Ḥadīth wa'l-Athar.*
——. "al-Mawāhib al-ʿAlīya fī Jamʿ al-Ḥikam al-Qur'āniyya wa'l-Ḥadīthiyya" [Divine gifts from on high that join the wisdom of the Qur'an with the wisdom of the Prophet]. MSS Istanbul: Suleymaniye, Esad Effendi 1769 folios 1–73. There
Muttaqī, ʿAlī ibn Ḥusām al-Dīn (*continued*)
is another MSS copy in Cairo at the archive of Dar al-Kutub, listed in the first catalog, vol. 7, no. 347.
——. "Minhāj al-ʿUmmāl fī Sunan al-Aqwāl" [The method of good works on the words of the Prophet Muhammad]. MSS Tonk, Rajasthan: APR 509 arabic; Lahore:

PU Arb. II 23/1602; and Hyderabad, Deccan: OML 105 arabic hadith. This book was finished by ʿAbd al-Wahhab Muttaqi after ʿAli Muttaqi died.
Muttaqī, ʿAlī ibn Ḥusām al-Dīn. "Mukhtaṣar Qaṭf al-Azhār" [A collection of hadith reports extracted from "A Fistful of Flowers" by al-Suyūṭī]. MSS Tonk, Rajasthan: APR 516.
——. *al-Nahj al-Atamm fī Tabwīb al-Ḥikam* [The most comprehensive method in collation of the wisdom sayings of Ibn ʿAṭā'allāh]. Damascus: Dār al-Qādiriyya, 1998.
——. "al-Naṣḥ al-Wāfī li'l-Qalb al-Shāfī" [Ample advice for a heart in healing]. MSS Lahore: PU 3923/871 and 4146/1094; and Aligarh: Azad, Subhanallah Collection 297.7/51 arabic. This is a commentary on Masʿūd Bakk, *Mir'āt al-ʿĀrifīn*.
——. "Naẓm al-Durar fī'l-Ḥikam al-Ghurar" [A string of pearls on wise and choice sayings]. MSS Hyderabad, Deccan: OML 121 arabic muḥāḍirāt; and Aligarh: Azad, Habibganj Collection 31/9 arabic khutab wa mawāʿiẓ. This is an arrangement of quotations from two earlier texts, "Aṭwāq al-Dhahab" of Zamakhsharī and "Aṭbāq al-Dhahab" of Aḥmad ibn ʿAlī al-Jawzī.
——. "Niʿam al-Miʿyār wa'l-Miqyās li-Maʿrifa bi-Marātib al-Nās" [The surest rule and guide to judging the different levels of people]. MSS Aligarh: Azad, Habibganj Collection 21/24 farsi. This text is also reproduced in ʿAli Muttaqi, "Ghāyat al-Maʿmūl."
——. "al-Raghā'ib fī'l-Ṣabr ʿalā al-Maṣā'ib" [Encouragements for patience in the face of disasters]. MSS Aligarh: Azad, Subhanallah Collection 297.7/51 farsi taṣawwuf.
——. "al-Ratba al-Fākhira fī Sulṭanat al-Dunyā wa'l-Ākhira" [The most superior station on authority in this world and the next"]. MSS Rampur: RL 3523. This work is known by the alternative title "al-Waṣīla al-Fākhira."
——. "Riqq al-Marqūm fī Ghāyat al-ʿUlūm" [A fine-lined parchment on the furthest goals of scholarship]. MSS Aligarh: Azad, Subhanallah Collection 297.7/51 farsi tasawwuf.
——. "Risāla dar Maʿrifat-e Dunyā" [On the true nature of the world]. Calcutta: Asiatic Society Collection 1080 and 1255 farsi, and Curzon Collection 399 farsi; Aligarh: Azad, University Collection 153 zamima; Islamabad: GB 7376; and Karachi: Mauzeh Milli N M 1959, and Hamdard Library R.122.
——. "Risāla dar Taṣawwuf" [Treatise on being a Sufi]. MSS Aligarh: Azad, Habibganj Collection 21/2. The initial portion of the manuscript is missing, obscuring its original title.
——. "Risālat al-Radd ʿalā man Qaḍā anna al-Mahdī al-Mawʿūd qad Ja'ā wa Maḍā" [Treatise refuting those who claim that the promised Mahdi has come and gone]. MSS Rampur: RL 1514g and 1975 arabic.
——. "Risālat-e Ḍurūriyāt dar Bāb-e Mubtadī-ye Ṭarīqat" [Treatise on the basics for a beginner on the path]. MSS Lahore: PU 4862/1842.
——. "Shamā'il al-Nabī" [Qualities of the Prophet Muhammad]. MSS Aligarh: Azad, Subhanallah Collection 297.7/22 hadith arabic; and Damascus: Maktaba Waṭaniyya 4822.
——. "Sharḥ Qawāʿid al-Ṭarīqa" [Commentary on Zarrūq's "Principles of Being a Sufi"]. MSS Berlin: DK 3031, PM, 547.1, folios 1–32a; and Paris: Escurial 2741,4.
——. "Sulūk al-Rijāl" [Soul training for real men]. MSS Khayrpur: Kitabkhana-ye

ʿUmumi, kaf lam ayn 297/6; and Hyderabad Sindh: Dargah Pir Syed Muhiballah Shah Rashidi.
——. "Tabwīb Sharḥ al-Ḥikam li-Ibn ʿAbbād al-Rundī" [Collation of the commentary of Ibn ʿAbbād on the wisdom sayings of Ibn ʿAṭāʾallāh]. MSS Istanbul: Suleymaniye, Hekim Oglu Millet 466.
——. "Tabyīn al-Rāfa fī-mā liʾllāh min al-Ḍiyāfa" [Illustrating graciousness about God's hospitable kindness]. MSS Aligarh: Azad, Subhanallah Collection 297.7/51.
——. "Tabyīn al-Ṭurūq ilā ʾllah" [Exposition of the paths to God]. MSS Lahore: PU 4146/1094 folios 71–72.
——. "Tajrīb al-Wāfī fī al-Ḥibr al-Ṣāfī" [Sufficient experiments on making pure ink]. MSS Aligarh: Azad, University Collection 7 farsi mutafarriqa.
——. "Taʿlīq ʿalā Sharḥ al-Ḥikam al-Khāmis ʿĀshar" [A commentary on the fifteenth commentary of Aḥmad Zarrūq on the wisdom sayings]. MSS Berlin: DK 869.6, We. 1757.2, folios 37a–50b.
——. "Talkhīṣ al-Bayān fī ʿAlāmāt Mahdī Ākhir al-Zamān" [The final clarification on the Mahdi of the end of time]. MSS Berlin: DK 2726/30; Princeton: GC Catalog II, 503 [no. 2] and supplement II, 518; and Rampur: RL 1514 and 1975 arabic. This is an abridgement of "ʿAlāmāt al-Mahdī Ṣāḥib al-Zamān" and was rendered into Persian as "Hashar Nāma." MSS Rampur: RL 405 farsi. Or "ʿAlāmāt-e Mahdī-ye Mawʿūd," MSS Islamabad: GB 2706, 6314, 3745, and 2825. Or "ʿAlāmāt-e Imām al-Mahdī," MSS Lahore: PU 4862/1842 folio 47.
——. "Tanbīh al-Aḥibba fī ʿAlāmāt al-Muḥabba" [Warning to lovers on the signs of sincere passion]. MSS Delhi: Shah Abuʾl Khayr Dargah 21 folios 1–9 tasawwuf.
——. "Tanbīh al-Ghāfilīn ʿan Sūʾ al-Sabīl al-Muḥarramīn wa al-ladhīna atbaʿahum Mutawāriyīn li-yarjiʿū ilā Sayyid al-Rashshād al-Amīn" [Admonition to the heedless to avoid the evil path of those led astray and those who pledge allegiance to follow them so that they might return to the true guide, Muhammad]. MSS Rampur: RL 1975.
——. "Tanbīh al-Raʾāfa fī-mā li-llah min al-Ḍiyāfa" [Reminder of graciousness about the limits of God's hospitality]. MSS Aligarh: Azad, Subhanallah Collection shamil 297.7/51, tasawwuf farsi.
——. "Taʿrīf al-Ṣirāṭ fī Sulūk al-Ghazāt" [Showing the path that is right for soul training of those who fight]. MSS Lahore: PU 3923/871 folios 178–91.
——. "al-Tawaṣṣul fīʾl-Yaqīn waʾl-Tawakkul" [Means to arrive at true faith and reliance upon God alone]. MSS Aligarh: Azad, Subhanallah Collection shamil 297.7/51 taṣawwuf farsi; and Lahore: PU 3923/871 folios 173–79. This is a Persian translation of parts of Ibn ʿAṭāʾallāh's *Kitāb al-Tanwīr.*
——. "Tidhkār al-Niʿam waʾl-ʿAṭāyā fīʾl-Ṣabr waʾl-Shukr ʿalā ʾl-Faqr waʾl-Balāyā" [Reminder of blessings and benedictions to be patient and grateful when in need and afflicted]. MSS Istanbul: Sulaymaniye 791/2; and Aligarh: Azad, Subhanallah Collection 297.7/51 folios 24a–25b arabic.
——. "ʿUnwān fī Sulūk al-Niswān" [An address on the soul training of women]. MSS Ahmedabad: Pir Mohammadshah Dargah; Islamabad: GB 3745; Hyderabad Sindh: Dargah Pir Syed Muhibballah Shah Rashidi; and Peshawar University.
——. "ʿUrwat al-Salaf waʾl-Khalaf fīʾl-Taṣawwuf al-Mustanbaṭ min al-Kitāb waʾl-Sunna wa Kalām al-Salaf" [The tightest bond of forefathers and descendants on

how to be a Sufi as derived directly from the Qur'an, the Prophet's example, and our pious ancestors]. MSS Princeton: GC Yahuda Collection 499 folios 86–97.
Muttaqī, ʿAlī ibn Ḥusām al-Dīn. "Zād al-Ṭālibīn" [The provision of the seekers]. MSS Patna: KB catalog, vol. 13, no. 957.
Muttaqī, Ḥusām al-Dīn ibn Muḥammad Multānī. "Ādāb al-Māʾida." MSS Islamabad: GB 9296.
——. "Ḥifẓ al-Īmān." MSS Islamabad: GB 3426.
Niẓāmī, Khalīq Aḥmad. *Ḥayāt-e Shaykh ʿAbd al-Ḥaqq Muḥaddith Dihlawī.* Delhi: Nadwat al-Muṣannifīn, 1964.
Niẓāmī, Miʿrāj Aḥmad. *Surūd-e Rūḥānī.* New Delhi: n.p., 1998.
Parwēz, Akhtar. *Shāh Bājan: Ēk Muṭāliʿa.* Burhanpur: private publication by the author, 2005.
Pātanī, Muḥammad ibn Ṭāhir. *Tadhkirat al-Mawḍūʿāt.* Bombay: al-Maktaba al-Qayyima, AH 1343.
Qādirī, Fuḍayl Aḥmad. *Tārīkh-e Mashrab-e Shaṭṭār.* Aligarh: Educational Book House, 1997.
Sajāwandī, ʿAbd al-Mālik. *Sirāj al-Abṣār.* Translated by Muṣṭafā Tashrīfallāhī. Chanchalguda, Hyderabad Deccan: private Mahdawi community publication, n.d.
Shāh Bājan Chishtī, Bahāʾ al-Dīn. "Khazāʾin-e Raḥmatallāh." (Also known by the title "Gulshan-e Raḥmat.") MSS Lahore: PU 2282/5289; and Delhi: Noor International Microfilm Institute.
Shāhjahānābādī, Kalīmallāh. *Maktūbāt-e Kalīmī.* Delhi: Matbaʿ Yūsufī, 1883–84.
Shaʿrānī, ʿAbd al-Wahhāb. *al-Ṭabaqāt al-Kubrā.* Beirut: Dār al-Jīl, 1988.
Shaṭṭārī, Bahāʾ al-Dīn. "Risāla-ye Shaṭṭāriyya." MSS Rampur: RL 905 farsi.
Shaṭṭārī, Faḍlallāh. "Manāqib-e Ghawthiyya." MSS Ahmedabad: BJI 294.
Sirhindī, Aḥmad. *Maktūbāt.* 6 vols. Edited by Nūr Aḥmad Amritsarī. Lahore: Nur Company, 1964.
Suyūṭī, Jalāl al-Dīn. *al-ʿArf al-Wardī fī Akhbār al-Mahdī.* Beirut: Dār al-Kutub al-ʿIlmiyya, 2006.
———. "al-Qawl al-Jalī fī Ḥadīth al-Walī." MSS Patna: KB catalog, vol. 25, no. 2774.
Tashrīfallāhī, Sayyid Maḥmūd. *Muqaddima-ye Sirāj al-Absār.* 3rd ed. Hyderabad: Aijaz Press, 1990.
Al-Tirmidhī, al-Ḥakīm Muḥammad. *Ṭabāʾi al-Nufūs.* Cairo: al-Maktab al-Thaqāfī, 1989.
Ulūghkhānī, Muḥammad ibn ʿUmar al-Makkī, "Ḥājjī Dabīr." *Ẓafar al-Wālih bi-Muẓaffar wa Ālihi.* Edited by E. Denison Ross. London: John Murray Publishers, 1910.
Ẓāhir al-Ḥaqq, Muḥammad, trans. *Manāqib-e Ghawthiyya.* Lithograph. Agra: Abū Maʿālī Press, 1933.
Zarrūq, Aḥmad. *Qawāʿid al-Taṣawwuf.* Beirut: Dār al-Jīl, 1992.
——. *Sharḥ Ṣaḥīḥ al-Bukhārī.* 6 vols. Edited by ʿIzzat ʿAli ʿAṭiya, and Mūsā Muḥammad ʿAli. Cairo: Maṭbaʿat Hisān, n.d.
——. "Sulūk al-Ṭarīq idhā fuqida al-Rafīq." MSS Ahmedabad: Pir Mohammadshah Dargah 70 dhayl; and Hyderabad: Salar Jung, Persian Kashkul 8, part 29.

Works in English and European Languages (Including Translations from Islamicate Texts)

Abū'l-Faḍl. *Akbar Nama*. Translated by Henry Beveredge. Calcutta: Asiatic Society, 1897.

Ahmad, Qazi Moin Uddin. *History of the Shattari Silsila*. PhD diss., Aligarh Muslim University, 1963.

Alam, Muzaffar. *Languages of Political Islam: India 1200–1800*. Chicago: University of Chicago Press, 2004.

Alam, Muzaffar, and Sanjay Subrahmanyam. "A View from Mecca: Notes on Gujarat, the Red Sea, and the Ottomans, 1517–39/923–946 AH." *Modern Asian Studies* 51, no. 2 (2017): 268–318.

——. *Writing the Mughal World: Studies on Culture and Politics*. New York: Columbia University Press, 2012.

Alam, Sarwar, ed. *Cultural Fusion of Sufi Islam: Alternative Paths to Mystical Faith*. London: Routledge, 2019.

Alvi, Sajida Sultana, trans. *Advice on the Art of Governance: An Indo-Islamic Mirror for Princes, or Mawʿiza-ye Jahangiri of Muhammad Baqir Najm-e Sani*. Albany: SUNY Press, 1989.

Anjum, Tanvir. "The Perpetually Wedded Wife of God: A Study of Shaykh Musa Sada Suhag." *Journal of Religious History* 39 (2015): 420–34.

Aquil, Raziuddin, and David Curley, eds. *Literary and Religious Practices in Medieval and Early Modern India*. Delhi: Manohar Publications, 2016.

Austin, Ralph W. J., trans. *The Bezels of Wisdom by Ibn Al 'Arabi*. New York: Paulist Press, 1980.

Badā'ūnī, ʿAbd al-Qādir. *Muntakhab al-Tawārīkh*. 3 vols. Translated by George S. A. Ranking, W. H. Lowe, and Wolseley Haig. Delhi: Renaissance Publishing House, 1986.

Balachandran, Jyoti. *Narrative Pasts: Making of a Muslim Community in Gujarat, 1400–1650*. New Delhi: Oxford University Press, 2020.

Bawa, Oudesh Rani. "The Role of Sufis and Saints in the Development of Deccani Urdu." *Deccan Studies Journal* 7, no. 2 (July–December 2009): 69–81.

Behl, Aditya. *Love's Subtle Magic: An Indian Islamic Literary Tradition, 1379–1545*. New York: Oxford University Press, 2012.

——. *Madhumalati: An Indian Sufi Romance*. New York: Oxford University Press, 2001.

Biagi, Elena, trans. *The Collection of Sufi Rules of Conduct by Abu Abd al-Rahman al-Sulami*. Cambridge: Islamic Texts Society, 2010.

Bigelow, Anna, ed. *Islam through Objects*. London: Bloomsbury Academic, forthcoming.

Blake, Stephen. *Time in Early Modern Islam: Calendar, Ceremony and Chronology in the Safavid, Mughal, and Ottoman Empires*. New York: Cambridge University Press, 2013.

Blecher, Joel. *Said the Prophet of God: Hadith Commentary across a Millennium*. Berkeley: University of California Press, 2017.

Brown, Jonathan. *Hadith: Muhammad's Legacy in the Medieval and Modern World*. Oxford: Oneworld, 2009.

Buehler, Arthur. *Sufi Heirs of the Prophet: The Indian Naqshbandiyya and the Rise of the Mediating Sufi Shaykh*. Columbia: University of South Carolina Press, 1998.

Burton-Page, John. *Indian Islamic Architecture: Forms and Typologies, Sites and Monuments*. Leiden, Neth.: Brill, 2008.

Campbell, James McNabb. *History of Gujarât: Gazetteer of the Bombay Presidency*. Bombay: Government Printing House, 1896.

Casale, Giancarlo. *The Ottoman Age of Exploration*. New York: Oxford University Press, 2010.

Chaube, J. *History of the Gujarat Kingdom, 1458–1537*. New Delhi: Munshiram Manoharlal, 1973.

Colby, Fredrick. *Narrating Muhammad's Night Journey: Tracing the Development of the Ibn ʿAbbas Ascension Discourse*. Binghamton: SUNY Press, 2008.

Commissariat, Manekshah Sorabshah. *History of Gujarat Including a Survey of Its Chief Architectural Monuments*. Vol. 1. Bombay: Longmans, Green and Company, 1938.

Currim, Mumtaz, and George Michell, eds. *Dargahs, Abodes of the Saints*. Delhi: Marg Publications, 2004.

Dallal, Ahmad. *Islam without Europe: Traditions of Reform in Eighteenth-Century Islamic Thought*. Chapel Hill: University of North Carolina Press, 2018.

Danner, Victor, trans. *The Book of Wisdom: Ibn ʿAtaʾallah*. New York: Paulist Press, 1978.

Dockrat, Mohammed Ashraf Ebrahim. *Between Orthodoxy and Mysticism: The Life and Works of Shaykh Muhammad ibn Tahir Fattani*. PhD diss., University of South Africa, 2002.

Eaton, Richard. *Social History of the Deccan, 1300–1761: Eight Indian Lives*. New York: Cambridge University Press, 2005.

——, ed. *India's Islamic Traditions, 711–1750*. New Delhi: Oxford University Press, 2003.

Elger, Ralf, and Yavuz Köse, eds. *Many Ways of Speaking about the Self: Middle Eastern Ego-Documents in Arabic, Persian, Turkish (14th–20th Century)*. Wiesbaden: Harrassowitz Verlag, 2010.

Ernst, Carl. *Eternal Garden: Mysticism, History, and Politics in a South Asian Sufi Center*. Albany: SUNY Press, 1992.

———. *Introduction to Sufism*. Boston: Shambala Publications, 1997.

———. *Refractions of Islam in India: Situating Sufism and Yoga*. Los Angeles: Sage, 2016.

Ernst, Carl, and Bruce Lawrence. *Sufi Martyrs of Love: The Chishti Order in South Asia and Beyond*. New York: Palgrave Press, 2002.

Farishta, Muhammad Qasim. *History of the Rise of the Mohammadan Power in India till the Year 1612*. Translated by John Briggs. New Delhi: Adam Publishers, 2006.

Faruqi, Lois Ibsen. "Music, Musicians and Muslim Law." *Asian Music* 10, no. 2 (1985): 3–36.

Findly, Ellison. *Nur Jahan: Empress of India*. New Delhi: Oxford University Press, 1993.

Fleischer, Cornell. "Mediterranean Apocalypse: Prophecies of Empire in the Fifteenth and Sixteenth Centuries." *Journal of the Economic and Social History of the Orient* 61 (2018): 18–90.

Friedmann, Yohanan. *Shaykh Aḥmad Sirhindi: An Outline of His Thought and a Study of His Image in the Eyes of Posterity.* Montreal: McGill University Press, 1971.

Gandhi, Supriya. *The Emperor Who Never Was: Dara Shukoh in Mughal India.* Cambridge, Mass.: Harvard University Press, 2020.

Geoffroy, Eric, ed. *La Voie Soufie des Shadhilis.* Paris: Maisonneuve and Larose, 2005.

Green, Nile. *Bombay Islam: The Religious Economy of the West Indian Ocean, 1840–1915.* New York: Cambridge University Press, 2011.

Gujarātī, Muṣṭafā. *Majālis-e Khamsa: Five Sessions of Emperor Akbar's Court.* Translated by Sayyid Ḍiyā'allāh. Chanchalguda, Hyderabad Deccan: Idāra-ye Shamsiyya, 1997.

Hanif, N. *Islamic Concept of Crime and Justice.* Vol. 2. New Delhi: Sarup and Sons, 1999.

Hermansen, Marcia, trans. *The Conclusive Argument from God: Shah Wali Allah's Hujjat Allah al-Baligha.* Leiden, Neth.: Brill, 1996.

Ho, Engseng. *The Graves of Tarim: Genealogy and Mobility across the Indian Ocean.* Berkeley: University of California Press, 2006.

Hodgson, Marshall G. S. *The Venture of Islam: Conscience and History in a World Civilization.* 3 vols. Chicago: University of Chicago Press, 1958.

Homerin, Th. Emil. *Aisha al-Baʿuniyya: A Life in Praise of Love.* Oxford: Oneworld Publications, 2019.

Huda, Qamarul. *Striving for Divine Union: Spiritual Exercises for Suhrawardi Sufis.* London: RoutledgeCurzon, 2003.

Ishaq, Muhammad. *India's Contribution to the Study of Hadith Literature.* Dacca, Bangladesh: University of Dacca, 1955.

Israel, Milton, and N. K. Wagle, eds. *Islamic Society and Culture: Essays in Honor of Professor Aziz Ahmad.* New Delhi: Manohar, 1983.

Jahangir. *Tuzuk-e Jahangiri.* Translated by Alexander Rogers. Delhi: Low Price Publications, 1989.

Johns, Anthony. *The Gift Addressed to the Spirit of the Prophet.* Canberra: Australian National University Press, 1965.

Kamali, Mohammad Hashim. *Principles of Islamic Jurisprudence.* Cambridge: Islamic Texts Society, 2000.

Karamustafa, Ahmet. *Sufism: The Formative Period.* Berkeley: University of California Press, 2007.

Khushaim, ʿAli Fahmi. *Zarruq the Sufi.* Tripoli, Libya: General Company for Publication, 1976.

Knight, Michael Muhammad. *Muhammad's Body: Baraka Networks and the Prophetic Assemblage.* Chapel Hill: University of North Carolina Press, 2020.

Knysh, Alexander D. *Ibn ʿArabi in the Later Islamic Tradition: The Making of a Polemical Image in Medieval Islam.* Albany: SUNY Press, 1999.

Kugle, Scott. "The Accidental Revivalist: Abd al-Haqq Muhaddith Dihlawi's Search for Islamic Knowledge and Power between Mecca and Delhi." *Journal of Islamic Studies* (Oxford Center for Islamic Studies) 19, no. 2 (2008): 196–246.

———. *The Book of Illumination: English Translation of "Kitab al-Tanwir fi Isqat al-Tadbir" by Shaykh Ibn ʿAta'allah al-Iskandari.* Louisville: Fons Vitae Press, 2005.

———. "Burhan al-Din Gharib: Enduring Sufi Example in the Eternal Garden of Khuldabad." *Deccan Studies* 7, no. 2 (2009): 82–111.

——. "Death before Death: Ahmad Zarruq's Critique of Spiritual Authority in Sufism." *Journal for Islamic Studies* (University of Cape Town) 26 (2006): 113–55.

——. "Heaven's Witness: The Uses and Abuses of Muhammad Ghawth Gwaliori's Ascension." *Journal of Islamic Studies* (Oxford Center for Islamic Studies) 14, no. 1 (2003): 1–36.

———. *Rebel between Spirit and Law: Ahmad Zarruq, Sainthood, and Authority in Islam.* Bloomington: Indian University Press, 2006.

——. *Sufis and Saints' Bodies: Mysticism, Corporeality, and Sacred Power in Islam.* Chapel Hill: University of North Carolina Press, 2007.

——. *When Sun Meets Moon: Gender, Eros, and Ecstasy in Urdu Poetry.* Chapel Hill: University of North Carolina Press, 2016.

Lambah, Abha Narain, and Alka Patel, eds. *Architecture of the Indian Sultanates.* Delhi: Marg Publications, 2006.

Lawrence, Bruce. "Early Indo-Muslim Saints and Conversion." In *Islam in Asia*, edited by Yohanan Friedmann and Raphael Israel, 109–45. Boulder, Colo.: Westview, 1984.

——, trans. *Morals for the Heart: Conversations of Nizam Ad-Din Awliya.* New York: Paulist Press, 1992.

——, ed. *The Rose and the Rock: Mystical and Rational Elements in the Intellectual History of South Asian Islam.* Durham: Duke University Program in Comparative Area Studies, 1979.

Lawrence, Bruce, and David Gilmartin, eds. *Beyond Turk and Hindu: Rethinking Religious Identities in Islamicate South Asia.* Gainesville: University Press of Florida, 2000.

Lindquist, Steven, ed. *Religion and Identity in South Asia and Beyond: Essays in Honor of Patrick Olivelle.* London: Anthem Press, 2011.

Maʿbarī, Zayn al-Dīn. *Tuḥfat al-Mujāhidīn: A Historical Epic of the Sixteenth Century.* 2nd ed. Translated by S. Muhammad Husayn Nainar. Kuala Lumpur: Islamic Book Trust, 2009.

Mayeur-Jaouen, Catherine, ed. *Adab and Modernity: A "Civilising" Process?* Leiden, Neth.: Brill, 2020.

Meisami, Julie Scott, trans. *The Sea of Precious Virtues "Bahr al-Fava'id": A Medieval Islamic Mirror for Princes.* Salt Lake City: University of Utah Press, 1991.

Meri, Josef, ed. *Medieval Islamic Civilization: An Encyclopedia.* Vol. 2. New York: Routledge, 2005.

Metcalf, Barbara Daily. *Moral Conduct and Authority: The Place of Adab in South Asian Islam.* Berkeley: University of California Press, 1984.

——. *Perfecting Women: Maulana Ashraf ʿAli Thanawi's "Bihishti Zewar," a Partial Translation with Commentary.* Boulder, Colo.: NetLibrary, 1990.

Moin, A. Azfar. *The Millennial Sovereign: Sacred Kingship and Sainthood in Islam.* New York: Columbia University Press, 2012.

Mojaddedi, Jawid, trans. *Rumi: The Masnavi, Book One.* Oxford: Oxford University Press, 2004.

Nicholson, Reynold, trans. *The Kitab al-Lumaʿ fīʾl-Taswwuf of Abu Nasr al-Sarraj.* Leiden, Neth.: Brill, 1914.

Nizami, Khaliq Ahmad. *Akbar and Religion.* Delhi: Idara-ye Adabiyat-e Delli, 1989.

Özbaran, Salih. *Ottoman Response to Portuguese Expansion.* Istanbul: Thelsis Press, 1994.

Pearson, Michael N. *The Indian Ocean*. New York: Routledge, 2001.
——. *Pious Passengers: The Hajj in Earlier Times*. New Delhi: Sterling Publishers, 1994.
Pollock, Sheldon, ed. *Literary Cultures in History: Reconstructions from South Asia*. Berkeley: University of California Press, 2003.
Qadri, Fozail Ahmad. "Mughal Relations with the Shattari Sufis: Abu'l-Fadl's treatment of Shaykh Muhammad Ghauth Gwaliori." *Islamic Culture* 72, no. 2 (April 1999): 79–114.
Qamaruddin. *The Mahdawi Movement in India*. Delhi: Idara-ye Adabiyat-e Delli, 1985.
Riddell, Peter. *Islam and the Malay-Indonesian World: Transmission and Responses*. London: Hurst and Company, 2001.
Rizvi, S. A. A. *History of Sufism in India*. 2 vols. Delhi: Munshiram Manoharlal, 1989.
——. *Muslim Revivalist Movements in Northern India in the Sixteenth and Seventeenth Centuries*. Lucknow: Balkrishna Book Company, 1965.
Schimmel, Annemarie. *And Muhammad Is His Messenger: The Veneration of the Prophet in Islamic Piety*. Chapel Hill: University of North Carolina Press, 1985.
——. *Mystical Dimensions of Islam*. Chapel Hill: University of North Carolina Press, 1975.
Shaikh, Saʿdiyya. *Sufi Narratives of Intimacy: Ibn ʿArabī, Gender, and Sexuality*. Chapel Hill: University of North Carolina Press, 2014.
Shaw, Marvin. *The Paradox of Intention: Reaching the Goal by Giving Up the Attempt to Reach It*. Atlanta: Scholars Press, 1988.
Sheikh, Samira. *Forging a Region: Sultans, Traders, and Pilgrims in Gujarat, 1200–1500*. Oxford: Oxford University Press, 2010.
Siddiqi, Muhammad Suleman. *The Bahmani Sufis*. Delhi: Idara-ye Adabiyat-e Delli, 1989.
——. *The Junaydi Sufis of the Deccan*. Delhi: Primus Books, 2014.
Steinfels, Amina. *Knowledge before Action: Islamic Learning and Sufi Practice in the Life of Sayyid Jalal al-Din Bukhari Makhdum-e Jahaniyan*. Columbia: University of South Carolina Press, 2012.
Wasserstein, David, and Ami Ayalon, eds. *Mamluks and Ottomans: Studies in Honor of Michael Winter*. London: Routledge, 2006.
Winter, Michael. *Society and Religion in Early Ottoman Egypt: Studies in the Writings of al-Shaʿrani*. New Brunswick: Transaction, 1982.
Zargar, Cyrus. "The Ten Principles: Theoretical Implications of Volitional Death in Najm al-Din Kubra's 'al-Usul al-ʿAshara.'" *Muslim World* 103 (2013): 107–30.

INDEX

Abbasid dynasty, 21
ʿAbd al-Ḥaqq Muḥaddith Dihlawī (d. 1642), 1–5; attachment to Qadir Order, 34, 93–94, 193–94, 198, 200, 202, 210, 215–16, 224–25; attachment to Naqshbandi Order, 209–11, 228–37, 238; autobiography of, 194, 195, 197; as biographer, 10, 35, 48, 58, 85, 119, 135, 176, 178, 182–83, 216; critique of Ahmad Sirhindi, 226, 228–35; as disciple of ʿAbd al-Wahhab Muttaqi, 200–203, 211; exile from Delhi, 224–26; in Gujarat, 198–99; hadith scholarship of, 200–201, 204, 208, 217–18, 220, 221, 224, 238; interactions with Jahangir's court, 211–13, 214–16, 217–24; letters of, 195, 203, 208–9, 211–13, 217, 226, 228–35; pilgrimage of, 192–93, 197, 199–200, 220; position at Akbar's court, 194–97, 203; reform of Sufism, 5, 8, 89, 94, 192, 196, 198–99, 204–11, 223, 228–35; relation to Ahmad Zarruq, 205–9, 212, 240; return to Delhi, 175–77, 192, 199, 200, 202, 203. *See also* Nūr al-Ḥaqq; Sufi hospice: of ʿAbd al-Haqq Muhaddith Dihlawi
ʿAbd al-Karīm al-Jīlī (d. 1403), 94, 203
ʿAbdallāh Anṣārī, 75
ʿAbdallāh ʿAydarusī, Sayyid, 268n16
ʿAbdallāh Sulṭānpūrī, 266n137
ʿAbd al-Qādir ʿAydarūsī (also known as Abū Bakr Muḥyī al-Dīn), 57, 268n22
ʿAbd al-Qādir Badāʾūnī (Mughal historian, d. 1605), 26, 165, 194, 196
ʿAbd al-Qādir al-Fākihī, 180, 183
ʿAbd al-Qādir Jīlānī (d. 1166), 4, 93, 95, 193, 200–203, 210, 215–16, 244, 252n59; conception of self-will, 33–34; tomb of, 175, 203. *See also* Qadiri Order
ʿAbd al-Raḥīm Khān-e Khānān (Mughal noble, d. 1627), 188
ʿAbd al-Wahhāb Muttaqī (d. 1593), 8, 91, 174–79, 209, 257n23; advocacy of moderation, 93–94, 202, 257n13, 257n15, 270n65; biographic sources, 10, 85, 176, 216, 251n38, 257n18; conception of *dhikr*, 30, 71; conflict with Mahdawi movement, 186, 192; giving initiation in the triple tariqa, 71, 93–94, 202, 245; reform of Sufism, 71–73, 88–89, 92–94, 127, 182, 196, 199–204, 210–11, 258n30; self-abnegation, 91–92, 200, 257n22; as successor to ʿAli Muttaqi, 71, 91, 127, 183, 192, 254n24, 258n29
Abū Bakr al-Ṣiddīq (first successor to Prophet Muhammad, d. 634), 185, 244, 268n16
Abū Ḥanīfa (jurist, d. 767), 201. *See also* Hanafi school of law
Abūʾl-ʿAbbās al-Mursī (d. 1287), 92, 245, 257n22
Abūʾl-Faḍl (d. 1602, Mughal noble), 187, 194, 212, 266n137, 269n36
Abūʾl-Fatḥ Sarmast (d. 1538), 122
Abūʾl-Ḥasan al-Shādhilī (d. 1258), 33, 92, 169, 245, 252n59. *See also* Shadhili Order
Abū Madyan Shuʿayb (d. 1198), 42, 245. *See also* Madyani Order
Abū Naṣr al-Sarrāj (d. 988), 125–26
adab, 5, 10, 13, 17, 21–22, 35, 117, 126, 213, 217, 219, 223, 232, 240–24. *See also* court: manners of; literature; Sufi discipline
Aden, 1, 52, 112, 268n16
advice (*naṣīḥ*), 10, 45, 63–65, 78, 108, 111, 189–90, 197, 208–9, 228, 266n142; in "mirror for princes" literature, 10, 99–102, 186, 217–24, 271n10
Afghanistan, 16, 28, 140
Afghans, 49, 53–54, 78, 122–23, 190, 263n71, 265n123. *See also* Lōdī dynasty

Agra, 172, 188, 190, 194, 203–4, 259n63, 269n42
Ahl-e Hadith, 241
Aḥmad. *See* Muhammad the Prophet: eternal presence of
Aḥmad ibn ʿUqbā al-Ḥaḍramī, 58–59, 64, 210, 245
Aḥmad Khattū (d. 1475), 42
Aḥmad Shāh I (second Sultan of Gujarat, d. 1442), 40, 41–42, 51, 243, 252n76, 267n149
Aḥmad Shāh II (fourth Sultan of Gujarat, d. 1458), 243
Aḥmad Shāh III (ninth Sultan of Gujarat, d. 1561), 243
Aḥmad Sirhindī (d. 1624), 10, 192, 216, 224–27, 240
Aḥmad Zarrūq (d. 1494), 58–59, 74–75, 87, 94, 151, 237, 240, 244–45, 254n23; epistle on death of self-will, 63–66; principles of being a Sufi, 68–71, 205, 207–12, 259n50, 270n79; grandmother of, 96, 104
Ahmedabad (Aḥmadābād), 11, 18, 42; map of, 40
Ahmednagar (Aḥmadnagar), 18, 53, 263n71; Niẓām Shāh ruler of, 172
Aḥrār, Khwāja ʿUbaydallāh (d. 1490), 209–10, 244, 271n92; grandson Khwāja Nūra, 261n13
ʿĀʾisha Bāʿūniyya (d. 1517), 96
Ajmer, 16, 41, 43, 215, 268n28
Akbar (d. 1605, third Mughal emperor), 136, 177, 187–96, 204, 211, 219–20, 259n63; conquest of Gujarat, 187, 243; decree of (*maḥḍar*), 191, 258n43, 269n39; interest in Mahdawi movement, 144, 187, 212, 262n56; interest in Nuqtawi movement, 266n140; religious ideology of, 190, 192, 196, 210, 212, 217–18, 268n28, 269n36
Akbar Nama, 55, 81
Akhbār al-Akhyār, 215–16
ʿAlāʾī, Shaykh, 262n5
alchemy, 64, 66, 92, 257n23; aromatic roots of (*ʿaqāqīr*), 77
ʿAlī ibn Abī Ṭālib (d. 661), 169, 245, 260n69, 271n97
ʿAlī Mahīmī (d. 1431), 51
ʿAlī Muttaqī (known by his full name as ʿAlī ibn Ḥusām al-Dīn ibn ʿAbd al-Mālik ibn Qāḍī Khān al-Hindī al-Muttaqī [d. 1567]), xvii, 5–11, 250n16; assessment of Mughals, 49, 258n43; assessment of Portuguese, 78–80; biographic sources, 48, 57, 135, 145, 176, 182–83, 192, 216, 251n38, 259n66, 267n9; critique of sainthood, 102–9; as "Enforcer of the Shariʿa," 118–19, 134, 154, 167–71; experiments with death, 32–35, 48, 63–67; final illness, 178–83; hadith scholarship, 56–57, 59, 61, 62, 74, 106–7, 148–50, 153–54, 156–60, 167, 183–84, 237–41, 254n24, 253n42, 264n94, 265n119; honorific name, 35–36, 91; ideal of scholar-saint, 59–60, 77–78, 94, 109, 119, 166–67; initiation in triple tariqa, 58–59, 86–87, 94, 244–45; opposition to Mahdawi movement, 26, 137, 140–41, 145–55, 158–67, 184–85, 231, 264n97; persecution of Muhammad Ghawth Gwaliori, 123–37, 162–67, 231, 237; reform of Sufism, 37–38, 62–78, 86–91, 94–102, 235, 237; rejection of existential philosophy, 89–91, 257n16; rejection of music, 87–89, 256n6; relation to Ahmad Zarruq, 59, 68–71, 74–75, 151, 210–12; relation to sultan of Gujarat, 43–45, 47–48, 49–54, 78–79, 83–86, 99–102, 109–14, 135, 154–55, 167–72, 177–78, 187, 190, 258n40, 260n74, 260n75, 265n109, 266n141; search for Sufi master, 24–25, 27–29, 31–32, 251n39; wisdom sayings, 74–77; youth, 14–17, 22–26, 27. *See also* Sufi hospice: of ʿAli Muttaqi; tomb-shrine: of ʿAli Muttaqi
Anas ibn Mālik (d. 712), 68
ancestors (*salaf*), 69, 223
aphorisms. *See* wisdom sayings
apocalypse (End of Time), 8–9, 26, 137–38, 146–50, 180, 185; hadith about, 9, 25, 142, 259n49, 264n87, 264n94, 264n100
Arabian Sea, 4, 7, 41–42, 46–47, 112–13, 256n76, 270n57

Arabic language, xi–xii, 10, 14, 20–21, 64, 74–75, 118–19, 156, 164, 194, 204–5, 208
architecture, xv, 7, 21, 29, 39, 60, 152–53; in Gujarat, 140, 191; in Mandu, 120; in Mughal empire, 203, 223, 261n6
army, 55, 99–101, 113, 203; of prayer, 115; salary of, 101, 223
Aṣaf Khān (prime minister of Gujarat), 45–47, 54, 79, 83, 99, 113, 171–72, 180, 253n93, 256n77, 258n40; murder of, 172, 267n148
ascension (*miʿrāj*), 126, 266n140; of Prophet Muhammad, 122–24, 149; of Muhammad Ghawth, 122–27, 129, 131–35, 164–65, 189, 191, 261n9; of saints, 77, 164, 231
asceticism (*zuhd*), 95, 101, 104, 125, 128, 132–33, 162, 166, 178, 237, 254n33, 262n49; and yoga, 121
Asīrgaṙh fortress, 18, 250n15
astrology, 10, 121, 127, 166; comets in, 263n59
authenticity (*aṣāla*), 69, 107, 109, 127, 153, 157, 178, 205; in sainthood, 82, 95, 98–102, 103–9, 128–29, 182, 189, 237, 266n137. *See also* saints: authenticity of
authority, 15, 24–25, 54, 73, 86–87, 97–98, 110–11, 117, 144, 153, 156–59, 209, 222–23, 234, 254n24; of Muhammad, 33, 90, 166–67; of rulers, 99–102, 136, 141, 154, 190–91, 196, 212, 218–19, 222, 224, 226, 258n41, 269n39; of saints, 18, 27, 34–36, 48, 59–62, 71, 91, 101–3, 119, 123–25, 139, 165–66, 206, 226, 228, 232, 237, 259n50; transcendent, 137–39, 163–67, 181, 187

Bābur (first Mughal emperor, d. 1530), 28, 43, 49, 53, 122, 136, 209, 259n60
backsliding (*istidrāj*), 104, 127–28
Bahāʾ al-Dīn Naqshband (d. 1398), 209, 244. *See also* Naqshbandi Order
Bahāʾ al-Dīn Zakariyā (d. 1262), 29, 252n74
Bahādur Shāh (seventh Sultan of Gujarat, d. 1537); 43–45, 47–55, 78–83, 102, 109, 113, 143–44, 243, 252n84, 253nn85–86, 253n2, 256n73, 256n76, 259nn60–61, 259n66; brother Chānd Khān, 253n2; brother Laṭīf, 43, 243; brother Sikandar, 43, 253n85
Bahlūl, Shaykh (also known as Shaykh Pĥūl, d. 1538), 122, 136, 261n11
Bahmani sultanate, 39, 42, 51, 259n63
Bājan. *See* Shāh Bājan, Bahāʾ al-Dīn
al-Bakrī, Abūʾl-Ḥasan (d. 1546), 56–59, 159, 180–82, 184, 254n23
al-Bakrī, Muḥammad Abū al-Makārim (d. 1585), 56, 58, 181, 254n32
Balachandran, Jyoti, 7
Bāqī Biʾllāh, Khwāja Muḥammad (d. 1603), 209–11, 226–31, 233, 236, 244, 270n67, 271n92; son Khwāja Khurd, 240
bathing, 38, 44, 65; for ritual ablution, 110–11, 180
Bāyazīd Bisṭāmī (d. 874), 33, 137, 229
Bayrām Khān (Mughal general, d. 1561), 188, 190
Behl, Aditya, 135, 137
Bektāshī Order, 98
Bharōch, 18, 44, 132, 134, 143, 252n75, 254n20, 260n77, 270n58. *See also* ports: in Gujarat
Bidar, 18, 258n29, 259n63
Bihār, 54, 78, 121–22, 167, 257n13
Bijapur, 18, 51, 78–79
biography, 5, 10, 48, 57, 58, 74, 93, 135, 182–83, 192, 236, 251n38; as memorial genre (*tadhkira*), 119, 176, 189, 198, 216, 225, 235, 267n5; of Prophet Muhammad, 4, 149
blessing, 17, 24, 34, 39, 49, 60–61, 63, 73, 92–93, 106, 111, 171, 190, 199, 216, 231, 260n69, 271n89; political efficacy of, 41–43, 117, 122, 169–71, 215, 220
blood, 85, 100, 111, 140
body, 4, 5, 14, 20, 34, 65–66, 211, 219, 236; of ruler, 203. *See also* blood; heart; Muḥammad the Prophet: body of
Bohras, 183, 185, 268n15, 268n22, 268n32
Bukhārā, 16, 209
Bukhārī, Shaykh Farīd (Mughal noble also known as Murtaḍā Khān, d. 1615), 211, 213, 217, 220, 222, 234
Bukhari sayyids, 42, 172, 252n77, 253n85

Burhān al-Dīn Gharīb (d. 1337), 13, 16–17, 250n15
Burhān al-Dīn Sharrābī (d. 1554), 172, 267n148
Burhānpūr, xviii, 1, 14–15, 17–19, 17, 22–24, 36, 61, 88, 91, 109, 140, 237–39, 250n15, 250n34, 256n9

Calicut (Kozhīkōde), 79–80. *See also* Malabar
Cambay (Kħambħāt or Kambaya), 18, 47, 78, 117, 155, 187, 252n75, 259n62; gulf of, 18, 41
caste, 87, 265n123, 267n148. *See also* Bohras; Hindus
caution (*wara*ʿ), 28, 31–32, 34, 45, 70, 108, 208, 258n30
Central Asia, 6, 16, 49, 120, 122, 136, 209; Afghanistan, 16, 28, 140; Uzbekistan, 16, 42
Champaner, 18, 42, 47, 53–55, 79, 243, 259n62, 261n18
charisma, 26, 59, 86, 97, 137, 225–26, 235; of Mahdi, 26, 139; of Muhammad, 10
charity, 37, 95, 152, 223, 260n1; education as, 60; in hadith, 177
Chaul (Chawl), 51–52
Chishti Order, xvii, 16–27, 31, 38, 59, 61, 100, 128, 136–37, 178–79, 183, 190–91, 209, 228, 232, 245, 271n89; early masters in (*Khwājagān*), 16–17, 215–16; in Sultanate of Gujarat, 18–20, 42, 145, 252n77; relation to Mahdawi movement, 27, 100, 139–40, 165, 263n57; use of music in, 12–15, 88
Chittor (Chittōrgāṙħ), 18, 49, 256n73
civil discord (*fitna*), 105, 124–27, 140–41, 143, 172; as moral corruption, 161–62, 168
coffee, 57, 254n30
court, 23, 56, 101, 107, 113–19, 139, 154, 167–71, 186; histories composed at, 136; manners of (*ādāb*), 21–22, 214, 217, 223, 234; of God, 232; of Mughals, 122, 144, 187, 190–98, 201, 203–4, 214–17, 220–21, 224–26, 269n40, 269n46, 269n51; scholars of, 42, 144, 190–91, 212, 266n137, 268n28
critique, 6, 141, 163, 166–67, 212, 241; by Sufis of other Sufis, 10, 29–30, 34, 88, 102–8, 119–20, 189, 210, 226–28, 237–38, 258n29; in hadith studies, 66–67; of Shattari Order, 123–37, 164–67, 178, 231; of Mahdawi movement, 146–62, 164–67, 179, 183–85, 231, 264n97, 268n21, 268n32

Dabul, 51–52
Dāniyāl Chishtī, 267n57
Dārā Shikōh (Mughal prince, d. 1659), 4, 225, 270n74, 272n13
dargah. *See* tomb-shrine
Daulatabad (Dawlatābād), 17, 24. *See also* Khandesh
death, 59, 64, 76, 87–88, 98, 104–5, 180–83, 210–12; by martyrdom, 60, 80–81, 83, 98, 136, 143; penalty of, 51, 110, 140, 143, 147, 154–56, 161, 186, 189, 229; of self-will, 27–28, 32–37, 63–66, 69, 71, 75–77, 99, 104, 210, 251n39, 252n59; by suicide, 134
Deccan, 7, 14–18, 24, 91, 167, 178, 232, 253n87; kingdoms of, 23, 39, 42, 51, 53, 56, 78, 172, 263n71; Mughals in, 224, 239; plateau of, 15; Shiʿism in, 100
Delhi, 2, 4, 8, 16–17, 27, 39–43, 46–47, 49, 54, 78, 89, 121, 122, 172, 177, 192–95, 198, 199, 200, 203–4, 209–11, 216, 220, 224–26, 236, 238, 269n40, 270n67
Delhi sultanate, 16–17, 22, 23, 27, 41–43, 56, 122, 203, 218, 243, 250n31. *See also* Lōdī dynasty; Sūrī dynasty; Tughlaq dynasty
Deoband, 240–41, 252n68
dhikr. *See* meditation: as repetition of God's names
Dilāwar, Shāh (d. 1538), 141, 144, 156, 265n110
Diu, 18, 46–49, 52–54, 78–80, 112, 154, 243, 252n75, 253n9, 259n66, 260n77
dreams. *See* sleep: dreams during
drowning, 2–3, 4, 12–13, 20, 61
drums, 12–13, 20, 116

East Africa, 52, 98; Ethiopians from, 54; Somali ports in, 52

ecstasy (*wajd*), 15, 17–18, 22–23. 26, 39, 64, 88, 105, 137, 178, 182, 193, 203, 237; absorption in (*istighrāq*), 105, 178–79; bliss, 15, 199; boasts uttered in (*shaṭḥiyāt*), 123, 229, 267n10; drunken (*sukr*), 203, 229; Sufi characterized by (*majdhūb*), 209. *See also* insanity
egoism, 31, 34, 35, 66, 102, 128, 130, 206. *See also* death: of self-will
Egypt, 33, 52–53, 59, 253n9, 267n5; Al-Azhar University, 254n23; hadith scholars from, 42, 56, 58, 146, 201, 254n23. *See also* Mamlūk dynasty
elephant, 154, 155
emanation, 90, 94, 272n31
Enforcer of the Shariʿa (*ḥākim al-sharʿ*), 114, 118, 120, 131, 134, 154, 167, 260n79
equality, 16, 56, 229–35
essence (*dhāt* or *jawhar*), 68, 70, 91, 130–31, 179, 227, 230–31, 257n22; as meaning (*maʿnā*), 204; of Sufism, 60, 66–69, 88. *See also* God; essence of
ethics (*akhlāq*), 5–7, 10, 16, 20–25, 28, 58, 67, 74, 99, 106, 127–31, 141, 189, 220–24, 240, 257n19
eunuch, 144; as false man (*nā mard*), 145
exile, 5–7, 16, 35, 48–49, 54, 78, 80, 83, 86, 92, 109, 113, 123, 154, 220, 224, 237, 239; of Humayun, 143, 172, 190; of Muhammad Ghawth, 191
existence (*wujūd*), 89, 104, 171, 218–19, 231; existential philosophy (*wujūdiyya*), 62, 87–94, 121, 129–32, 166, 198–99, 203, 256n16; existential unity (*waḥdat al-wujūd*), 129–31, 179, 203, 208, 229. *See also* emanation

faith (*īmān*), 20, 27, 29–31, 48, 130, 141, 158, 207, 257n13; eclipse of, Islamic attestation of (*kalima*), 138, 147, 189
Fārūqī dynasty, 17, 109, 253n2, 259n61; Nāṣir Khān Fārūqī (second king, d. 1437), 250n15; Mīrān ʿĀdil Khān II (fifth king, d. 1503), 17
Fatehpur Sikri, 136, 194, 197, 203, 259n63; religious debates at (*ʿibādat-khāna*), 144, 194, 196, 268n28
fatwa, 57, 96, 140, 146–48, 156, 161–62, 189, 235, 264n87, 264n90, 265n126; inquiry for (*istiftāʾ*), 146
Fayḍī (Mughal noble and poet, d. 1595), 187, 194, 212, 266n137, 269n36
Firozabad, 259n63
Fleisher, Cornell, 8–9
food, 24, 28, 44, 70, 134, 178, 251n43, 257n7; minimal intake of, 27, 31, 32
Freud, Sigmund, 178
Fuḍayl ibn ʿIyāḍ (d. 803), 183

gender, 96–98, 144–45, 162–63. *See* men; women
Ghawthī Shaṭṭārī, Muḥammad (d. 1562), 189, 198, 236–37, 259n66
Ghiyāth al-Dīn Khiljī. *See* Malwa
greed, 38, 53, 117, 168, 172, 200
God: essence of (Ar. *dhāt*; Gj. *param*), 179, 230–31; intimacy with (*qurb*), 6, 37–38, 104, 127, 132, 134, 150, 163–65, 167; invoking names of (*daʿwat-e asmāʾ*), 122, 127; names of, 130, 188; throne of, 2, 122, 124–27, 164–65, 232
Gujarat, 5, 7–9, 18, 24–27, 32, 35–39, 41–45, 46–54, 56, 78–82, 86–87, 91, 103, 108–14, 119–20, 123, 127, 135–37, 139–46, 153–55, 162, 167, 169–72, 176–78, 183–92, 197–98, 232, 237–39, 243, 252n74, 258n45, 259n60, 259n66, 263n71, 267n149; coast of, 1, 7–9, 15, 27, 46, 51–52, 78–79, 198, 259n66; manuscripts in, 63, 118–19, 260n1; Saurashtra region in, 266n77. *See also* Muẓaffar-Shāhī dynasty; ports: in Gujarat
Gujari. *See* Urdu
Gulbadan Begum (Mughal princess, d. 1603), 136

ḥadīth, 4–8, 54–62, 146–62, 166–67, 183–85, 189–92, 198–201, 217–21, 240–41; with authentic narration (*ṣaḥīḥ*), 146–47, 157, 160, 233; chain of transmission of (*isnād*) 107, 151, 175, 221; with single narrator (*āḥād*), 153; collections of, 4, 31, 43, 57, 70, 148–49, 151, 159–60, 175, 178, 200, 204, 224, 238, 254n20, 265n119; confirmed by multiple narrators (*mutawātir*), 147, 156;

ḥadīth (*continued*)
contradiction between multiple reports, 149, 156–57; critique of narrators of (*jarḥ wa taʿdīl*), 106–7, 156, 233; with divine origin (*qudsī*), 227; as false (*mawḍūʿ*), 157, 160, 184–85, 264n87, 268n19; fusion with Sufism, 5–6, 8–10, 30, 59–78, 86, 94, 95, 106, 113–14, 153, 165, 184, 203, 207–8, 237–40; recording of, 201, 237, 255n42; Sufis as scholars of, 14, 16, 18, 43, 90, 124–25, 131–32, 156, 192, 198, 209, 237, 249n10; in wisdom sayings, 64–65, 75–76. *See also* legal reasoning
Hafiz Shirazi (Sufi poet, d. 1390), 13, 249n2
Hajj. *See* pilgrimage
Ḥallāj (d. 922), 229, 267n10
Ḥamīd Ẓuhūr al-Ḥaqq, Ḥājjī, 136–37, 261n11
Hanafi school of law, 148, 201–2, 209, 262n55, 264n89, 268n15, 270n66; *Hidāya* as authoritative text of, 209, 270n65
Hanbali school of law, 148, 264n89, 270n66
Ḥasan Baṣrī (d. 728), 260n69
Ḥasan ibn ʿAlī (grandson of Prophet Muhammad, d. 670), 215
Ḥasan Muḥammad Chishtī, 140
heart, xvii, 20, 35–36, 60, 92, 97, 128, 175–76, 181, 193–97, 200, 209, 230, 241; hardening of, 128, 197; as locus of piety, 1, 5–6, 31, 150, 184; purity of, 13, 16, 36–38, 65, 85, 104, 206–7, 211; of saints, 77; as subtle energy (*laṭīfa*), 212, 266n130; vision of, 126
heresy, 119, 129, 157, 164–65, 171, 188, 195–96, 266n137; accusation of against Mahdawis, 140, 142, 147, 150, 152, 161–63, 186–88, 268n22; anathematization of (*takfīr*), 68, 208, 266n137. *See also* innovation
Hijaz, 1, 56, 200. *See also* Mecca; Medina
ḥikam. *See* wisdom sayings
Hindus, 16, 17, 24, 42, 79, 121, 133–34, 137, 212; Brahmin, 24, 116, 121; Jain, 42, 116; Rajput, 39, 53, 212
Hodgson, Marshall, 21
homosexuality, 172, 256n9, 267n148. *See also* eunuch; meditation: on human beauty
Hujwīrī, ʿAlī (d. 1072), 229
Humāyūn (second Mughal emperor, d. 1540), 122–23, 131, 136, 172, 190–91, 261nn12–13; invasion of Gujarat, 47, 49–50, 53–55, 78, 80, 184, 256n76, 259n60
Ḥusām al-Dīn Muttaqī (d. 1553), 27–32, 58, 73, 133–34, 141, 251nn42–43, 251n47, 254n33,
Ḥusayn ibn ʿAlī (d. 680), 215
hypocrite (*zindīq*), 38, 67, 98, 129, 185–86

Ibn ʿArabī (d. 1240), 89–91, 94, 96, 203, 257nn12–13, 257nn15–16, 269n33, 271n97
Ibn ʿAṭāʾallāh al-Iskandarī (d. 1310), 59, 65, 69, 74–77, 128, 241, 245. *See also* wisdom sayings
Ibn Ḥajar al-ʿAsqalānī (d. 1449); hadith commentary *Fatḥ al-Bārī*
Ibn Ḥajar al-Haythamī (d. 1566), 56, 59, 79, 146–49, 184, 254nn23–24, 264n89
Ibn Suwayda, Wajīh al-Dīn Muḥammad (hadith scholar, d. 1504), 56, 254n20, 260n79
Imam, 16, 225; as prayer leader, 84; in Shiʿism, 100, 215, 234
inerrancy (*ʿiṣma*), 141, 150, 181, 233
infidels (*kāfir*), 53, 83, 130, 142, 150–54, 171, 222; anathematization of (*takfīr*), 26, 30, 142, 146–48, 151, 160–61, 186, 189, 262n56
innovation, 57, 86, 136, 137, 191, 204–5, 259n51, 269n36; as inauthentic practices (*bidʿa*), 87, 151–53, 157, 187–88, 196; innovator (*mubtadiʿ*), 129, 152, 161. *See also* heresy
insanity, 88, 181, 195; as overpowering attraction to God (*jadhba*), 196–98
intoxication (*sukr*), 204, 212; by substances, 57, 171–72, 224; by ecstasy, 182, 189, 203, 229
Iran, 6, 16, 21, 42, 53, 123, 172, 190, 212, 244, 260n1; Shiraz, 125. *See also* Safavid dynasty
Iraq, 6; Baghdad, 94, 175, 203, 215, 218

Islamic norms (*sharīʿa*), 20–21, 26, 30, 37, 60–61, 72–73, 100, 104, 129–32, 138, 141, 147, 162–66, 187, 189–90, 194, 204–8, 212, 226; in royal court, 44, 83–86, 113–14, 115–18, 168–70, 194, 216, 217–18, 220, 260n69
isolation, 93, 104, 116, 126, 180, 194, 201, 203, 222, 251n39; as ritual retreat in Sufism (*khalwa*), 24, 29–30, 71–73, 92, 96, 101
Iʿtiād Khān (noble of Gujarat), 139, 186

Jahānārā (Mughal princess, d. 1681), 225
Jahāngīr (fourth Mughal emperor, d. 1627), 10, 204, 214–16, 217–19, 221, 223–26, 271n10; as Prince Salīm, 211, 213
Jalāl al-Dīn al-Suyūṭī (d. 1505), 56–57, 62, 146, 148–49, 159, 178, 254n24, 259n49, 264n87, 264n94, 265n119
Jalāl al-Dīn Makhdūm-e Jahāniyān (d. 1384), 41, 252n74, 252n76
Jalore (Jālōr), 143
Junayd (d. 910), 205–7, 229
jurisprudence. *See* legal reasoning
jurists, 16, 21, 44, 56–59, 61, 68–69, 87–88, 95–97, 144, 160–61, 190–91, 205–6, 235, 237, 257n12, 257n15, 261n18, 264n89; Akbar's judgment about, 196, 209, 258n43; authoritative (*mujtahid*), 157, 159, 191. *See also* legal reasoning
justice (*ʿadl*), 21–22, 24, 29, 68, 99–101, 118, 212–13, 214–15, 217–19, 221–23, 232; court of (*maḥkama*), 114; brought by the Mahdi, 158. *See also* moderation

Kaʿba, 139, 171, 180, 199; circumambulation of, 4, 54, 174; as "House of God," 170, 193; Maqām Ḥanafī at, 174, 176
Khandesh (Khāndēsh), 14, 17, 23, 49, 53, 109, 224, 243, 250n15, 253n2, 259n61, 260n1. *See also* Fārūqī dynasty
Khiḍr, 122, 139, 165
Khudāwand Khān (also known as Ṣūfī Āghā Turk, governor of Surat), 112, 260n73, 267n148
Khundamīr, Sayyid (Mahdawi leader, d. 1524), 140–43, 263n72
knowledge, i, xviii, 108, 130–32, 205; inner intuitive (*maʿrifa*), 29, 67–68,103, 193, 206–7; outer scholarly (*ʿilm*), 8, 16, 28–32, 57, 60–62, 67–68, 90–92, 126, 152, 164, 182, 204, 223; as struggle for learning (*ijtihād*), 4, 61, 74, 92, 152, 196, 218. *See also* madrasa
Konkan, 51; Goa, 18, 52, 78–79, 260n77
Kubrāwī Order, 120, 252n59

law (*qānūn*), 69, 99, 111, 116, 218
legal reasoning (*fiqh*), 201; imitative custom in (*taqlīd*), 159; role of hadith in, 241, 270n65, 270n66
letters, 88, 123, 134, 155, 162, 203, 226, 228, 235, 272n39; collection of Sufi's (*maktūbāt*), 74, 195, 204, 208–17, 222, 229, 234, 236, 269n50
literature (*adabiyāt*), 21–22, 167, 217; of Sufism, 33, 65, 107, 135
Lōdī dynasty, 41–43, 49, 53, 122–23, 203, 263n71, 265n123, 266n137; Ibrāhīm Lōdī (d. 1526), 43, 253n84; Sikandar Lōdī (d. 1517), 41
long sixteenth century, 5, 8, 10
love (*ʿishq*), xvii, 13, 70, 107–8, 170, 197, 205; erotic, 38, 61–62, 172; in poetry, 2, 13, 178–79, 181, 193; in Sufism, 15, 16, 31, 37, 74, 88–89, 120, 137, 175, 193–94, 199, 215, 228, 230–31

madrasa, 4, 8, 68, 83, 91, 113, 120, 184, 204, 209, 235, 240; at Ahmedabad, 132, 135, 261n18; at Calcutta, 119; at Deoband, 240–41; named after ʿAli Muttaqi, 238–39
Madyani Order, 58, 86, 202, 209, 245, 271n89
Maghribi Order, 42
Mahdawī movement, 10, 24–27, 100, 108, 137–39, 154, 155–62, 166–67, 177–78, 183–90, 192, 224, 226, 234, 237, 258n45, 262n55, 263n61, 263n72, 265n109, 265n123, 268n21, 269n36; Ajuman-e Mahdawiyya and, 263n68, 263n77; circles (*dāʾira*) of, 140–41, 143, 144; relations with Bohras, 268n22, 268n32; relations with Shattari Order, 119–20, 137, 162–67, 266n136

Mahdī, 8, 57, 137–55, 156–62, 185, 191; ʿAli Muttaqi's delusion of being, 179–82; living person specified as (*tashkhīṣ*), 149–50, 153–54; as related to sainthood, 138, 149–50, 165, 226, 262n56, 264n97; as related to Shiʿism, 100, 264n83; Sayyid Muhammad Jawnpūrī as, 9, 24–26, 138–41, 143, 151, 156, 158, 263n59, 265n101, 265n126. *See also* apocalypse
Mahīm, 18, 51, 252n75. *See also* Konkan
Maḥmūdābād (now Mehmedabad), 18, 40, 110, 172, 243, 259n62
Maḥmūd Bēgṛā (fifth Sultan of Gujarat, also known as Maḥmūd Shāh I, d. 1511), 40, 42, 51–52, 139, 142, 243, 258n45, 259n62, 260n79, 263n61, 263n71; sisters Rājī Murādī and Rājī Sūn, 139
Maḥmūd Shāh III (eighth Sultan of Gujarat, d. 1554), 83–86, 96, 99, 102–3, 109–14, 118, 154–55, 162, 169, 177–78, 243, 259nn62–63, 260nn74–75, 267n149; fight with Portuguese, 112–13, 260n77; murder of, 155, 171–73, 186
maktūbāt. *See* letters, collection of Sufi's
Malabar, 51–52, 79–80
malfūẓāt. *See* oral teachings
Mālik Ayāz (governor of Diu), 52–53
Mālik ibn Anas (jurist, d. 795), 208
Mālik Muḥammad Jaysī (Sufi poet, d. 1542), 165
Malwa (Mālwā), 23–24, 46–47, 49, 53–54, 120, 188, 198, 253n2; under Ghiyāth al-Dīn Khiljī (fifth sultan, d. 1500), 23; under Hōshang Shāh Ghōrī (first sultan, d. 1435), 250n31; under Nāṣir al-Dīn (sixth sultan, d. 1512), 23. *See also* Mandu
Mamluk dynasty, 52–53, 56; naval policy of, 52, 253n9
Mandsaur (Mañdsawr), 18, 54
Mandu (Māñdū), 18, 23–24, 36, 40, 47, 49, 54, 91, 120–22, 127, 140, 198, 259n66
men, 35, 53, 84, 116, 144–45, 171, 212; potency of, 144, 171, 175, 181; real men (*rijāl*), 97, 109, 144–45, 258n37, 263n74. *See also* women
Maraj al-Baḥrayn, 204, 270n75
marriage, 44, 63, 91, 96, 179; as blessed with children, 145, 194, 253n90, 267n11; as politically strategic, 49, 51, 224, 253n2; polygamous, 109, 120
martyrdom. *See* death: by martyrdom
mediator (*miyānjī*), 25, 44, 101–2, 124, 220, 227–34; intermediary (*wāsiṭa*), 228, 234
medicine, 13, 30–31, 44, 71, 91, 104, 172; abortion-inducing, 110
Medina, 2, 112, 116, 147, 174–75, 185, 197, 199, 201, 227, 268n21, 269n50, 270n58; history of, 4; origin of Sufism in, 16. *See also* tomb-shrine: of Prophet Muhammad
meditation, 26, 29, 72, 128, 269n43; as continuous in the heart, 139; musical, 16, 87–88; on human beauty (*shāhid-bāzī*), 88, 256n8; as repetition of God's names (*dhikr*), 20; silent, 74, 139
millenarianism, 136, 138, 149
millennialism, ideology of, 9, 27, 137–55, 172, 191–92, 226–27, 240, 266n140, 269n39
millennium, 25, 148, 151, 166, 183, 224, 233, 238; as "End of Time," 137–38, 146, 185; Islamic (on October 19, 1591), 8–9, 25–26, 203, 264n87
mind, 5, 20, 92, 181; peace of, 94, 197, 221; as susceptible to temptation, 85
miracles (*khawāriq al-ʿāda*), 4, 65, 95, 149; of Prophet, 122; of saints (*karamāt*), 18, 29–30, 92, 97, 104–5, 107, 127–29, 229, 259n50, 267n11
Mīrān Muḥammad Khān Fārūqī, 243, 253n2, 259n61
mirror for princes, 101, 217
Mīr Sayyid Manjhan (Sufi poet, d. after 1545), 137
Mirzā ʿAzīz Kōkā (Mughal noble, d. 1624), 187, 198
Mirzā Hindāl (Mughal prince, d. 1551), 122, 136
Mirzā Ḥusām al-Dīn, 225
Miṣrāta, 59
Miyān Ghiyāth, 44, 253n89
Miyān Mīr (d. 1635), 224–25

Miyān Muṣṭafā Gujarātī (d. 1578), 144, 187, 262n56
Miyān Sajāwandī, ʿAbd al-Mālik (d. 1573), 156–62, 164, 265n110, 265n116
moderation (*iʿtidāl*), 192, 208, 213, 224–26, 241
Moin, A. Azfar, 10, 101–2, 127, 135–37, 191
monsoon, 270n57
Mōrbī, 187
mosque, 16, 21, 32, 40, 44, 60, 96, 135; congregational (*jāmiʿ masjid*), 17, 42, 178. *See also* prayer
Mubārak Nāgōrī, Shaykh (Mughal noble, d. 1593), 187, 212, 266n137, 269n36
Mubārak Sayyid Bukharī, 172
Muḥammad Ghawth Gwāliyarī, 121–37, 138, 164, 166, 167, 188–89, 191, 198, 231, 237, 262n39; brothers of, 261n11; mosque of, 40, 135
Muḥammad ibn Faḍlallāh Burhānpūrī, 132, 256n9
Muḥammad ibn Khafīf (d. 982), 124–26, 261n21
Muḥammad ibn Ṭāhir Pāṫanī (d. 1578), 8, 68, 132, 177, 183–90, 192, 253n89, 268n16, 268n19; Mālik al-Muḥaddithīn as nickname of, 184; as Sunni Bohra, 268n15, 268n22, 268n32
Muḥammad Jawnpūrī, Sayyid (d. 1505), 24–26, 137–43, 145, 148–61, 164, 167, 179, 185, 226, 231, 233–34, 262n56, 263n57, 263nn64–65, 264n97, 265n101; controversy over name of, 156, 265n126; legal authority of, 138, 185, 262n55; relations with rulers, 139, 142, 258n45, 263n61; son and successor Sayyid Maḥmūd, 140, 142–43, 150, 263n71. *See also* Mahdī: Sayyid Muhammad Jawnpūrī as
Muḥammad Ṣādiq Hamadānī (d. circa 1614), 235, 271n92
Muḥammad Shāh II (third Sultan of Guajrat, d. 1451), 243
Muḥammad Tāj Ganj-e Shakarī, 140, 263n64
Muḥammad the Prophet, 244, 256n89; biography of, 4; birthday of (*mawlid*), 171; body of, 10, 227–28; death of; eternal presence of (*Aḥmad*), 166, 227, 231, 272n17; example of (*sunna*), 15–16, 28, 90, 160, 163–65, 189, 257n15; individuation of (*taʿayyun*), 227; light of, 220, 230; miracles of, 122; mission of, 138–39; reality of (*ḥaqīqat-e muḥammadiyya*), 230–31, 272nn31; spirit of, 138–39, 141, 158, 272n30; virtues of, 24–26, 64, 73, 208, 234; reports about (see *ḥadīth*). *See also* ascension; tomb-shrine: of Prophet Muhammad
Muḥammad Zamān Mīrzā (Mughal prince, d. 1539), 49, 259n60
al-Muḥāsibī (d. 857), 259n51
Muʿīn al-Dīn Chishtī, Khwāja (d. 1236), 12, 16, 100, 190–91, 215–16, 245; tomb-shrine of, 41, 43, 190. *See also* Chishti Order
Multan, 27–29, 32, 141, 251n47
Mūsā Jīlānī, Shaykh, 193–94, 197, 244, 269n42, 269n46
Mūsā Sadā Sohāg, 40, 145
music, xvii, 14, 17–19, 31, 64, 66, 74, 87–88, 108, 116, 121, 167, 198; legality of in Islam, 16, 38, 59, 87–89; Qawwali, xv, 12–14, 22, 178, 249n1; Sufi ritual of listening to (*mehfil-e samāʿ*), 16–17, 21–22, 27–28, 96. *See also* drums
Mutawakkil, ʿAzīzallāh (d. 1506), 24–25, 28, 245
Mutawakkil, Raḥmatallāh, 250n20, 250n34
Muṫhiya, Shaykh, 184
Muttaqī. *See* ʿAbd al-Wahhāb Muttaqī; ʿAlī Muttaqī; Ḥusām al-Dīn Muttaqī
Muttaqi community, xvii, 4–5, 7–8, 10, 71, 93–94, 135, 189, 193, 204, 207, 209–10, 235, 238–40, 257n13, 258n29, 267n5
Muzaffar Alam, 10, 21
Muẓaffar Shāh I (first Sultan of Gujarat, formerly known as Muẓaffar Khān, d. 1407), 39–42, 243, 252n74, 252n76; son Muḥammad Shāh I, 41
Muẓaffar Shah II (sixth Sultan of Gujarat, d. 1526), 42–43, 52, 142–43, 243
Muẓaffar Shah III (tenth and last Sultan of Gujarat, d. 1573), 186, 243, 267n149

Muẓaffar-Shāhī dynasty, 39–48, 139–40; struggle of, against Portuguese, 49–54; terminal phase of, 171–73, 186–87, 243

Najm al-Dīn Kubrā (d. 1221), 37, 252n59. *See also* Kubrāwī Order
Naqshbandi Order, 10, 122, 136, 209–11, 216, 217, 226–32, 235–38, 244, 261nn12–13, 270n67
Nāṣir al-Dīn al-Laqānī, 254n23
Nawanagar, 18, 260n77
Niẓām al-Dīn Aḥmad Bakhshī (Mughal noble, d. 1621), 194, 198
Niẓām al-Dīn Awliyā (d. 1325), 16–17, 22, 31, 34, 128, 245, 249n10, 252n77,
Nizami, Khaliq Ahmed, 192, 209, 225, 266n140, 269n36, 269n39
North Africa, 42, 59, 205, 240, 267n5; Morocco, 58–59; Tarabulus (Libya), 59. *See also* Egypt
Nūr al-Ḥaqq, Muḥammad (son and successor of ʿAbd al-Ḥaqq Dihlawi, d. 1663), 208, 224, 228, 233, 269n47
Nūrjahān (Mughal queen, d. 1645), 215, 224–25; building of, 120

ocean, 7, 159; as metaphor for divinity, 20, 178, 204, 220; Indian Ocean, 7, 9, 43, 48, 51, 53, 80, 144, 201, 232, 253n9, 254n30
oral teachings (*malfūẓāt*), 10, 17, 22, 34–35, 74, 85, 97, 184, 256n6, 265n101
Ottoman Empire, 98–99, 181; campaigns of, in Indian Ocean, 53, 112–13, 253n9, 260n73; funds of, to Sufis in Mecca, 58, 254n33, 260n74, 260n76; religious ideology of, 9, 80, 218, 269n39; Sulayman the Magnificent as ruler of, 53, 112, 113

Palanpur (Pālanpūr), 18, 139, 143
partisanship, 8, 99, 131, 160, 186, 189, 192, 215, 226, 258n41; in Sufi communities, 72, 87, 90, 93–94, 132, 202, 257n13, 258n29. *See also* sectarianism
Patan (Pāṭan), 41, 142–44, 183–84, 186–88, 190, 252n77, 263n72
pearls, 41, 120, 148
persecution, 119–20, 266n136; against Mahdawi movement, 26, 137, 141–48, 154–56, 160–62, 167, 182, 186–89, 265n109, 265n116, 266n137; against Muhammad Ghawth, 131–37, 189, 191, 198, 237–38; of Sufis by other Sufis, 123
Persian language, xi, 4, 77; hadith commentary in, 57, 151, 204, 220, 224, 264n100; manuscripts in, 10, 254n34, 275; and Persianate literature, 21; relation to Indian vernacular, 19–21, 23, 137; Sufi poetry in, 75, 89, 93, 158–59, 178, 250n20
Persian Gulf, 42, 52
piety (*taqwā*), 18, 237; as deceptive display, 67, 152–53, 164; in early Sufism, 21, 35–38, 206; in Muttaqi community, 4–5, 7, 28–31, 37, 44, 91–92, 95, 104–6, 259n54; in Qur'an, 1, 5, 6, 216; as related to caution, 133–34; as related to renunciation, 16, 18–19
pilgrimage, 4–6, 16, 22, 32, 48, 152, 193; as banishment, 110, 112, 190; as Hajj to Mecca, 1, 5, 6, 54, 58, 79, 91, 93, 112–13, 143, 184–85, 198–200, 260n74; significance of in advent of Mahdi, 25, 139. *See also* tomb-shrine: visit to
pirates, 1, 9, 51, 79
poetry, 2, 13, 16–20, 22, 38–39, 179; as argumentation, 57, 117–18,159, 209; epic, 137, 166–67; as related to wisdom sayings, 74–75; in song, xv, 17, 20–21, 23, 31, 64, 87–89, 93, 103
ports, 1, 7, 41, 45–48, 154; in Gujarat, 41, 51–52, 139, 183, 190–91, 252n75; Portuguese capture of, 9, 49–52, 143, 187, 260n73, 260n77. *See also* Bharōch; Diu; Surat
Portuguese, 51–53, 78–80, 109, 112–13, 143–44, 155, 243, 253n9, 259n66, 260n73, 260n77; colonialism of, 9, 79, 98, 187; as pirates, 1, 47, 79, 256n76
prayer, 3–4, 13, 37, 84, 115, 117, 145, 152, 175–76, 231; ablutions before, 110–11; call to, 269n46; direction of (*qibla*),

189; plea to God in (*munājāt*), 200, 204, 228. *See also* Imam
pride (*kibr*), 25, 37–38, 67, 108, 234. *See also* egoism
principle (*qaʿida*), 62–63, 68, 76, 105–6, 131, 158, 163, 189, 201, 205–6, 213, 234; scriptural root of (*aṣl*), 69, 157. *See also* Usuli scholarship
prophets before Muhammad, 122, 169, 218, 222; Abraham, 235; Jesus, 146, 185; Job, 65, 266n130; Moses, 188; relation to saints, 226, 230, 233
punishment, 37, 147–48, 154, 158, 161–62, 186–87, 189, 225, 241
purity, 70, 72, 84–85, 108, 119, 167, 206, 220, 221; of body, 38; of food, 31–32, 133–34. *See also* bathing; heart: purity of

Qāḍī ʿAbdallāh Sindhī, 44–45, 253n1, 267n9
Qāḍī Aḥmad Jūd, 42
Qāḍī Ḥamīd Muḥaddith, 44, 253n1, 267n9
Qadiri Order, 28, 33, 87, 93, 165, 193, 202, 206, 209, 228, 232, 244, 251n41, 268n16; female authorities in, 96
Qawāʾid al-taṣawwuf, 68–69, 205, 270n79
Qawwali. *See* music: Qawwali
Qurʾan, xi, 1–2, 5–6, 14, 15, 20, 48, 60, 86, 90, 105, 159, 163, 183–84, 200, 222, 223, 237, 238; as cited in wisdom sayings, 75–76, 255n69; interpretation of, 24, 29, 42–43, 88, 134, 135, 138, 141, 144, 151–52, 164, 257n16, 261n24, 265n101; recitation of, 30, 85, 171, 262n39; writing of, 252n84
Qutb-e ʿĀlam, Sayyid Burhān al-Dīn (d. 1452), 40, 41–42, 252n76, 263n65,

Rādhanpūr, 142
Raḥmatallāh Sindhī 44, 68
rain, 3–4, 14, 34, 95, 145
Rajasthan (Rājasthān), 139, 143
reason (*ʿaql*), xvii, 66, 89, 103, 130, 141, 174, 191, 193, 195–98, 203, 205, 220, 232; in hadith, 257n15; vs. opinion (*rāʾī*), 157, 164, 201, 264; vs. speculation (*ẓann*), 153, 157, 158, 201
rebellion, 39, 110, 122, 172, 213, 217, 219, 224, 256n73, 267n148; in discourse, 142, 195; against God, 68, 163
Red Sea, 1, 52, 53, 112, 143. *See also* Arabian Sea; Persian Gulf
reform, 5, 7–9, 37, 58–59, 62–63, 69, 71, 74–75, 77–78, 82, 86–95, 102–9, 118–19, 132, 137–38, 166–73, 176–78, 182–84, 192, 196, 198–202, 210–13, 216–17, 223, 226, 235–41, 255n39, 267n5, 271n12; Mahdawi conceptions of, 24, 26. *See also* revivalism
regent, 43, 109, 111, 186, 188, 190, 143. *See also* vice-regent
reliance on God (*tawakkul*), 18–19, 24, 32, 70, 77, 102, 169, 195, 206, 251n39; in Mahdawi movement, 25–26, 141; as renunciation, 16, 70; in Shattari Order, 130
repentance (*tawba*), 48; before God, 74, 124, 128, 181; as recanting of prior belief, 147, 162
revelation, 24, 30, 68, 75, 90, 96, 130, 158, 164, 169, 227; inner meaning of, 25. *See also* Qurʾan
revivalism, 5, 189, 199, 205, 211, 236, 241; of Mahdawi movement, 9, 26, 120; of Ahmad Sirhindi, 10, 192
rivers, 16, 27, 133–34; Indus, 27; Narmada, 24; Sabarmati, 18, 41, 47, 115; Tapti, 250n15

Saʿdī Shīrāzī (Persian poet, d. 1291), 75, 159
Safavid Empire, 6, 9, 42, 53, 172; Shah Tahmasp in, 190
Ṣaḥīḥ al-Bukhārī, 43, 254n20
Ṣaḥīḥ Muslim, 190
saints (*walī*, plural *awliyāʾ*), 5, 13, 15, 38, 76–77; authenticity of, 27, 29, 31–32, 35, 54, 103, 127–29; axial (*quṭb*), 92, 102, 258n40; in Chishti Order, 16–18, 22–24, 100; Mahdawi view of, 25, 143, 149–50, 165–66, 262n56; scholar-saints (*jāmiʿ*), 59–62, 67, 80–82, 86–87, 91, 94–95, 102,

saints (*continued*)
109, 118–19, 123, 167, 223, 236, 271n88; in Shattari Order, 123–24, 129–30, 132–35, 138, 165–66, 188–89
sainthood (*wilāya*), 30, 33, 37, 62–64, 102–9, 184, 191, 223, 235; as publicly displayed, 88–89, 179–82, 259n50; stages of (*maqāmāt*), 37, 92, 103–6, 129–30, 149, 264n97
al-Sakhāwī, Muḥammad ibn Muḥammad, 58, 87, 245, 254n34
al-Sakhāwī, Shams al-Dīn Muḥammad (d. 1497), 58, 254n23
salvation (*saʿāda*), 37, 64, 94, 163, 169, 182, 199, 216, 218; of society, 61, 99–101, 219–23
samāʿ. *See* music
Sārangpūr, 18, 188; Sarangpur Gate of Ahmedabad, 40, 135
Satan. *See* tempter
satchel (*kharīṭa*), 1–3, 6; as chapter divisions, 7, 11, 14–15, 48, 86, 119–20, 176–77, 216–17; as derwish purse (*kinf*), 34, 252n60; as reminder of death, 34–35, 59, 173, 177, 183
Sayf al-Dīn, Shaykh, 193, 206, 208
sayyids, 16, 42, 154, 157, 171–72, 215, 251n41, 253n85. *See also* Muḥammad Jawnpūrī, Sayyid
scripture (*kitāb*), xi, 64, 68–71, 73, 76, 126, 156, 163, 166–67. *See also* Qurʾan; revelation
seal (*khātam*): of prophethood, 165; of sainthood, 138, 165, 262n56
sectarianism, 27, 67, 147, 151, 153, 160, 185, 234. *See also* partisanship
Shadhili Order, 58–59, 86, 87, 92, 169, 202, 209, 245, 254n34
Shafiʿi school of law, 147, 201–2, 262n55, 264n89, 270n65
Shāh ʿAbd al-Raḥīm Dihlawī (d. 1719), 240
Shāh Bājan, Bahāʾ al-Dīn (d. 1507), xviii, 12–14, 17–24, 245, 250n20, 250n34; son and successor ʿAbd al-Ḥakīm, 23
Shāh Chālinda, 140
Shāh-e ʿĀlam, Sayyid Sirāj al-Dīn (d. 1475), 40, 42, 252n77, 252n83. *See also* Bukhari sayyids
Shāhjahān (fifth Mughal emperor, d. 1666), 224
Shāhpūr Gate of Ahmedabad, 40, 44, 135, 14
Shāhriyār (Mughal prince, d. 1628), 224
Shāh Walīʾllāh Dihlawī (d. 1762), 240, 270n66
sharīʿa. *See* Islamic norms
Shaṭṭār, Shāh ʿAbdallāh (d. 1485), 120–21, 136. *See also* Shattari Order
Shattari Order, 10, 88, 108, 119, 120–37, 138, 178–79, 191, 198, 232, 237–38, 253n87, 261n7, 261nn11–13, 262n28, 270n58; also known as ʿIshqī Order, 215; relations with Mahdawi movement, 162–66, 188–89, 266n136
Shaykh Jī Bukhārī 140
Sheikh, Samira, 7, 39
Shēr Khān Fulādī (governor of Patan), 186
Shēr Shāh Sūrī. *See* Sūrī dynasty
Shīʿa, 100, 116, 146, 234, 264n83, 268n22; as state religion, 6; in Mughal Empire, 188, 190, 212, 224–25, 271n12; Ismāʿīlī movement of, 42, 268n15
ship, 1–3, 7, 43, 48, 54, 110, 113, 117, 143, 154, 168, 260n74; as metaphor for state, 116, 204, 221
Ṣibghatallāh, 132, 270n58
sincerity (*ṣidq* or *ikhlāṣ*), 5–6, 27–29, 31–32, 74, 92, 95, 97–99, 102–3, 105, 107–9, 118, 128–29, 131, 153, 158, 169, 180–81, 195, 207, 216, 229, 251n39, 259n49
Sindh, 27, 140, 142, 243; scholars from, 44, 68, 253n87
sleep, 66, 212; deprivation of, 126, 193; dreams during, 22, 134, 135, 176, 193, 210, 253n85, 253n89
sobriety (*ṣaḥw*), 39, 124–25, 204–5, 229. *See also* intoxication
soul (*nafs*), 5, 14, 20, 60, 66, 77, 95–99, 104, 131, 139, 199, 200, 207, 212, 219, 257n16; as trapped by egoism, 35–36. *See also* Sufi training
South Asia, xv, 2, 4–10, 29; importance of Gujarat to, 39, 43, 47; Sufism in, 15–22, 42

Southeast Asia, 8, 167; Aceh, 8; Indonesia, 232, 270n58; Sumatra, 80, 272n30
spirit (*rūḥ*), 20, 65, 165, 197, 211–12, 230, 236; of Prophet, 26, 158, 167, 199, 227, 232, 272n30; of one's shaykh, 91
spiritual reality (*ḥaqīqa*), 20, 126, 210, 230, 232
spiritual state (*ḥāl*), 29, 70–72, 74, 102, 105, 124, 130–31, 133, 140, 150, 174, 179–80, 182, 204, 206, 229–30, 267n11
spiritual struggle (*mujāhida*), 33, 48, 64, 77, 105, 133, 197, 201; as greater jihad, 212
Sufi disciples (*murīd*), 5, 28, 29, 30, 59, 68, 200, 227–28, 233; relation with master, 31–32, 71–73, 93–94, 97–98, 198, 211, 226; known as "impoverished ones" (*fuqarāʾ*), 100; rulers as, 112, 122, 191
Sufi discipline (*adab*), 5, 8, 10, 21–22, 24, 32, 34, 39, 48, 58, 63, 66, 77, 117, 184, 209, 213, 230
Sufi hospice (*khānqāh*), 12, 17, 120; of ʿAbd al-Haqq Muhaddith Dihlawi, 8, 204, 215; of ʿAli Muttaqi, 40, 68, 113, 178, 179; as related to tomb-shrine, 21
Sufi master (*shaykh*, *murshid*, or *pīr*), 24, 35, 86, 94, 97, 139, 153, 196, 197, 200, 232–33; absorption in personality of (*fanāʾ fī'l-shaykh*), 91; techniques of, granted without initiation (*istifāda*), 198. *See also* saint
Sufi orders (*ṭarīqa*), 5, 27–28, 56, 82, 103, 137, 167, 237, 238; completion of (*takmīl*), 25, 165; fusion of multiple, 62, 86, 89, 94; initiation in, 123; initiatory lineage in (*silsila*), 124, 244, 252n59; as mystical training, 20
Sufism (*taṣawwuf*), 8, 9–10, 15–16, 21, 24, 66
Sufi training (*sulūk*), 23, 28–32, 37, 54, 58–59, 62–63, 67–68, 70–77, 95–100, 107, 141, 219; aspirant to (*sālik*), 37, 71; as traveling path, 63, 92, 105–16, 200, 210, 231–32, 234
Suhrawardi Order, 28, 29, 136, 137; in Gujarat, 41–42, 172, 252n83, 252n85
Sulaymān Pāshā (Ottoman admiral), 112
sultanate of Gujarat. *See* Muẓaffar-Shāhī dynasty
Sunnis, 16, 53, 100, 131, 139, 225, 233, 235, 268n15; in hadith studies, 56, 124–25; in Mughal political theory, 190–91, 212, 217–18, 220, 226; relations with Mahdawi movement, 26–27, 138, 140–42, 146–48, 151, 153, 161, 163, 263n72, 265n126, 268n21
Surat, 18, 52, 110, 112, 154, 187, 198, 252n75, 260n73, 270n57
Sūrī dynasty, 266n137; Shēr Shāh Sūrī (d. 1545), 54, 78, 123, 256n73; son Salīm Shāh Sūrī (d. 1554), 172. *See also* Afghans

tempter (*shayṭān*), 97, 195; as dominating heart, 85, 104; throne of, 124–27
Tīmūr (d. 1405), 41, 83; rulers descended from, 9, 49, 53
al-Tirmidhī, al-Ḥakīm (d. 869), 35–38
tomb-shrine (*rawḍa* or *dargah*), xviii, 19, 21, 29, 40, 42, 94, 120–21, 133, 145, 172, 183, 191, 203, 236, 249n1; custodians of, xviii, 101; of ʿAli Muttaqi, 176, 183; of Prophet Muhammad, 92, 174, 185, 199, 200, 227, 268n21; of royalty, 120, 140; visits to (*ziyārat*), 17, 22, 41, 43, 96, 175, 190
treasurer (*mīr bakhshī*), 198, 211
triple *tarīqa*, 58, 71, 83, 86–87, 93–94, 177, 199, 202, 209, 211, 244. *See also* Sufi orders: fusion of multiple
truth (*ḥaqq*), i, 106, 125–26, 138, 158, 169, 215, 228; as quality of God, 68, 93, 147, 202, 205, 231; as rights (*ḥuqūq*), 39, 41, 97, 108, 170, 206, 222; void of, 233
Tughlaq dynasty, 39, 243; Fīrōz Shāh Tughlaq (d. 1388), 39. *See also* Delhi sultanate

Ujjain, 18, 40, 188
Ulūghkhānī, Muḥammad ibn ʿUmar al-Makkī al-Āṣafī (also known as Ḥājjī Dabīr, d. after 1611), 80, 85–86, 110, 118–19, 171, 172, 260n1, 266n141
Umayyad dynasty, 237
union (*ittiḥād*), 88, 134, 179, 193, 229–32, 234, 272n17
unity (*tawḥīd*), 130–31, 178, 188–89, 195, 203, 229

Urdu, 10, 21, 192, 206, 249n14, 250n19, 256n81, 257n15, 267n143; Gujari dialect of, xi, 13, 17, 19, 20, 22, 131, 267n7
Usuli scholarship, 69, 207, 209

vanity (*riyā*), 195, 206, 232, 234, 256n7
Vatva, 40, 253n85. *See also* Qutb-e ʿAlam, Sayyid Burhān al-Dīn
veil (*parda*), 61–62, 125, 130, 193; as separation (*ḥijāb*), 104, 105, 138, 179, 205, 230
vernacular, 21, 22; as cultural process, 17, 137, 238. *See also* Urdu: Gujari dialect of
vice-regent (*khalīfa*), 99–100, 142; as successor in Sufi order, 71, 193; as Sunni political leader, 185, 218
virtue (*iḥsān*), 24, 25, 28, 45, 57, 60, 68, 91, 106, 141, 158, 206, 208, 230, 241; equated with manhood, 145, 263n74; hadith as reservoir of, 70, 73–74; for rulers, 98, 101–2, 109, 218, 223
visions (*mushāhida*), 71, 92, 176, 230, 257n22, 271n92; in Mahdawi movement, 140, 163–65; in Shattari Order, 121–27, 165. *See also* sleep: dreams during

Wajīh al-Dīn ʿAlawī (d. 1590), 40, 124, 131–35, 165, 188–89, 198, 237, 247, 261n18, 269n33, 270n58
Walī'llāh (father of ʿAbd al-Wahhab Muttaqi), 91, 127
wealth, 23, 39, 41, 47, 58, 65, 77, 97, 152, 183, 228; in coinage, 24, 32, 108, 119, 168, 184, 256n7; denounced in Mahdawi movement, 25, 139; from inheritance, 175, 269n42; from land grant (*jāgīr*), 117, 215–16, 196; as stipend, 23, 58, 112–13, 115, 184, 254n33, 260n74; from taxes, 28–29, 52, 54, 78, 101, 118, 251n42, 260n79
wisdom sayings (*ḥikam*), 64–66, 74–77, 87, 88; of Ibn ʿAṭāʾallāh Iskandari, 59, 65, 69, 74, 128, 241
women, 163, 171; as co-wives, 109, 120; fertility of, 110, 145, 267n11; in Sufism, 96–98; transgender, 145; as wives, 44, 49, 96, 145, 175, 183, 212, 224. *See also* gender
world (*dunyā*), 15, 20, 23, 26, 39, 54, 70, 97, 99–102, 117, 119, 122, 139, 165, 170, 196, 200, 220–21; as abode of trials, 105, 144, 168–69; as abode of deception, 38, 61, 104, 167, 169, 188; as abode of virtues, 60, 95, 167, 169; as composed of God's names, 127–28, 130; end of, 146, 149, 166, 188; hadith about, 17, 64, 175, 177, 212; history of, 8, 112; next (*ākhira*), 44, 99–101, 105, 109, 126, 129, 134, 169, 211; unseen (*ghayb*), 33

Yemen, 1, 56, 112, 168, 257, 260n73; soldiers from, 54, 98; Sufis from, 42, 57, 92
yoga, 121

Zād al-Muttaqīn, 10, 135, 144, 249n3, 249n14, 250n16, 251n38
Zarruq. *See* Aḥmad Zarrūq
Zaynābād, 18, 250n15
Zayn al-Dīn Maʿbarī, Makhdūm (d. 1583), 79–80
Zayn al-Din Shirazi (d. 1370), 250n15

Islamic Civilization and Muslim Networks

Scott Kugle, *Hajj to the Heart: Sufi Journeys across the Indian Ocean* (2021)

Michael Muhammad Knight, *Muhammad's Body: Baraka Networks and the Prophetic Assemblage* (2020).

Kelly A. Hammond, *China's Muslims and Japan's Empire: Centering Islam in World War II* (2020).

Zachary Valentine Wright, *Realizing Islam: The Tijaniyya in North Africa and the Eighteenth-Century Muslim World* (2020).

Alex Dika Seggerman, *Modernism on the Nile: Art in Egypt Between the Islamic and the Contemporary* (2019).

Babak Rahimi and Peyman Eshaghi, *Muslim Pilgrimage in the Modern World* (2019)

Simon Wolfgang Fuchs, *In a Pure Muslim Land: Shiʿism between Pakistan and the Middle East* (2019).

Gary R. Bunt, *Hashtag Islam: How Cyber Islamic Environments Are Transforming Religious Authority* (2018).

Ahmad Dallal, *Islam without Europe: Traditions of Reform in Eighteenth-Century Islamic Thought* (2018).

Irfan Ahmad, *Religion as Critique: Islamic Critical Thinking from Mecca to the Marketplace* (2017).

Scott Kugle, *When Sun Meets Moon: Gender, Eros, and Ecstasy in Urdu Poetry* (2016).

Kishwar Rizvi, *The Transnational Mosque: Architecture, Historical Memory, and the Contemporary Middle East* (2015).

Ebrahim Moosa, *What Is a Madrasa?* (2015).

Bruce Lawrence, *Who Is Allah?* (2015).

Edward E. Curtis IV, *The Call of Bilal: Islam in the African Diaspora* (2014).

Sahar Amer, *What Is Veiling?* (2014).

Rudolph T. Ware III, *The Walking Qur'an: Islamic Education, Embodied Knowledge, and History in West Africa* (2014).

Saʿdiyya Shaikh, *Sufi Narratives of Intimacy: Ibn ʿArabī, Gender, and Sexuality* (2012).

Karen G. Ruffle, *Gender, Sainthood, and Everyday Practice in South Asian Shiʿism* (2011).

Jonah Steinberg, *Ismaʿili Modern: Globalization and Identity in a Muslim Community* (2011).

Iftikhar Dadi, *Modernism and the Art of Muslim South Asia* (2010).

Gary R. Bunt, *iMuslims: Rewiring the House of Islam* (2009).

Fatemeh Keshavarz, *Jasmine and Stars: Reading More Than "Lolita" in Tehran* (2007).

Scott Kugle, *Sufis and Saints' Bodies: Mysticism, Corporeality, and Sacred Power in Islam* (2007).

Roxani Eleni Margariti, *Aden and the Indian Ocean Trade: 150 Years in the Life of a Medieval Arabian Port* (2007).

Sufia M. Uddin, *Constructing Bangladesh: Religion, Ethnicity, and Language in an Islamic Nation* (2006).

Omid Safi, *The Politics of Knowledge in Premodern Islam: Negotiating Ideology and Religious Inquiry* (2006).

Ebrahim Moosa, *Ghazālī and the Poetics of Imagination* (2005).

miriam cooke and Bruce B. Lawrence, eds., *Muslim Networks from Hajj to Hip Hop* (2005).

Carl W. Ernst, *Following Muhammad: Rethinking Islam in the Contemporary World* (2003).

www.ingramcontent.com/pod-product-compliance
Lightning Source LLC
Chambersburg PA
CBHW021649230426
43668CB00008B/559